Toshiaki Iwashiro

I'm over 30 now, and I still have trouble writing the symbol "&." I wish I could get some pointers from whoever came up with the symbol "&."

Toshiaki Iwashiro was born December 11, 1977, in Tokyo and has the blood type of A. His debut manga was the popular *Mieru Hito*, which ran from 2005 to 2007 in Japan in *Weekly Shonen Jump*, where *Psyren* was also serialized.

PSYREN VOL. 6
SHONEN JUMP Manga Edition

STORY AND ART BY TOSHIAKI IWASHIRO

Translation/Camellia Nieh
Lettering/Annaliese Christman
Design/Matt Hinrichs
Editor/Joel Enos

PSYREN © 2007 by Toshiaki Iwashiro
All rights reserved.
First published in Japan in 2007 by SHUEISHA Inc., Tokyo.
English translation rights arranged by SHUEISHA Inc.

The rights of the author(s) of the work(s) in this publication to be so
identified have been asserted in accordance with the Copyright, Designs
and Patents Act 1988. A CIP catalogue record for this book is available
from the British Library.

Printed in the U.S.A.

Published by VIZ Media, LLC
P.O. Box 77010
San Francisco, CA 94107

10 9 8 7 6 5 4 3 2 1
First printing, September 2012

www.viz.com

THE WORLD'S
MOST POPULAR MANGA

www.shonenjump.com

SHONEN JUMP MANGA EDITION

PSYREN

6
FLAME

Story and Art by
Toshiaki Iwashiro

AGEHA YOSHINA

SAKURAKO AMAMIYA

HIRYU ASAGA

OBORO MOCHIZUKI

KABUTO KIRISAKI

Characters

MARI

FREDRIKA

KYLE

VAN

SHAO

THE ELMORE WOOD GANG

Story

AGEHA YOSHINA IS A NORMAL HIGH SCHOOL STUDENT UNTIL HE
HAPPENS UPON A RED TELEPHONE CARD EMBLAZONED WITH THE
WORD PSYREN, WHICH ULTIMATELY TRANSPORTS HIM TO PSYREN
WORLD WHERE HE'S QUICKLY EMBROILED IN A DANGEROUS
GAME OF LIFE OR DEATH.

DURING THEIR LATEST JOURNEY TO PSYREN, AGEHA, ALONG
WITH HIS FRIEND SAKURAKO AND OTHER PLAYERS THEY'VE MET
ALONG THE WAY, SEARCH DESPERATELY FOR CLUES TO TELL
THEM HOW AND WHY THEIR OWN WORLD HAS BECOME THE
WASTELAND OF PSYREN. IN KABUTO'S UNCLE'S CABIN, THEY
FIND A VIDEO WITH FOOTAGE OF ELMORE WOOD'S CHILDREN
CHALLENGING THE MYSTERIOUS ORGANIZATION W.I.S.E–AND
BEING BRUTALLY DESTROYED. THEIR HORROR AND SHOCK ARE
INTERRUPTED BY DOLKEY, A MEMBER OF W.I.S.E, WHOSE
POWERFUL ATTACKS OVERWHELM THE GROUP. BUT WITH THE
HELP OF KABUTO'S VISIONS AND AGEHA'S NEW MELZEZ LANCE,
THE GROUP SURVIVES THE BATTLE AND MAKES IT SAFELY HOME.

PSYREN

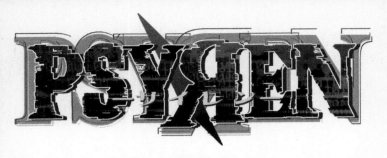

VOL. 6
FLAME
CONTENTS

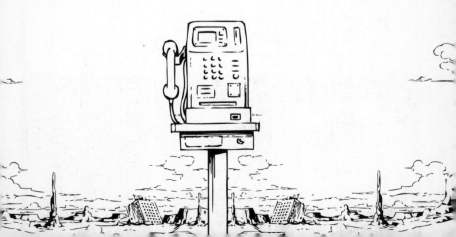

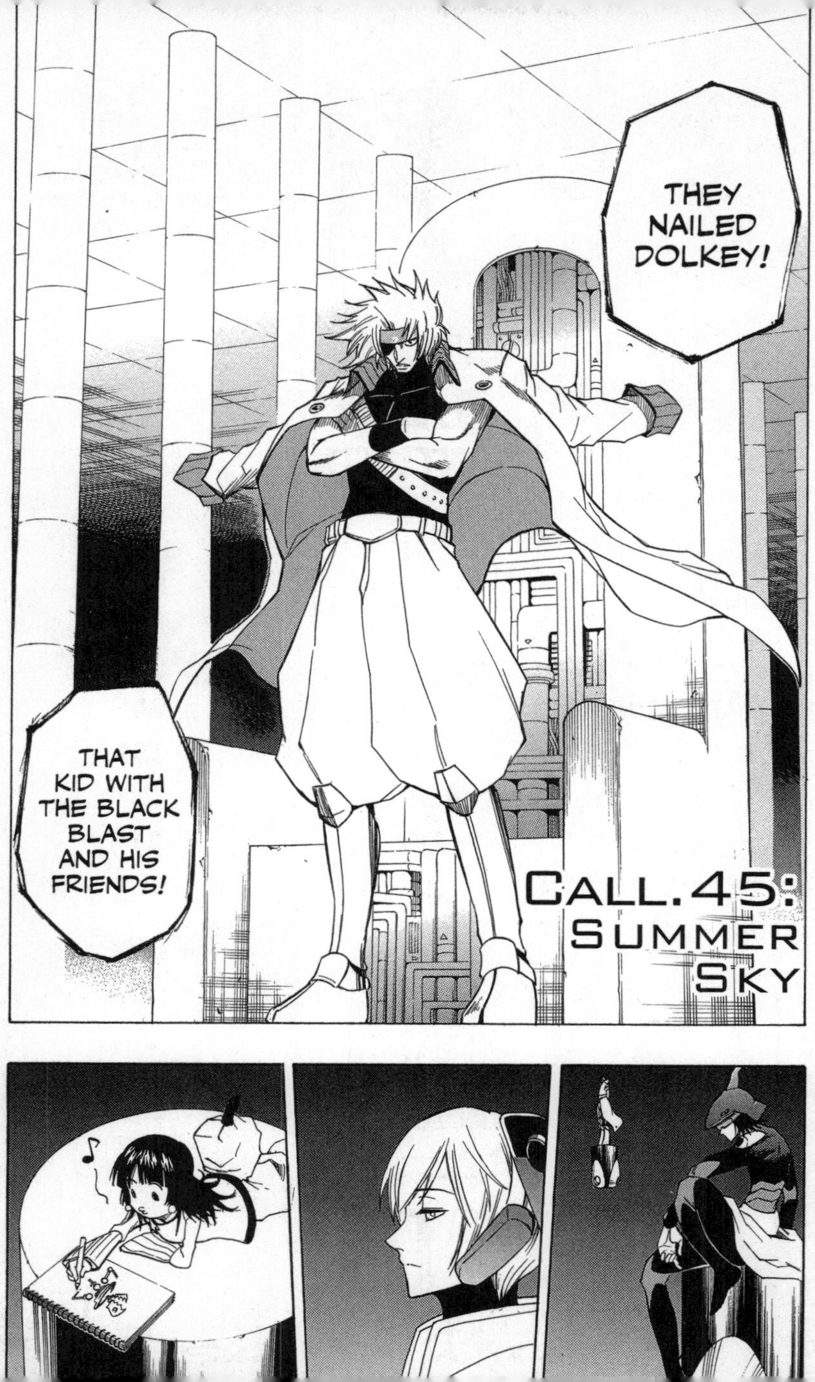
THEY NAILED DOLKEY!
THAT KID WITH THE BLACK BLAST AND HIS FRIENDS!
CALL. 45: SUMMER SKY

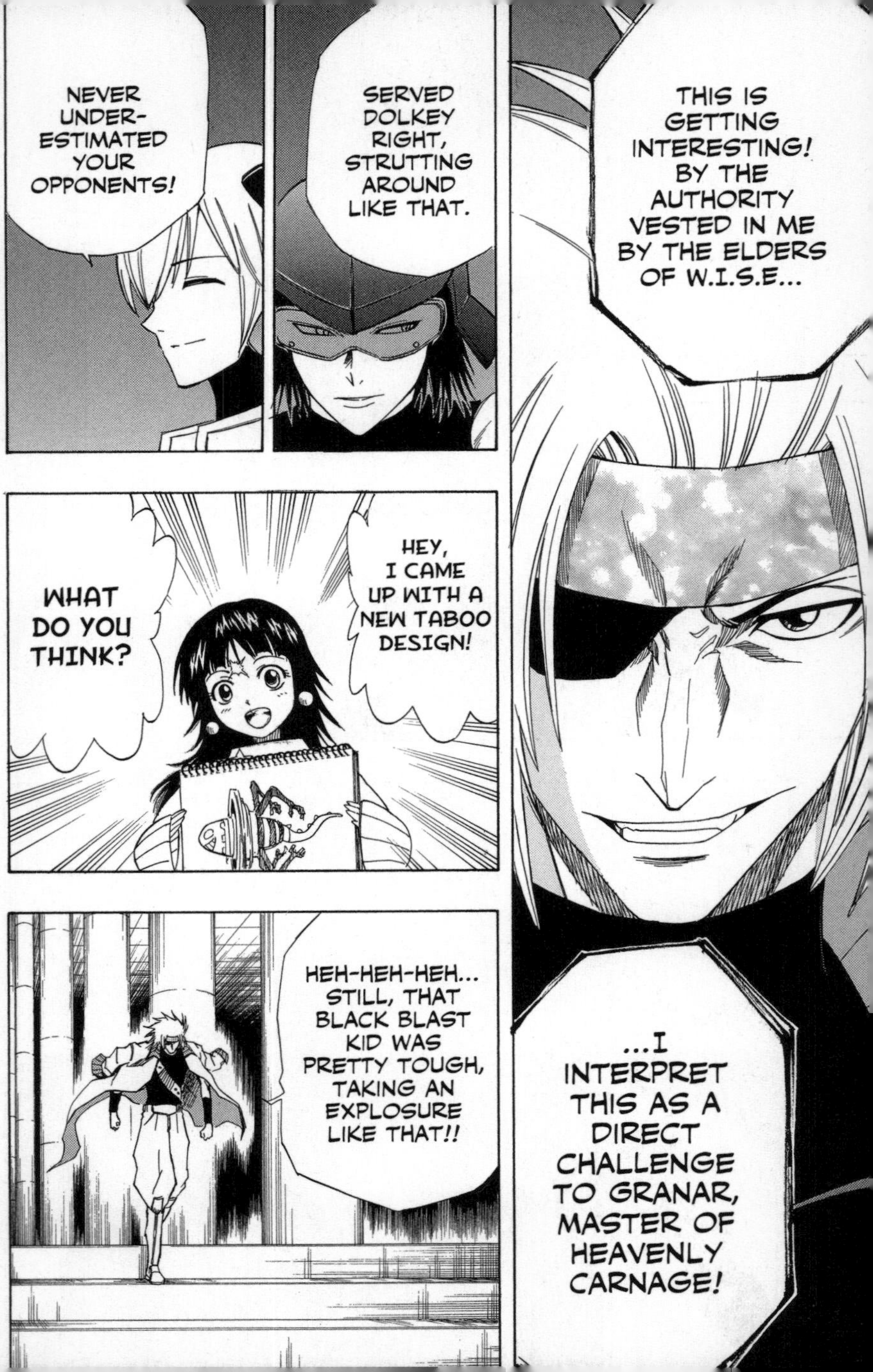
THIS IS GETTING INTERESTING! BY THE AUTHORITY VESTED IN ME BY THE ELDERS OF W.I.S.E...
...I INTERPRET THIS AS A DIRECT CHALLENGE TO GRANAR, MASTER OF HEAVENLY CARNAGE!
SERVED DOLKEY RIGHT, STRUTTING AROUND LIKE THAT.
NEVER UNDER-ESTIMATED YOUR OPPONENTS!
HEY, I CAME UP WITH A NEW TABOO DESIGN!
WHAT DO YOU THINK?
HEH-HEH-HEH... STILL, THAT BLACK BLAST KID WAS PRETTY TOUGH, TAKING AN EXPLOSURE LIKE THAT!!

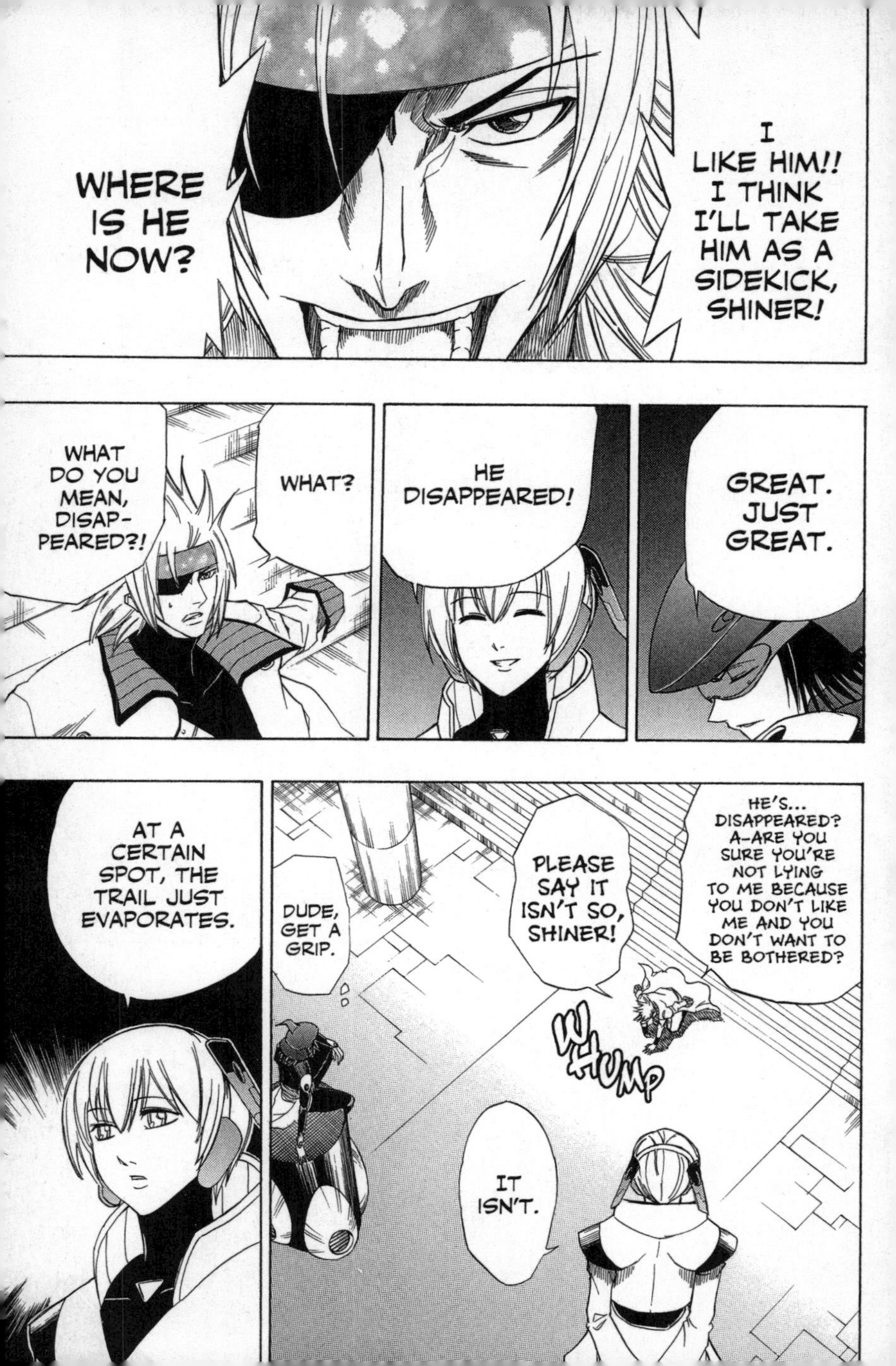
I LIKE HIM!! I THINK I'LL TAKE HIM AS A SIDEKICK, SHINER!
WHERE IS HE NOW?
GREAT. JUST GREAT.
HE DISAPPEARED!
WHAT?
WHAT DO YOU MEAN, DISAP-PEARED?!
HE'S... DISAPPEARED? A-ARE YOU SURE YOU'RE NOT LYING TO ME BECAUSE YOU DON'T LIKE ME AND YOU DON'T WANT TO BE BOTHERED?
PLEASE SAY IT ISN'T SO, SHINER!
DUDE, GET A GRIP.
WHUMP
IT ISN'T.
AT A CERTAIN SPOT, THE TRAIL JUST EVAPORATES.

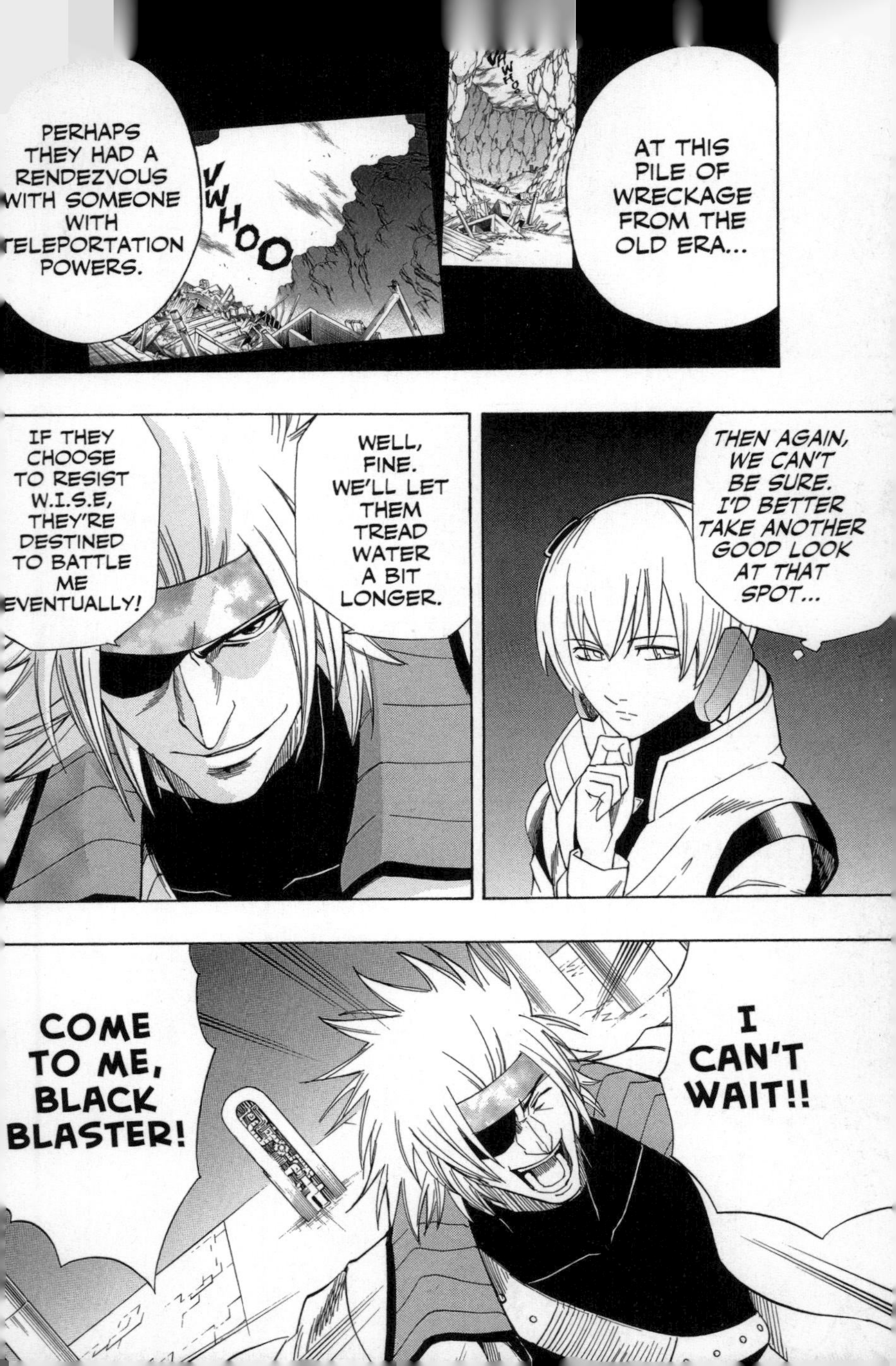
AT THIS PILE OF WRECKAGE FROM THE OLD ERA...
VWHOO
PERHAPS THEY HAD A RENDEZVOUS WITH SOMEONE WITH TELEPORTATION POWERS.
THEN AGAIN, WE CAN'T BE SURE. I'D BETTER TAKE ANOTHER GOOD LOOK AT THAT SPOT...
WELL, FINE. WE'LL LET THEM TREAD WATER A BIT LONGER.
IF THEY CHOOSE TO RESIST W.I.S.E, THEY'RE DESTINED TO BATTLE ME EVENTUALLY!
I CAN'T WAIT!!
COME TO ME, BLACK BLASTER!

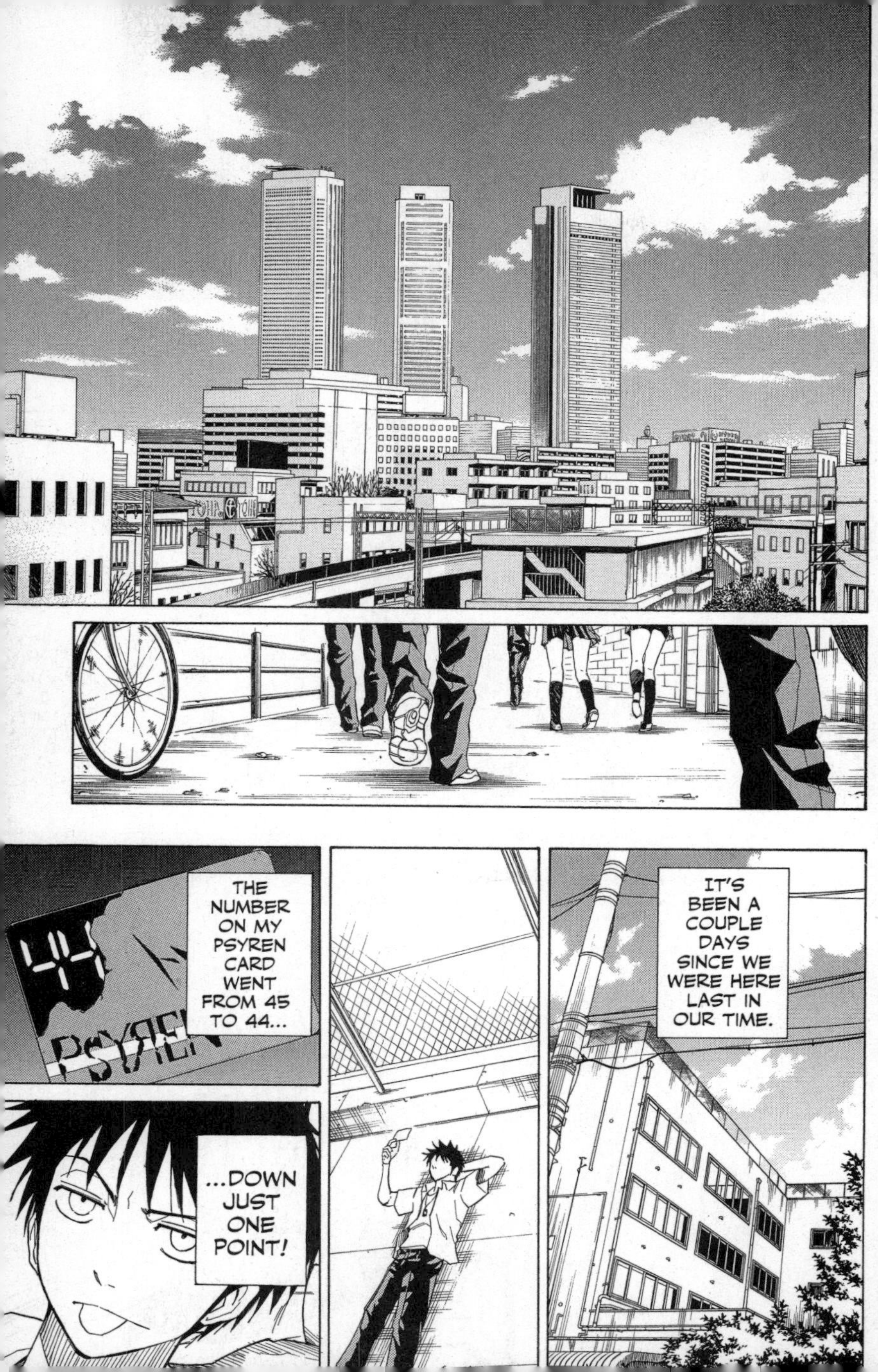
IT'S BEEN A COUPLE DAYS SINCE WE WERE HERE LAST IN OUR TIME.
THE NUMBER ON MY PSYREN CARD WENT FROM 45 TO 44...
...DOWN JUST ONE POINT!

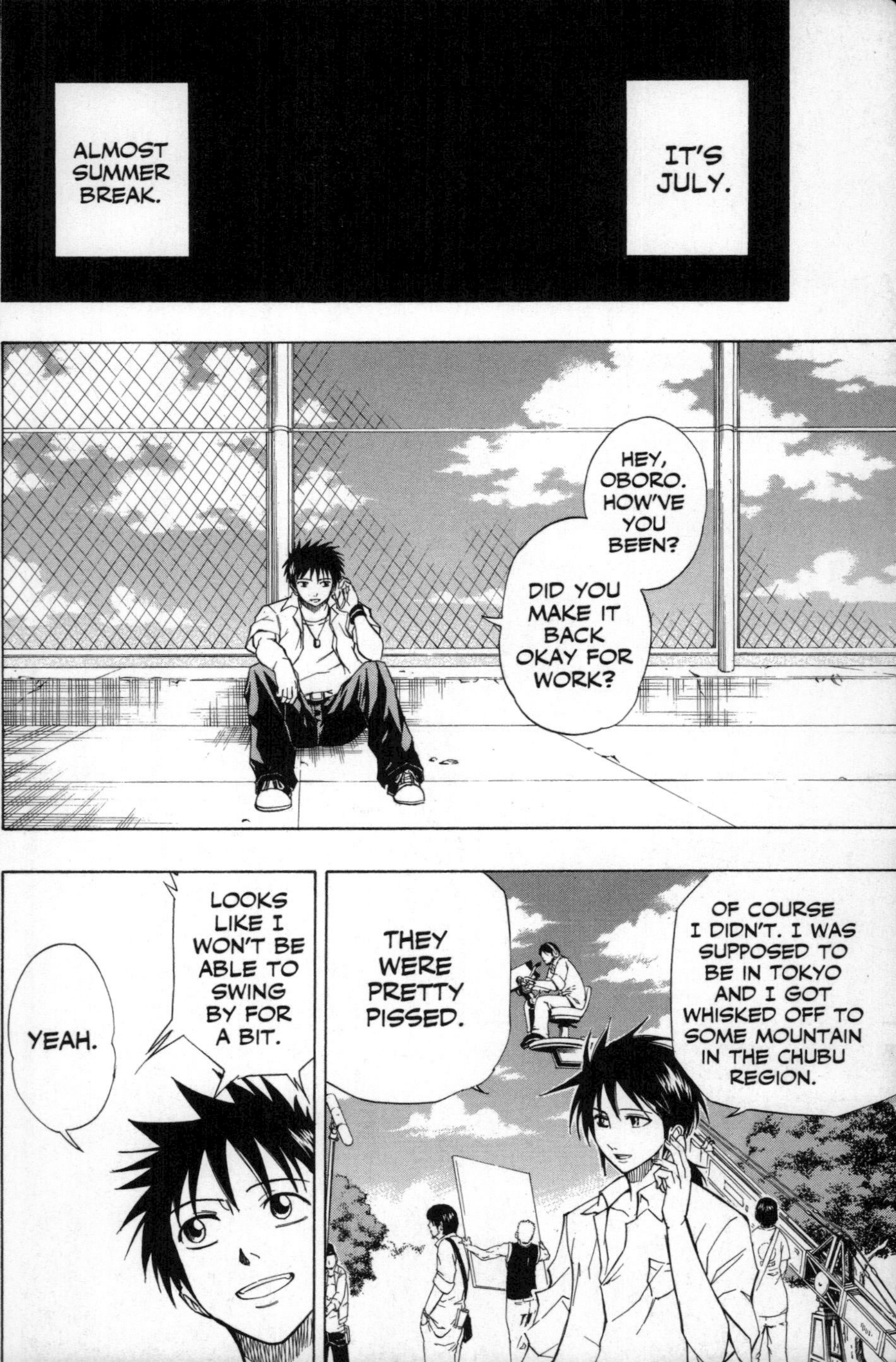
IT'S JULY.
ALMOST SUMMER BREAK.
HEY, OBORO. HOW'VE YOU BEEN?
DID YOU MAKE IT BACK OKAY FOR WORK?
OF COURSE I DIDN'T. I WAS SUPPOSED TO BE IN TOKYO AND I GOT WHISKED OFF TO SOME MOUNTAIN IN THE CHUBU REGION.
THEY WERE PRETTY PISSED.
LOOKS LIKE I WON'T BE ABLE TO SWING BY FOR A BIT.
YEAH.

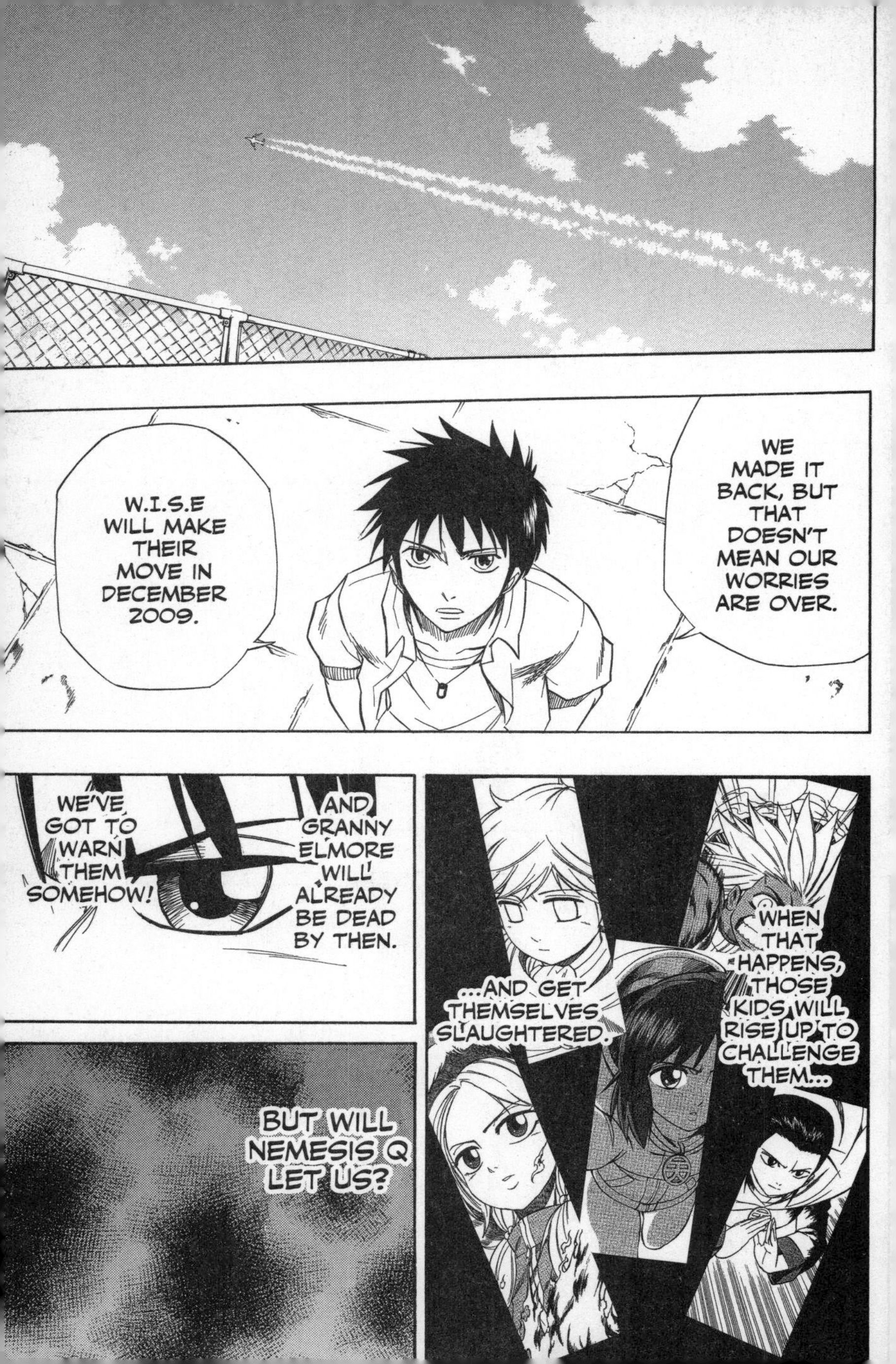
WE MADE IT BACK, BUT THAT DOESN'T MEAN OUR WORRIES ARE OVER.
W.I.S.E WILL MAKE THEIR MOVE IN DECEMBER 2009.
WHEN THAT HAPPENS, THOSE KIDS WILL RISE UP TO CHALLENGE THEM...
...AND GET THEMSELVES SLAUGHTERED.
AND GRANNY ELMORE WILL ALREADY BE DEAD BY THEN.
WE'VE GOT TO WARN THEM SOMEHOW!
BUT WILL NEMESIS Q LET US?

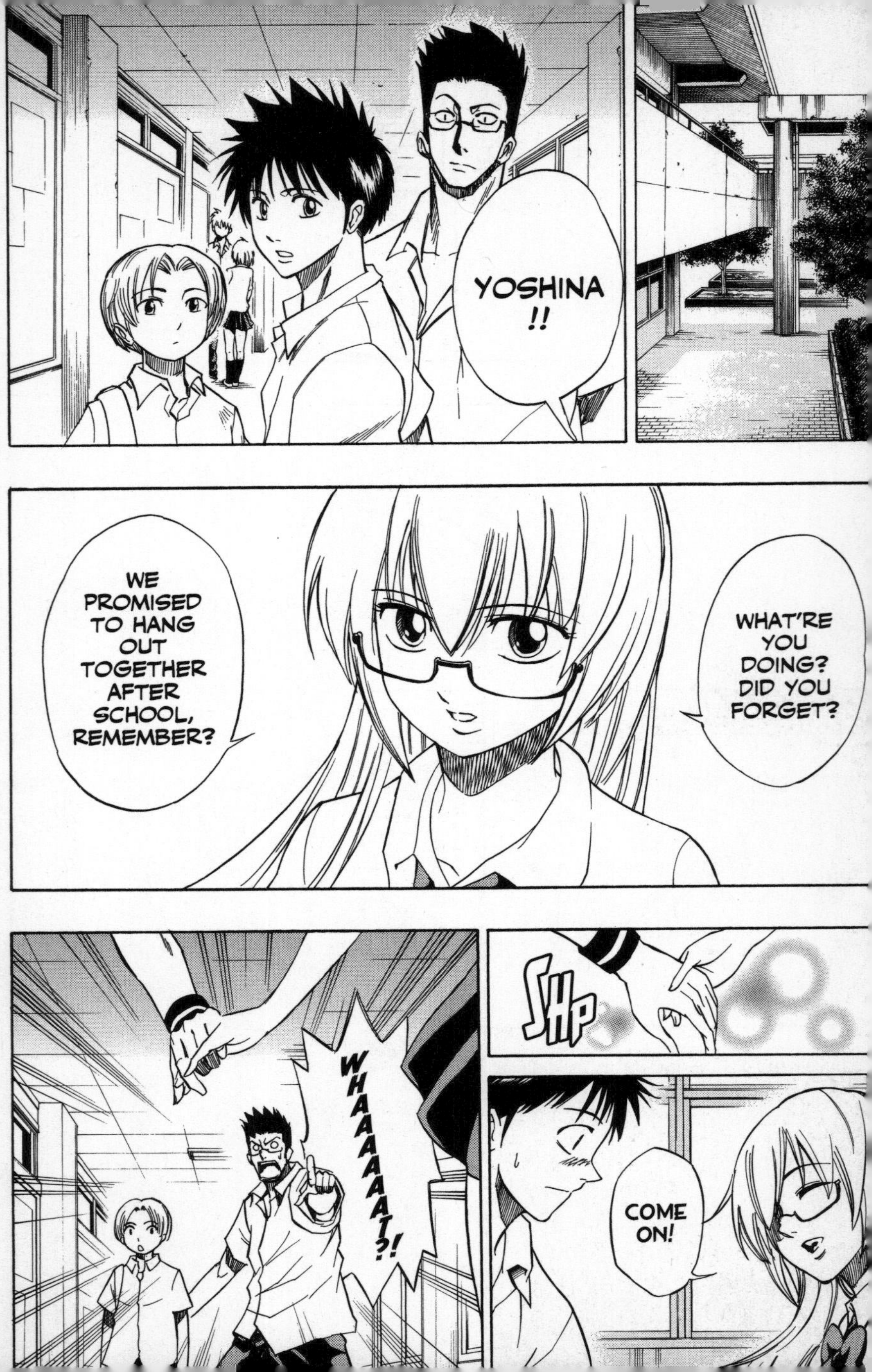
YOSHINA !!
WHAT'RE YOU DOING? DID YOU FORGET?
WE PROMISED TO HANG OUT TOGETHER AFTER SCHOOL, REMEMBER?
SHP
COME ON!
WHAAAAAAT?!

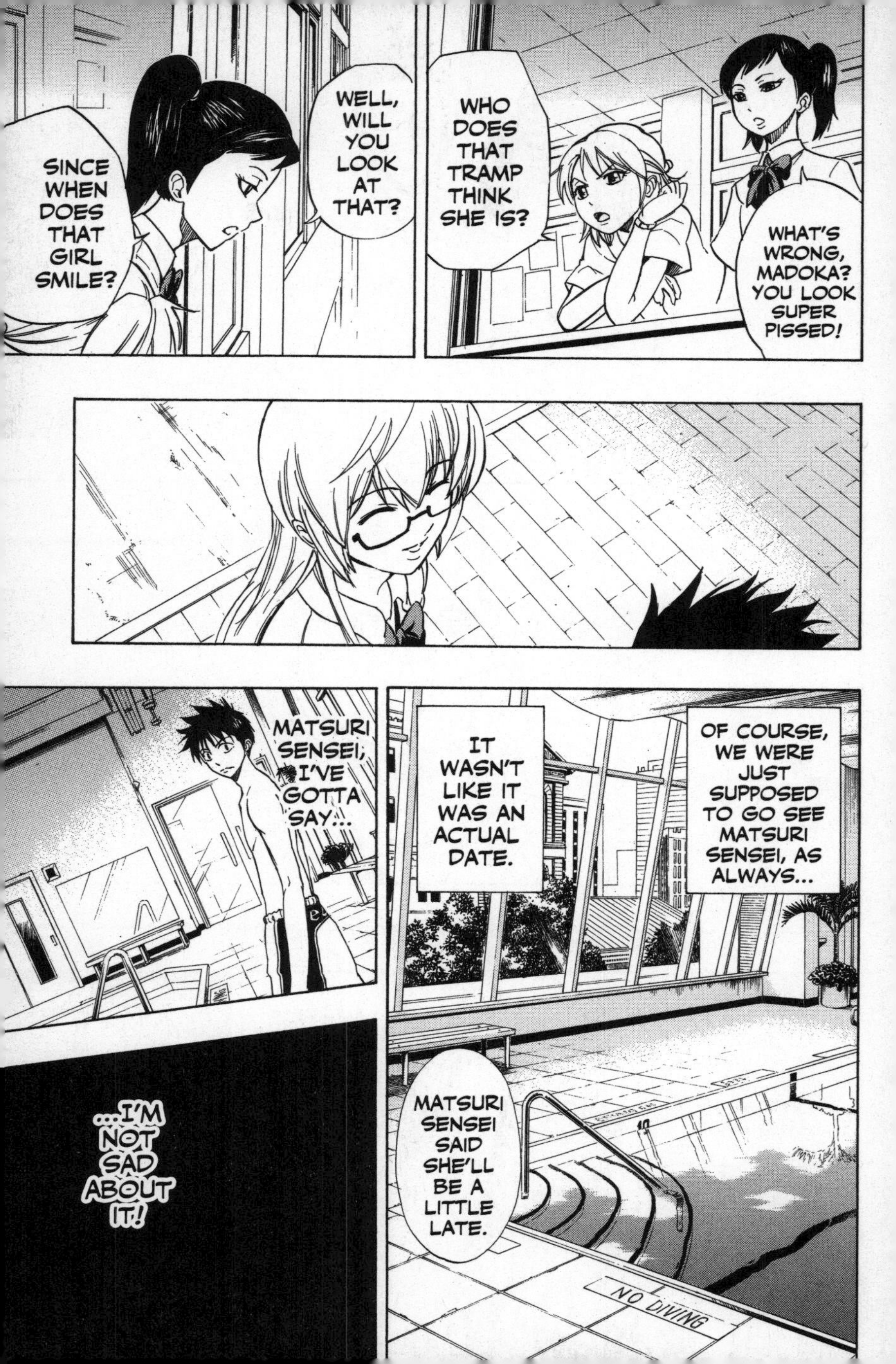
WHAT'S WRONG, MADOKA? YOU LOOK SUPER PISSED!
WHO DOES THAT TRAMP THINK SHE IS?
WELL, WILL YOU LOOK AT THAT?
SINCE WHEN DOES THAT GIRL SMILE?
OF COURSE, WE WERE JUST SUPPOSED TO GO SEE MATSURI SENSEI, AS ALWAYS...
IT WASN'T LIKE IT WAS AN ACTUAL DATE.
MATSURI SENSEI SAID SHE'LL BE A LITTLE LATE.
NO DIVING
MATSURI SENSEI, I'VE GOTTA SAY...
...I'M NOT SAD ABOUT IT!

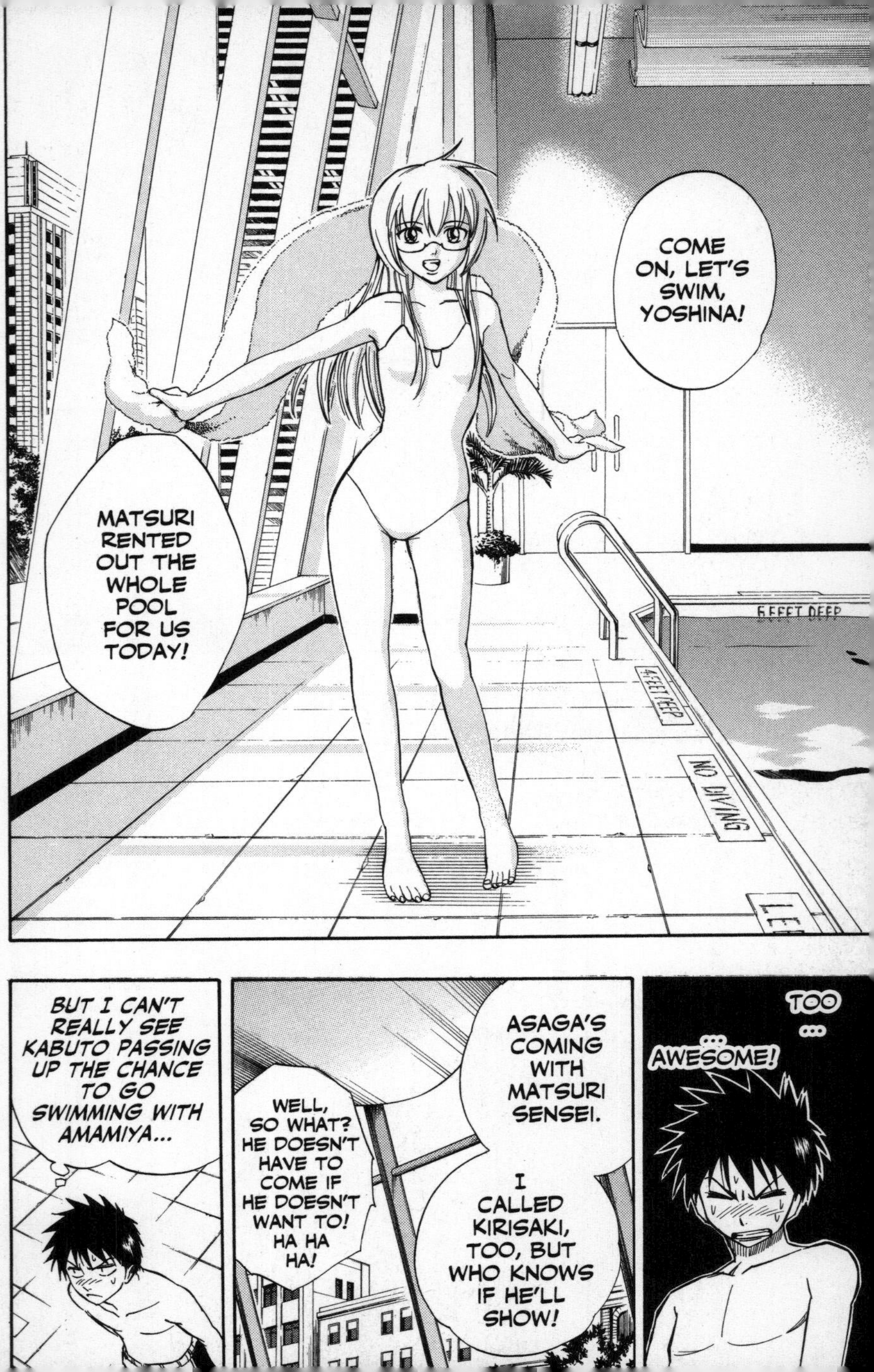
COME ON, LET'S SWIM, YOSHINA!
MATSURI RENTED OUT THE WHOLE POOL FOR US TODAY!
6 FEET DEEP
4 FEET DEEP
NO DIVING
TOO... ... AWESOME!
ASAGA'S COMING WITH MATSURI SENSEI.
I CALLED KIRISAKI, TOO, BUT WHO KNOWS IF HE'LL SHOW!
WELL, SO WHAT? HE DOESN'T HAVE TO COME IF HE DOESN'T WANT TO! HA HA HA!
BUT I CAN'T REALLY SEE KABUTO PASSING UP THE CHANCE TO GO SWIMMING WITH AMAMIYA...

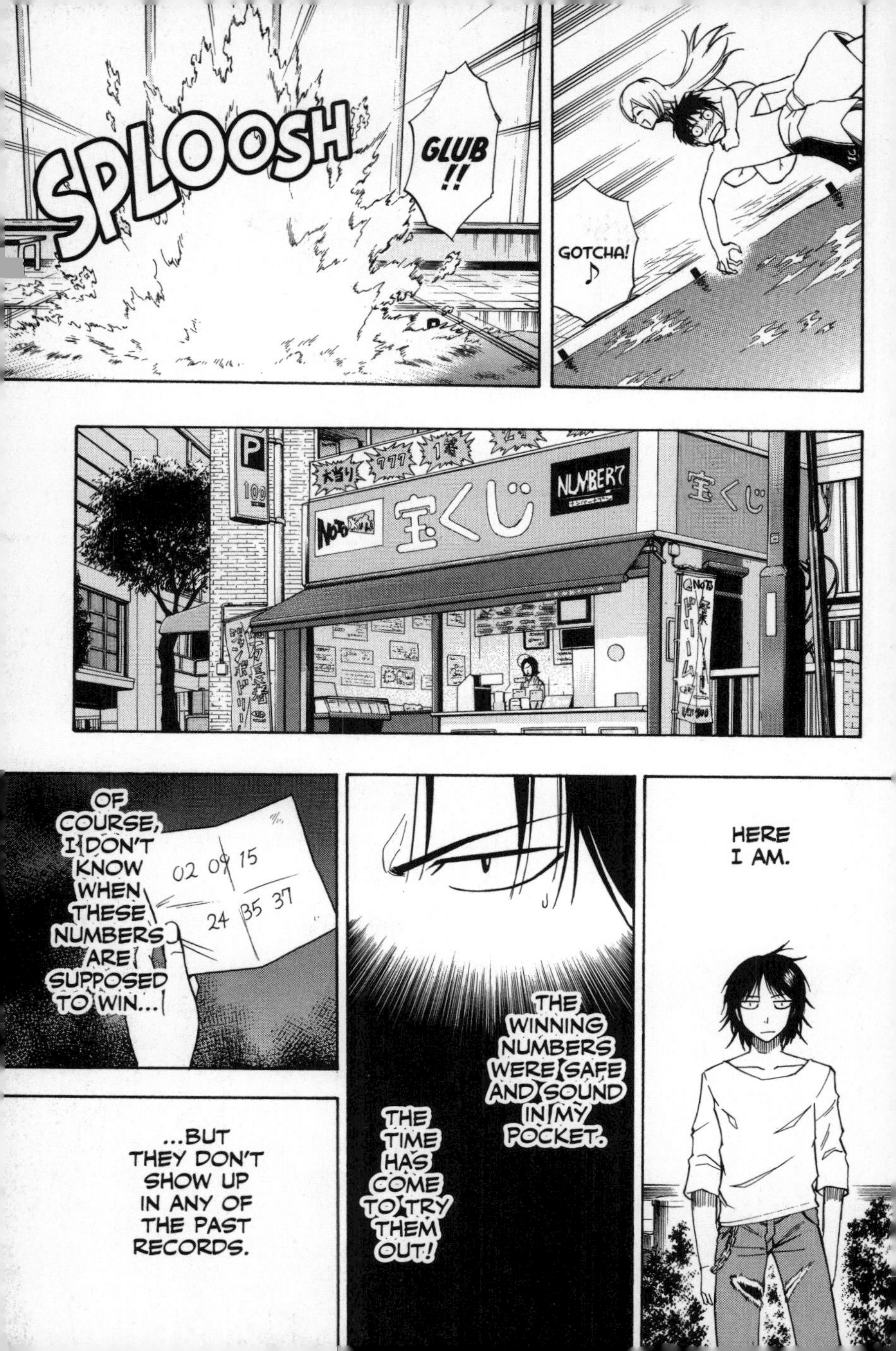

GOTCHA! ♪
GLUB !!
SPLOOSH
大当り
777
1等
NUMBER7
宝くじ
宝くじ
HERE I AM.
THE WINNING NUMBERS WERE SAFE AND SOUND IN MY POCKET.
THE TIME HAS COME TO TRY THEM OUT!
OF COURSE, I DON'T KNOW WHEN THESE NUMBERS ARE SUPPOSED TO WIN...
02 09 15
24 35 37
...BUT THEY DON'T SHOW UP IN ANY OF THE PAST RECORDS.

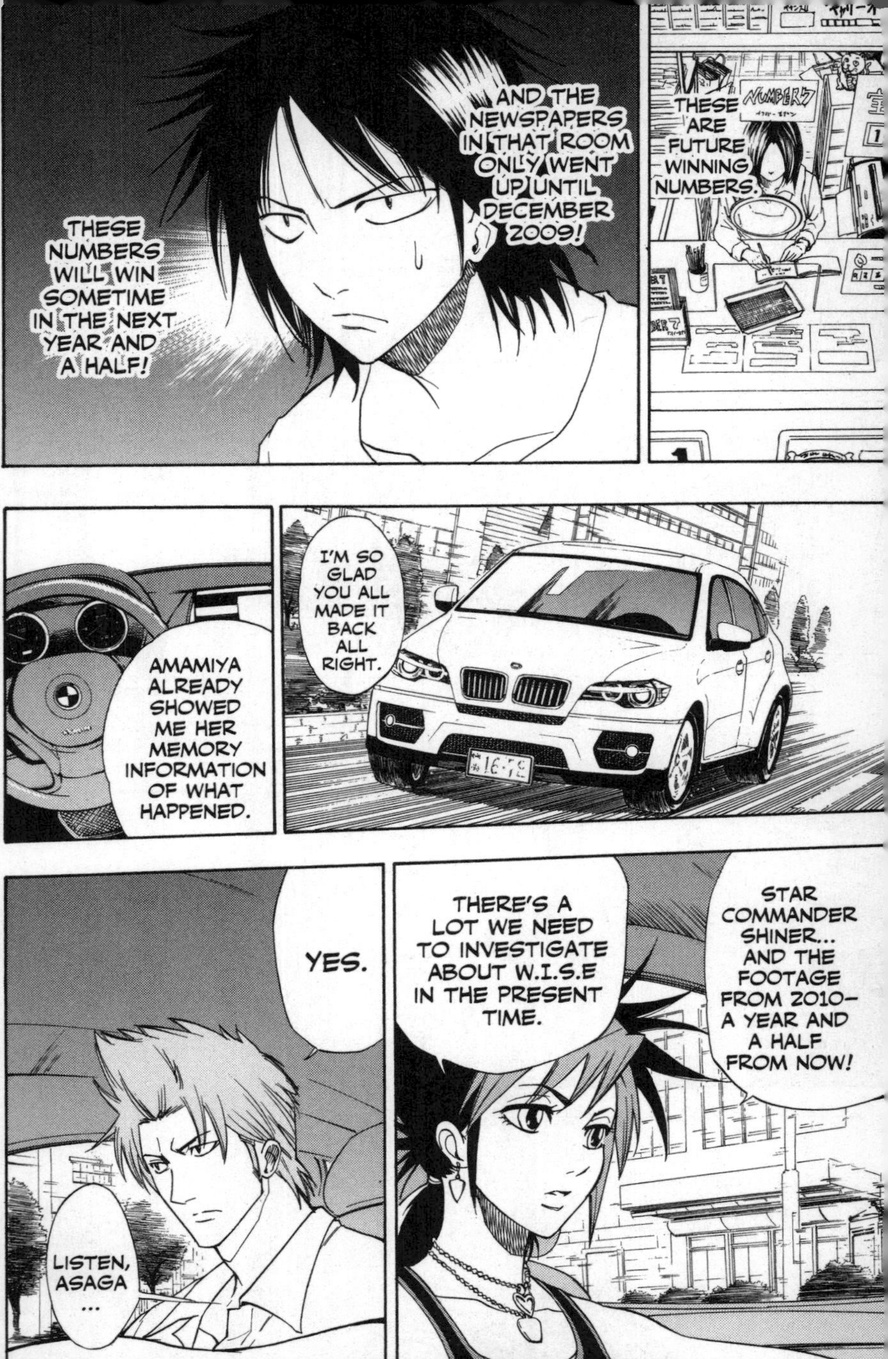
THESE ARE FUTURE WINNING NUMBERS.
AND THE NEWSPAPERS IN THAT ROOM ONLY WENT UP UNTIL DECEMBER 2009!
THESE NUMBERS WILL WIN SOMETIME IN THE NEXT YEAR AND A HALF!
I'M SO GLAD YOU ALL MADE IT BACK ALL RIGHT.
AMAMIYA ALREADY SHOWED ME HER MEMORY INFORMATION OF WHAT HAPPENED.
STAR COMMANDER SHINER... AND THE FOOTAGE FROM 2010— A YEAR AND A HALF FROM NOW!
THERE'S A LOT WE NEED TO INVESTIGATE ABOUT W.I.S.E IN THE PRESENT TIME.
YES.
LISTEN, ASAGA ...

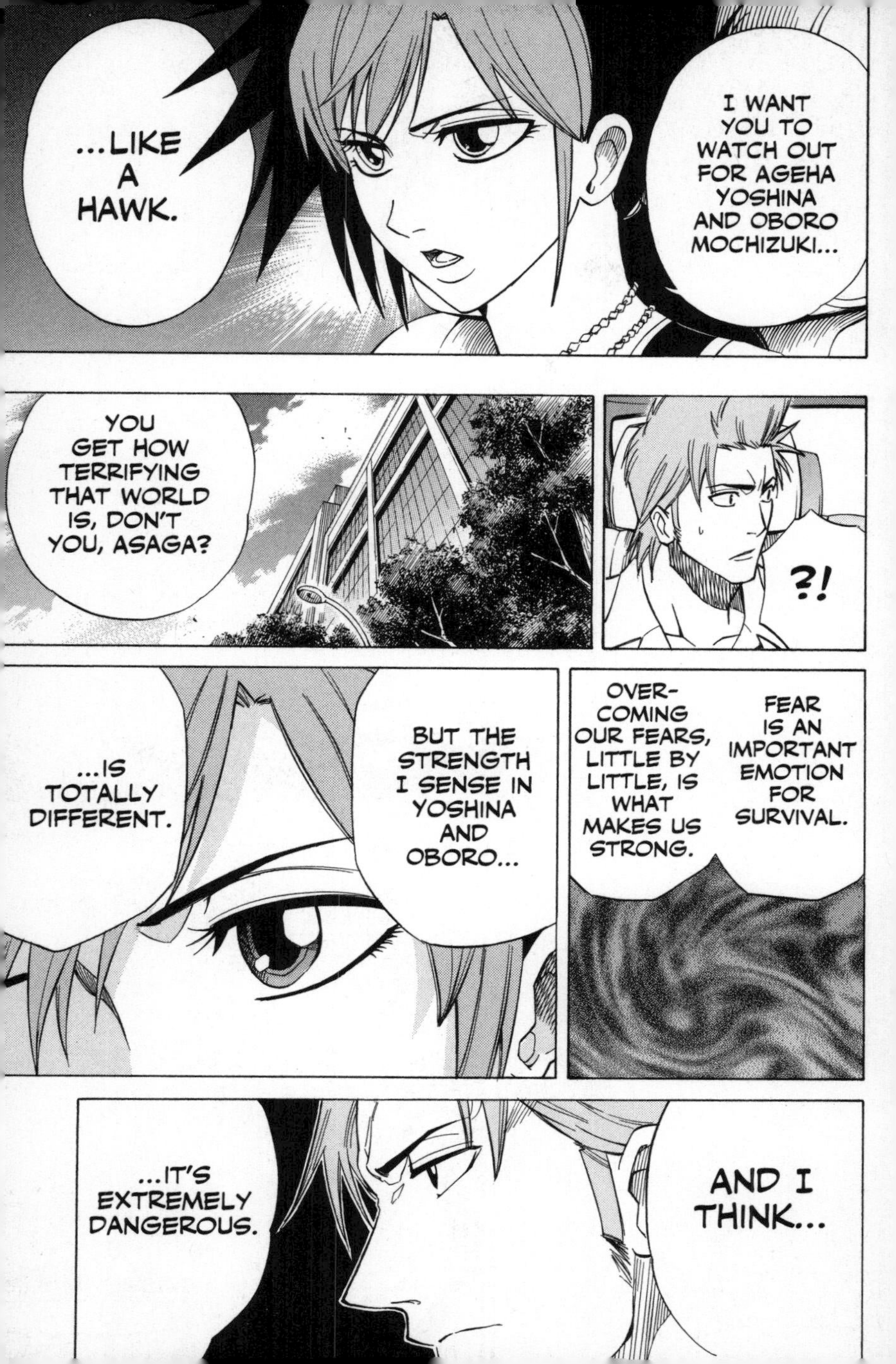
I WANT YOU TO WATCH OUT FOR AGEHA YOSHINA AND OBORO MOCHIZUKI...
...LIKE A HAWK.
?!
YOU GET HOW TERRIFYING THAT WORLD IS, DON'T YOU, ASAGA?
FEAR IS AN IMPORTANT EMOTION FOR SURVIVAL.
OVER-COMING OUR FEARS, LITTLE BY LITTLE, IS WHAT MAKES US STRONG.
BUT THE STRENGTH I SENSE IN YOSHINA AND OBORO...
...IS TOTALLY DIFFERENT.
AND I THINK...
...IT'S EXTREMELY DANGEROUS.

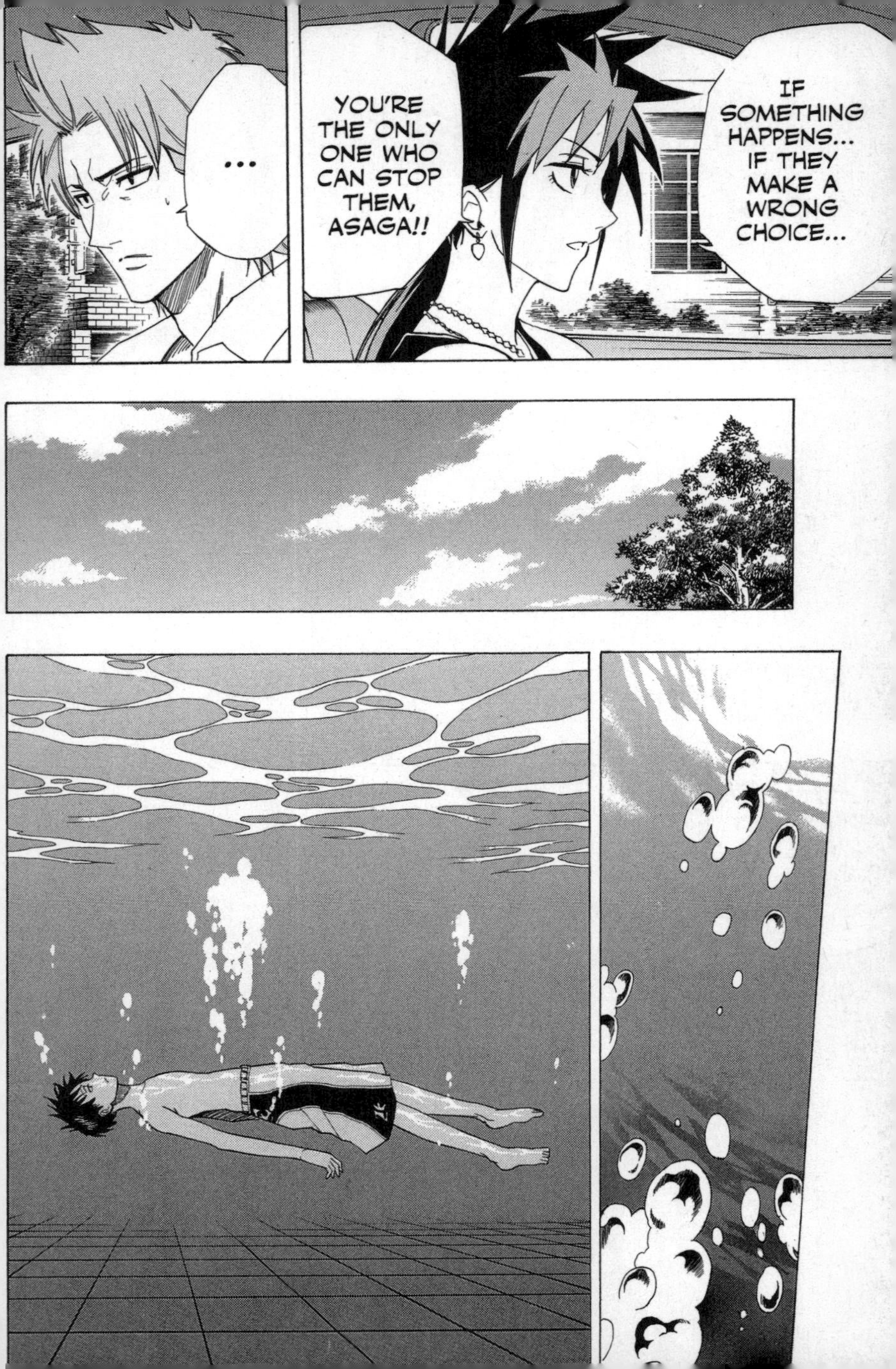
IF SOMETHING HAPPENS... IF THEY MAKE A WRONG CHOICE...
YOU'RE THE ONLY ONE WHO CAN STOP THEM, ASAGA!!
...

MAN, THIS FEELS GREAT.

SPLOOSH

...SEEMS LIKE A FARAWAY DREAM.

THAT BATTLE...

YOU'VE GOTTEN STRONGER...

...YOSHINA!

ZOOP

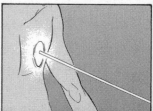

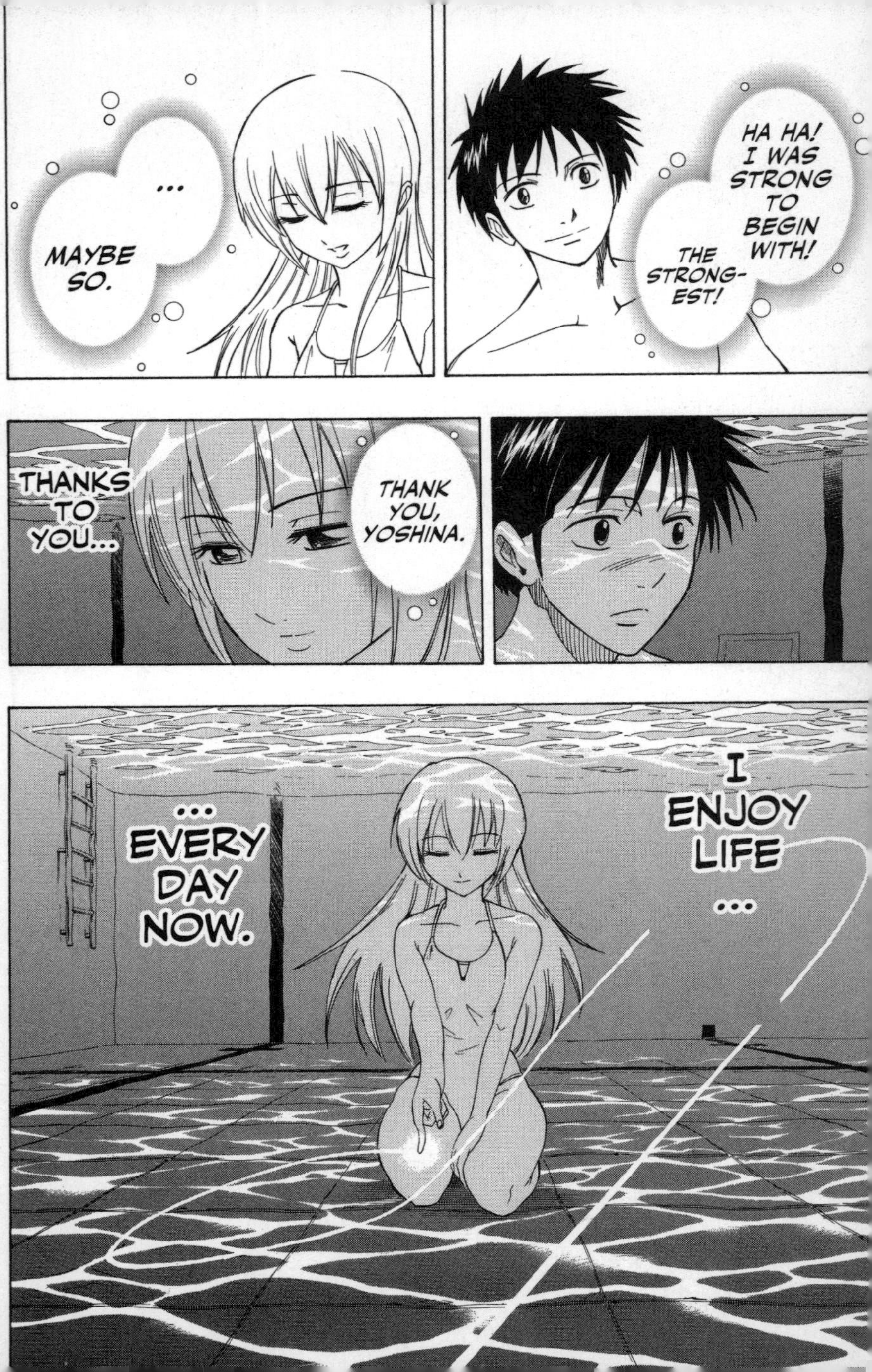
HA HA! I WAS STRONG TO BEGIN WITH!
THE STRONGEST!
...
MAYBE SO.
THANK YOU, YOSHINA.
THANKS TO YOU...
I ENJOY LIFE ...
... EVERY DAY NOW.

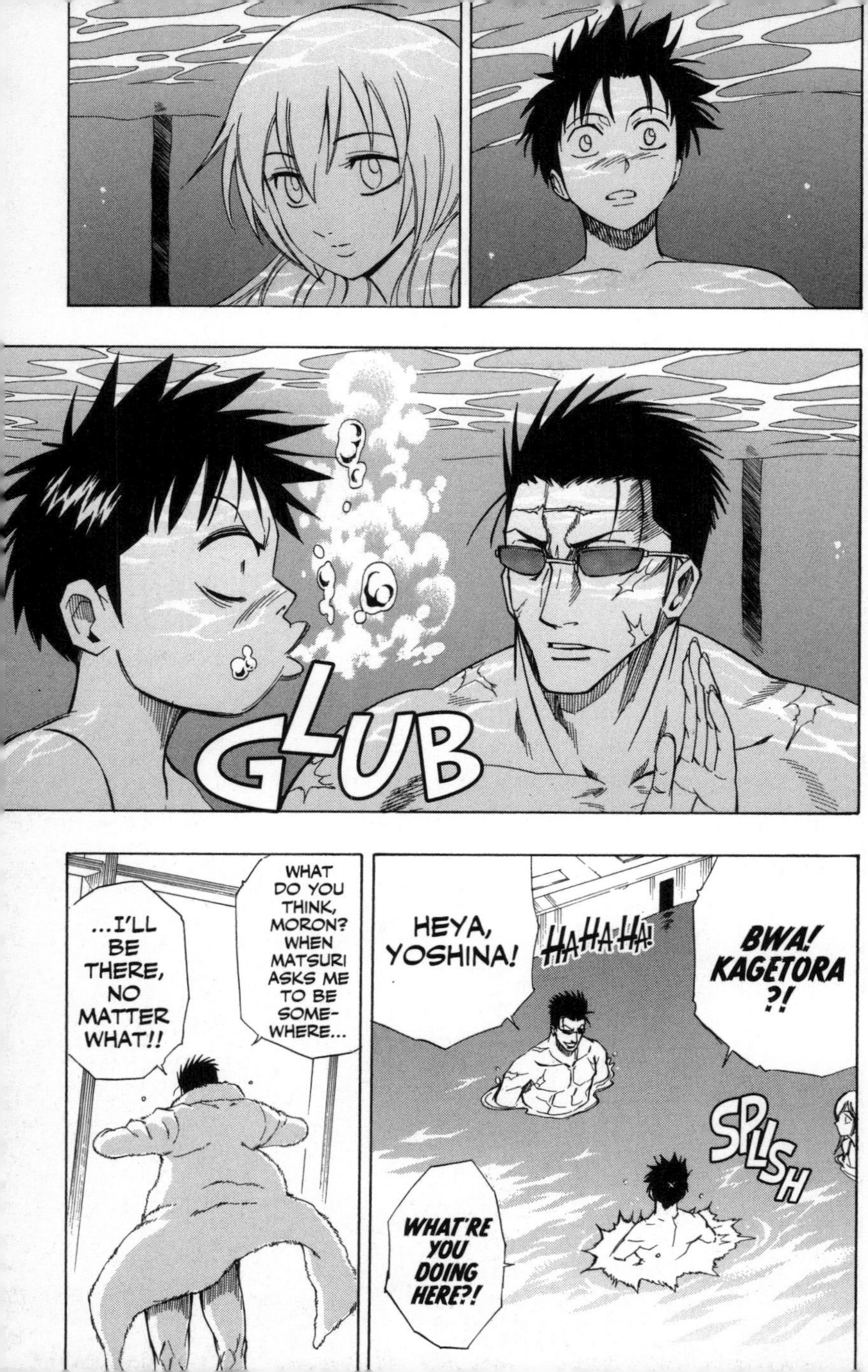
GLUB
BWA! KAGETORA?!
HAHAHA!
HEYA, YOSHINA!
SPLSH
WHAT'RE YOU DOING HERE?!
WHAT DO YOU THINK, MORON? WHEN MATSURI ASKS ME TO BE SOME-WHERE...
...I'LL BE THERE, NO MATTER WHAT!!

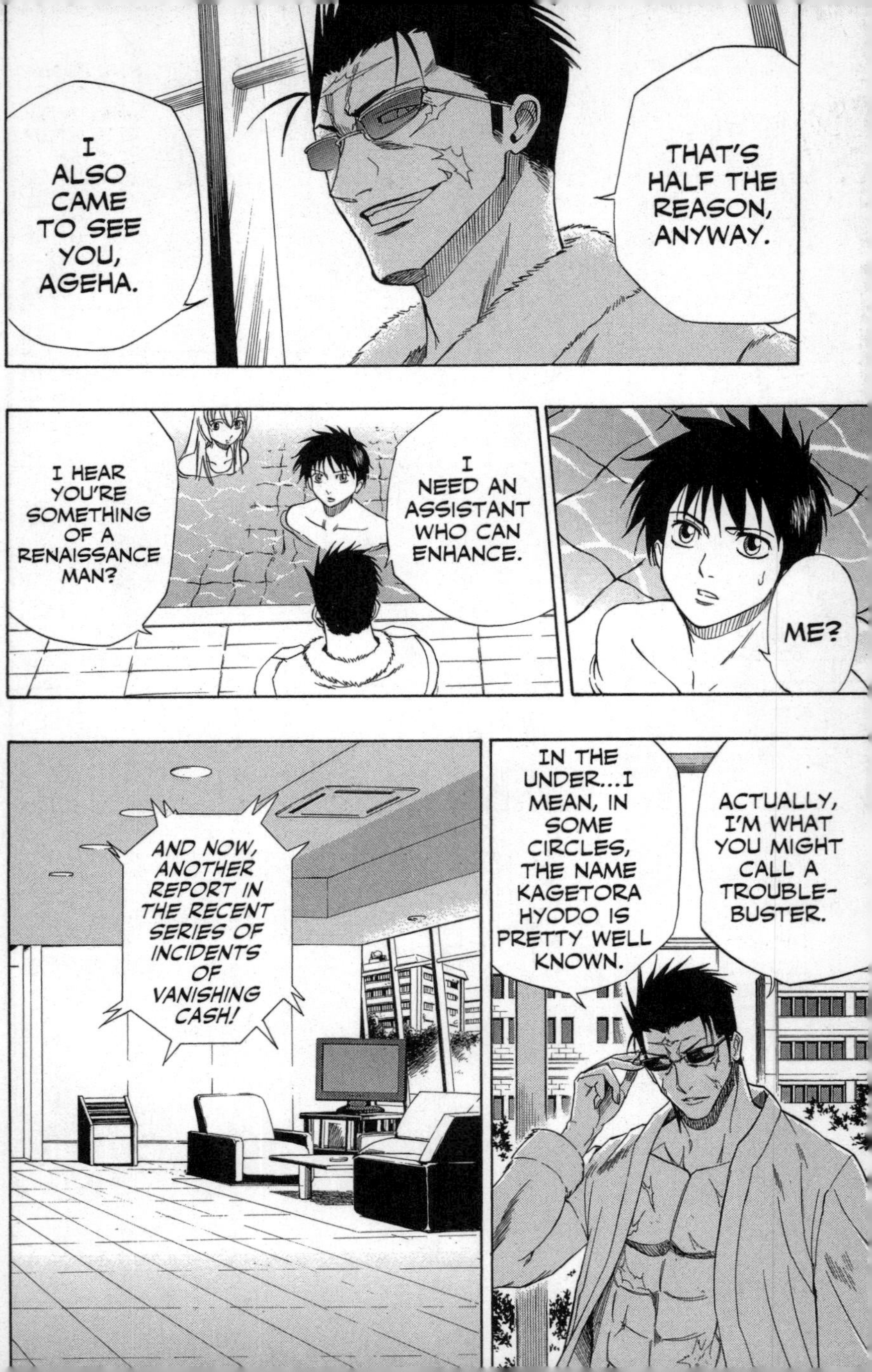
THAT'S HALF THE REASON, ANYWAY.
I ALSO CAME TO SEE YOU, AGEHA.
ME?
I NEED AN ASSISTANT WHO CAN ENHANCE.
I HEAR YOU'RE SOMETHING OF A RENAISSANCE MAN?
ACTUALLY, I'M WHAT YOU MIGHT CALL A TROUBLE-BUSTER.
IN THE UNDER...I MEAN, IN SOME CIRCLES, THE NAME KAGETORA HYODO IS PRETTY WELL KNOWN.
AND NOW, ANOTHER REPORT IN THE RECENT SERIES OF INCIDENTS OF VANISHING CASH!

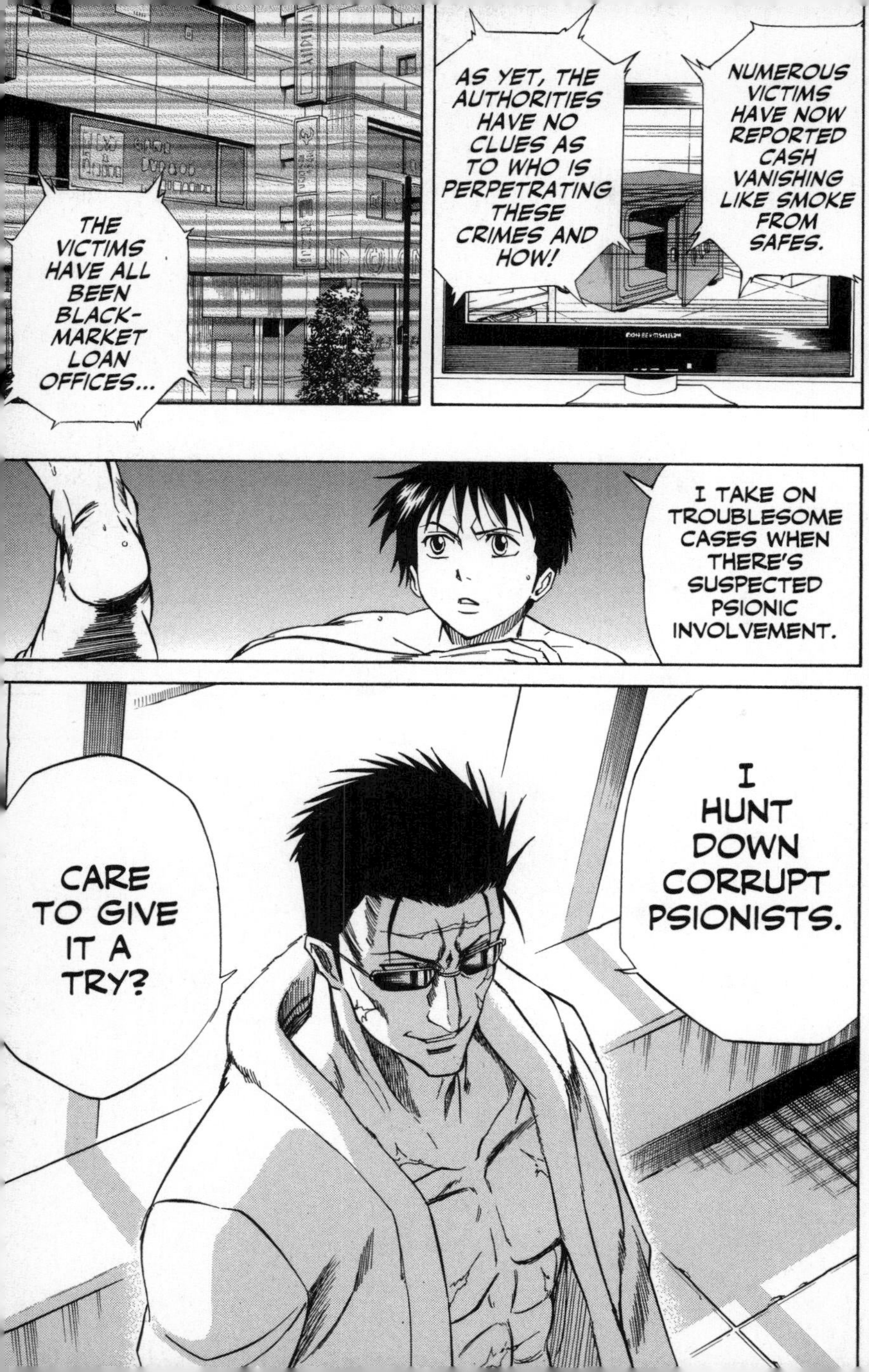
NUMEROUS VICTIMS HAVE NOW REPORTED CASH VANISHING LIKE SMOKE FROM SAFES.
AS YET, THE AUTHORITIES HAVE NO CLUES AS TO WHO IS PERPETRATING THESE CRIMES AND HOW!
THE VICTIMS HAVE ALL BEEN BLACK-MARKET LOAN OFFICES...
I TAKE ON TROUBLESOME CASES WHEN THERE'S SUSPECTED PSIONIC INVOLVEMENT.
I HUNT DOWN CORRUPT PSIONISTS.
CARE TO GIVE IT A TRY?

Mutters and mumblings...

STRUGGLES

THE PRESENT-DAY STORY THAT BEGINS IN THIS
VOLUME INVOLVED THE INS AND OUTS OF SO MANY
CHARACTERS THAT DRAFTING THE STORYBOARDS WAS
A HUGE CHALLENGE. BIT BY BIT, I HAD TO WEAVE IN
THE NECESSARY FORESHADOWING AND INTRODUCE THE
NEW CHARACTERS WHILE GIVING EACH OF THE KIDS A
CHANCE TO APPEAR. IT WAS HARD, BUT THANKS TO
THAT EXPERIENCE MY STORYBOARDING ABILITIES HAVE
IMPROVED (OR AT LEAST I'VE DEVELOPED THE ABILITY
TO SHRUG IN THE FACE OF POTENTIAL FAILURE).

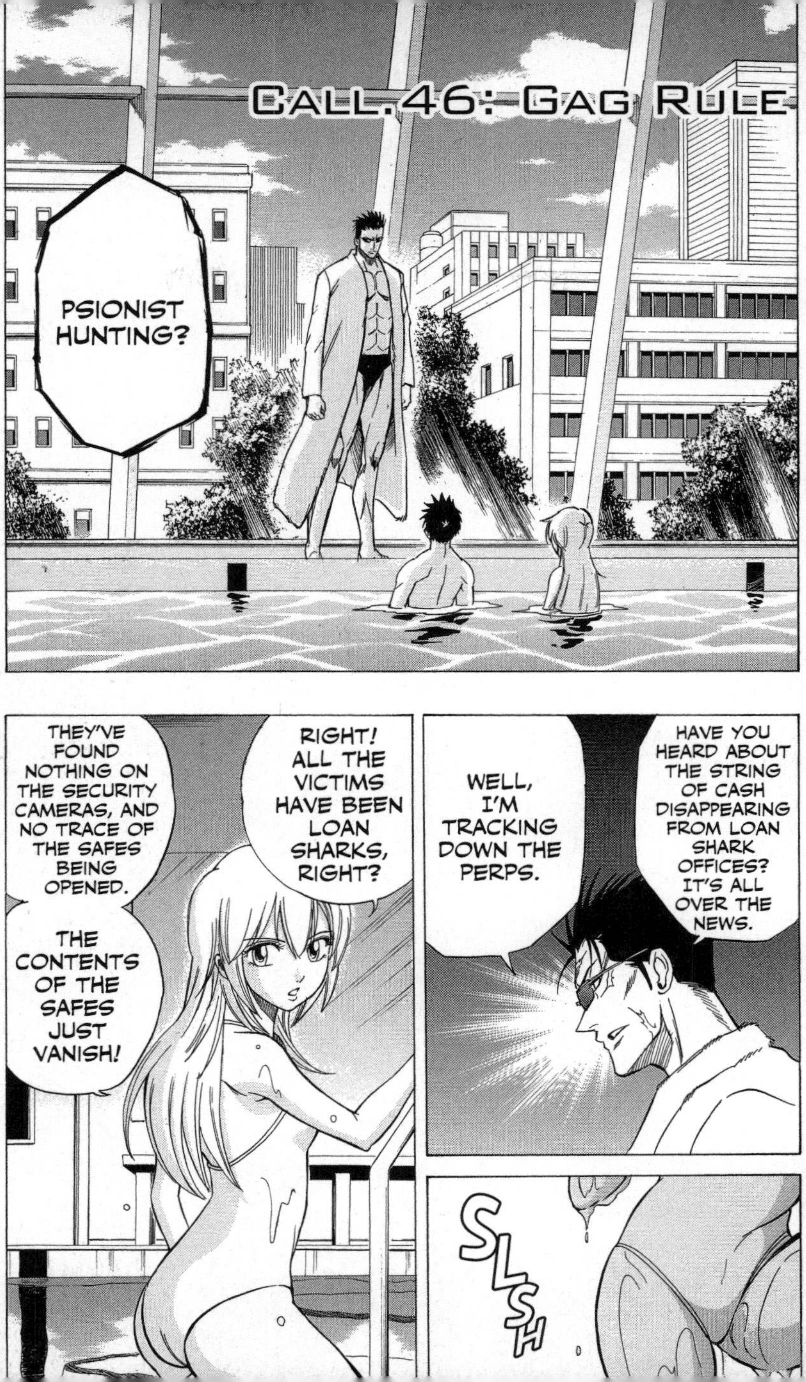
CALL.46: GAG RULE
PSIONIST HUNTING?
HAVE YOU HEARD ABOUT THE STRING OF CASH DISAPPEARING FROM LOAN SHARK OFFICES? IT'S ALL OVER THE NEWS.
WELL, I'M TRACKING DOWN THE PERPS.
SLSH
RIGHT! ALL THE VICTIMS HAVE BEEN LOAN SHARKS, RIGHT?
THEY'VE FOUND NOTHING ON THE SECURITY CAMERAS, AND NO TRACE OF THE SAFES BEING OPENED.
THE CONTENTS OF THE SAFES JUST VANISH!

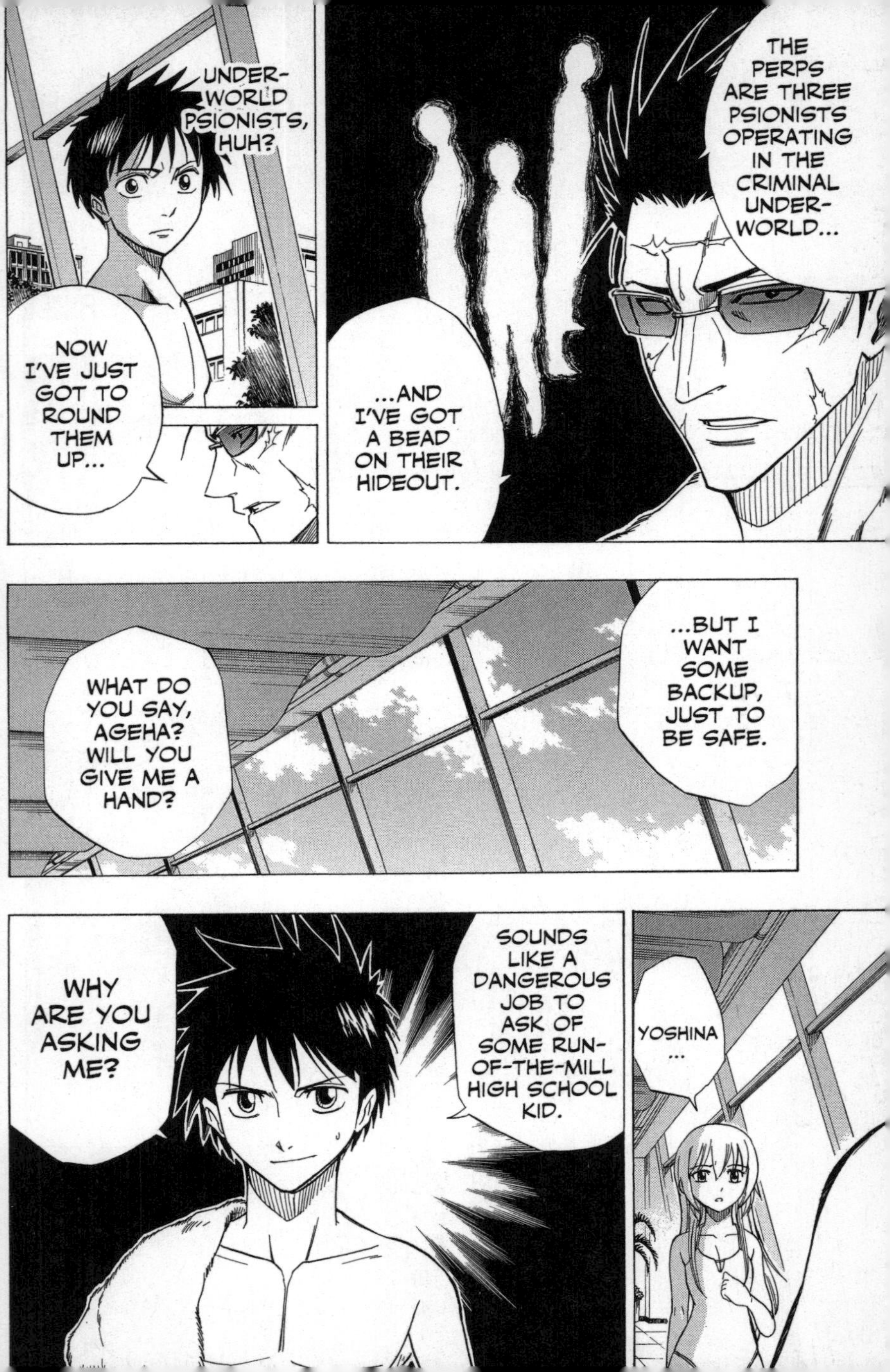
THE PERPS ARE THREE PSIONISTS OPERATING IN THE CRIMINAL UNDER-WORLD...
...AND I'VE GOT A BEAD ON THEIR HIDEOUT.
UNDER-WORLD PSIONISTS, HUH?
NOW I'VE JUST GOT TO ROUND THEM UP...
...BUT I WANT SOME BACKUP, JUST TO BE SAFE.
WHAT DO YOU SAY, AGEHA? WILL YOU GIVE ME A HAND?
YOSHINA ...
SOUNDS LIKE A DANGEROUS JOB TO ASK OF SOME RUN-OF-THE-MILL HIGH SCHOOL KID.
WHY ARE YOU ASKING ME?

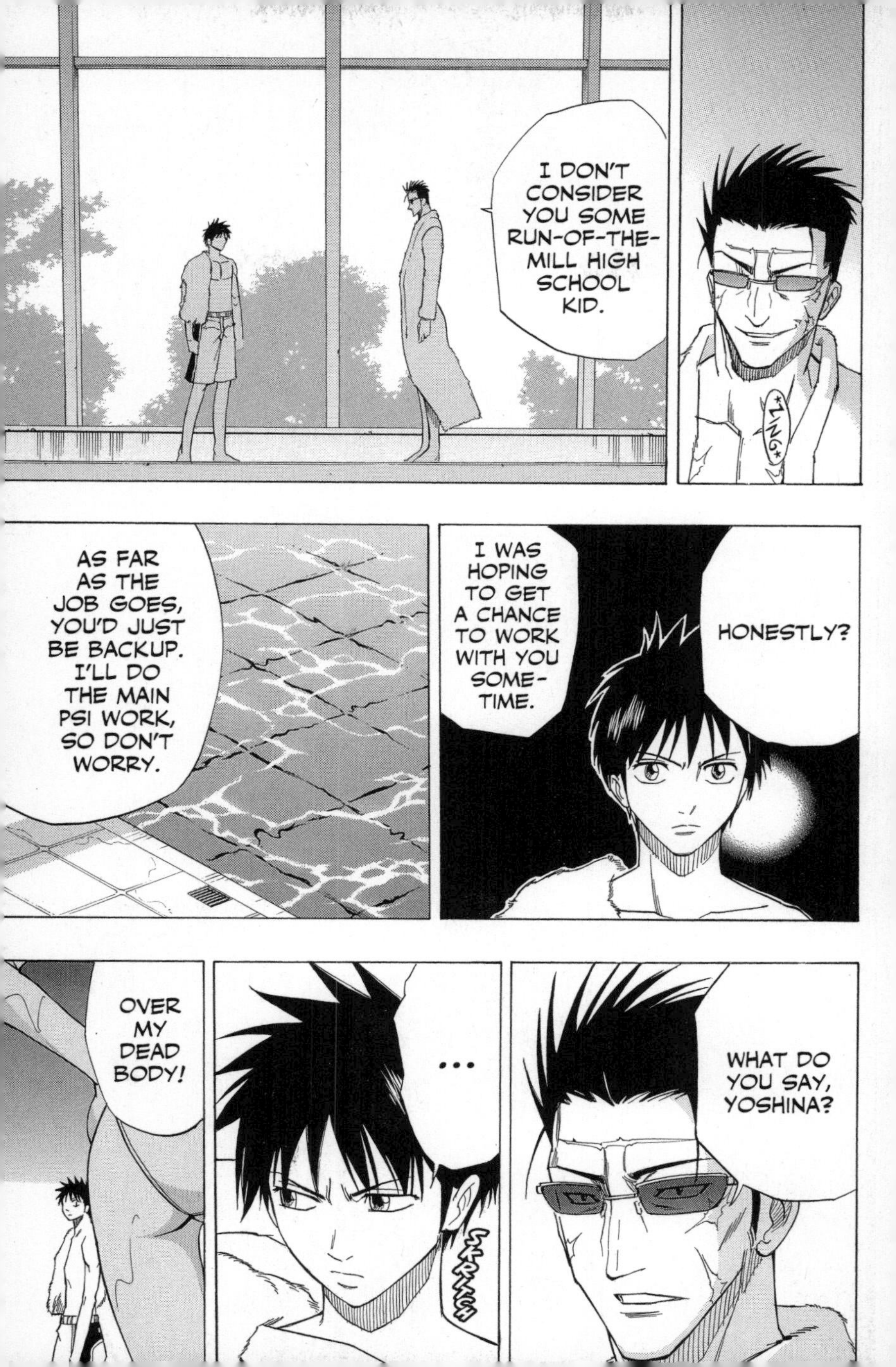
ZING
I DON'T CONSIDER YOU SOME RUN-OF-THE-MILL HIGH SCHOOL KID.
HONESTLY?
I WAS HOPING TO GET A CHANCE TO WORK WITH YOU SOME-TIME.
AS FAR AS THE JOB GOES, YOU'D JUST BE BACKUP. I'LL DO THE MAIN PSI WORK, SO DON'T WORRY.
WHAT DO YOU SAY, YOSHINA?
...
SKRITCH
OVER MY DEAD BODY!

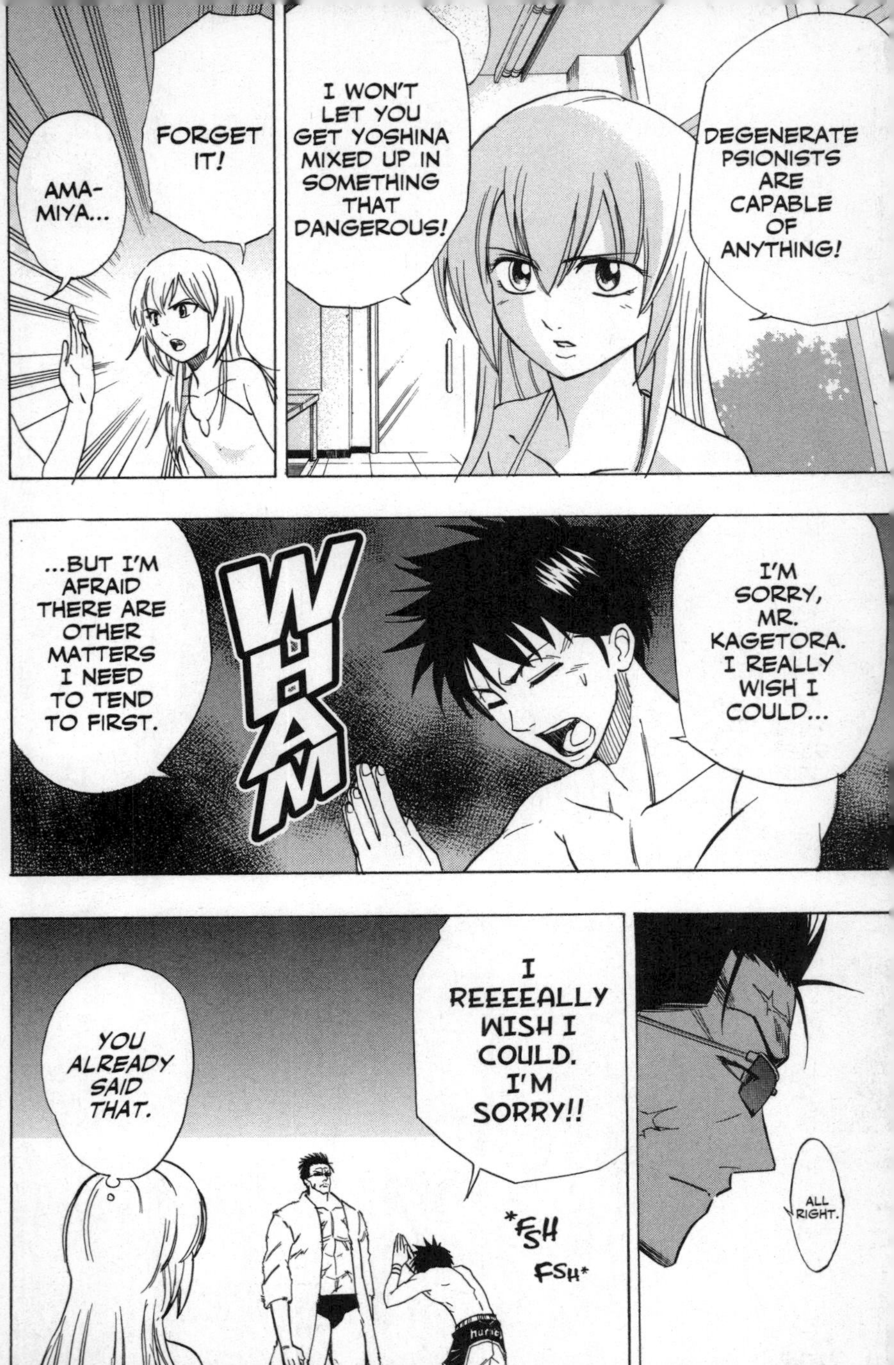
DEGENERATE PSIONISTS ARE CAPABLE OF ANYTHING!
I WON'T LET YOU GET YOSHINA MIXED UP IN SOMETHING THAT DANGEROUS!
FORGET IT!
AMA-MIYA...
I'M SORRY, MR. KAGETORA. I REALLY WISH I COULD...
WHAM
...BUT I'M AFRAID THERE ARE OTHER MATTERS I NEED TO TEND TO FIRST.
ALL RIGHT.
I REEEEALLY WISH I COULD. I'M SORRY!!
FSH FSH
YOU ALREADY SAID THAT.

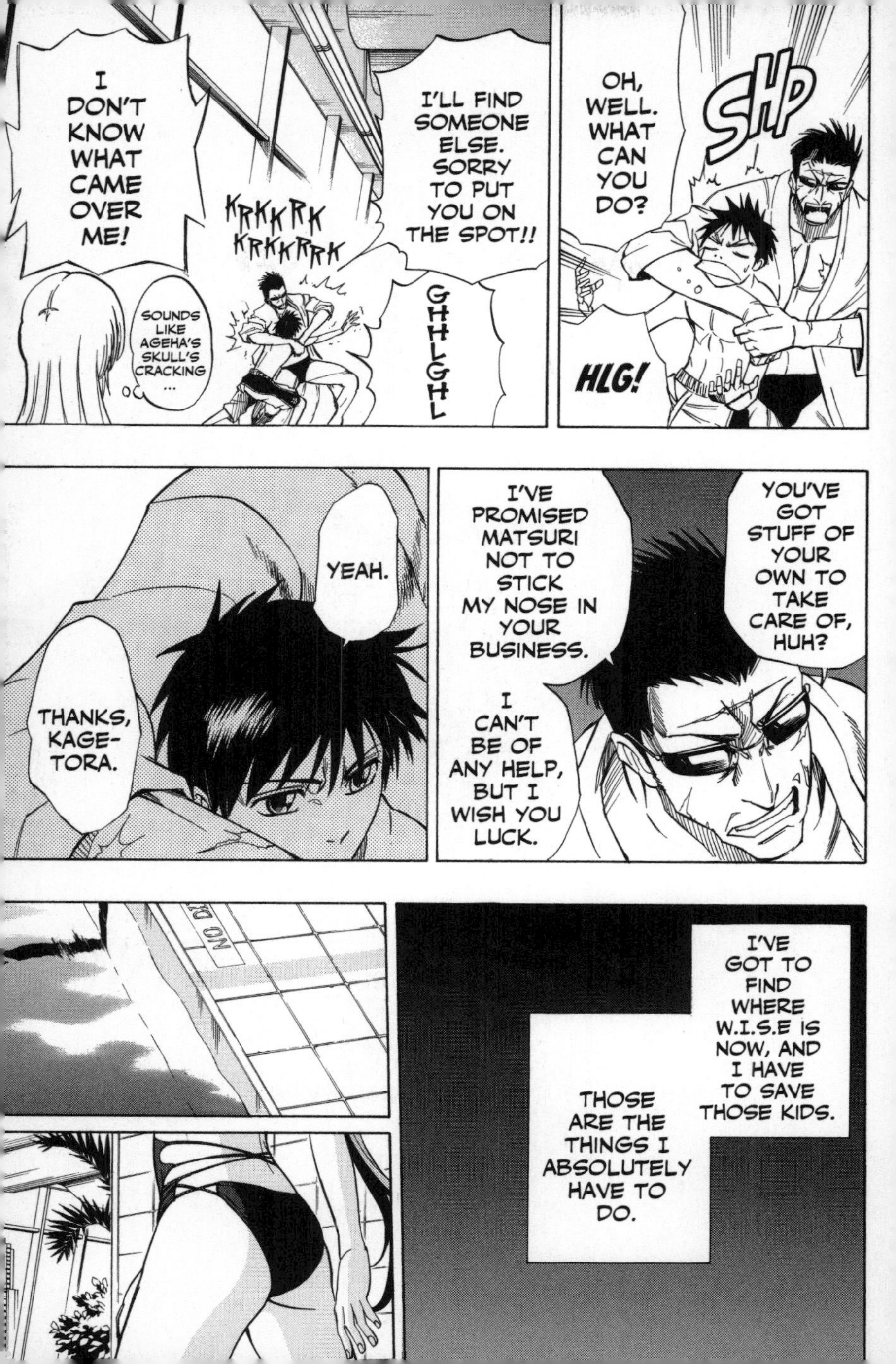
SHP
OH, WELL. WHAT CAN YOU DO?
HLG!
I'LL FIND SOMEONE ELSE. SORRY TO PUT YOU ON THE SPOT!!
GHHLGHL
KRKKRK KRKKRRK
I DON'T KNOW WHAT CAME OVER ME!
SOUNDS LIKE AGEHA'S SKULL'S CRACKING ...
YOU'VE GOT STUFF OF YOUR OWN TO TAKE CARE OF, HUH?
I'VE PROMISED MATSURI NOT TO STICK MY NOSE IN YOUR BUSINESS.
I CAN'T BE OF ANY HELP, BUT I WISH YOU LUCK.
YEAH.
THANKS, KAGE-TORA.
I'VE GOT TO FIND WHERE W.I.S.E IS NOW, AND I HAVE TO SAVE THOSE KIDS.
THOSE ARE THE THINGS I ABSOLUTELY HAVE TO DO.

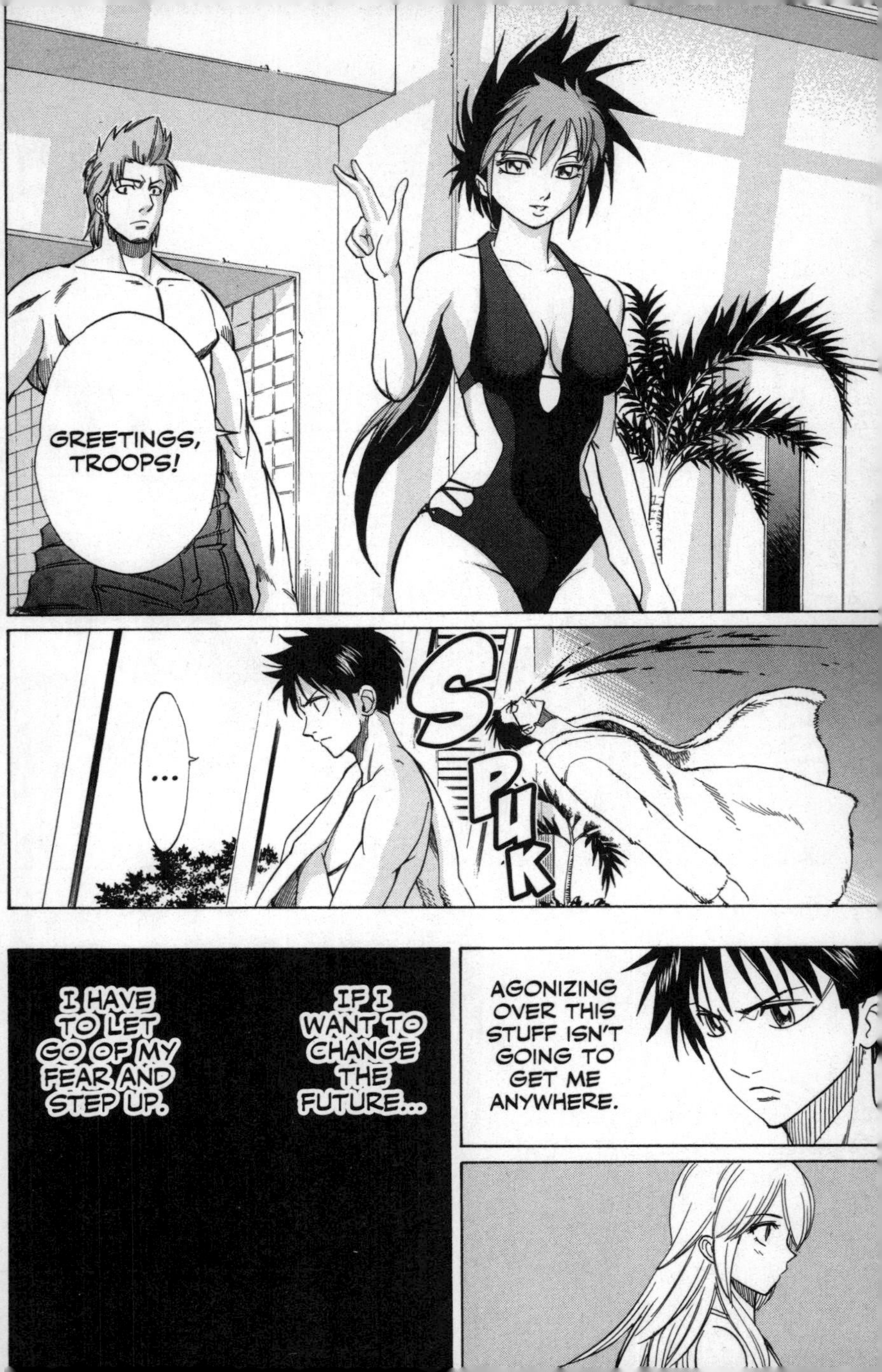
GREETINGS, TROOPS!
SPUK
...
AGONIZING OVER THIS STUFF ISN'T GOING TO GET ME ANYWHERE.
IF I WANT TO CHANGE THE FUTURE...
I HAVE TO LET GO OF MY FEAR AND STEP UP.

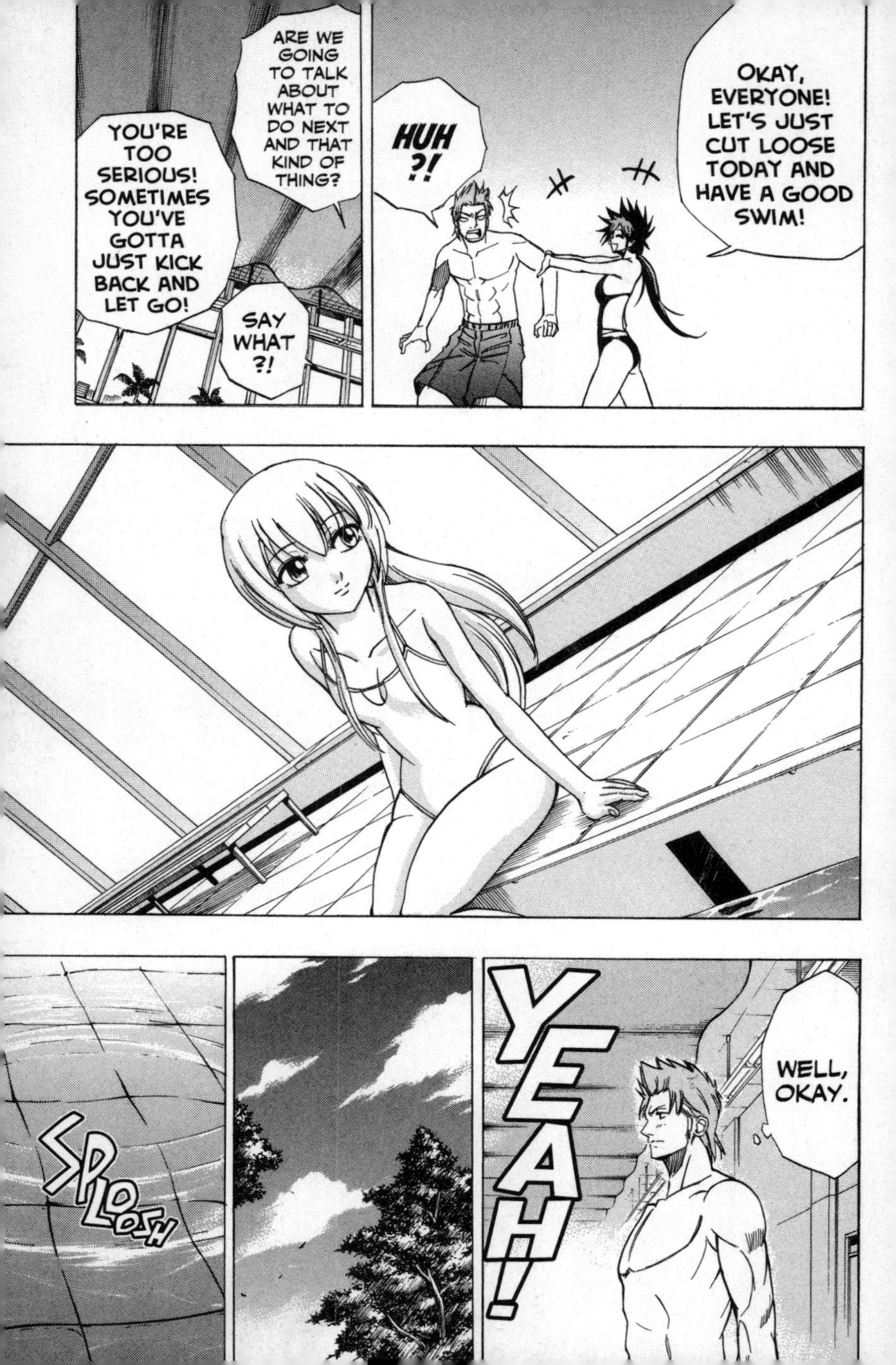
OKAY, EVERYONE! LET'S JUST CUT LOOSE TODAY AND HAVE A GOOD SWIM!
HUH ?!
ARE WE GOING TO TALK ABOUT WHAT TO DO NEXT AND THAT KIND OF THING?
YOU'RE TOO SERIOUS! SOMETIMES YOU'VE GOTTA JUST KICK BACK AND LET GO!
SAY WHAT ?!
WELL, OKAY.
YEAH!
SPLOSH

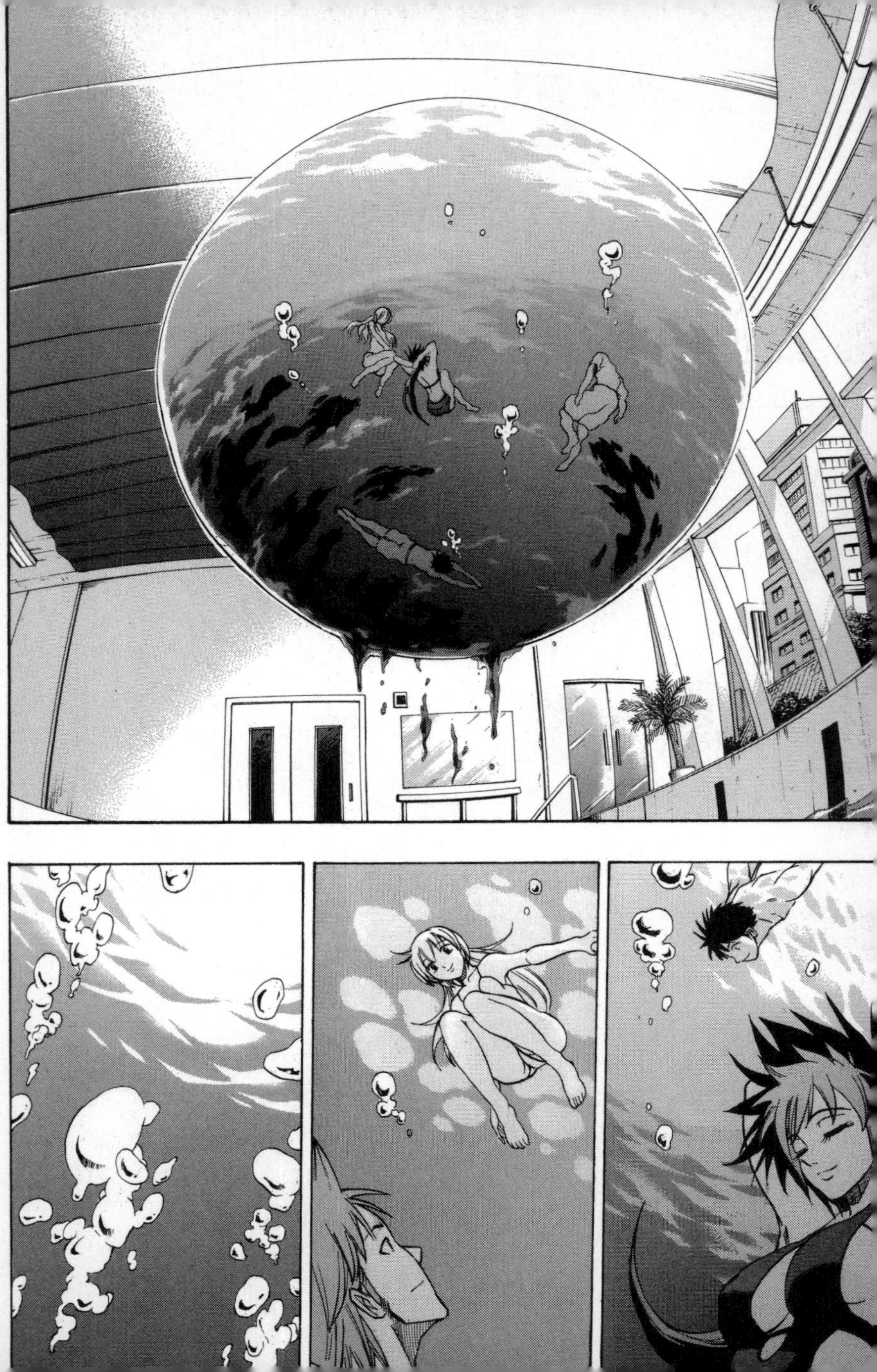

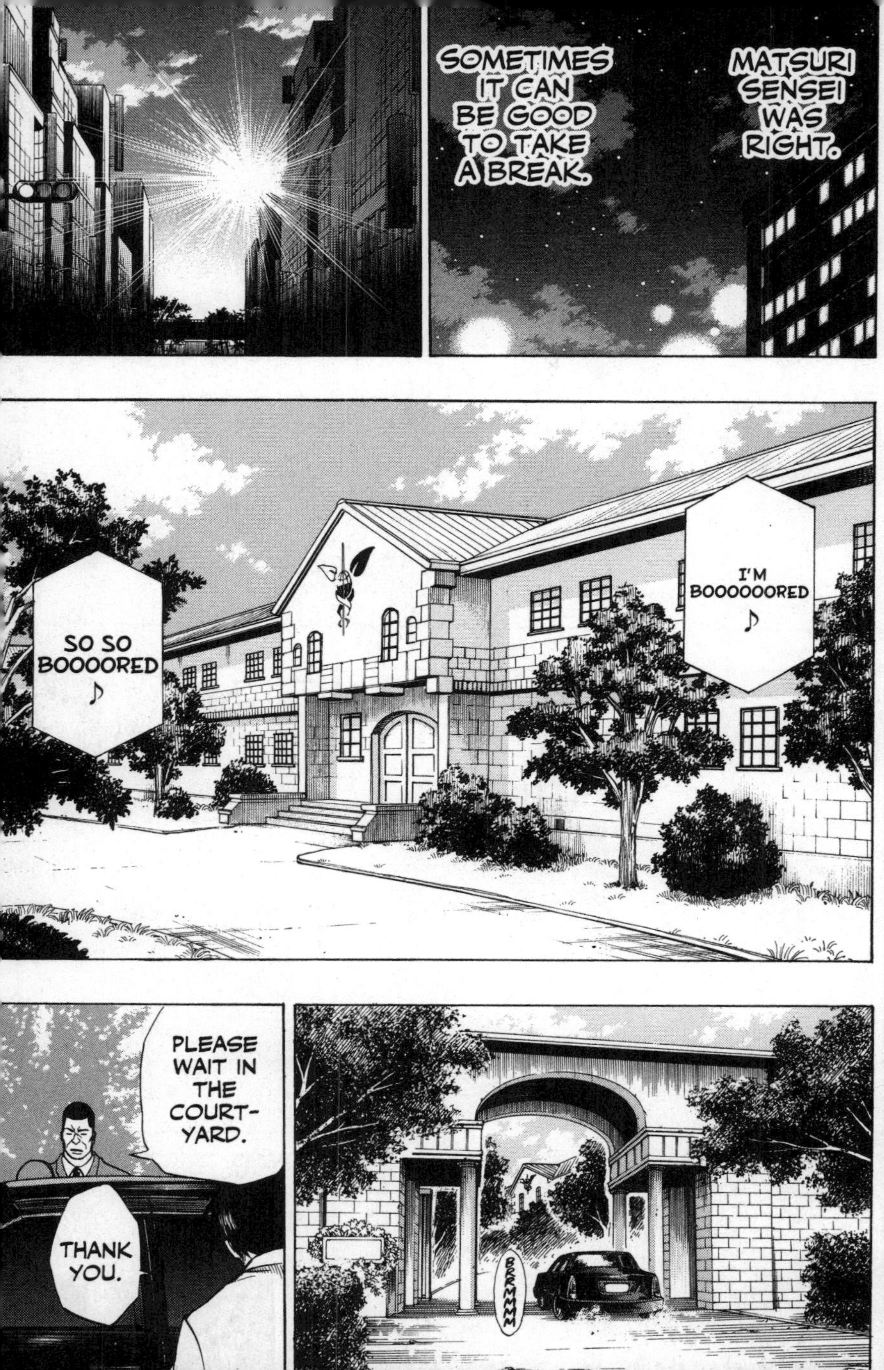
MATSURI SENSEI WAS RIGHT.
SOMETIMES IT CAN BE GOOD TO TAKE A BREAK.
I'M BOOOOOORED ♪
SO SO BOOOORED ♪
BRRMMMM
PLEASE WAIT IN THE COURT-YARD.
THANK YOU.

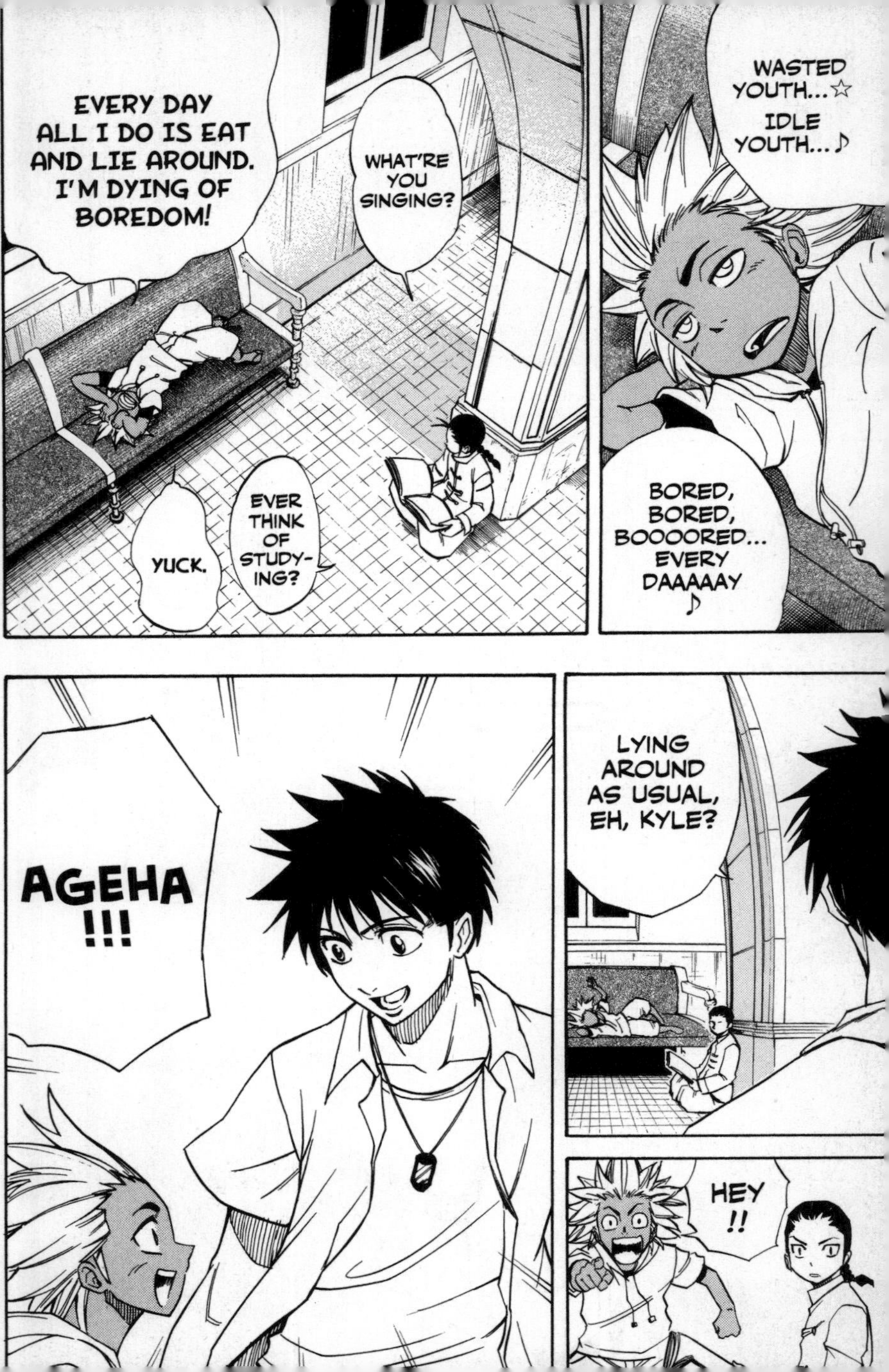

WASTED YOUTH...☆ IDLE YOUTH...♪
BORED, BORED, BOOOORED... EVERY DAAAAAY ♪
WHAT'RE YOU SINGING?
EVERY DAY ALL I DO IS EAT AND LIE AROUND. I'M DYING OF BOREDOM!
EVER THINK OF STUDYING?
YUCK.
LYING AROUND AS USUAL, EH, KYLE?
HEY !!
AGEHA !!!

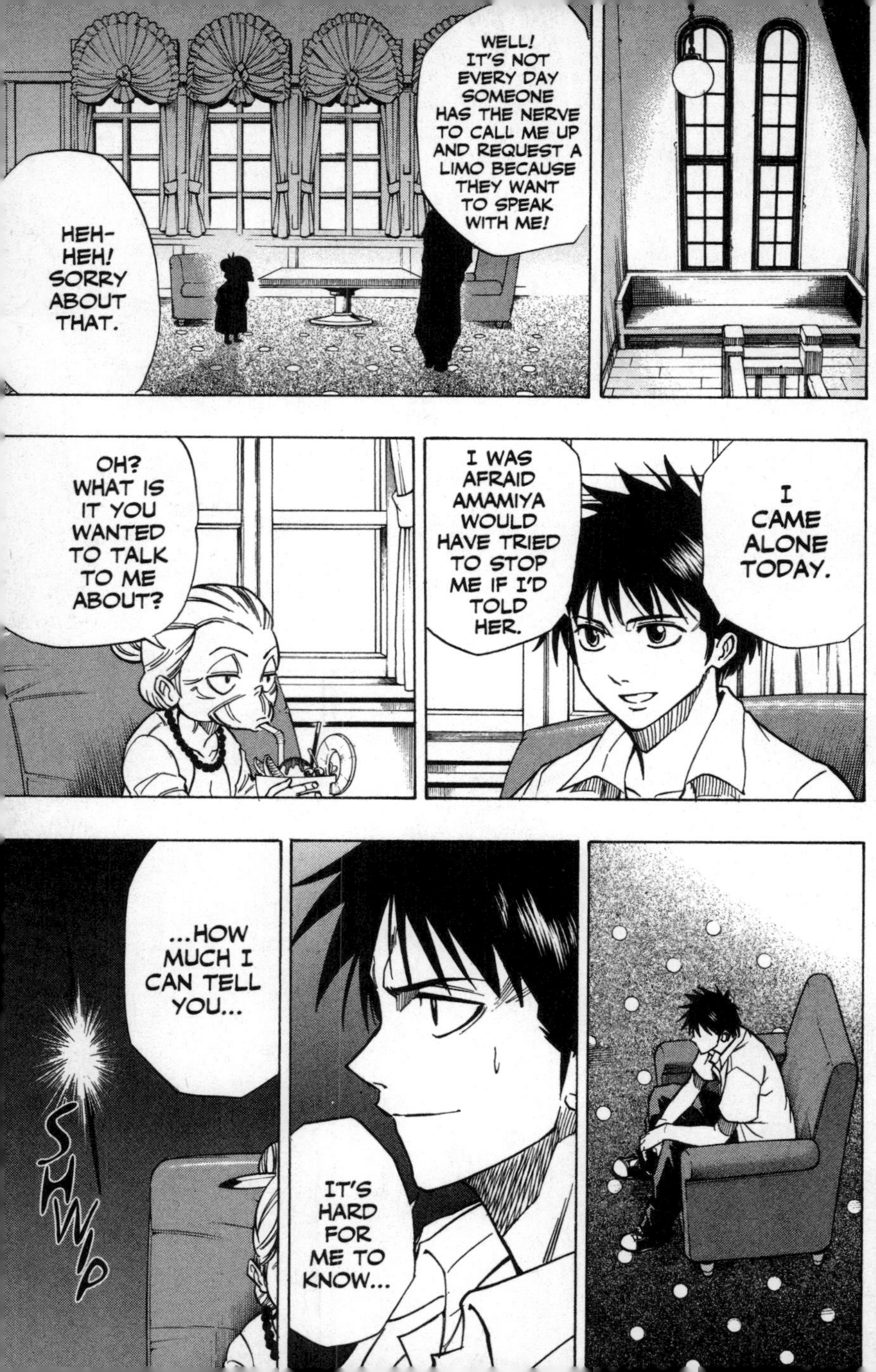
WELL! IT'S NOT EVERY DAY SOMEONE HAS THE NERVE TO CALL ME UP AND REQUEST A LIMO BECAUSE THEY WANT TO SPEAK WITH ME!
HEH-HEH! SORRY ABOUT THAT.
I CAME ALONE TODAY.
I WAS AFRAID AMAMIYA WOULD HAVE TRIED TO STOP ME IF I'D TOLD HER.
OH? WHAT IS IT YOU WANTED TO TALK TO ME ABOUT?
IT'S HARD FOR ME TO KNOW...
...HOW MUCH I CAN TELL YOU...
SHWIP

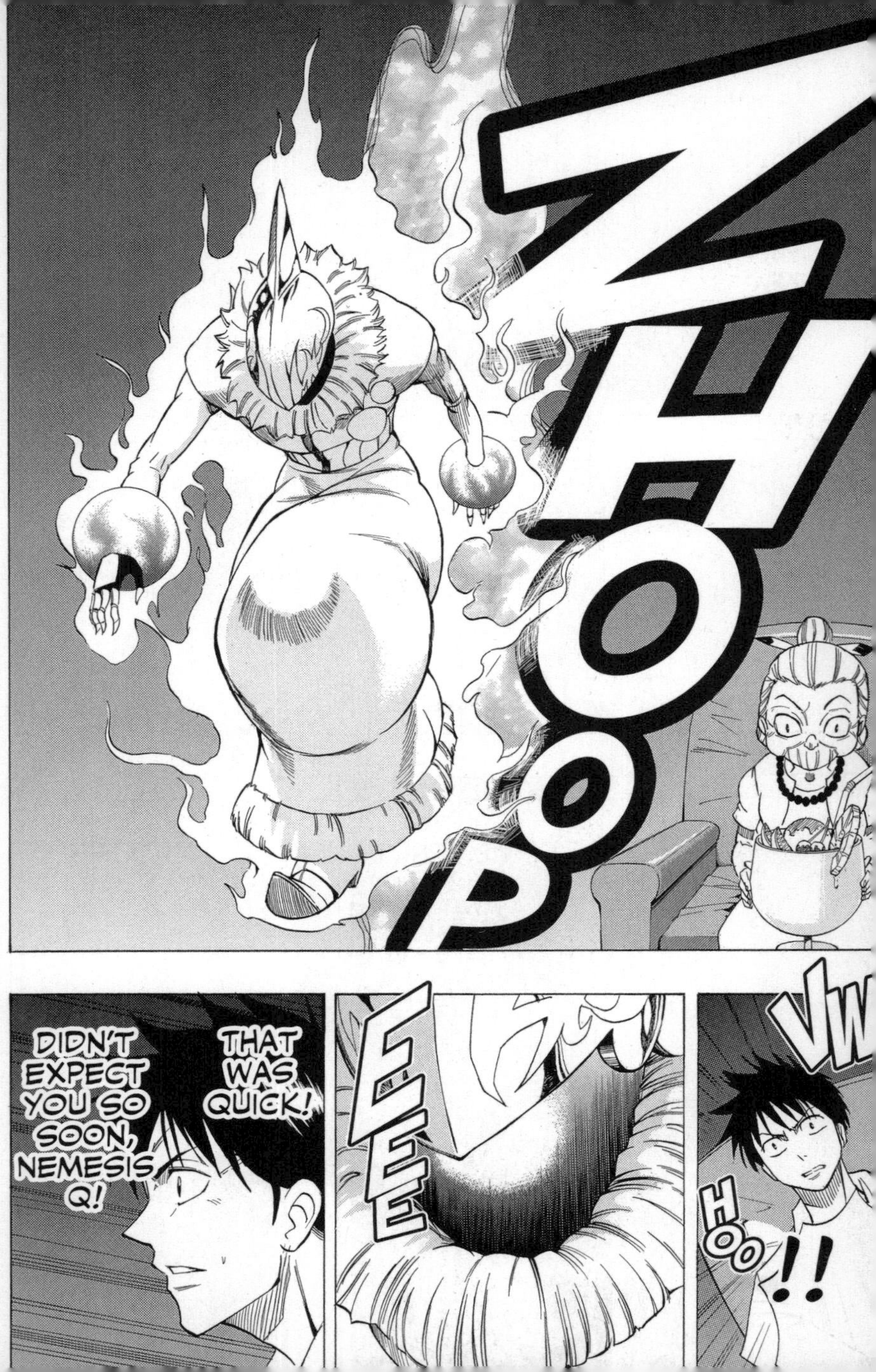
ZHOOOP
VW
HOO!!
EEEE
THAT WAS QUICK!
DIDN'T EXPECT YOU SO SOON, NEMESIS Q!

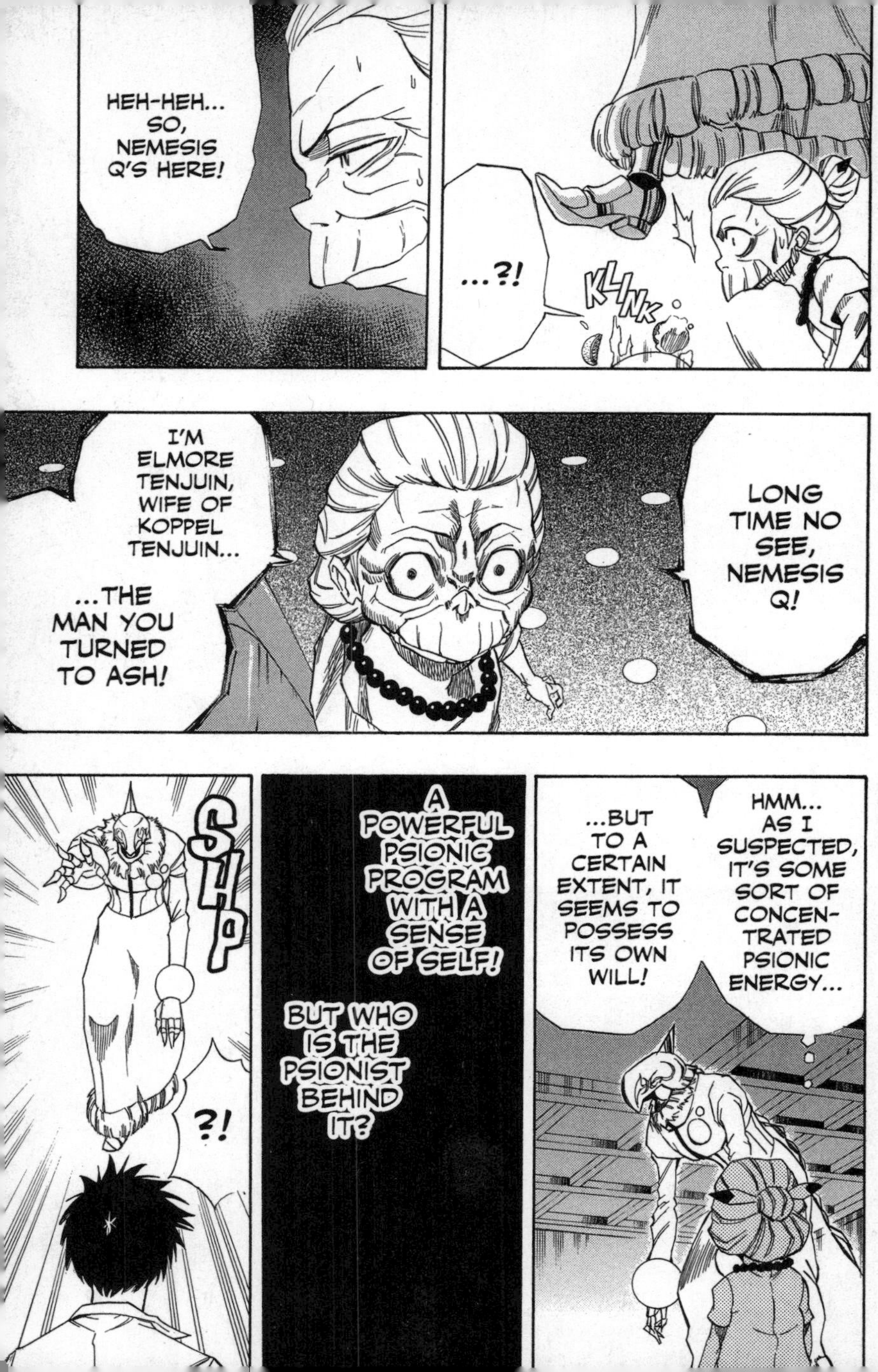
...?!
KLINK
HEH-HEH... SO, NEMESIS Q'S HERE!
LONG TIME NO SEE, NEMESIS Q!
I'M ELMORE TENJUIN, WIFE OF KOPPEL TENJUIN...
...THE MAN YOU TURNED TO ASH!
HMM... AS I SUSPECTED, IT'S SOME SORT OF CONCEN-TRATED PSIONIC ENERGY...
...BUT TO A CERTAIN EXTENT, IT SEEMS TO POSSESS ITS OWN WILL!
A POWERFUL PSIONIC PROGRAM WITH A SENSE OF SELF!
BUT WHO IS THE PSIONIST BEHIND IT?
SLIP
?!

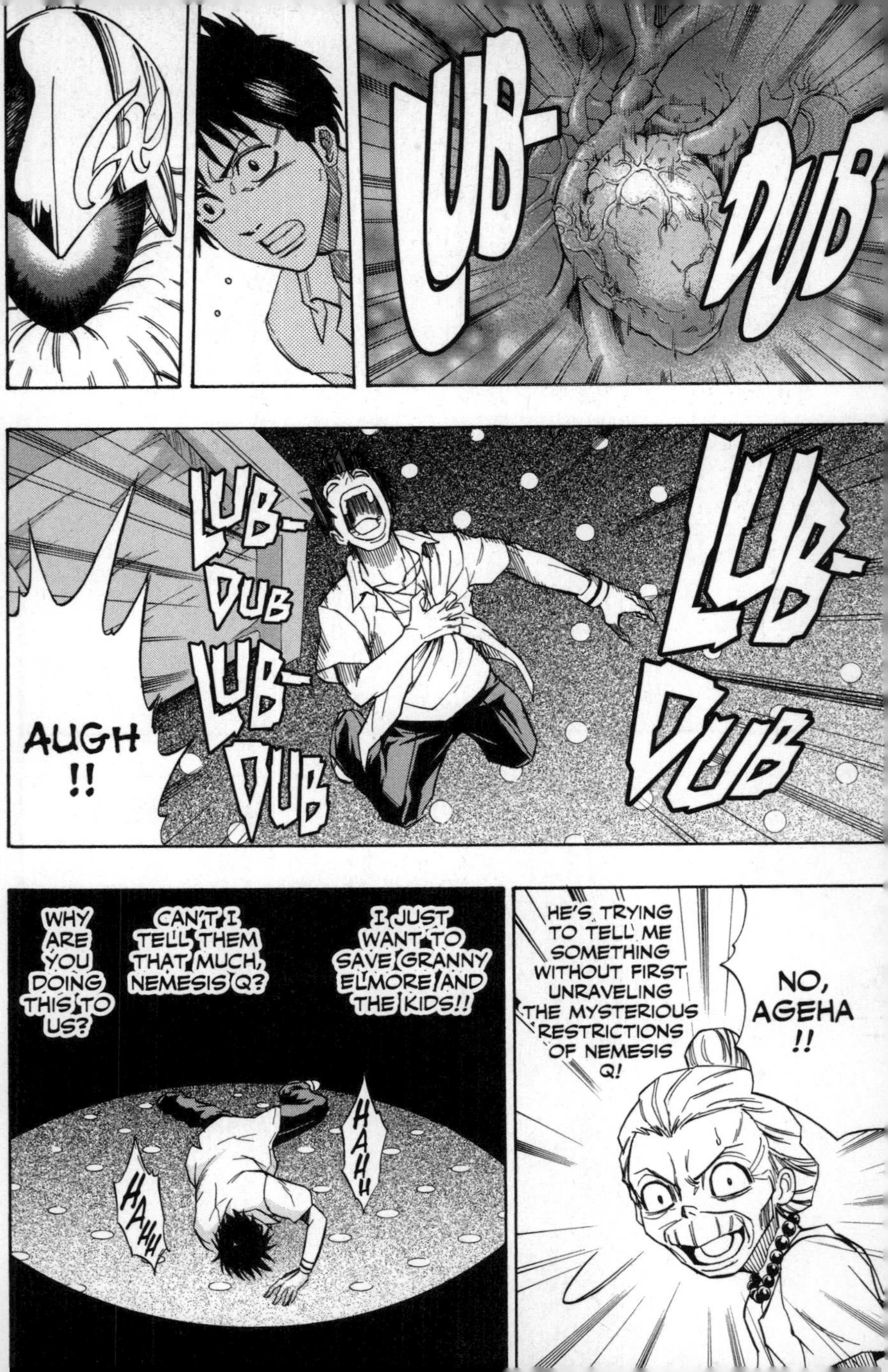
LUB-
DUB
LUB-
DUB
LUB-
DUB
LUB-
DUB
AUGH!!
NO, AGEHA!!
HE'S TRYING TO TELL ME SOMETHING WITHOUT FIRST UNRAVELING THE MYSTERIOUS RESTRICTIONS OF NEMESIS Q!
I JUST WANT TO SAVE GRANNY ELMORE AND THE KIDS!!
CAN'T I TELL THEM THAT MUCH, NEMESIS Q?
WHY ARE YOU DOING THIS TO US?
HAHH
HAHH

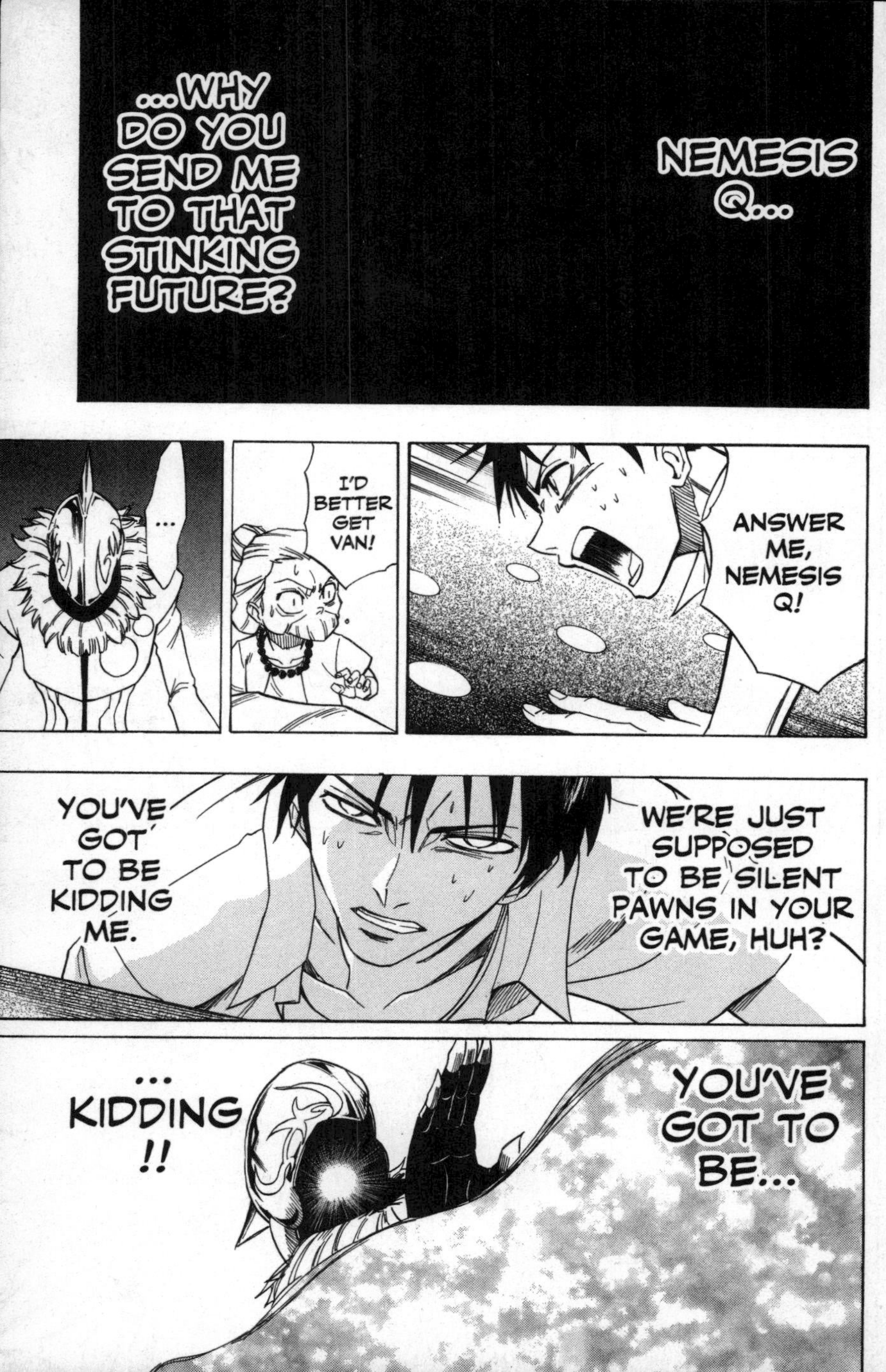
NEMESIS Q...
...WHY DO YOU SEND ME TO THAT STINKING FUTURE?
ANSWER ME, NEMESIS Q!
I'D BETTER GET VAN!
...
WE'RE JUST SUPPOSED TO BE SILENT PAWNS IN YOUR GAME, HUH?
YOU'VE GOT TO BE KIDDING ME.
YOU'VE GOT TO BE...
...KIDDING!!

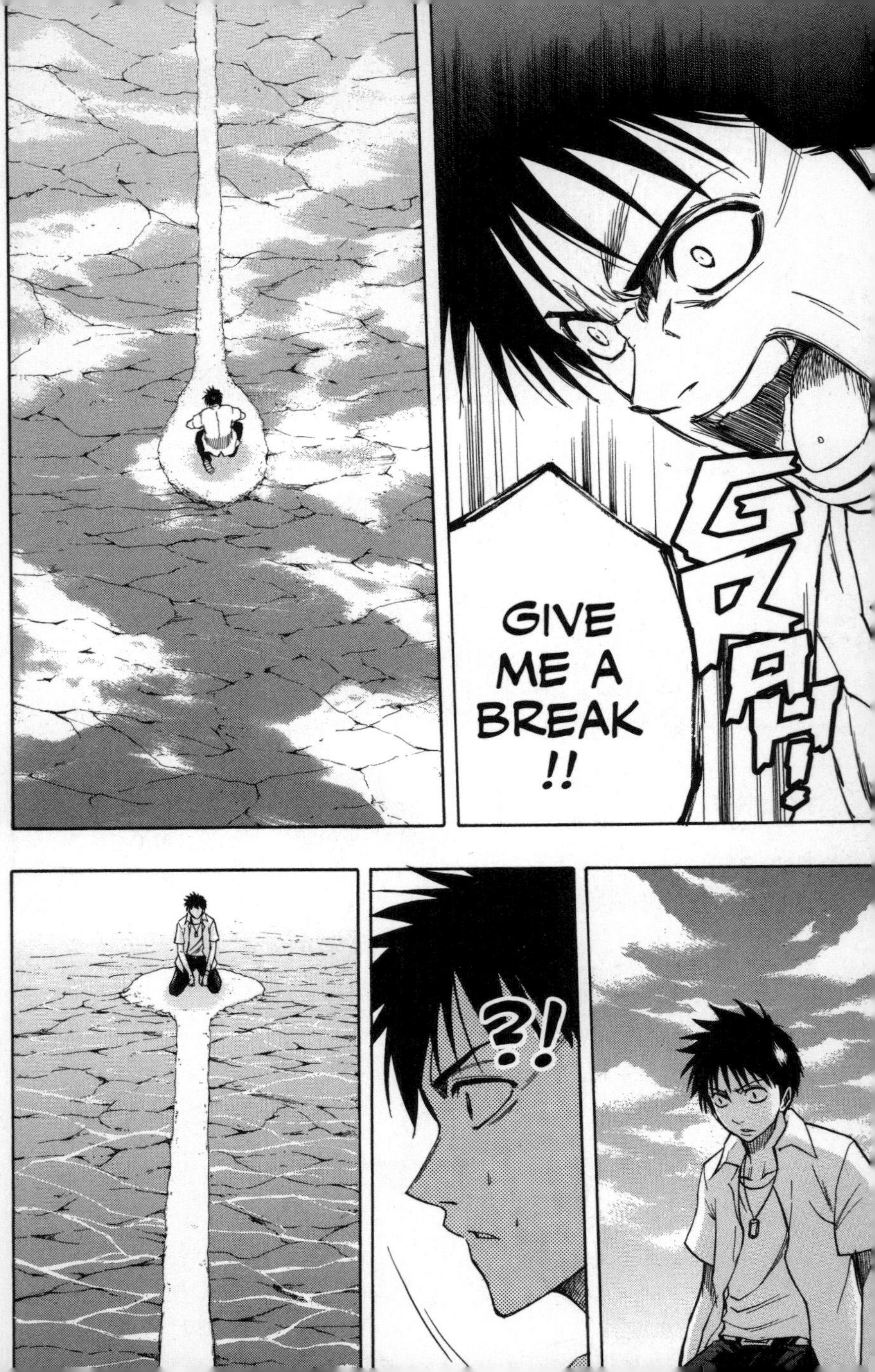
GIVE ME A BREAK !!
GRAH!
?!

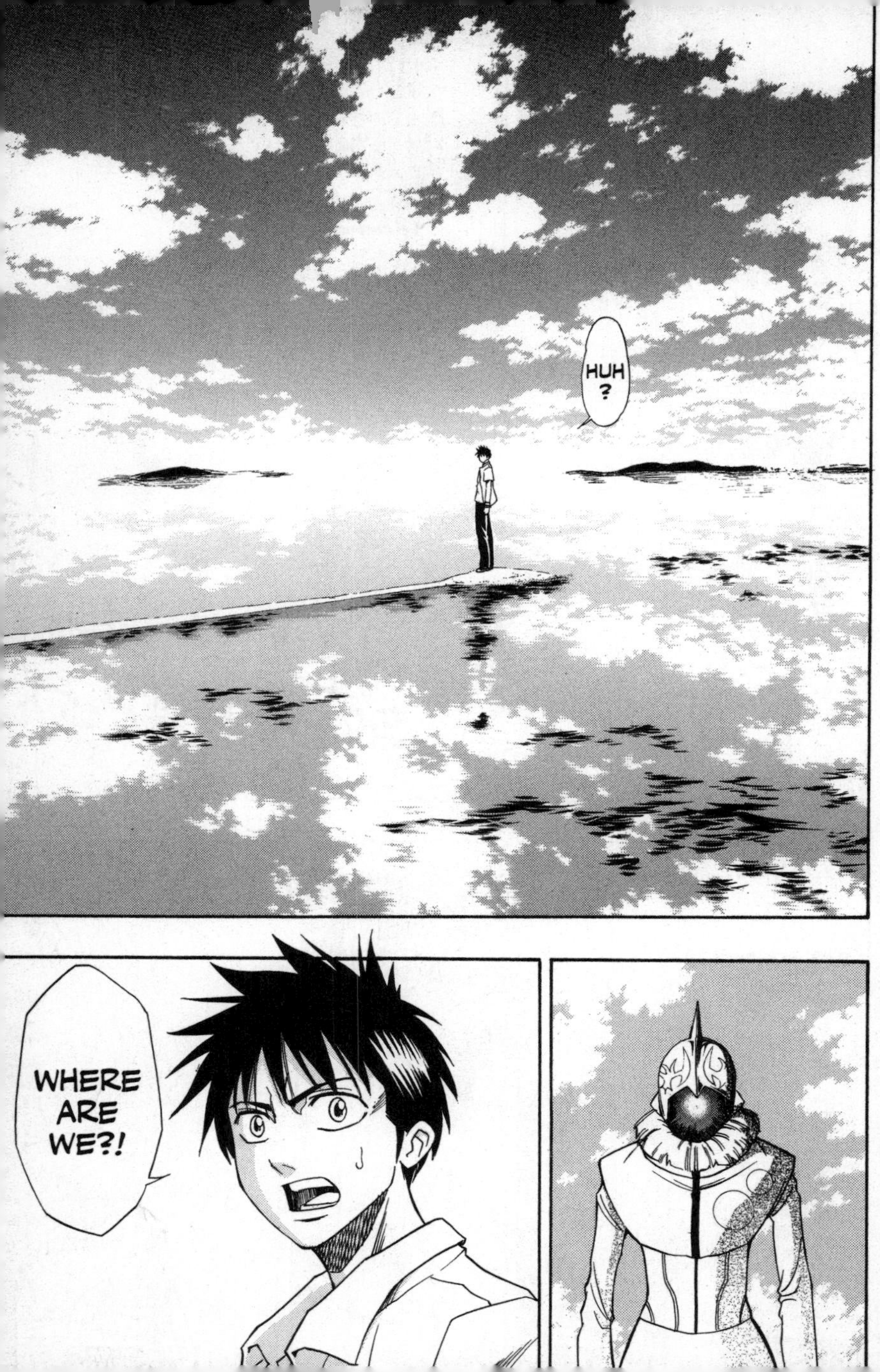
HUH ?
WHERE ARE WE?!

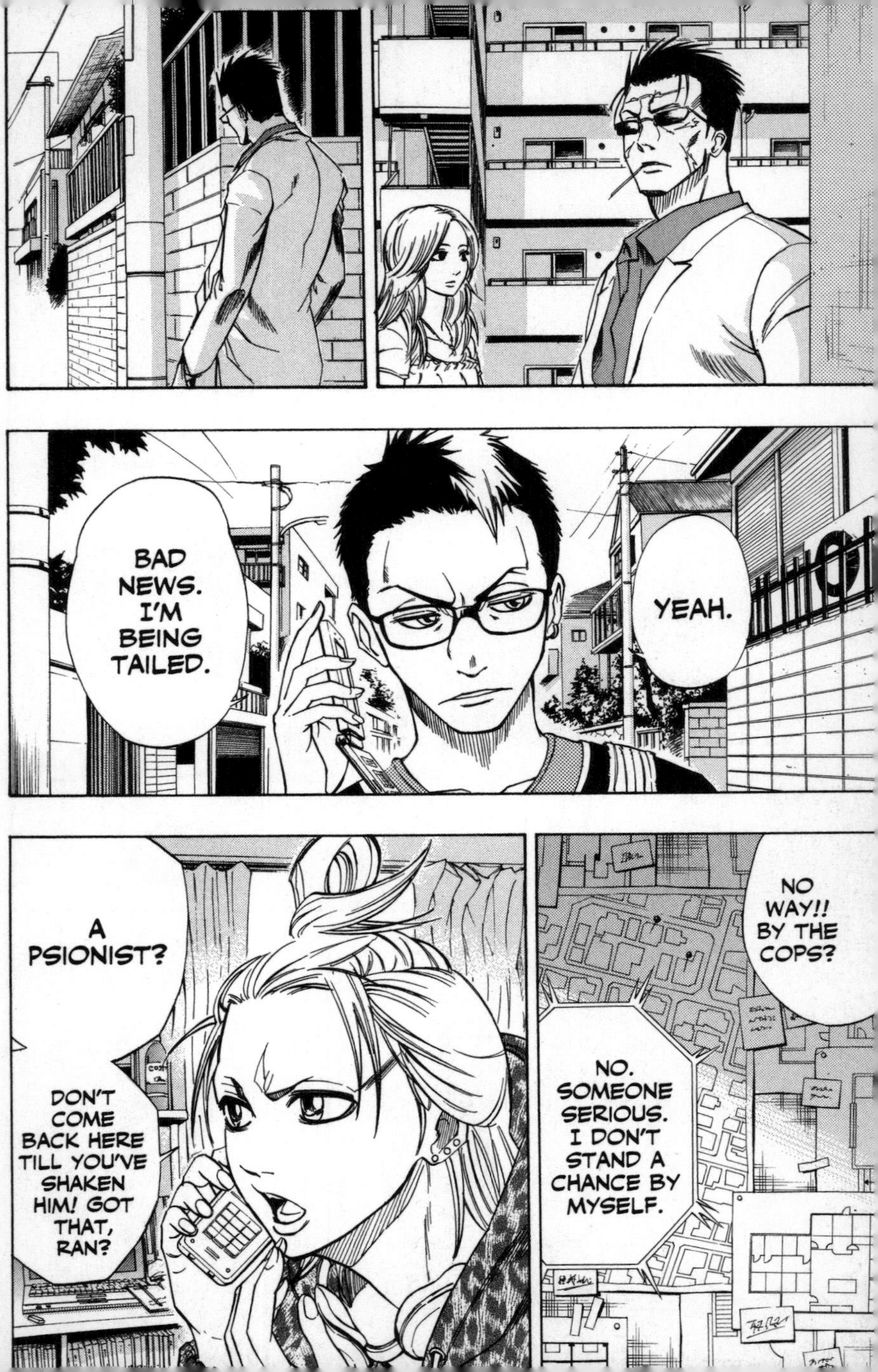
YEAH.
BAD NEWS. I'M BEING TAILED.
NO WAY!! BY THE COPS?
NO. SOMEONE SERIOUS. I DON'T STAND A CHANCE BY MYSELF.
A PSIONIST?
DON'T COME BACK HERE TILL YOU'VE SHAKEN HIM! GOT THAT, RAN?

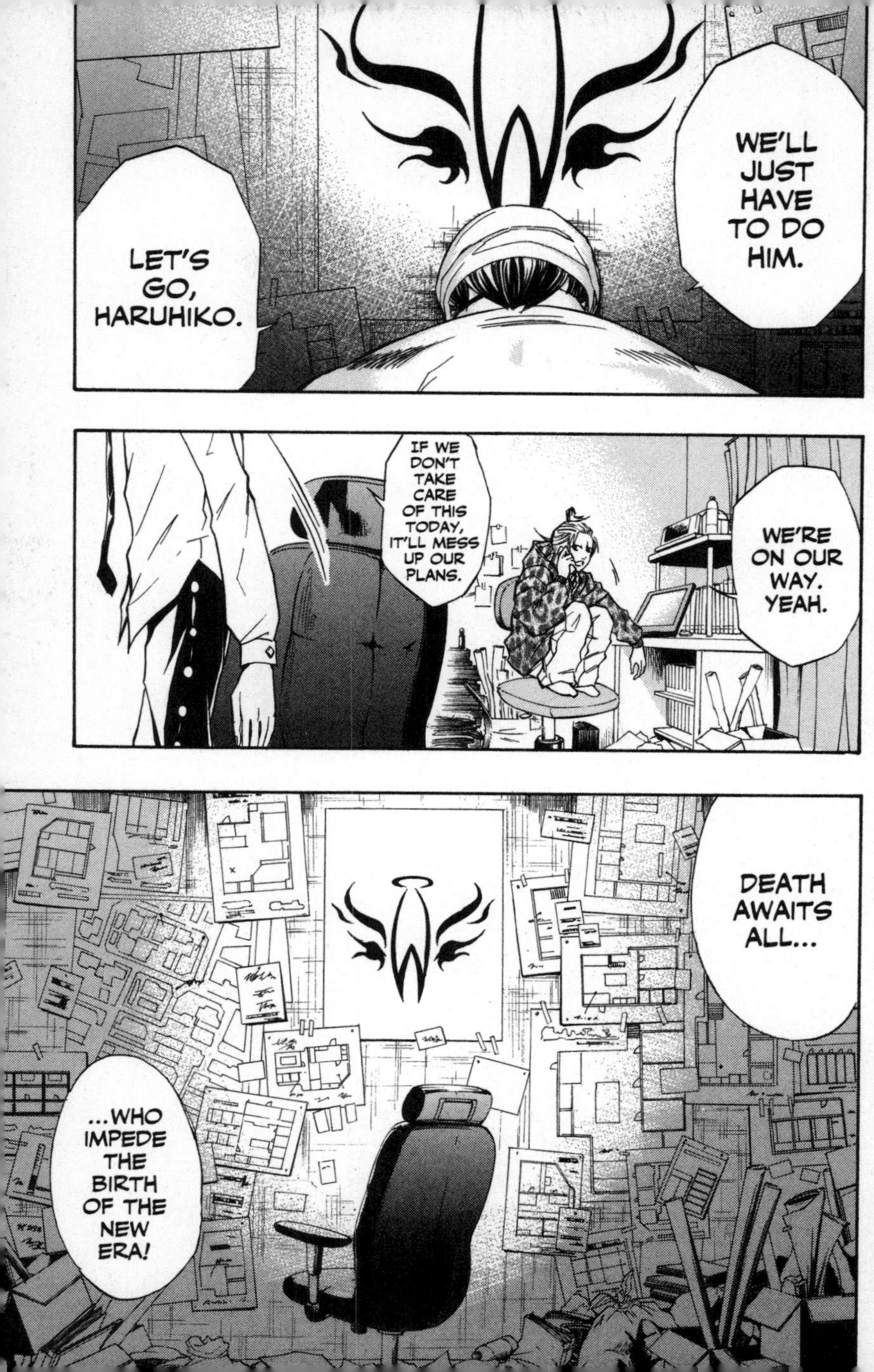
WE'LL JUST HAVE TO DO HIM.
LET'S GO, HARUHIKO.
WE'RE ON OUR WAY. YEAH.
IF WE DON'T TAKE CARE OF THIS TODAY, IT'LL MESS UP OUR PLANS.
DEATH AWAITS ALL...
...WHO IMPEDE THE BIRTH OF THE NEW ERA!

GRRR

unh

I HAD TO ADD IN SOME
SHADING I FORGOT TO DO WHEN
THIS WAS PUBLISHED IN *JUMP*.
GLAD I CAUGHT THAT! SORRY
ABOUT THAT, AMAMIYA!!

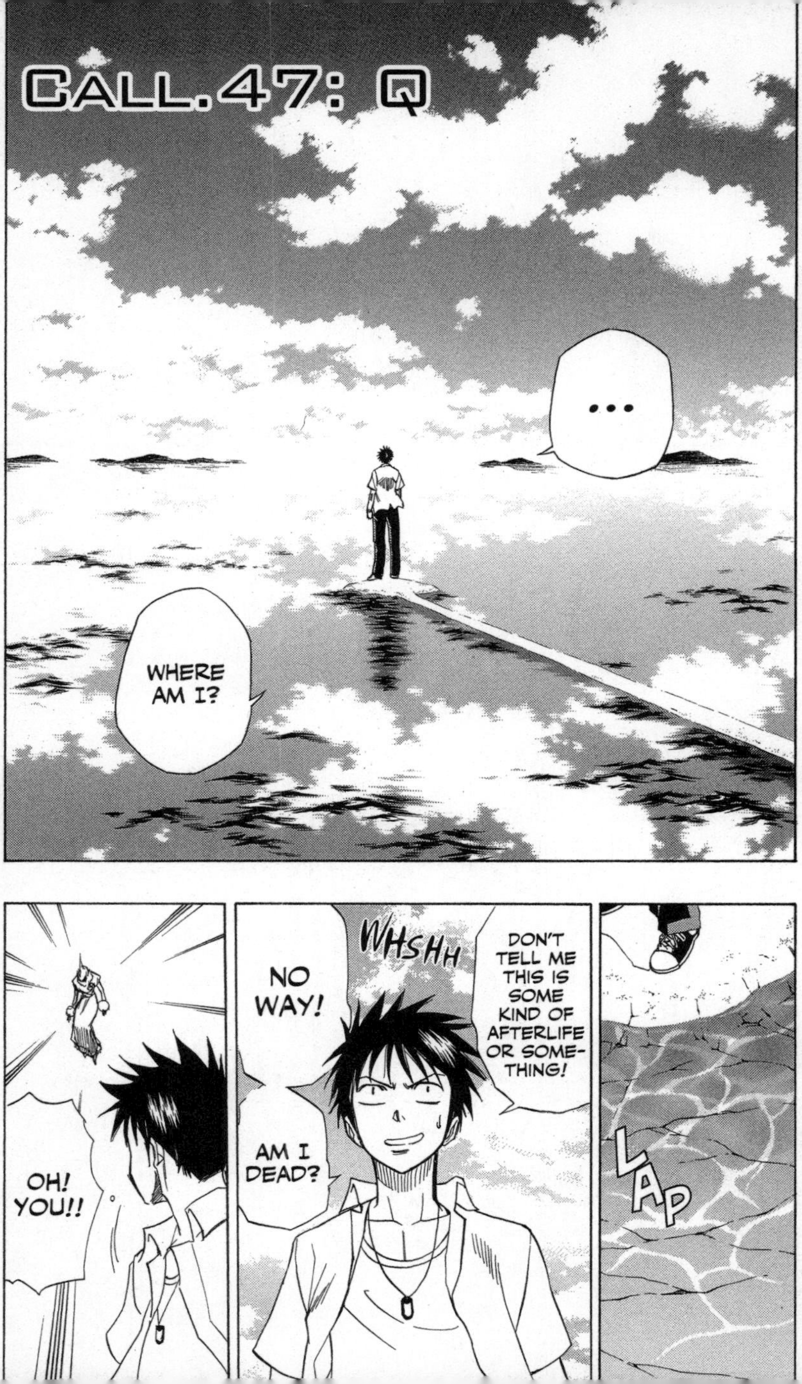
CALL.47: Q
...
WHERE AM I?
LAP
DON'T TELL ME THIS IS SOME KIND OF AFTERLIFE OR SOME-THING!
WHSHH
NO WAY!
AM I DEAD?
OH! YOU!!

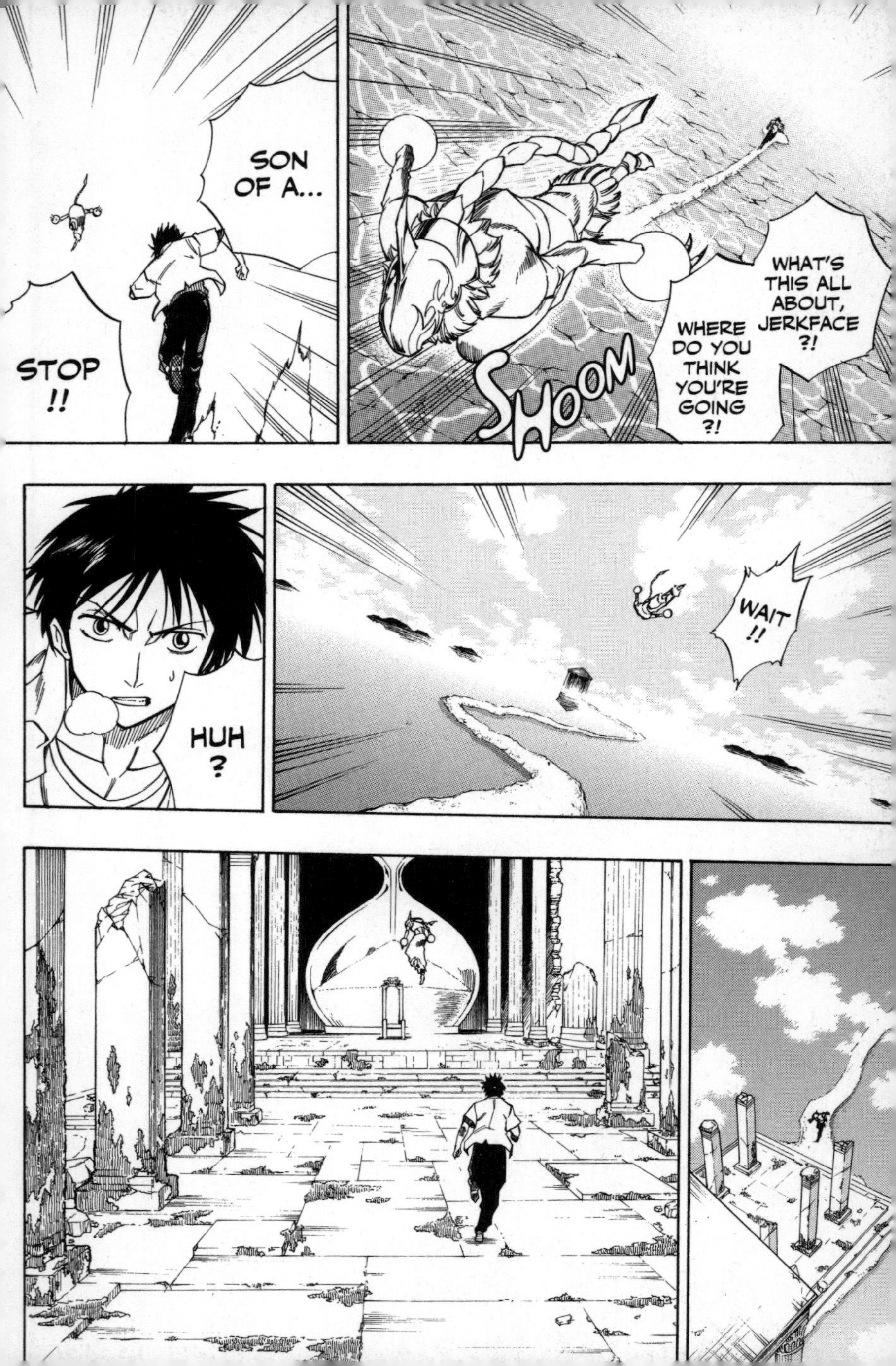
WHAT'S THIS ALL ABOUT, JERKFACE ?!
WHERE DO YOU THINK YOU'RE GOING ?!
SHOOM
SON OF A...
STOP !!
WAIT !!
HUH ?

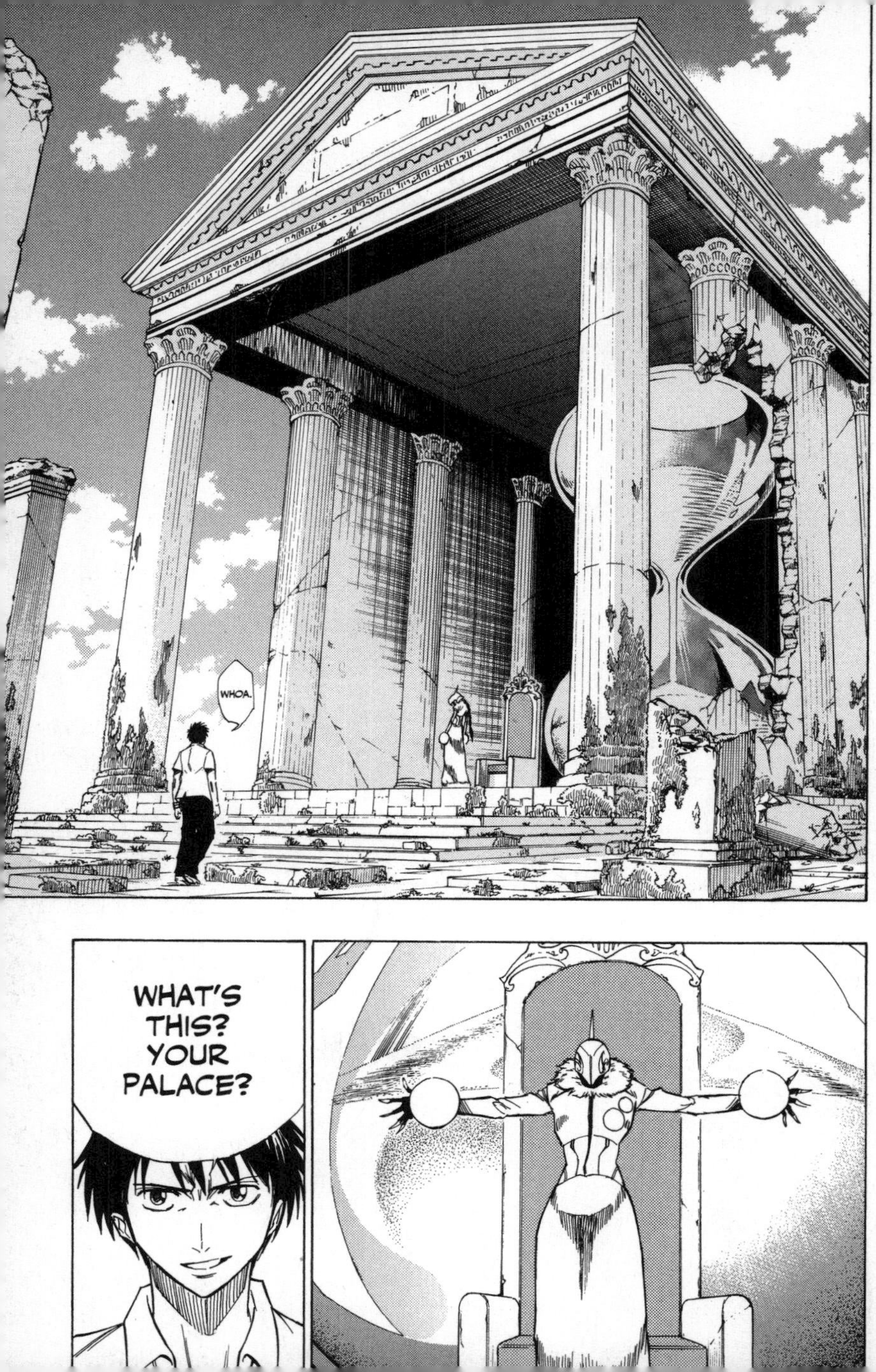
WHOA.
WHAT'S THIS? YOUR PALACE?

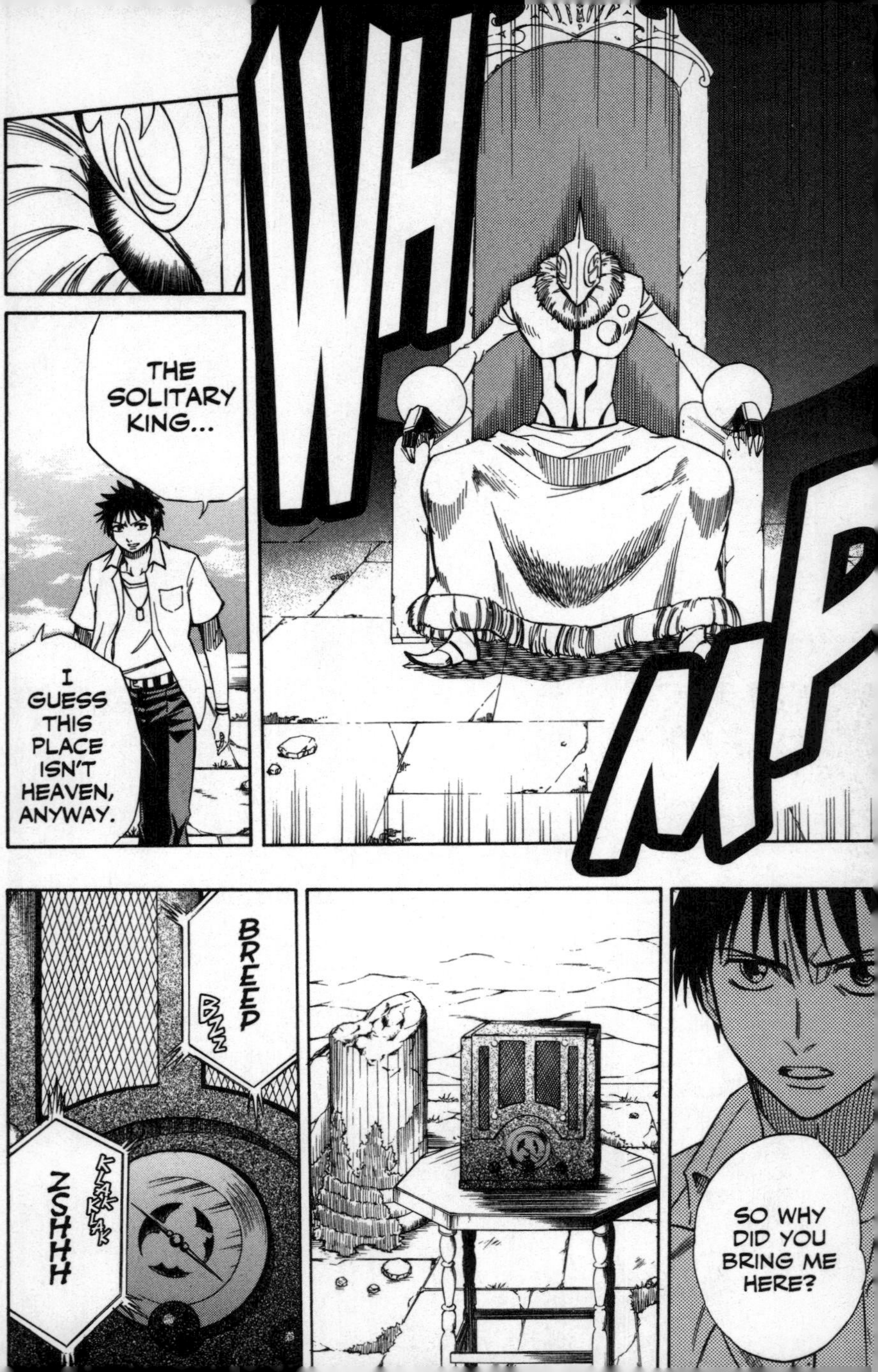
WH
MP
THE SOLITARY KING...
I GUESS THIS PLACE ISN'T HEAVEN, ANYWAY.
SO WHY DID YOU BRING ME HERE?
BREEEP
BZZ
KLAKKLAK
ZSHHH

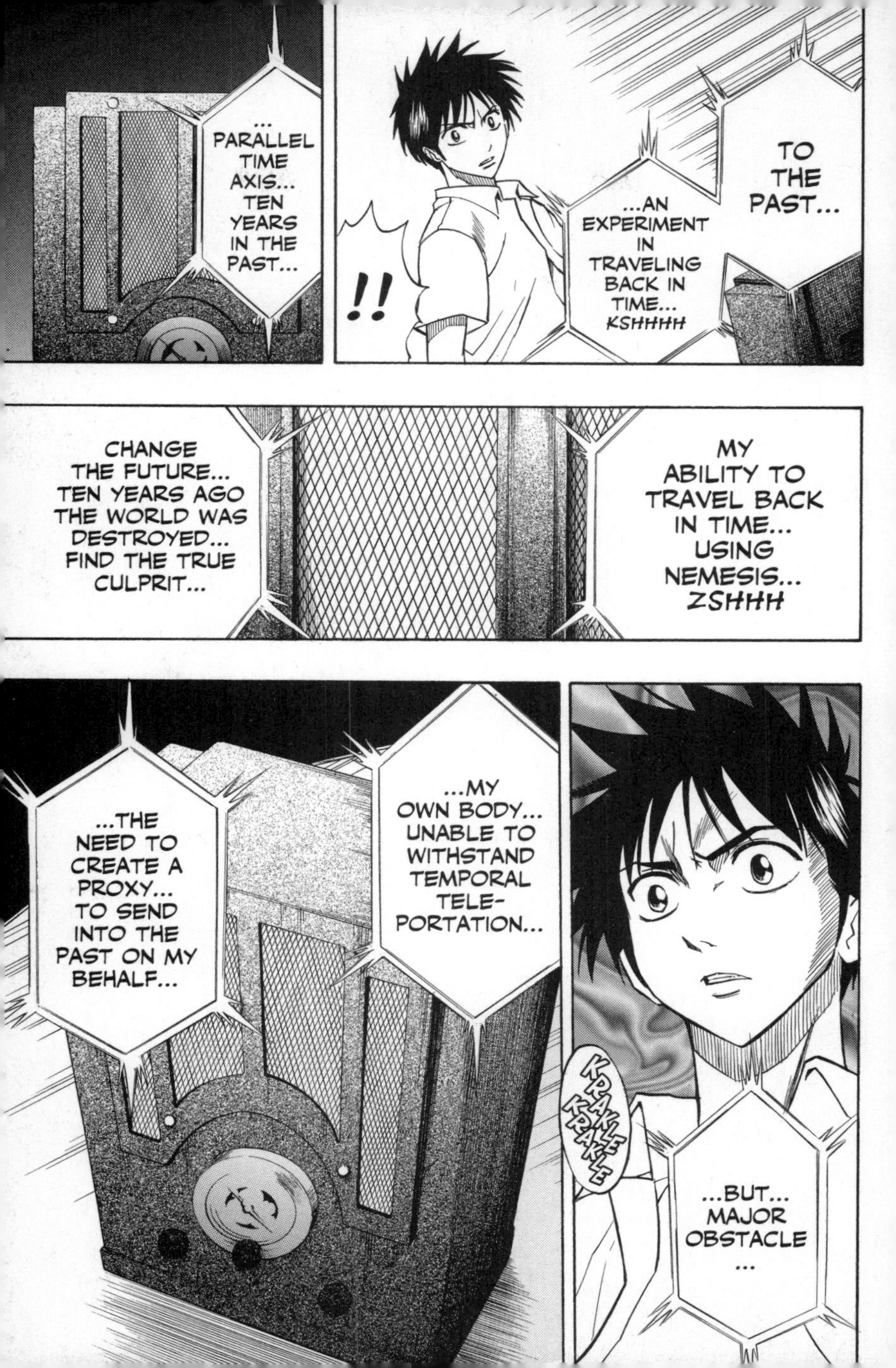
TO THE PAST...
...AN EXPERIMENT IN TRAVELING BACK IN TIME... KSHHHH
!!
... PARALLEL TIME AXIS... TEN YEARS IN THE PAST...
MY ABILITY TO TRAVEL BACK IN TIME... USING NEMESIS... ZSHHH
CHANGE THE FUTURE... TEN YEARS AGO THE WORLD WAS DESTROYED... FIND THE TRUE CULPRIT...
KRAKLE KRAKLE
...BUT... MAJOR OBSTACLE ...
...MY OWN BODY... UNABLE TO WITHSTAND TEMPORAL TELE-PORTATION...
...THE NEED TO CREATE A PROXY... TO SEND INTO THE PAST ON MY BEHALF...

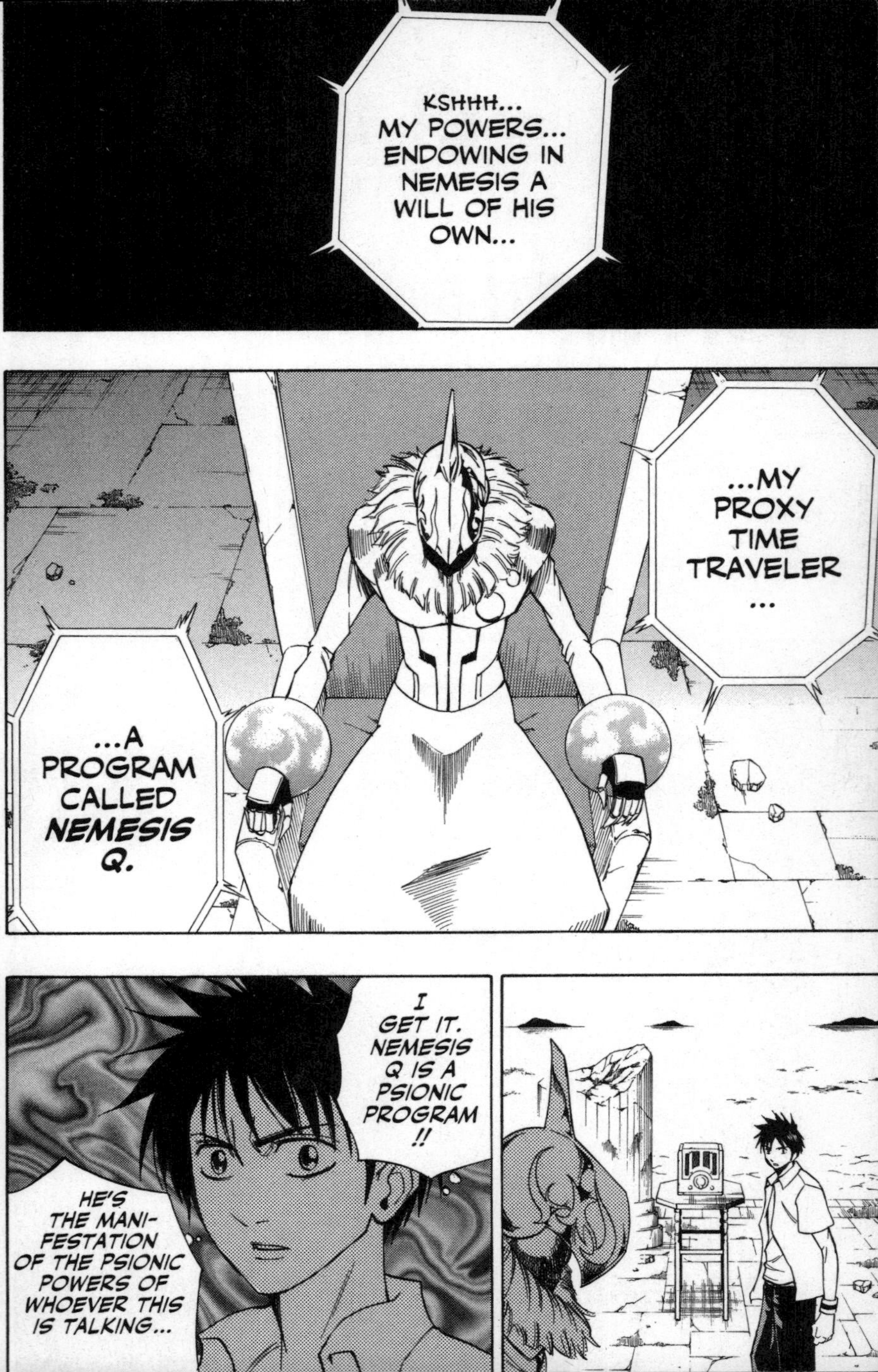
KSHHH... MY POWERS... ENDOWING IN NEMESIS A WILL OF HIS OWN...
...MY PROXY TIME TRAVELER ...
...A PROGRAM CALLED NEMESIS Q.
I GET IT. NEMESIS Q IS A PSIONIC PROGRAM !!
HE'S THE MANI-FESTATION OF THE PSIONIC POWERS OF WHOEVER THIS IS TALKING...

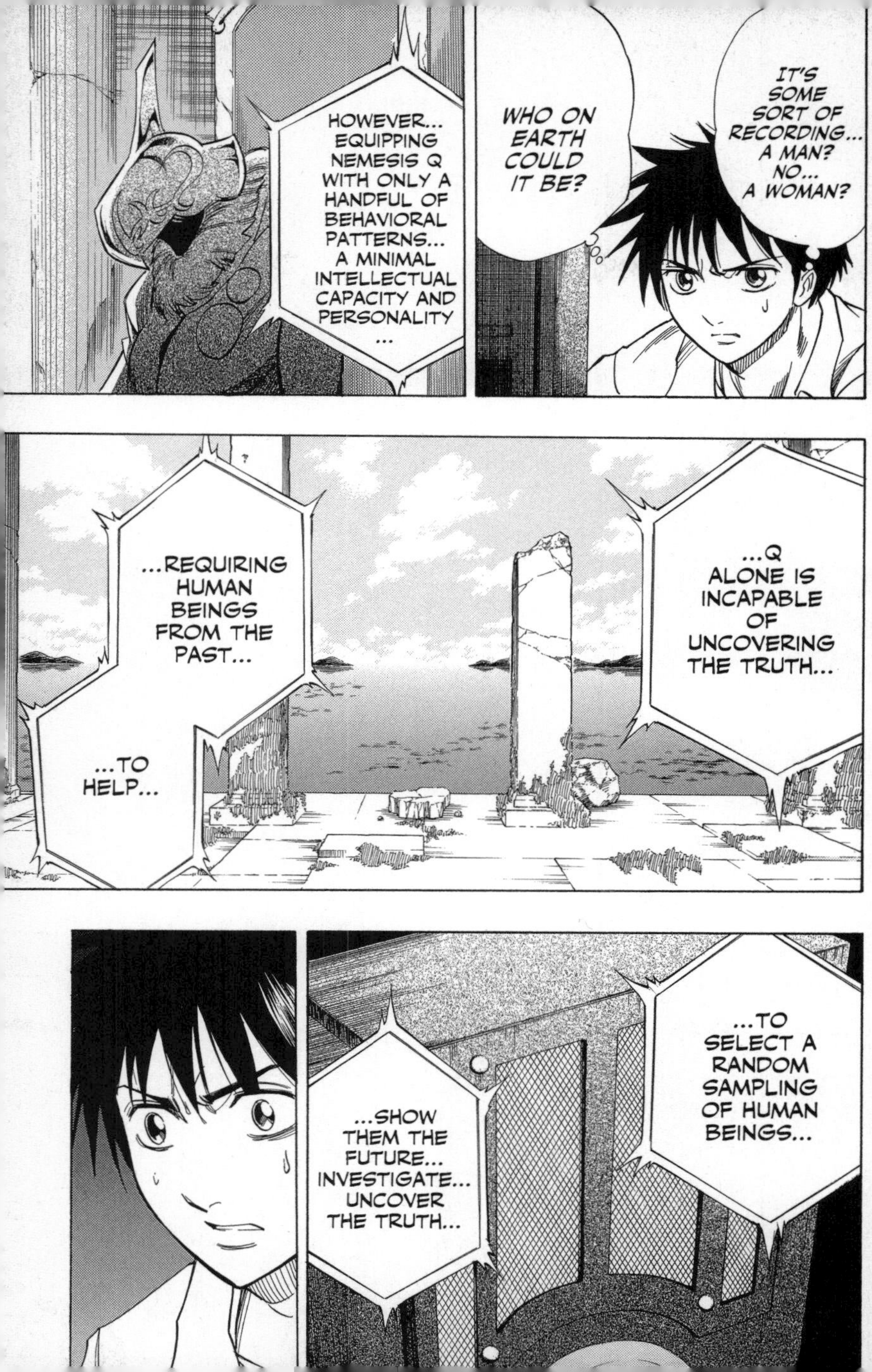
IT'S SOME SORT OF RECORDING... A MAN? NO... A WOMAN?
WHO ON EARTH COULD IT BE?
HOWEVER... EQUIPPING NEMESIS Q WITH ONLY A HANDFUL OF BEHAVIORAL PATTERNS... A MINIMAL INTELLECTUAL CAPACITY AND PERSONALITY ...
...Q ALONE IS INCAPABLE OF UNCOVERING THE TRUTH...
...REQUIRING HUMAN BEINGS FROM THE PAST...
...TO HELP...
...TO SELECT A RANDOM SAMPLING OF HUMAN BEINGS...
...SHOW THEM THE FUTURE... INVESTIGATE... UNCOVER THE TRUTH...

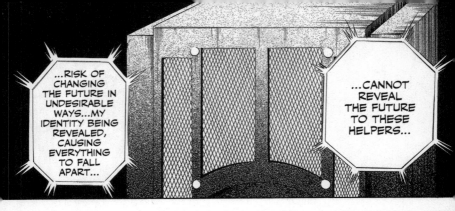

...CANNOT REVEAL THE FUTURE TO THESE HELPERS...
...RISK OF CHANGING THE FUTURE IN UNDESIRABLE WAYS...MY IDENTITY BEING REVEALED, CAUSING EVERYTHING TO FALL APART...
...NEMESIS Q WILL BE PROGRAMMED ...
...TO KILL ANY HELPERS WHO THREATEN TO REVEAL THE FUTURE...
BREEP
KSHHHH
CLIK

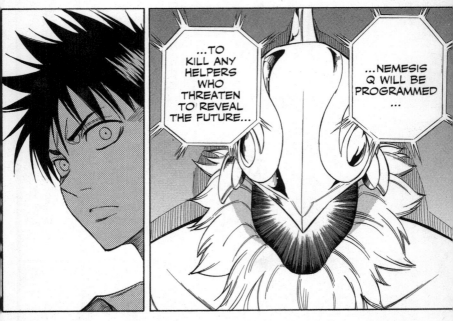

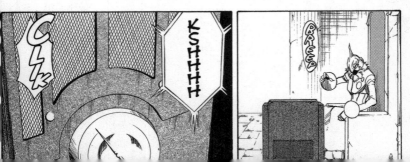

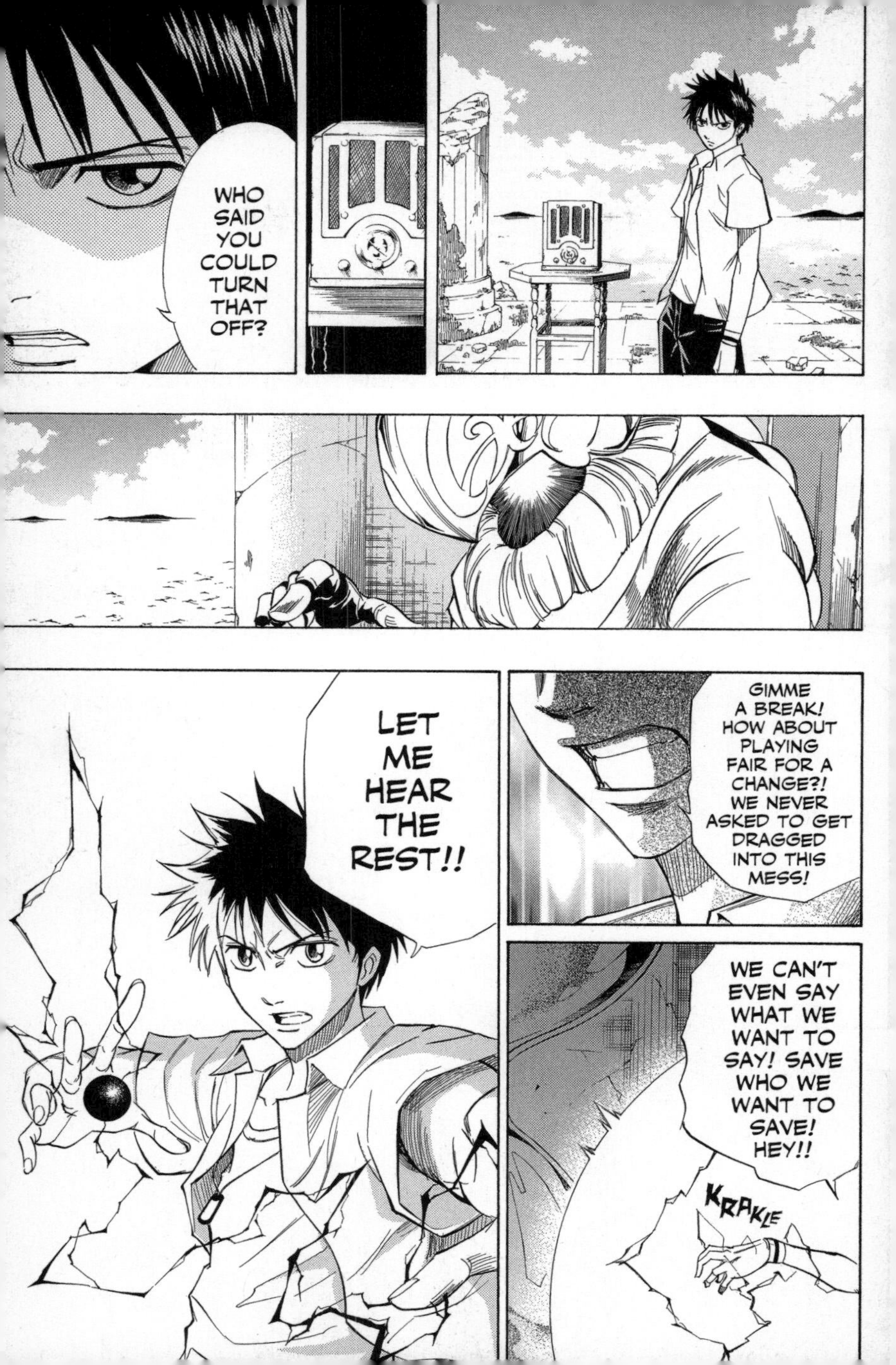
WHO SAID YOU COULD TURN THAT OFF?
GIMME A BREAK! HOW ABOUT PLAYING FAIR FOR A CHANGE?! WE NEVER ASKED TO GET DRAGGED INTO THIS MESS!
WE CAN'T EVEN SAY WHAT WE WANT TO SAY! SAVE WHO WE WANT TO SAVE! HEY!!
KRAKLE
LET ME HEAR THE REST!!

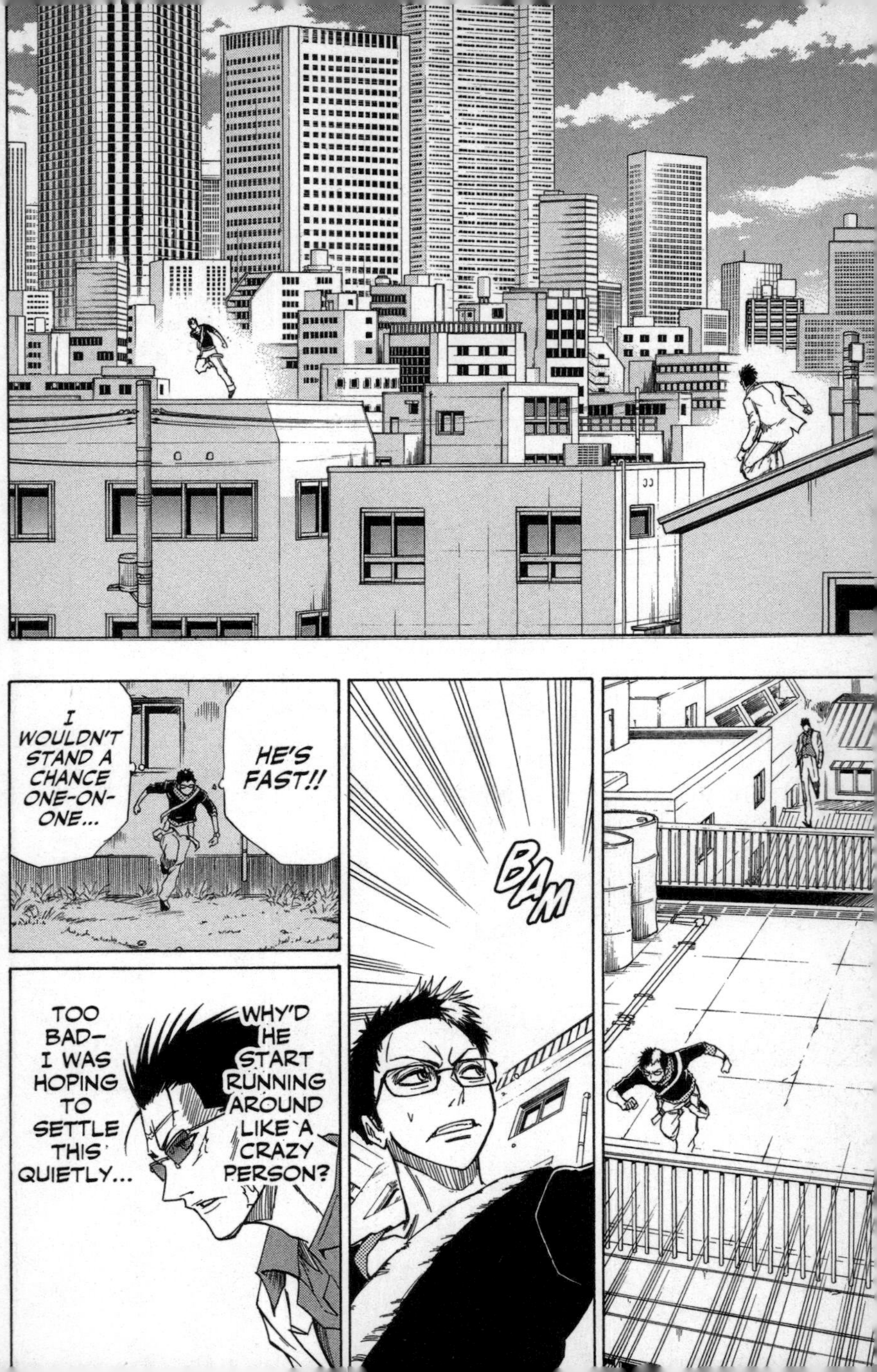
BAM
HE'S FAST!!
I WOULDN'T STAND A CHANCE ONE-ON-ONE...
WHY'D HE START RUNNING AROUND LIKE A CRAZY PERSON?
TOO BAD— I WAS HOPING TO SETTLE THIS QUIETLY...

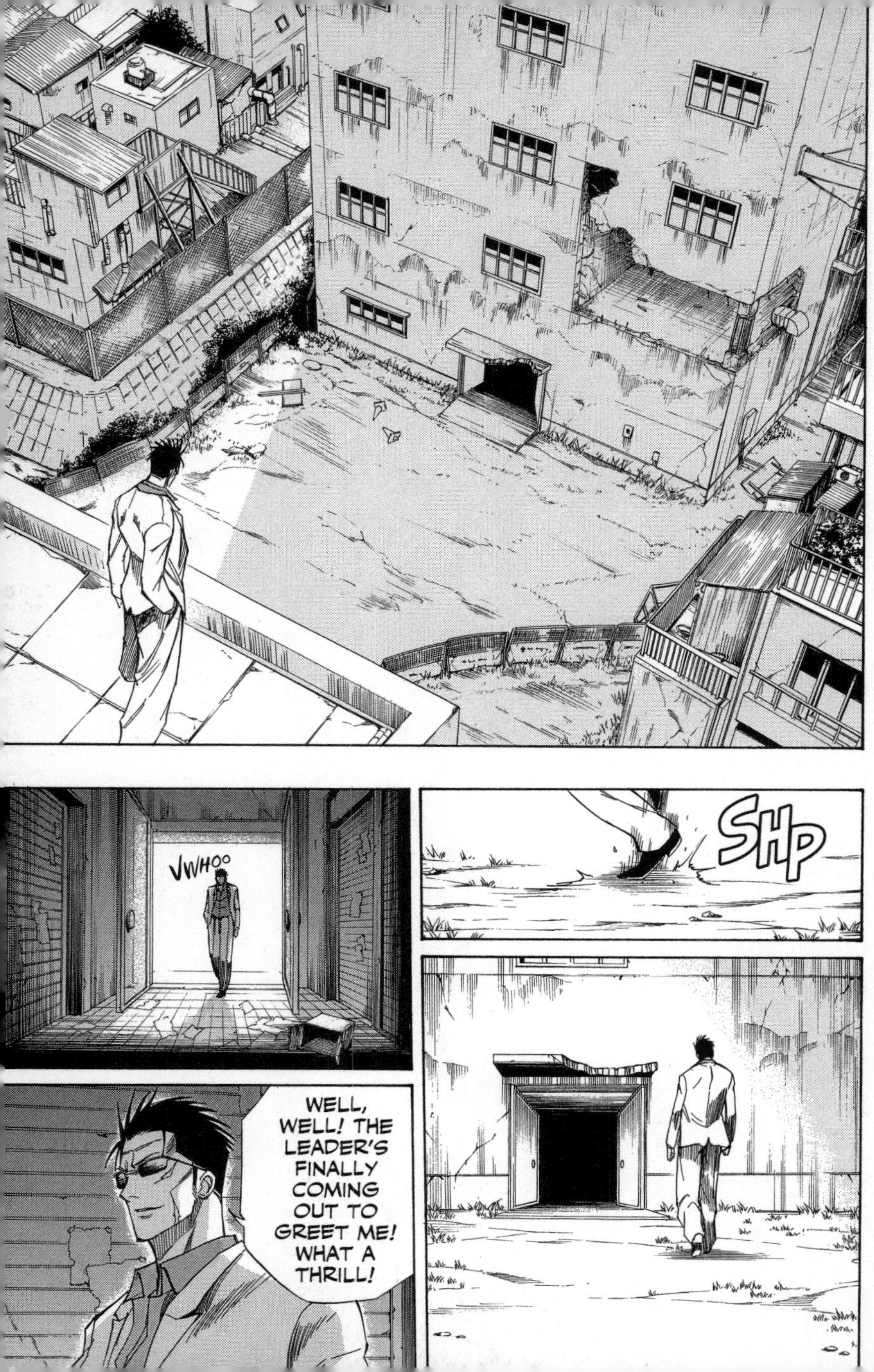
SHP
VWHOO
WELL, WELL! THE LEADER'S FINALLY COMING OUT TO GREET ME! WHAT A THRILL!

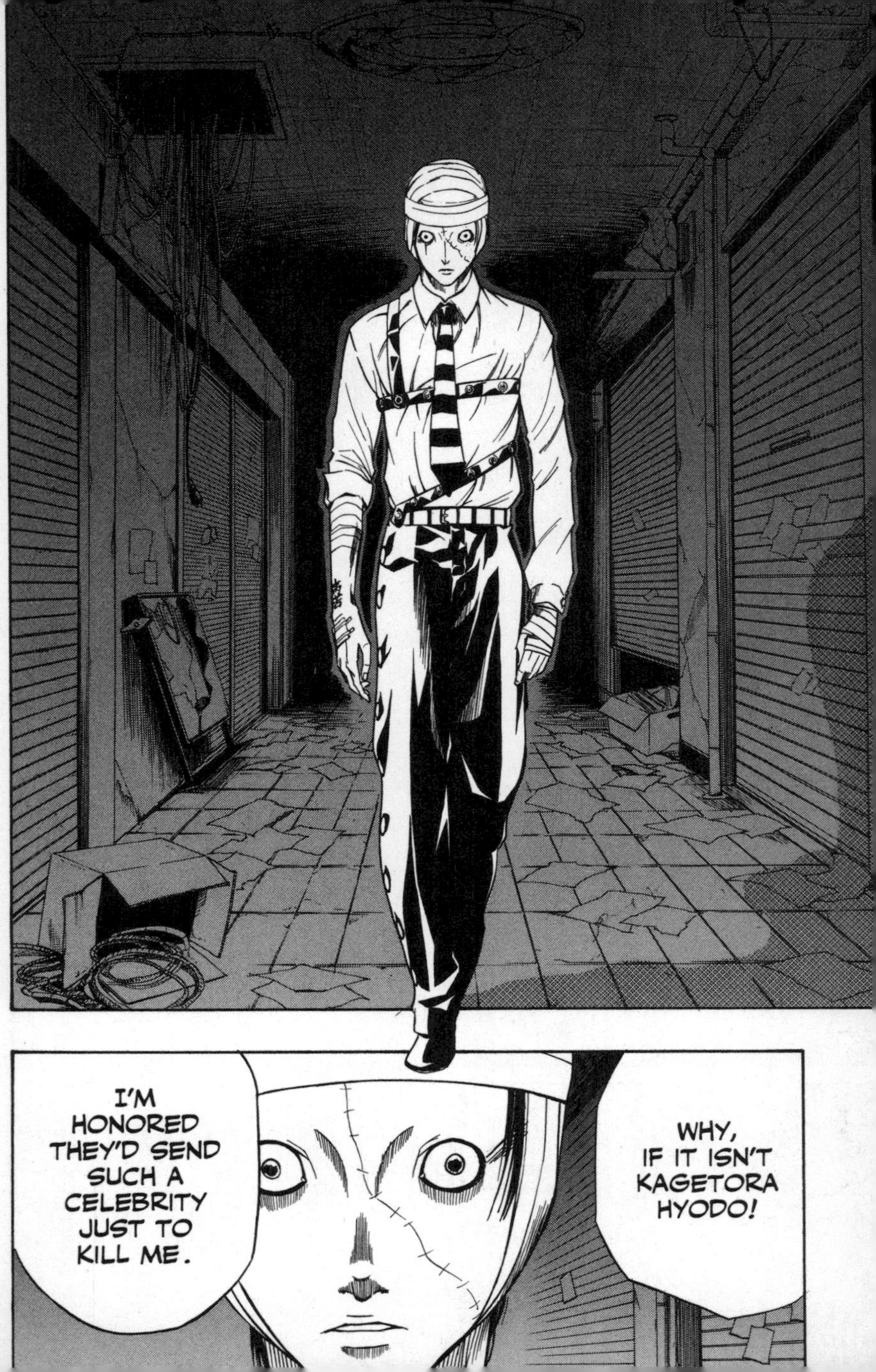
WHY, IF IT ISN'T KAGETORA HYODO!
I'M HONORED THEY'D SEND SUCH A CELEBRITY JUST TO KILL ME.

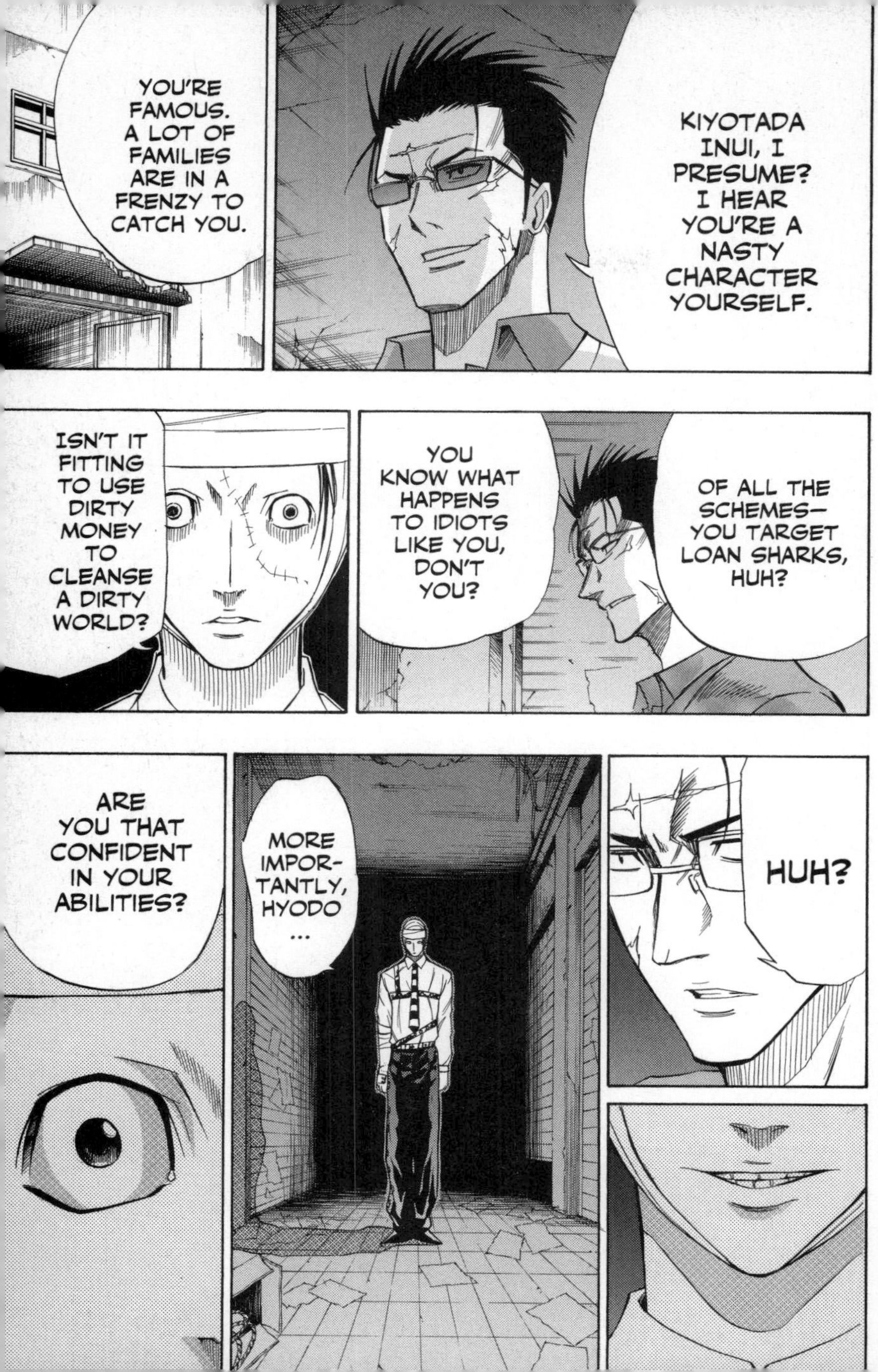
KIYOTADA INUI, I PRESUME? I HEAR YOU'RE A NASTY CHARACTER YOURSELF.
YOU'RE FAMOUS. A LOT OF FAMILIES ARE IN A FRENZY TO CATCH YOU.
OF ALL THE SCHEMES— YOU TARGET LOAN SHARKS, HUH?
YOU KNOW WHAT HAPPENS TO IDIOTS LIKE YOU, DON'T YOU?
ISN'T IT FITTING TO USE DIRTY MONEY TO CLEANSE A DIRTY WORLD?
HUH?
MORE IMPORTANTLY, HYODO ...
ARE YOU THAT CONFIDENT IN YOUR ABILITIES?

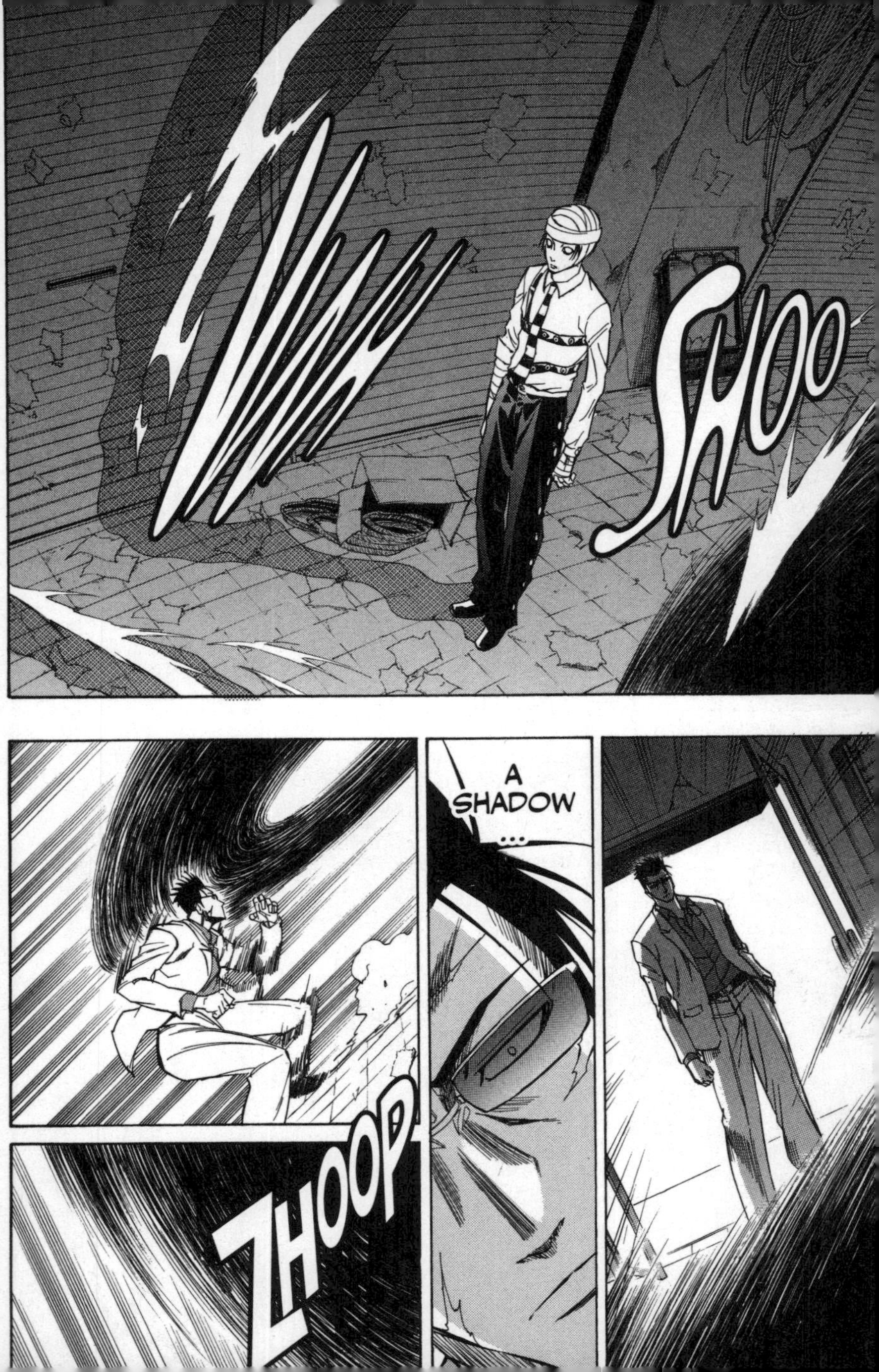
SHOO
A SHADOW
...
ZHOOP

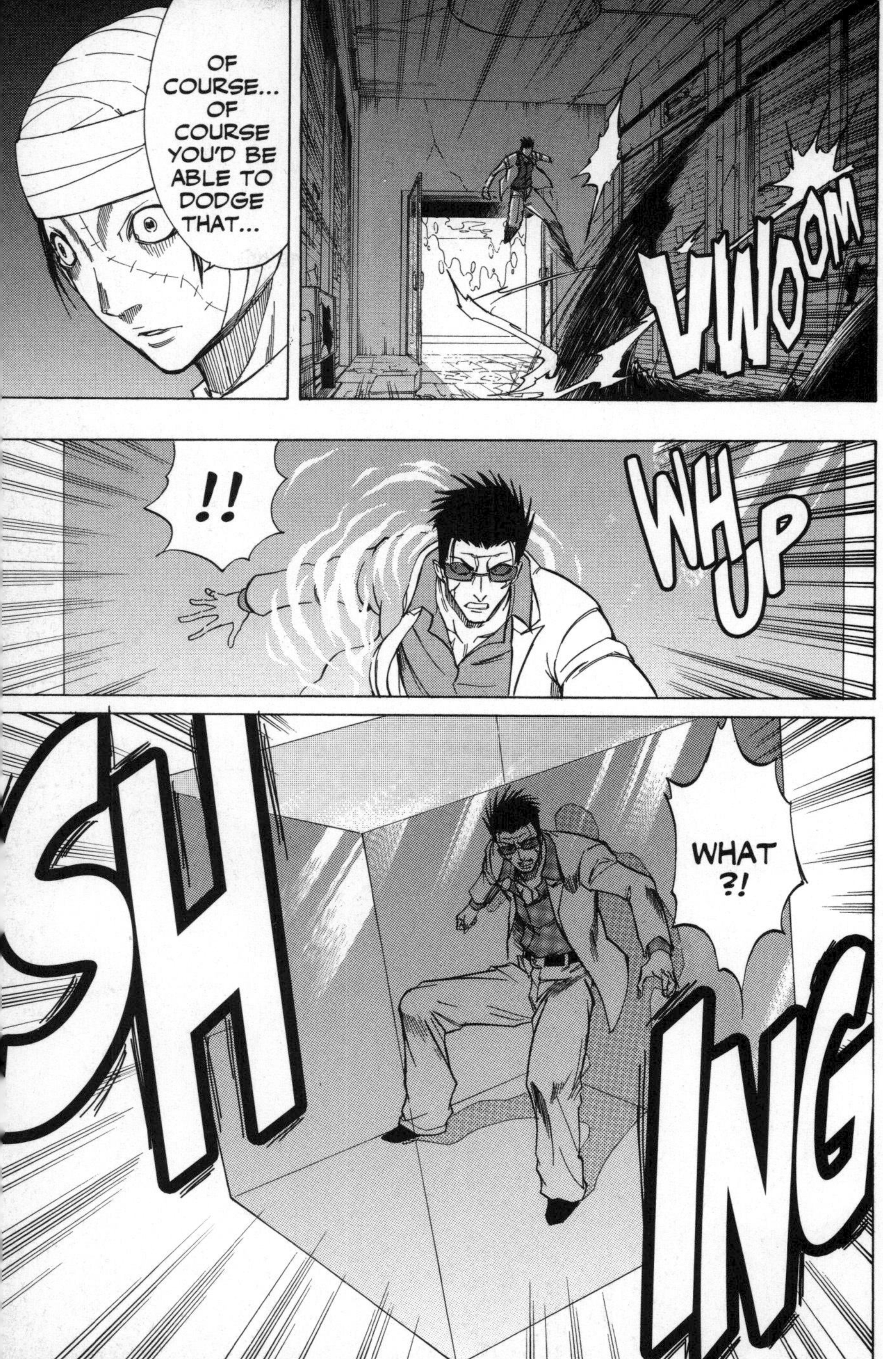
VWOOM
OF COURSE... OF COURSE YOU'D BE ABLE TO DODGE THAT...
WHUP
!!
SHING
WHAT?!

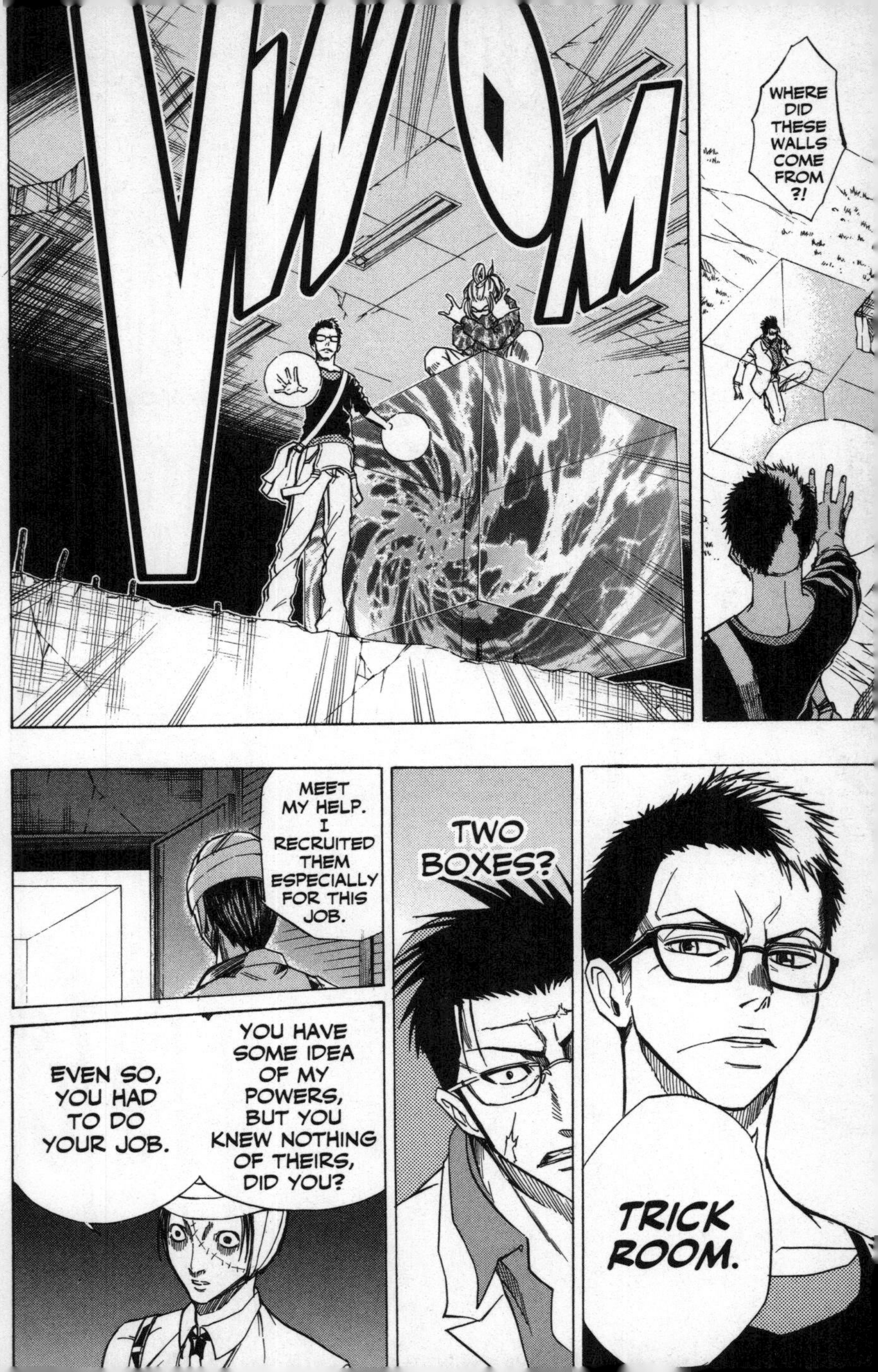

WHERE DID THESE WALLS COME FROM ?!
VWOM
TRICK ROOM.
TWO BOXES?
MEET MY HELP. I RECRUITED THEM ESPECIALLY FOR THIS JOB.
YOU HAVE SOME IDEA OF MY POWERS, BUT YOU KNEW NOTHING OF THEIRS, DID YOU?
EVEN SO, YOU HAD TO DO YOUR JOB.

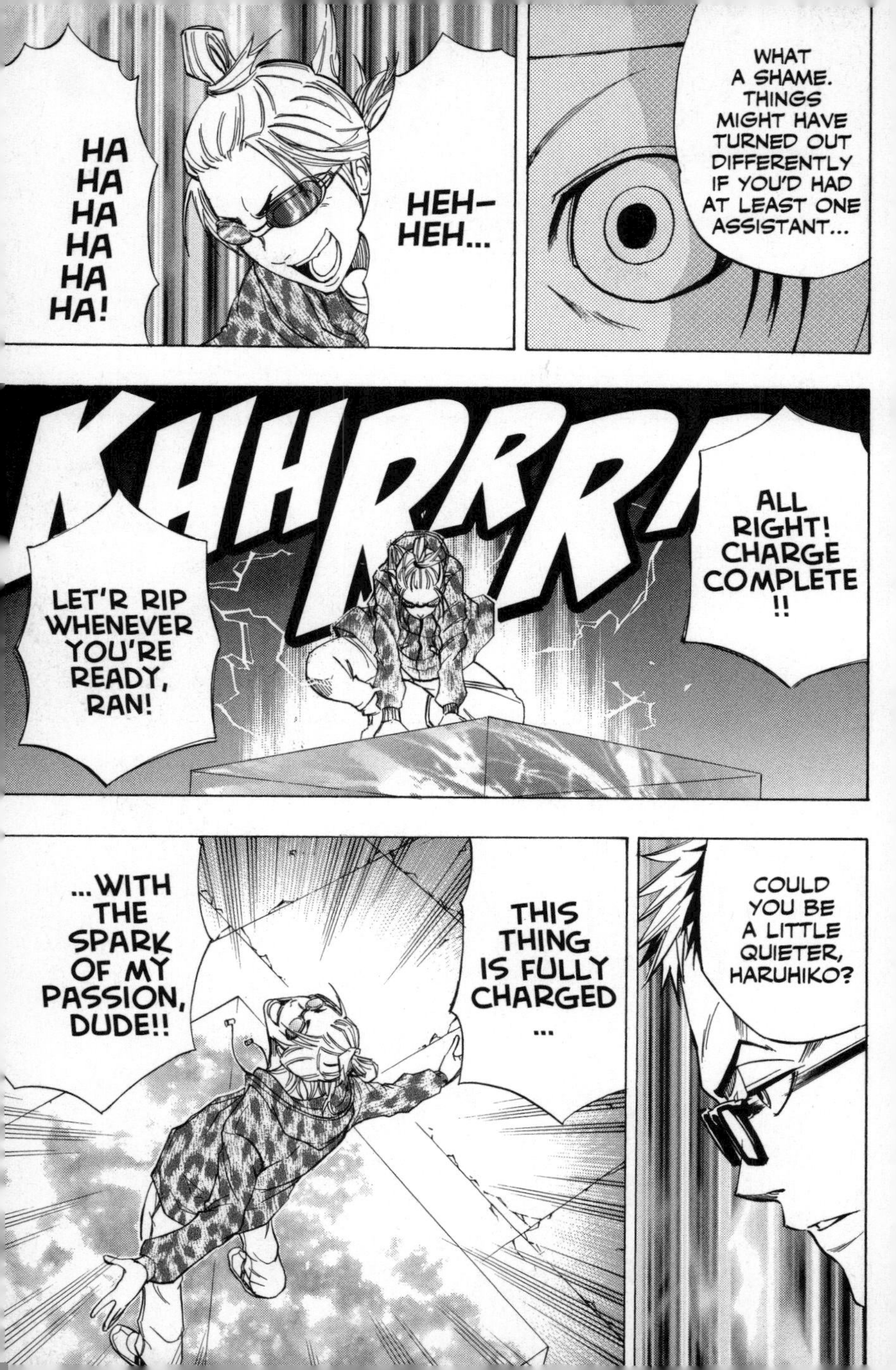
WHAT A SHAME. THINGS MIGHT HAVE TURNED OUT DIFFERENTLY IF YOU'D HAD AT LEAST ONE ASSISTANT...
HEH-HEH...
HA HA HA HA HA HA!
ALL RIGHT! CHARGE COMPLETE!!
KHRRR
LET'R RIP WHENEVER YOU'RE READY, RAN!
COULD YOU BE A LITTLE QUIETER, HARUHIKO?
THIS THING IS FULLY CHARGED...
...WITH THE SPARK OF MY PASSION, DUDE!!

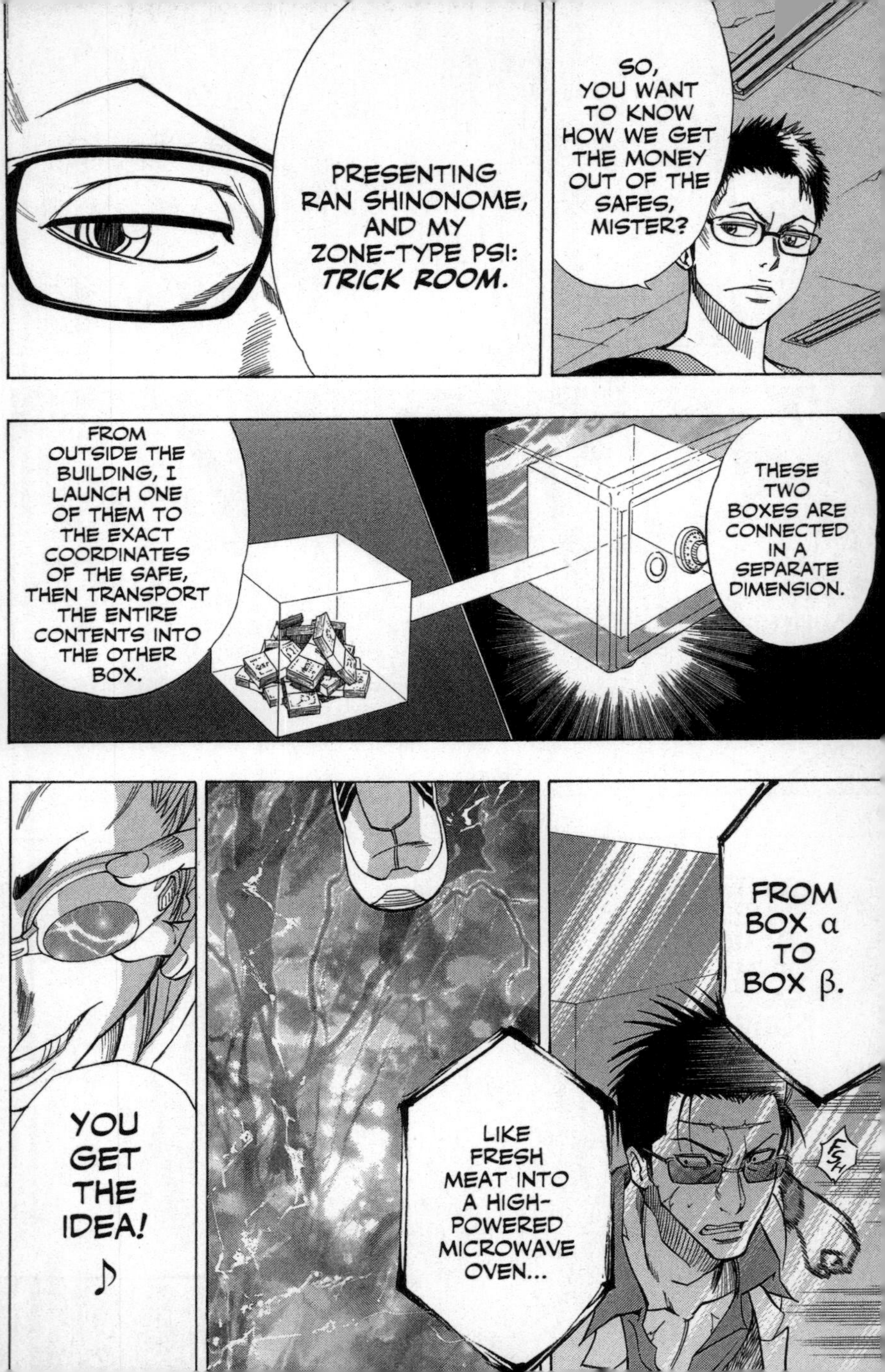
SO, YOU WANT TO KNOW HOW WE GET THE MONEY OUT OF THE SAFES, MISTER?
PRESENTING RAN SHINONOME, AND MY ZONE-TYPE PSI: *TRICK ROOM*.
THESE TWO BOXES ARE CONNECTED IN A SEPARATE DIMENSION.
FROM OUTSIDE THE BUILDING, I LAUNCH ONE OF THEM TO THE EXACT COORDINATES OF THE SAFE, THEN TRANSPORT THE ENTIRE CONTENTS INTO THE OTHER BOX.
FROM BOX α TO BOX β.
FSH
LIKE FRESH MEAT INTO A HIGH-POWERED MICROWAVE OVEN...
YOU GET THE IDEA! ♪

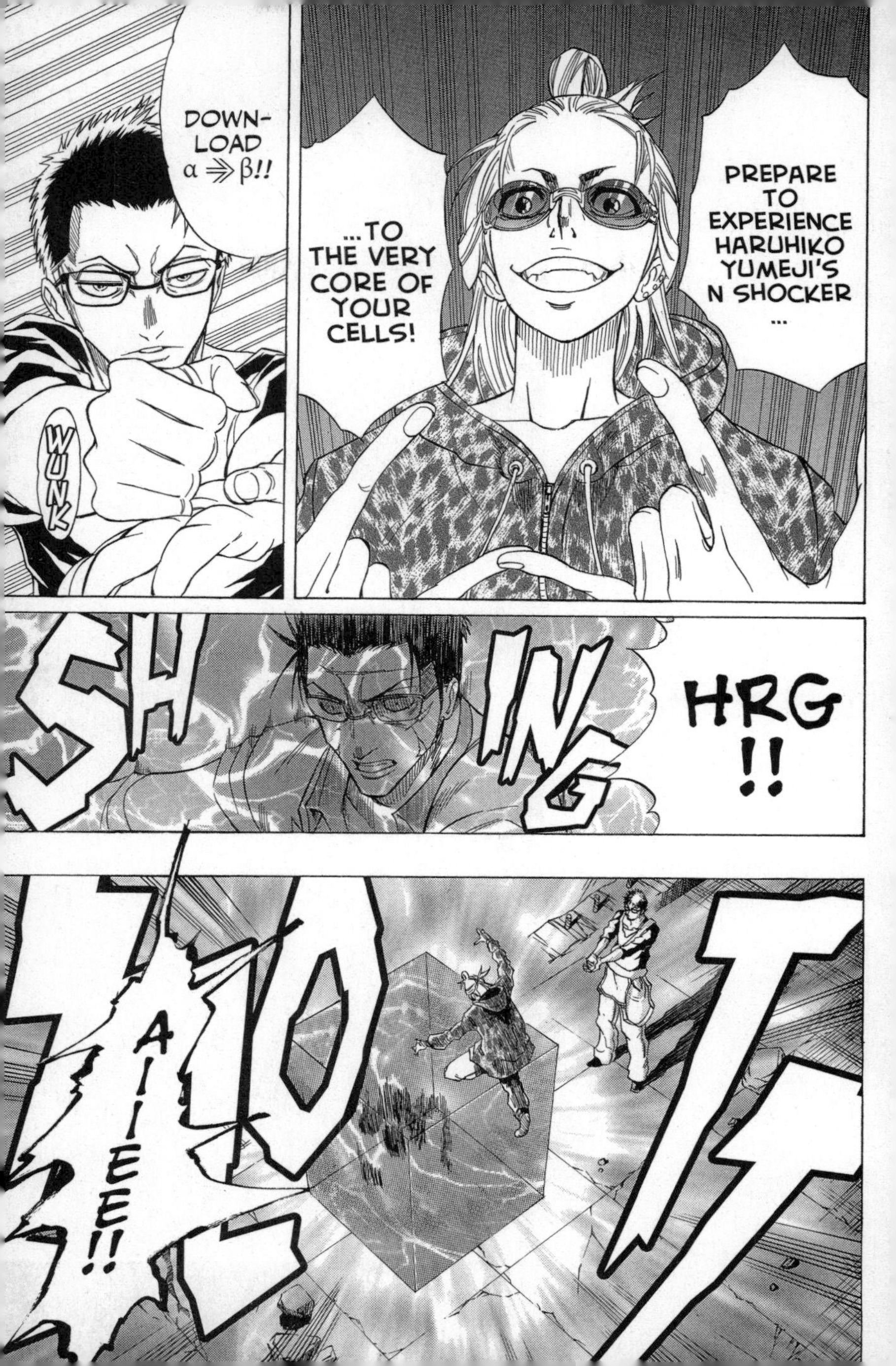

PREPARE TO EXPERIENCE HARUHIKO YUMEJI'S N SHOCKER ...
...TO THE VERY CORE OF YOUR CELLS!
DOWN-LOAD α ⇛ β!!
WUNK
HRG !!
SHING
ZOT
AIIEEE!!

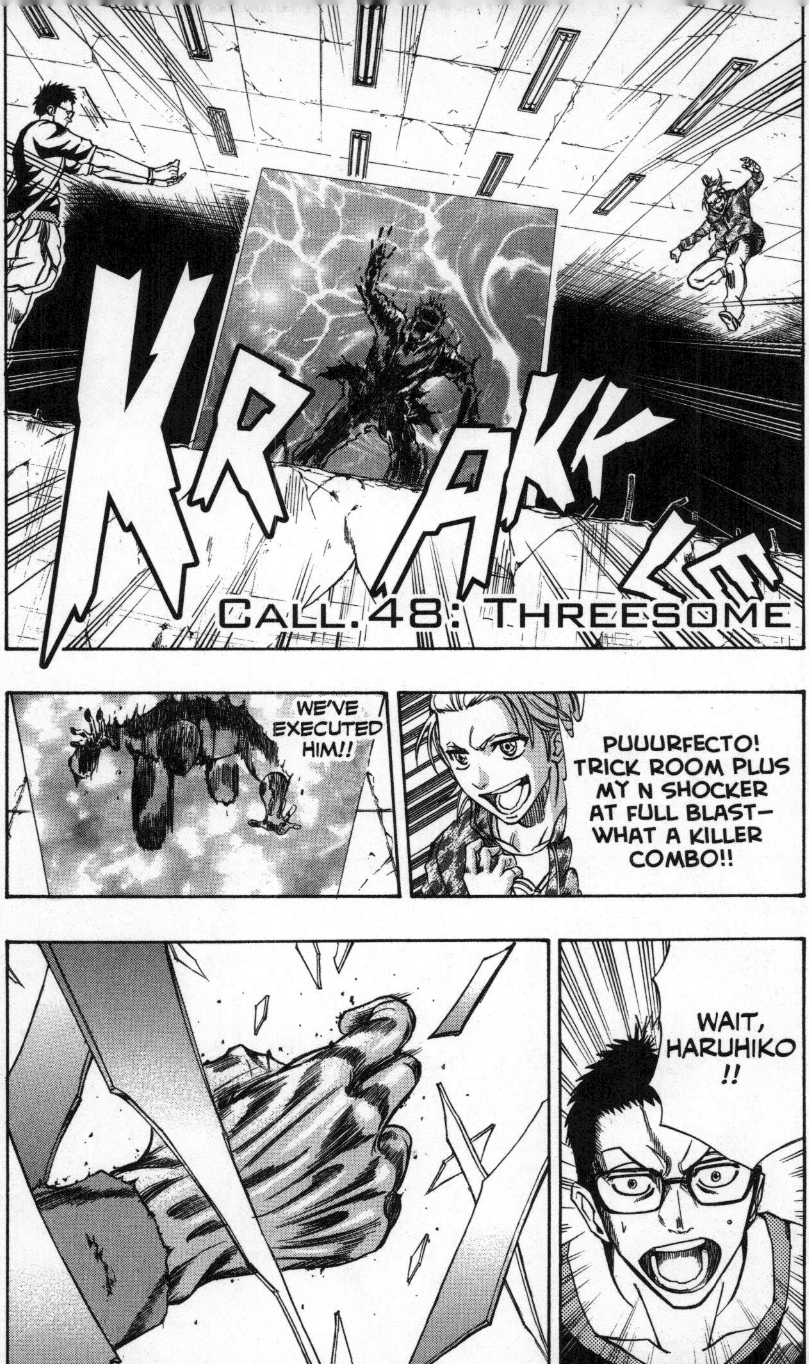
KRAKKLE
CALL.48: THREESOME
PUUURFECTO! TRICK ROOM PLUS MY N SHOCKER AT FULL BLAST—WHAT A KILLER COMBO!!
WE'VE EXECUTED HIM!!
WAIT, HARUHIKO!!

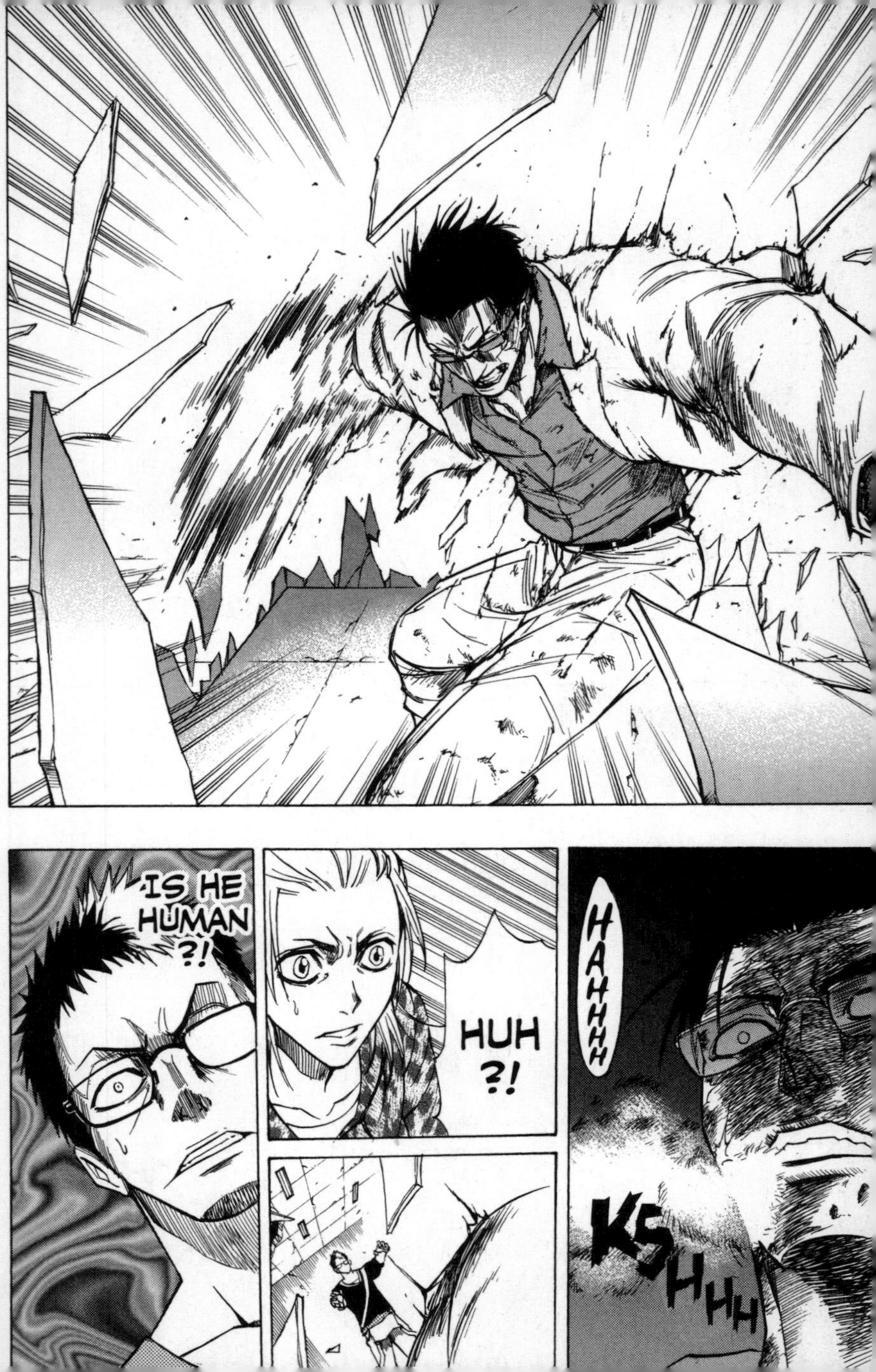
HAHHHH
KSHHHH
HUH ?!
IS HE HUMAN ?!

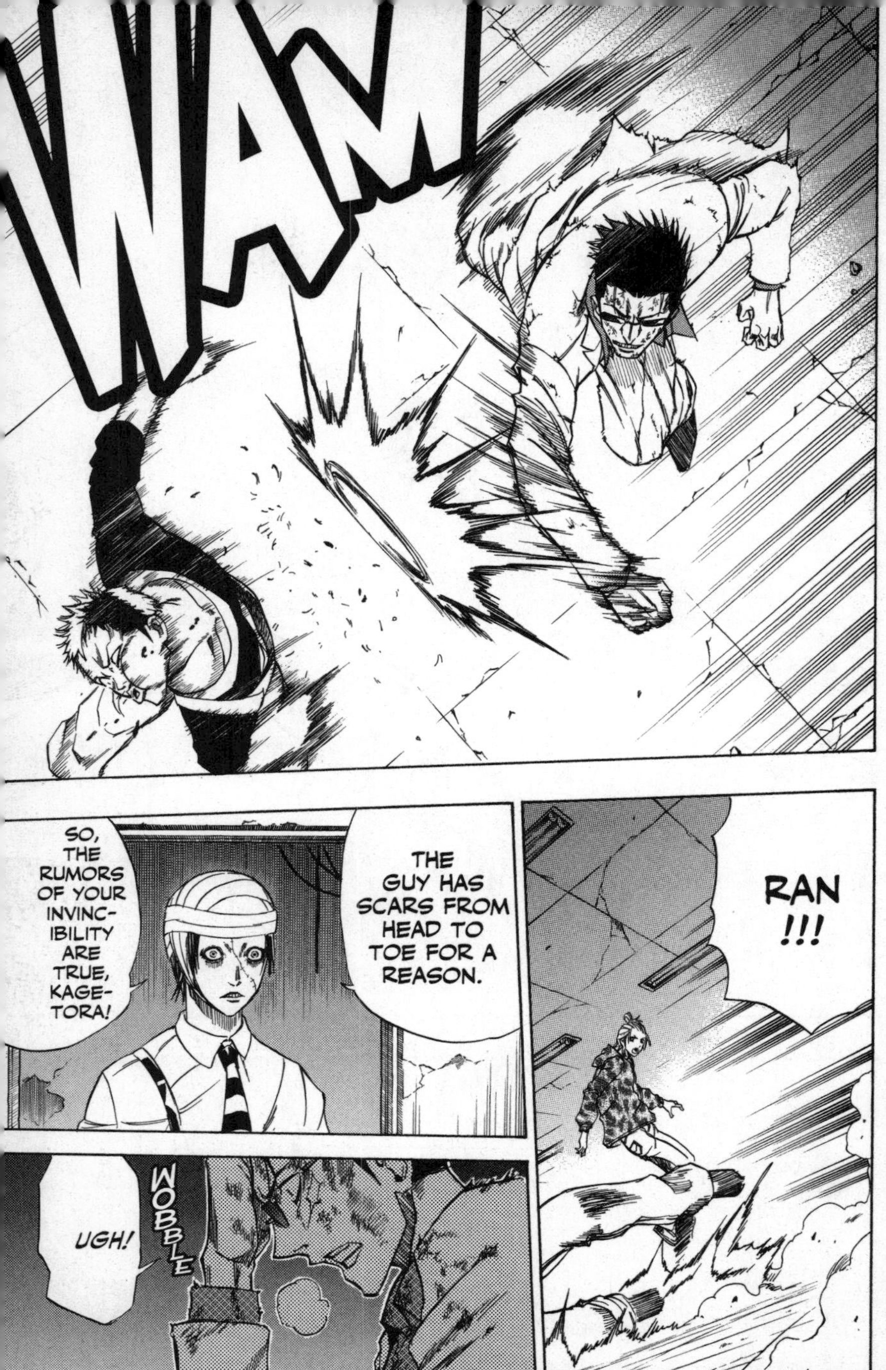
WAM
RAN!!!
THE GUY HAS SCARS FROM HEAD TO TOE FOR A REASON.
SO, THE RUMORS OF YOUR INVINCIBILITY ARE TRUE, KAGETORA!
WOBBLE
UGH!

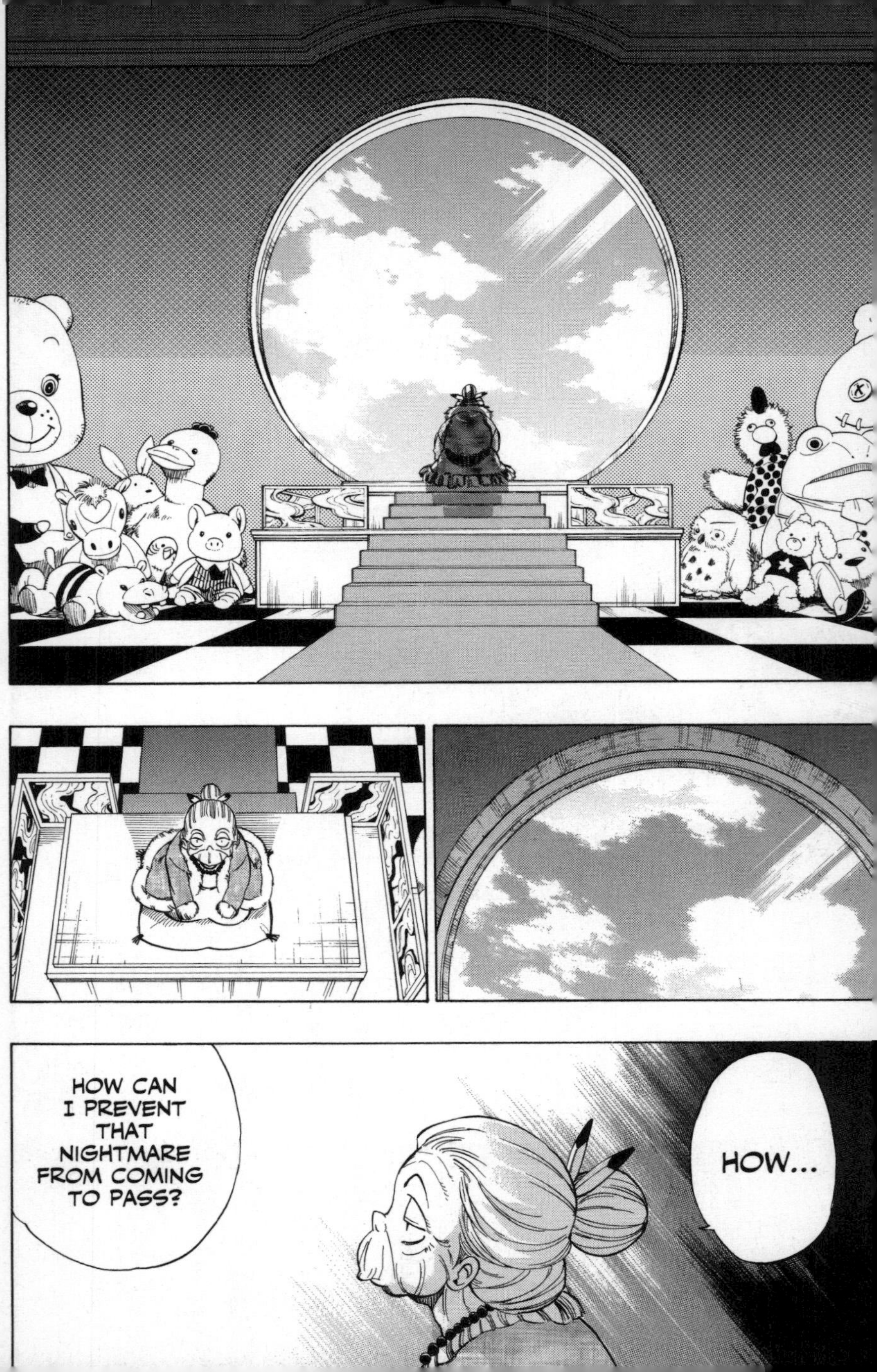
HOW...
HOW CAN I PREVENT THAT NIGHTMARE FROM COMING TO PASS?

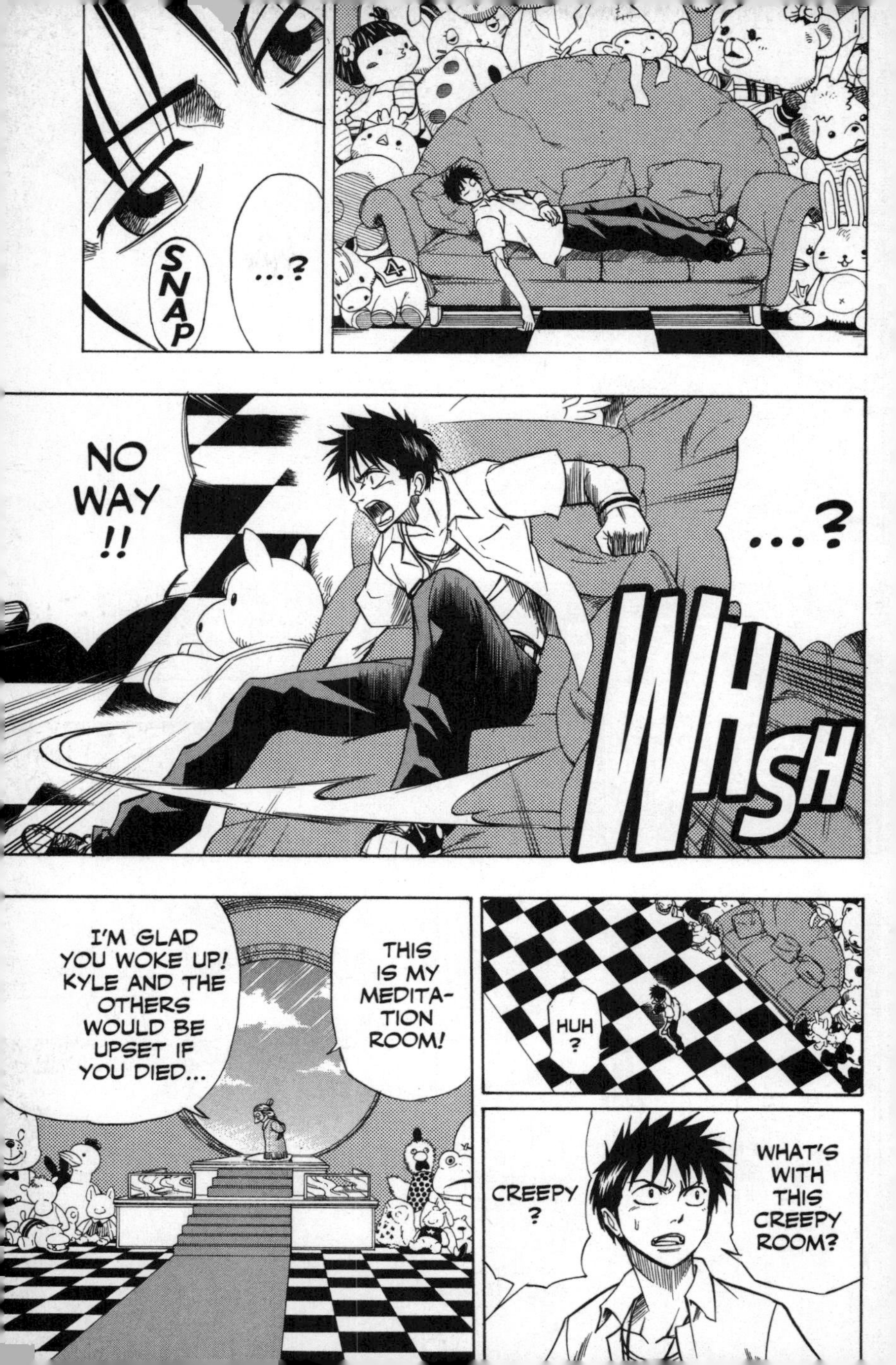
...?
SNAP
...?
WHSH
NO WAY !!
HUH ?
WHAT'S WITH THIS CREEPY ROOM?
CREEPY ?
THIS IS MY MEDITATION ROOM!
I'M GLAD YOU WOKE UP! KYLE AND THE OTHERS WOULD BE UPSET IF YOU DIED...

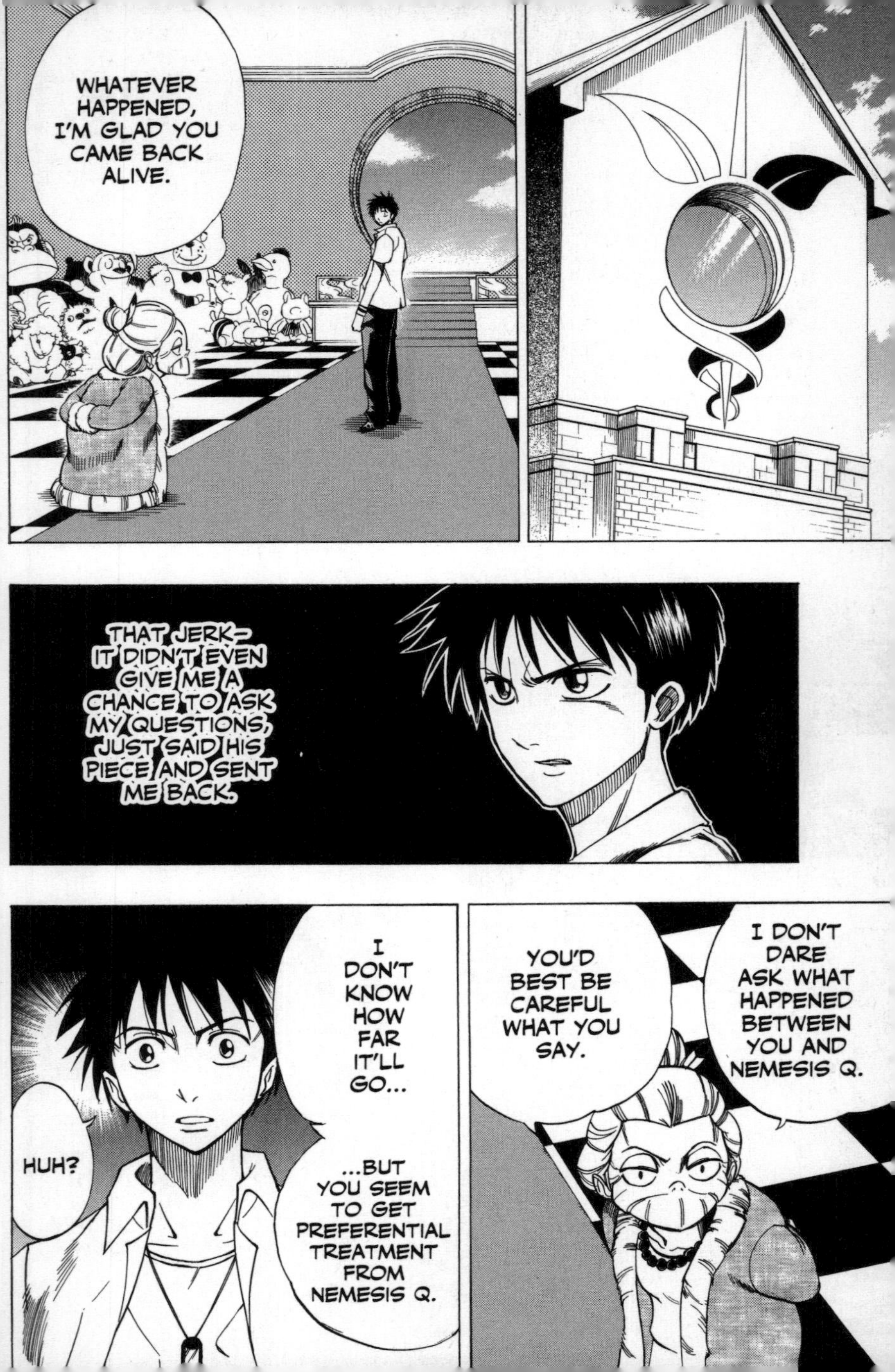
WHATEVER HAPPENED, I'M GLAD YOU CAME BACK ALIVE.
THAT JERK—IT DIDN'T EVEN GIVE ME A CHANCE TO ASK MY QUESTIONS, JUST SAID HIS PIECE AND SENT ME BACK.
I DON'T DARE ASK WHAT HAPPENED BETWEEN YOU AND NEMESIS Q.
YOU'D BEST BE CAREFUL WHAT YOU SAY.
I DON'T KNOW HOW FAR IT'LL GO...
...BUT YOU SEEM TO GET PREFERENTIAL TREATMENT FROM NEMESIS Q.
HUH?

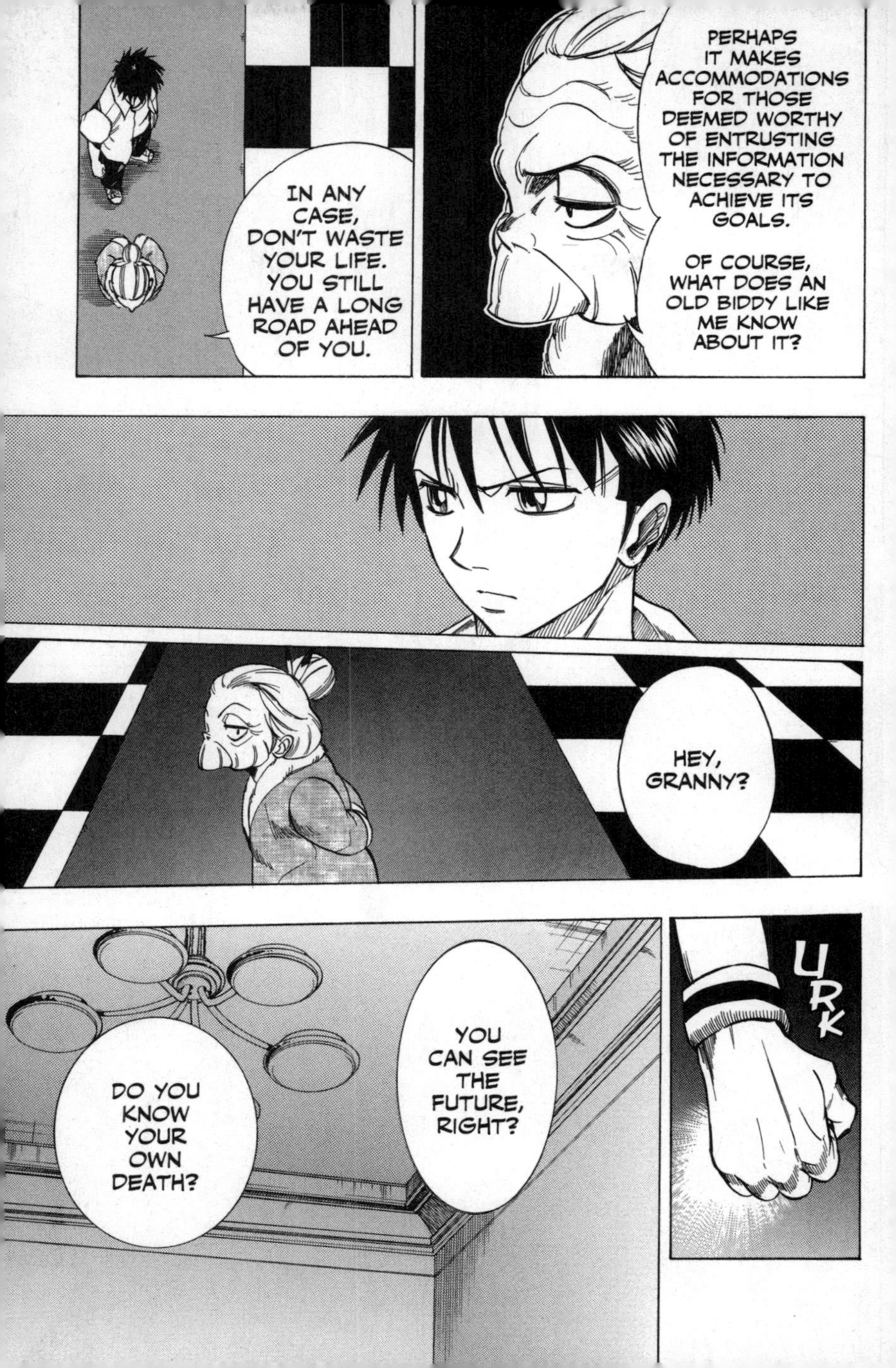
PERHAPS IT MAKES ACCOMMODATIONS FOR THOSE DEEMED WORTHY OF ENTRUSTING THE INFORMATION NECESSARY TO ACHIEVE ITS GOALS.
OF COURSE, WHAT DOES AN OLD BIDDY LIKE ME KNOW ABOUT IT?
IN ANY CASE, DON'T WASTE YOUR LIFE. YOU STILL HAVE A LONG ROAD AHEAD OF YOU.
HEY, GRANNY?
URK
YOU CAN SEE THE FUTURE, RIGHT?
DO YOU KNOW YOUR OWN DEATH?

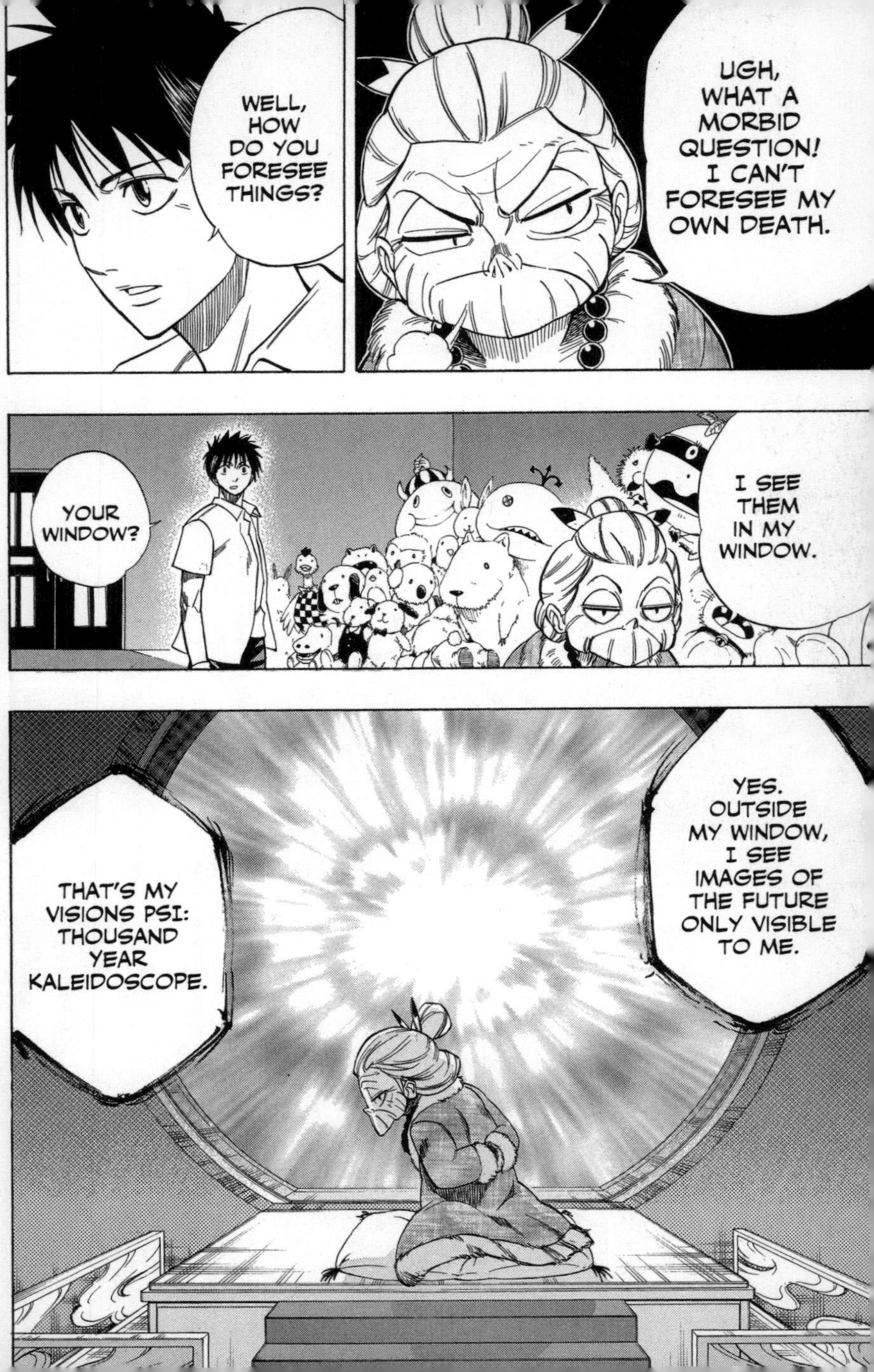
UGH, WHAT A MORBID QUESTION! I CAN'T FORESEE MY OWN DEATH.
WELL, HOW DO YOU FORESEE THINGS?
I SEE THEM IN MY WINDOW.
YOUR WINDOW?
YES. OUTSIDE MY WINDOW, I SEE IMAGES OF THE FUTURE ONLY VISIBLE TO ME.
THAT'S MY VISIONS PSI: THOUSAND YEAR KALEIDOSCOPE.

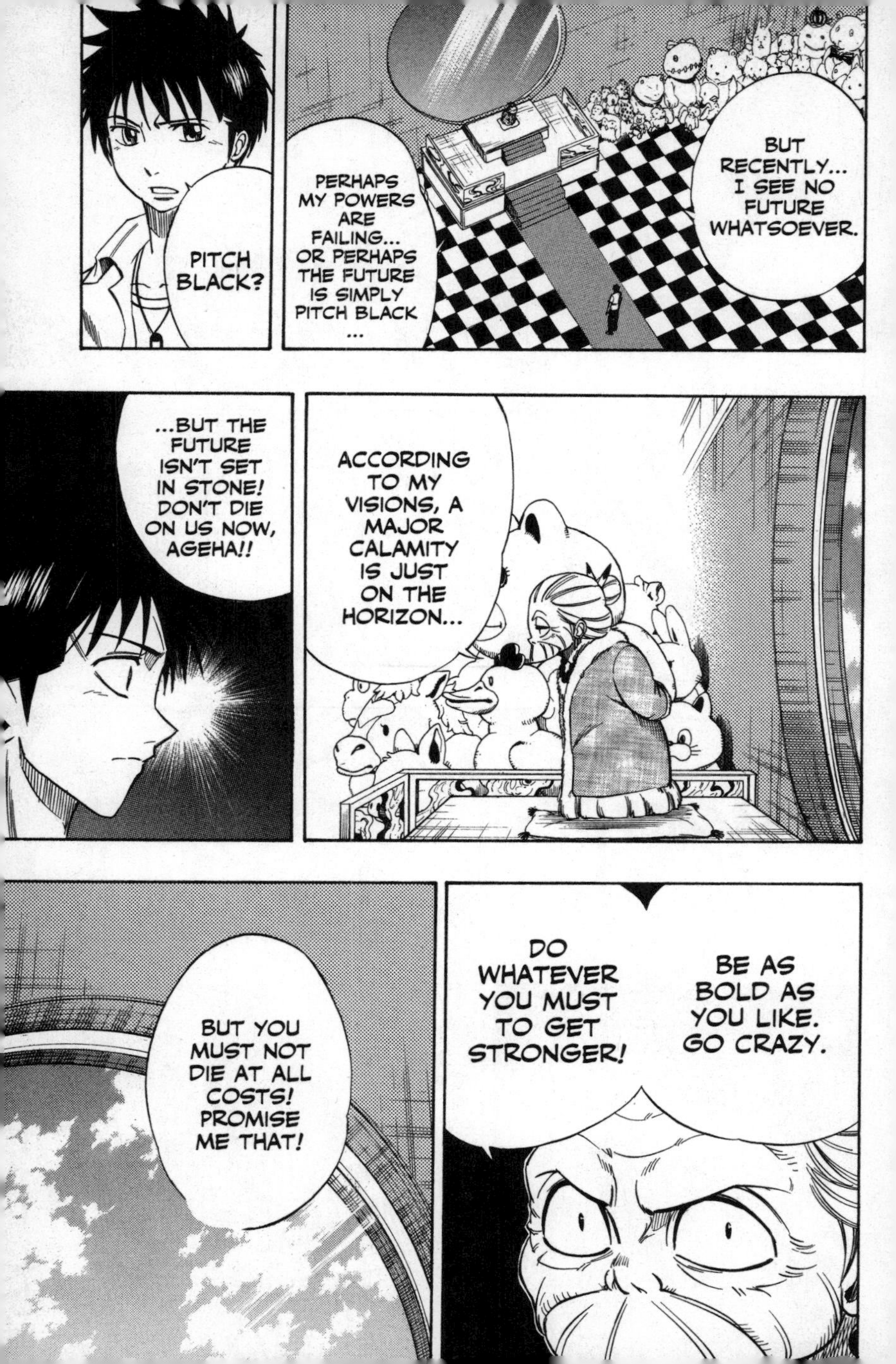
BUT RECENTLY... I SEE NO FUTURE WHATSOEVER.
PERHAPS MY POWERS ARE FAILING... OR PERHAPS THE FUTURE IS SIMPLY PITCH BLACK...
PITCH BLACK?
ACCORDING TO MY VISIONS, A MAJOR CALAMITY IS JUST ON THE HORIZON...
...BUT THE FUTURE ISN'T SET IN STONE! DON'T DIE ON US NOW, AGEHA!!
BE AS BOLD AS YOU LIKE. GO CRAZY.
DO WHATEVER YOU MUST TO GET STRONGER!
BUT YOU MUST NOT DIE AT ALL COSTS! PROMISE ME THAT!

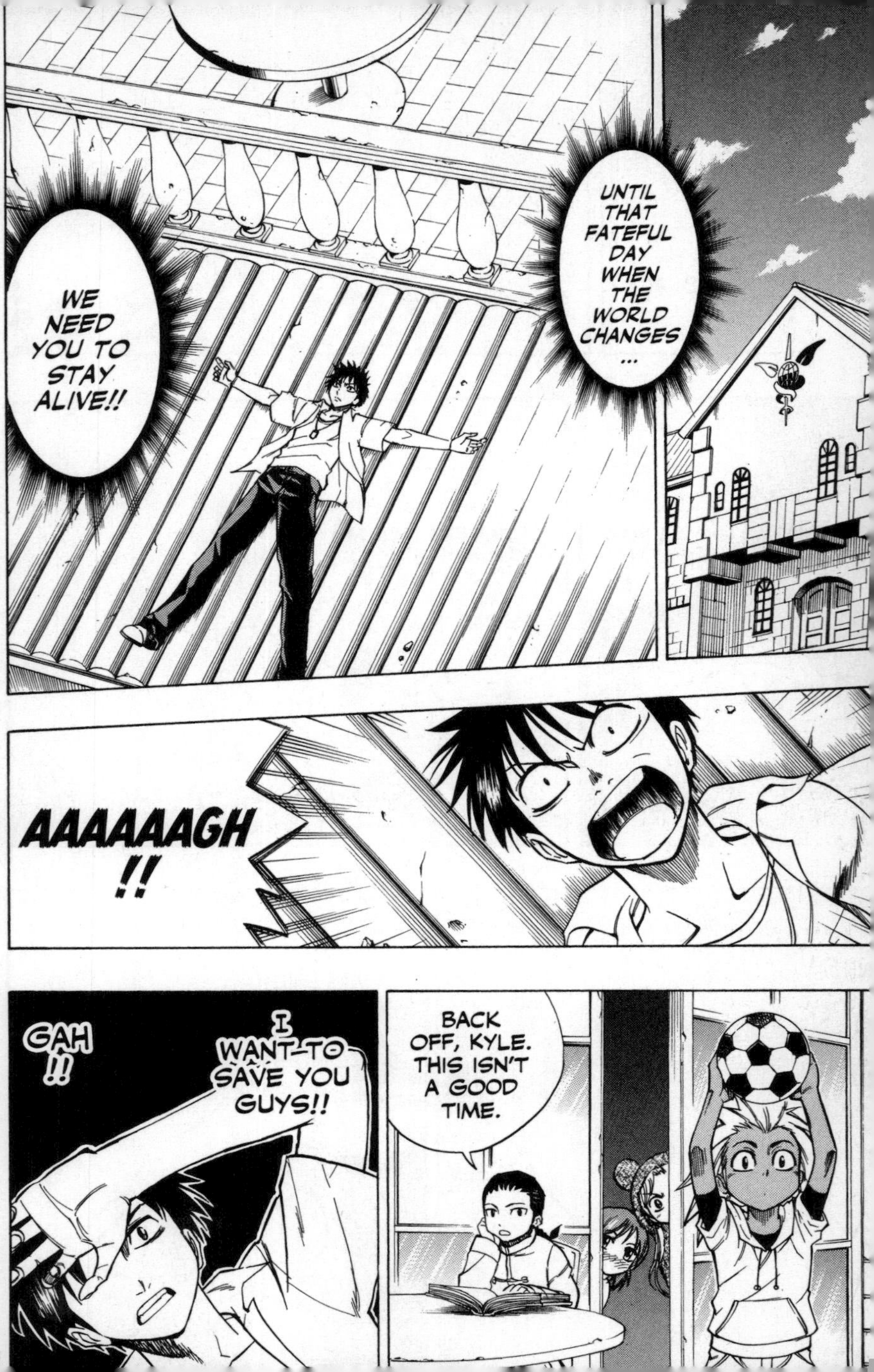

UNTIL THAT FATEFUL DAY WHEN THE WORLD CHANGES...
WE NEED YOU TO STAY ALIVE!!
AAAAAAGH!!
BACK OFF, KYLE. THIS ISN'T A GOOD TIME.
I WANT TO SAVE YOU GUYS!!
GAH!!

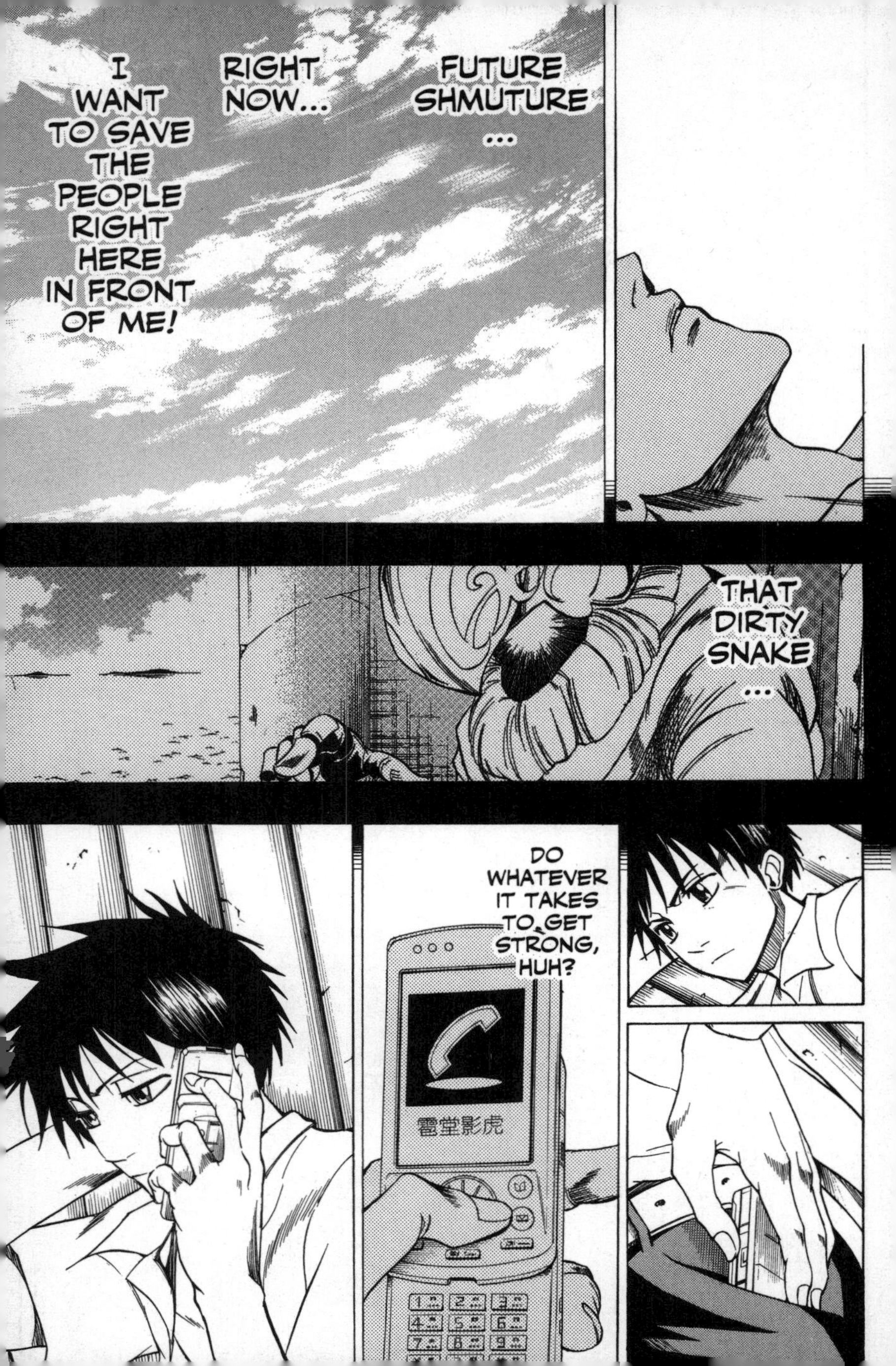
FUTURE SHMUTURE ...
RIGHT NOW...
I WANT TO SAVE THE PEOPLE RIGHT HERE IN FRONT OF ME!
THAT DIRTY SNAKE ...
DO WHATEVER IT TAKES TO GET STRONG, HUH?
霞堂影虎

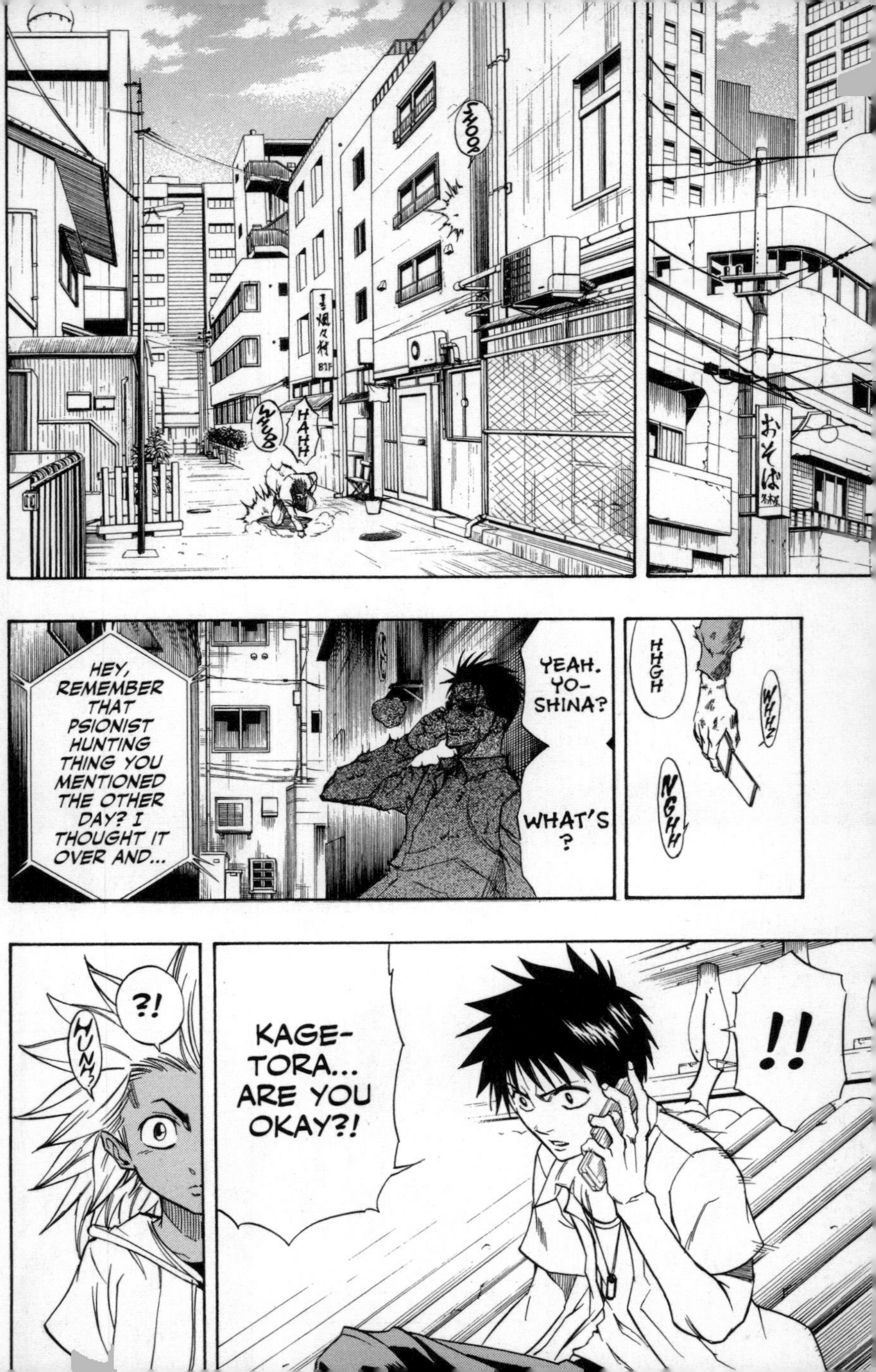
SHOOP
HAHH
WHUD
おそば
HHGH
WHHZ
NGHH
YEAH. YO-SHINA?
WHAT'S ?
HEY, REMEMBER THAT PSIONIST HUNTING THING YOU MENTIONED THE OTHER DAY? I THOUGHT IT OVER AND...
!!
KAGE-TORA... ARE YOU OKAY?!
?!
HUNH?

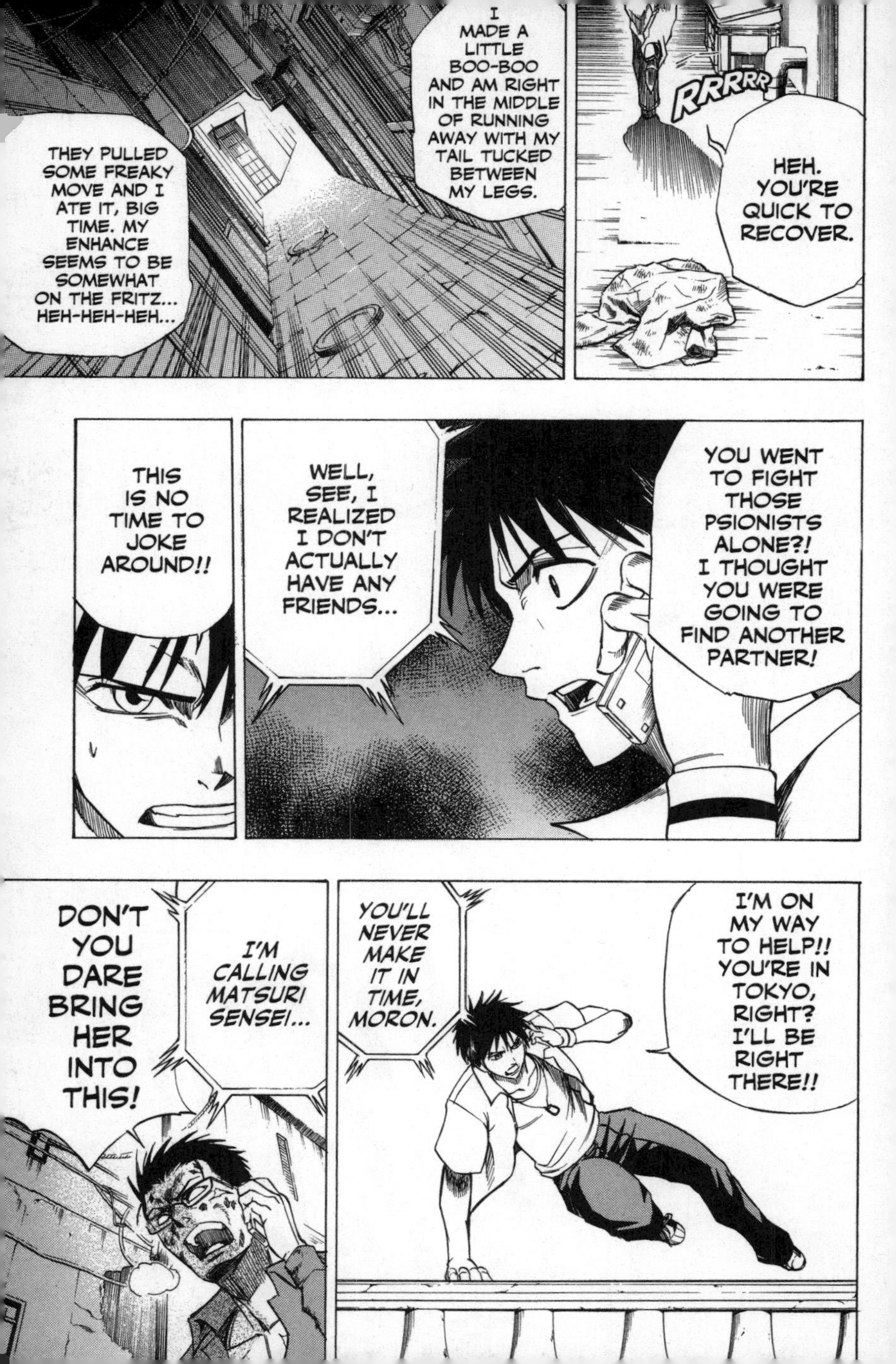
RRRRR
HEH. YOU'RE QUICK TO RECOVER.
I MADE A LITTLE BOO-BOO AND AM RIGHT IN THE MIDDLE OF RUNNING AWAY WITH MY TAIL TUCKED BETWEEN MY LEGS.
THEY PULLED SOME FREAKY MOVE AND I ATE IT, BIG TIME. MY ENHANCE SEEMS TO BE SOMEWHAT ON THE FRITZ... HEH-HEH-HEH...
YOU WENT TO FIGHT THOSE PSIONISTS ALONE?! I THOUGHT YOU WERE GOING TO FIND ANOTHER PARTNER!
WELL, SEE, I REALIZED I DON'T ACTUALLY HAVE ANY FRIENDS...
THIS IS NO TIME TO JOKE AROUND!!
I'M ON MY WAY TO HELP!! YOU'RE IN TOKYO, RIGHT? I'LL BE RIGHT THERE!!
YOU'LL NEVER MAKE IT IN TIME, MORON.
I'M CALLING MATSURI SENSEI...
DON'T YOU DARE BRING HER INTO THIS!

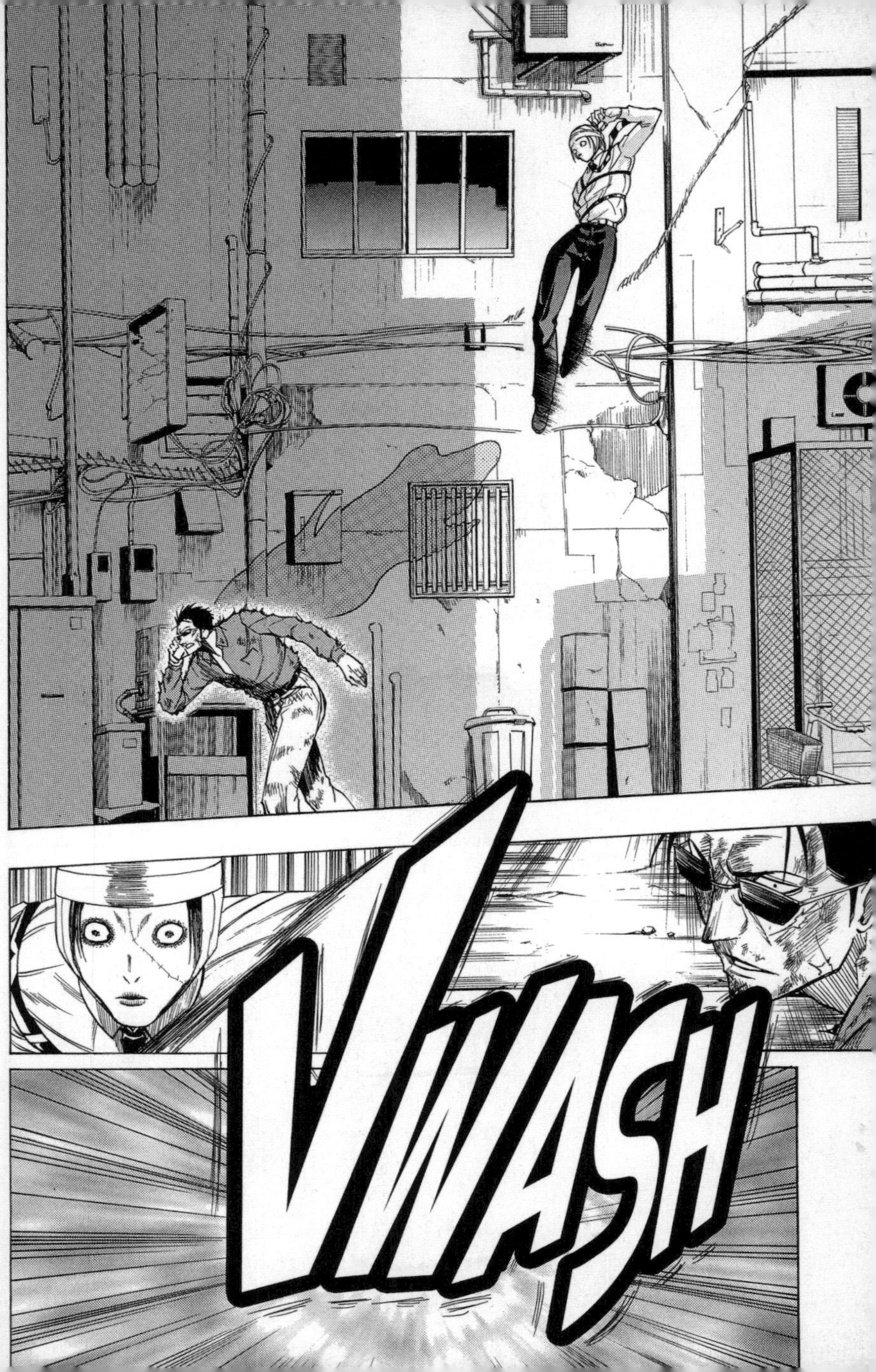
VWASH

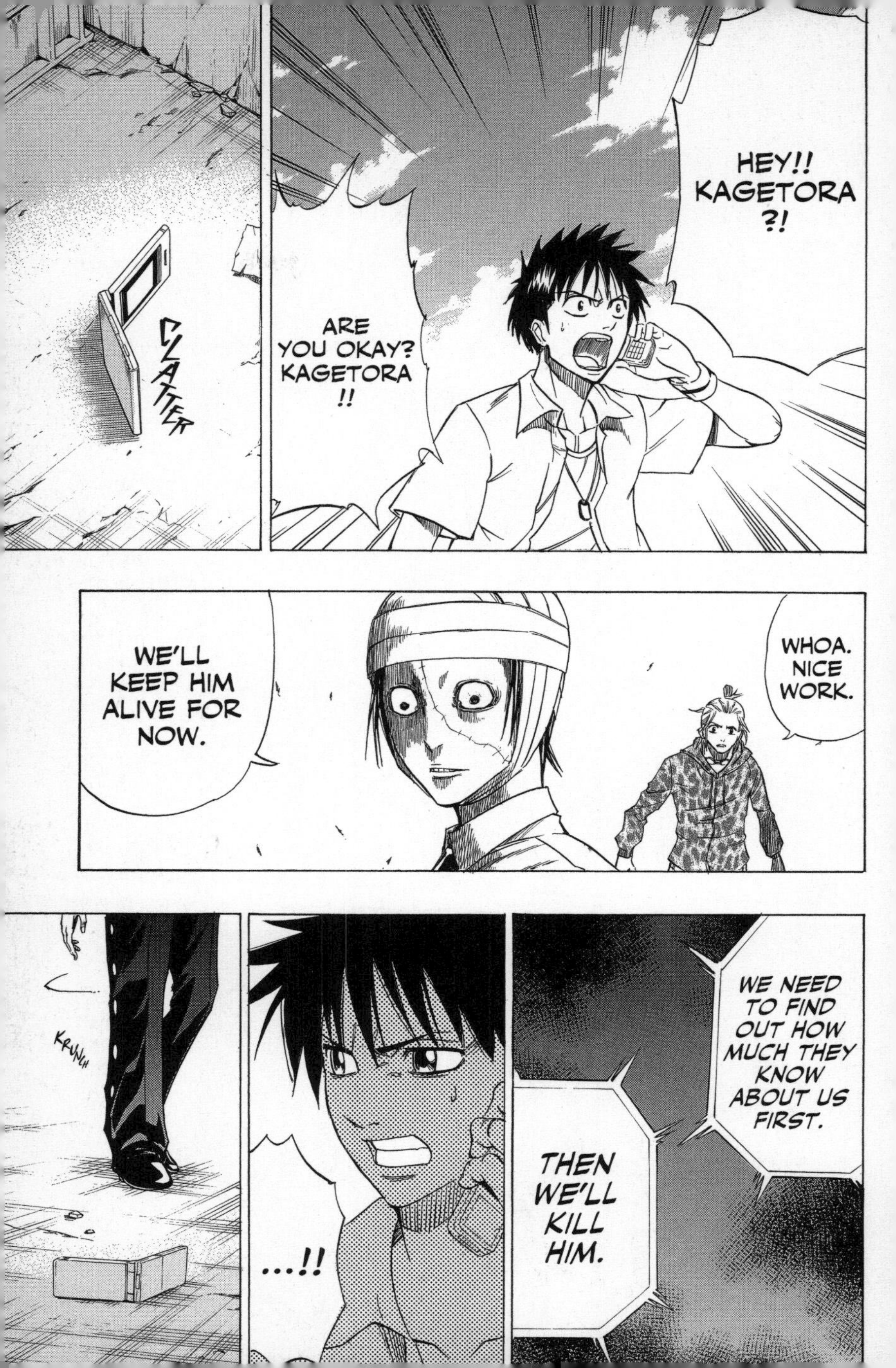
HEY!! KAGETORA ?!
ARE YOU OKAY? KAGETORA !!
CLATTER
WHOA. NICE WORK.
WE'LL KEEP HIM ALIVE FOR NOW.
WE NEED TO FIND OUT HOW MUCH THEY KNOW ABOUT US FIRST.
THEN WE'LL KILL HIM.
...!!
KRUNCH

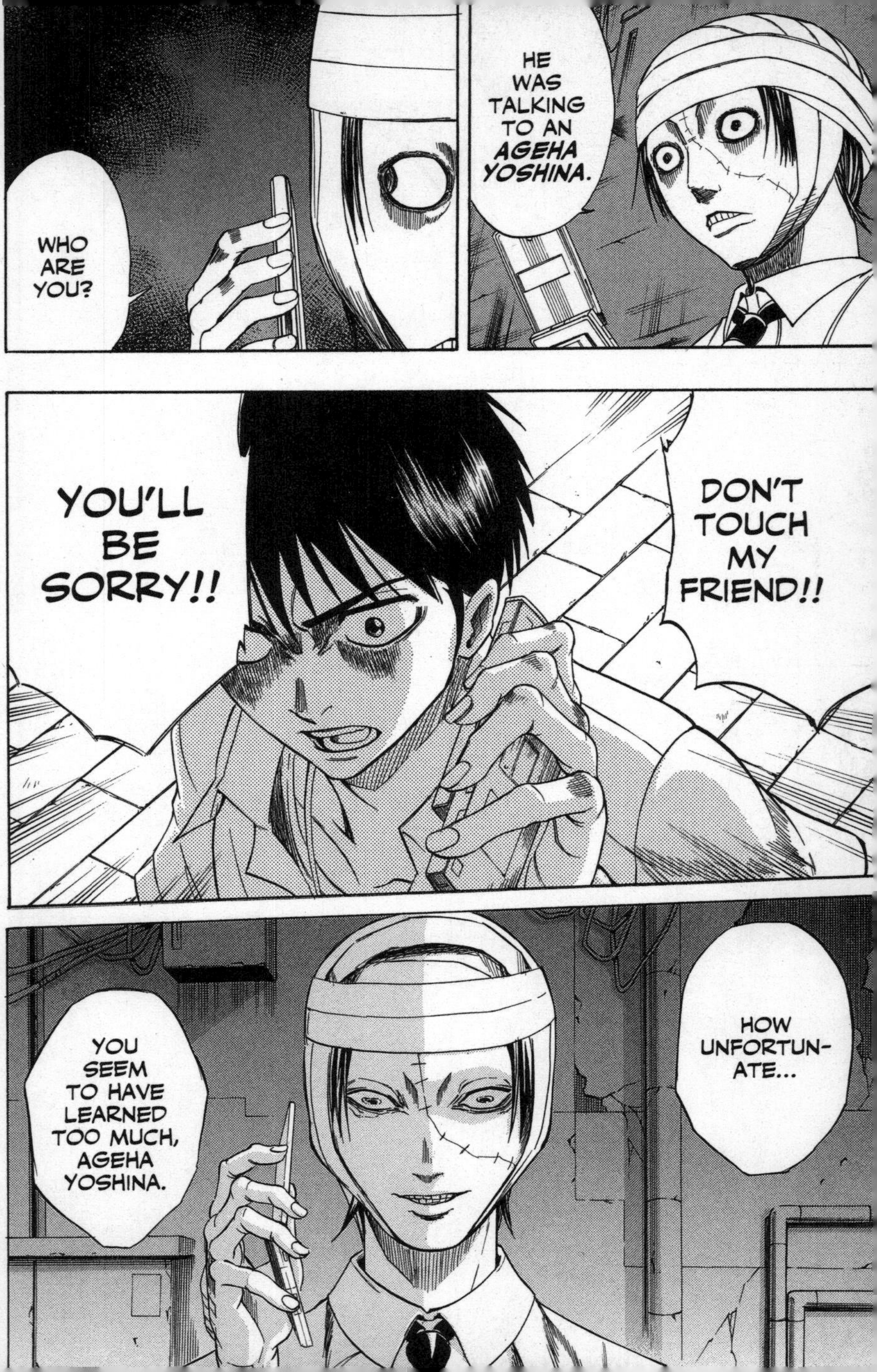
HE WAS TALKING TO AN *AGEHA YOSHINA.*
WHO ARE YOU?
DON'T TOUCH MY FRIEND!!
YOU'LL BE SORRY!!
HOW UNFORTUN-ATE...
YOU SEEM TO HAVE LEARNED TOO MUCH, AGEHA YOSHINA.

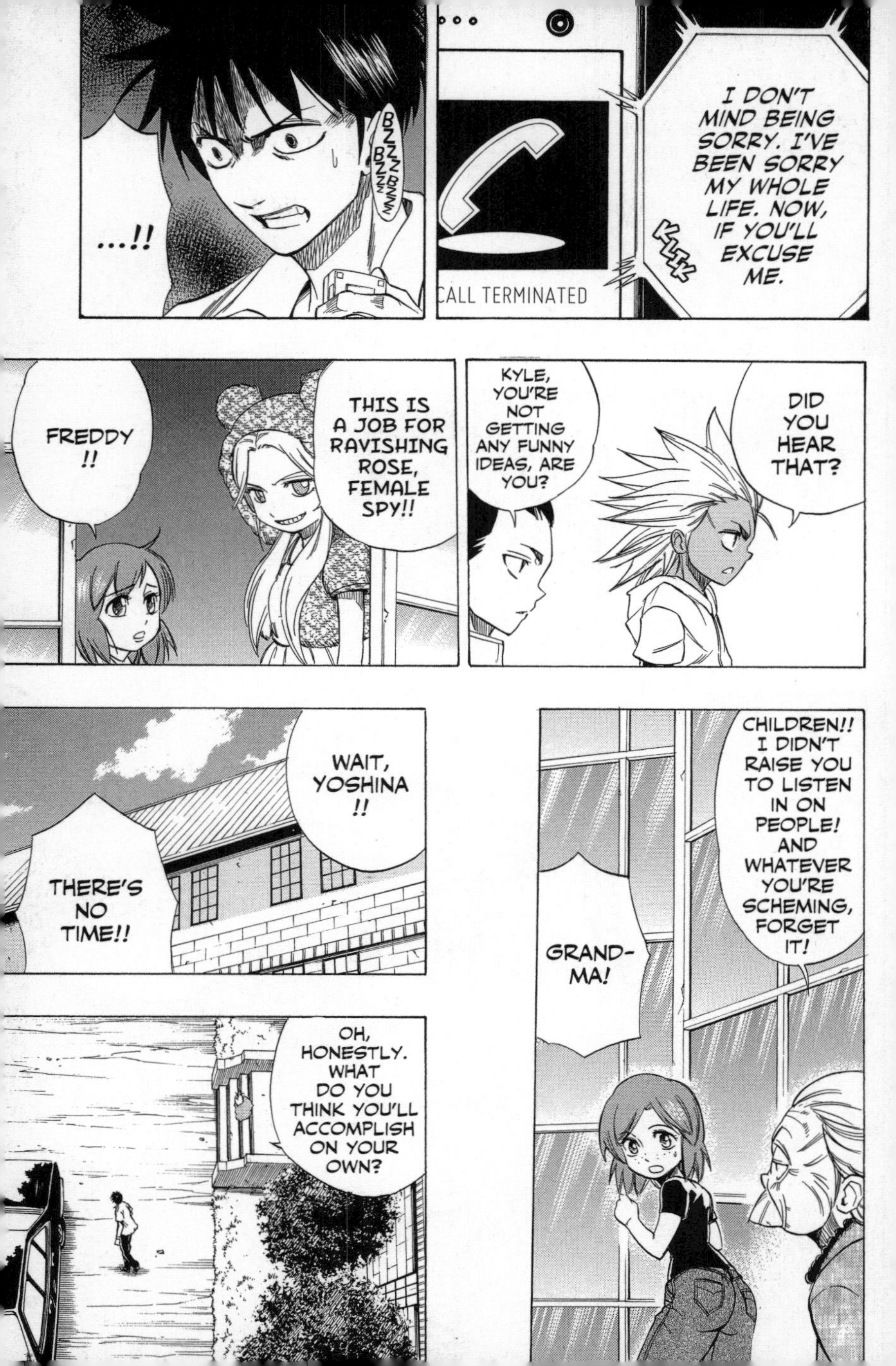
I DON'T MIND BEING SORRY. I'VE BEEN SORRY MY WHOLE LIFE. NOW, IF YOU'LL EXCUSE ME.
KLIK
CALL TERMINATED
...!!
DID YOU HEAR THAT?
KYLE, YOU'RE NOT GETTING ANY FUNNY IDEAS, ARE YOU?
THIS IS A JOB FOR RAVISHING ROSE, FEMALE SPY!!
FREDDY!!
CHILDREN!! I DIDN'T RAISE YOU TO LISTEN IN ON PEOPLE! AND WHATEVER YOU'RE SCHEMING, FORGET IT!
GRAND-MA!
WAIT, YOSHINA!!
THERE'S NO TIME!!
OH, HONESTLY. WHAT DO YOU THINK YOU'LL ACCOMPLISH ON YOUR OWN?

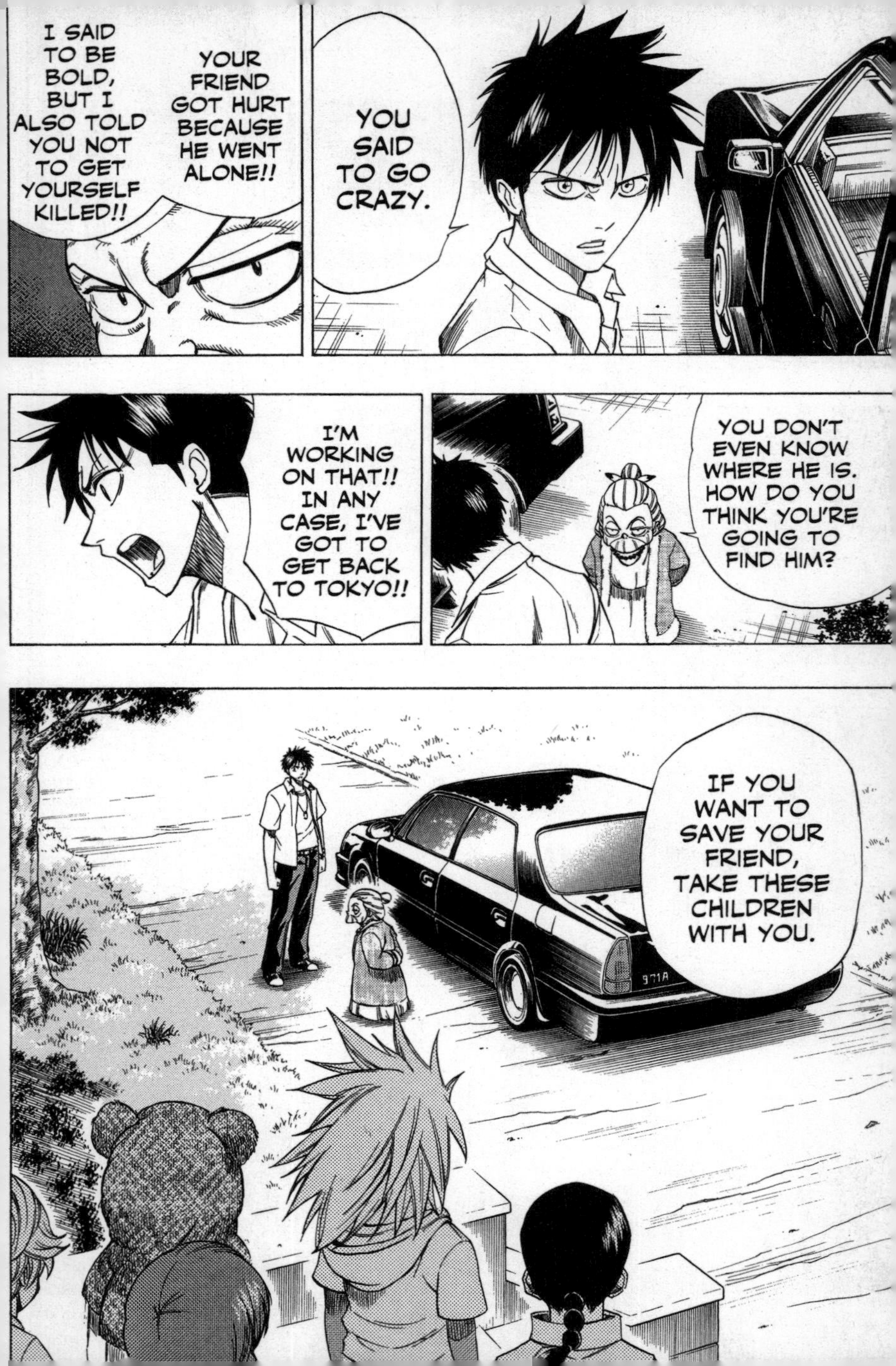
YOU SAID TO GO CRAZY.
YOUR FRIEND GOT HURT BECAUSE HE WENT ALONE!!
I SAID TO BE BOLD, BUT I ALSO TOLD YOU NOT TO GET YOURSELF KILLED!!
YOU DON'T EVEN KNOW WHERE HE IS. HOW DO YOU THINK YOU'RE GOING TO FIND HIM?
I'M WORKING ON THAT!! IN ANY CASE, I'VE GOT TO GET BACK TO TOKYO!!
IF YOU WANT TO SAVE YOUR FRIEND, TAKE THESE CHILDREN WITH YOU.
971A

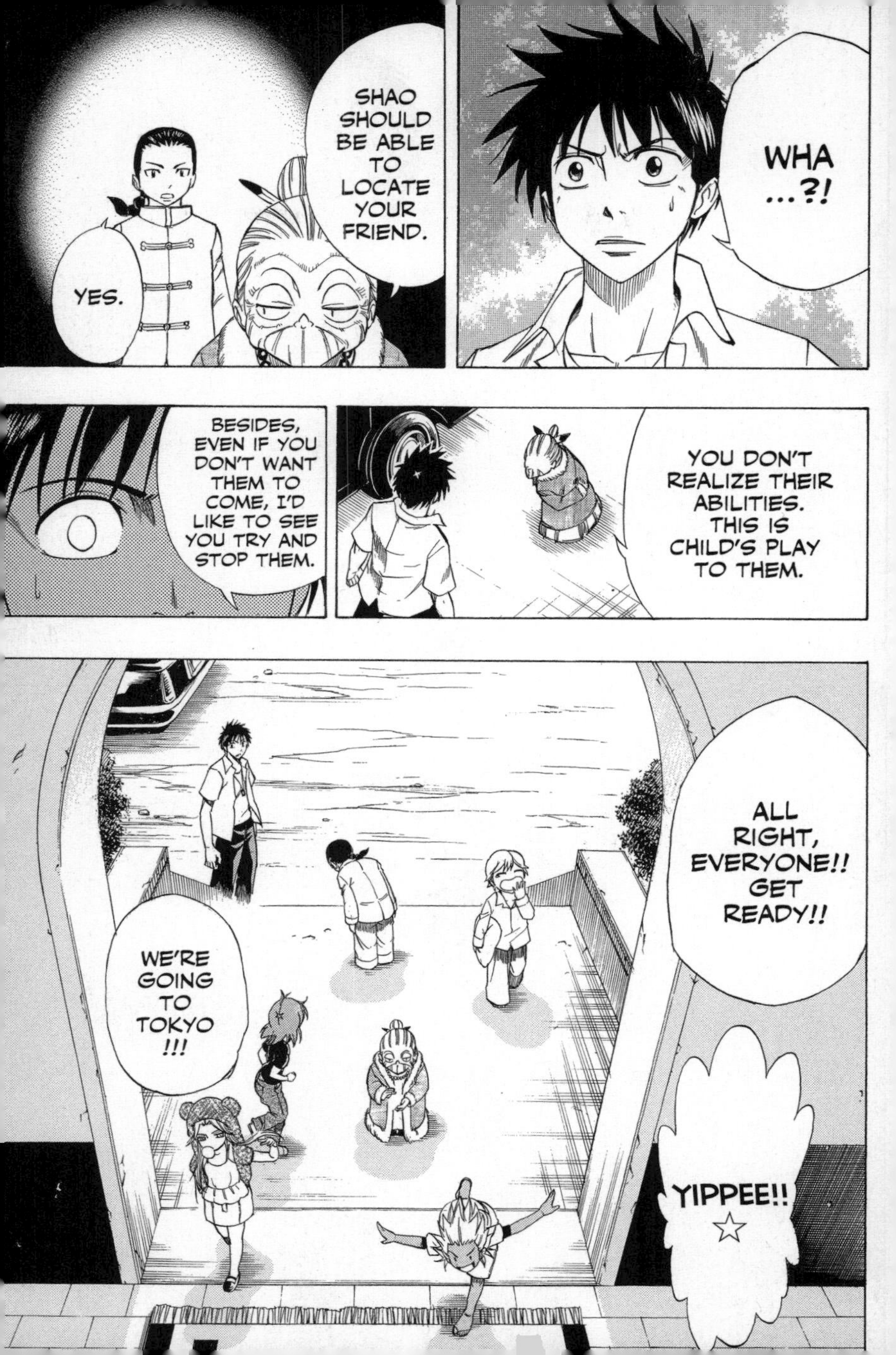
WHA ...?!
SHAO SHOULD BE ABLE TO LOCATE YOUR FRIEND.
YES.
YOU DON'T REALIZE THEIR ABILITIES. THIS IS CHILD'S PLAY TO THEM.
BESIDES, EVEN IF YOU DON'T WANT THEM TO COME, I'D LIKE TO SEE YOU TRY AND STOP THEM.
ALL RIGHT, EVERYONE!! GET READY!!
WE'RE GOING TO TOKYO!!!
YIPPEE!! ☆

Mutters and mumblings...

NOVELS I LOVE:

RIKU ONDA: BLACK AND TAN FANTASY
               THE ELEPHANT AND
                    THE TINNITUS

MIYUKI MIYABE: GAMO-HOUSE CASES
                CAR FIRE

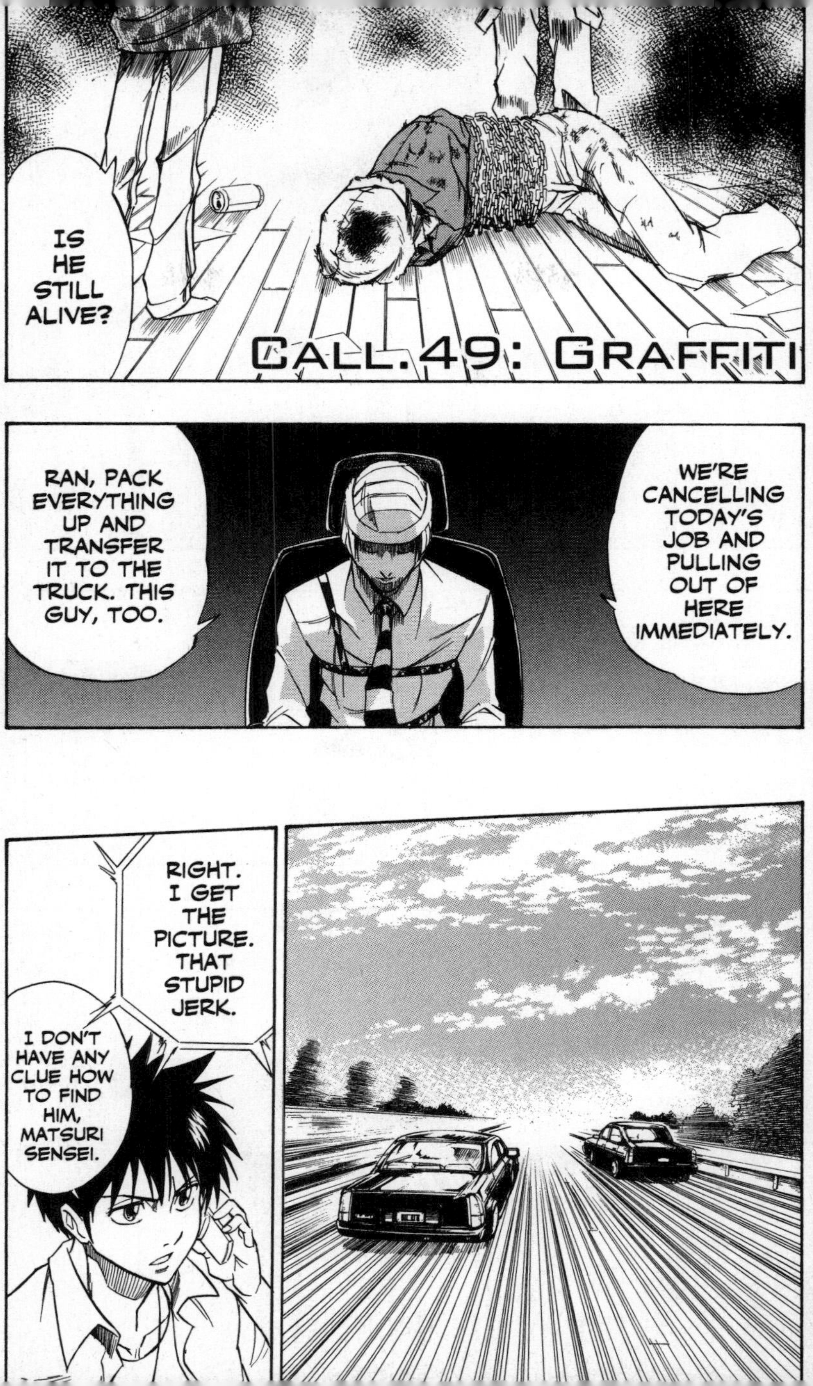
IS HE STILL ALIVE?
CALL.49: GRAFFITI
WE'RE CANCELLING TODAY'S JOB AND PULLING OUT OF HERE IMMEDIATELY.
RAN, PACK EVERYTHING UP AND TRANSFER IT TO THE TRUCK. THIS GUY, TOO.
RIGHT. I GET THE PICTURE. THAT STUPID JERK.
I DON'T HAVE ANY CLUE HOW TO FIND HIM, MATSURI SENSEI.

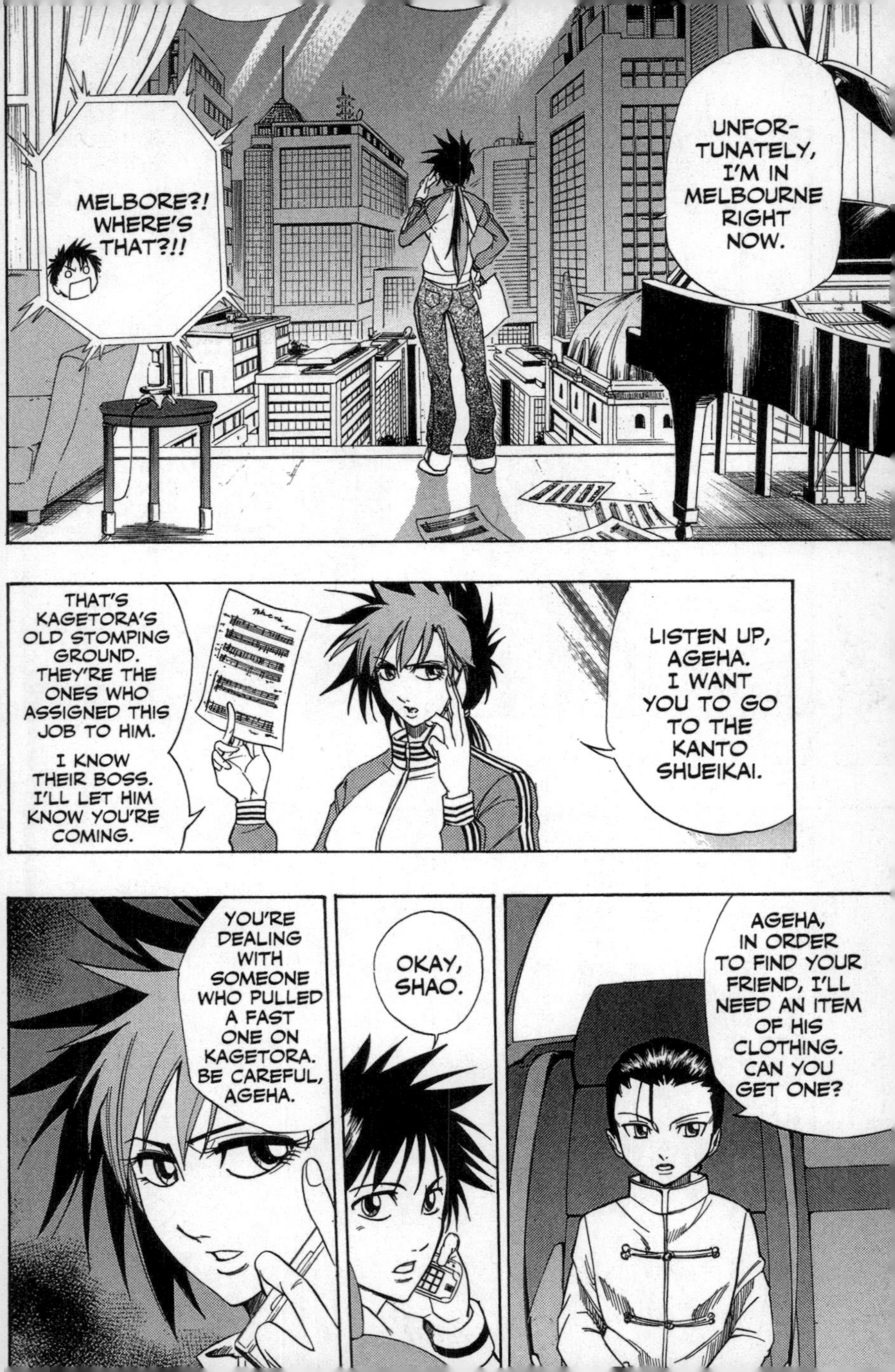
UNFORTUNATELY, I'M IN MELBOURNE RIGHT NOW.
MELBORE?! WHERE'S THAT?!!
LISTEN UP, AGEHA. I WANT YOU TO GO TO THE KANTO SHUEIKAI.
THAT'S KAGETORA'S OLD STOMPING GROUND. THEY'RE THE ONES WHO ASSIGNED THIS JOB TO HIM.
I KNOW THEIR BOSS. I'LL LET HIM KNOW YOU'RE COMING.
AGEHA, IN ORDER TO FIND YOUR FRIEND, I'LL NEED AN ITEM OF HIS CLOTHING. CAN YOU GET ONE?
OKAY, SHAO.
YOU'RE DEALING WITH SOMEONE WHO PULLED A FAST ONE ON KAGETORA. BE CAREFUL, AGEHA.

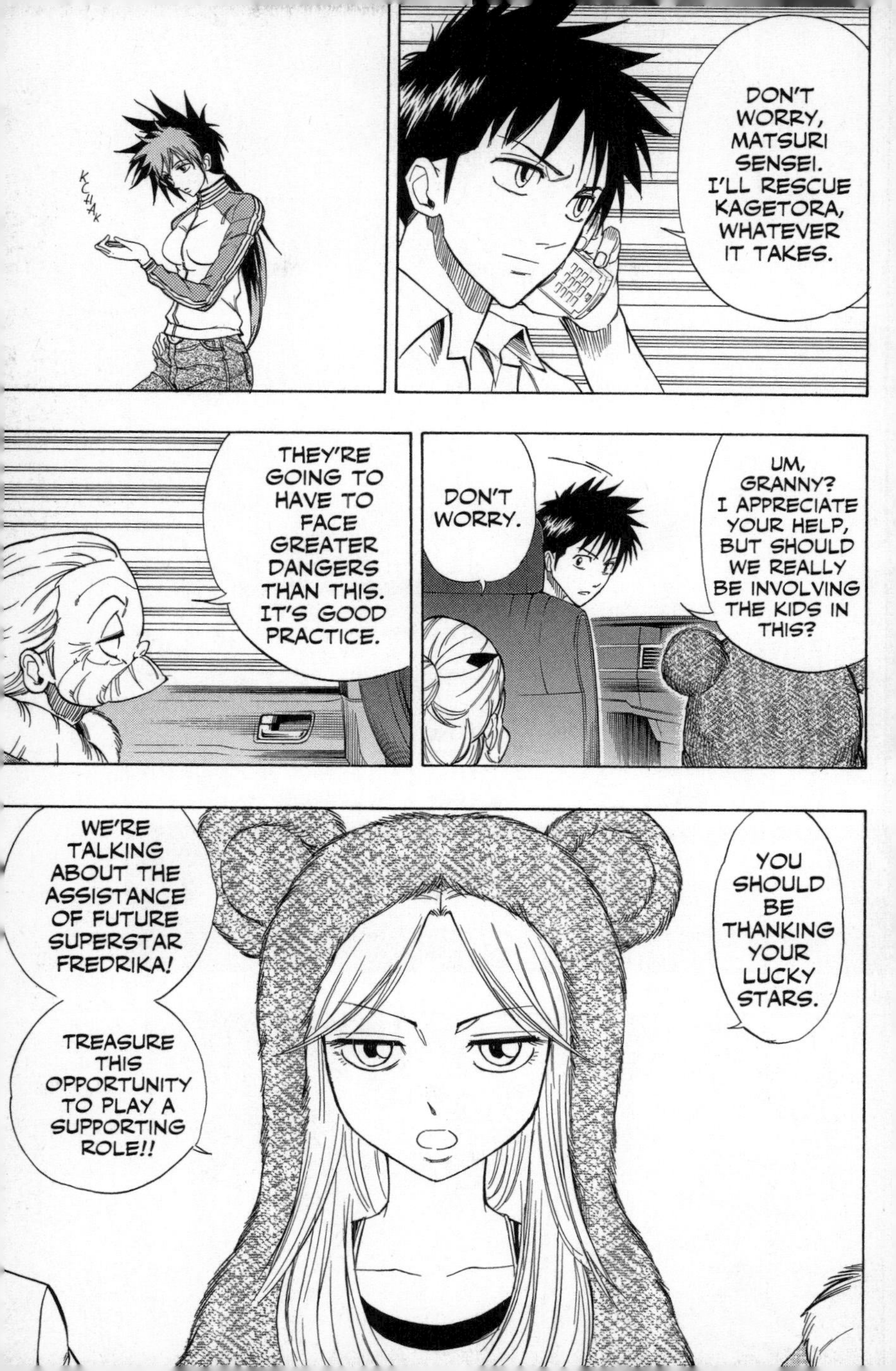
DON'T WORRY, MATSURI SENSEI. I'LL RESCUE KAGETORA, WHATEVER IT TAKES.
KCHAK
UM, GRANNY? I APPRECIATE YOUR HELP, BUT SHOULD WE REALLY BE INVOLVING THE KIDS IN THIS?
DON'T WORRY.
THEY'RE GOING TO HAVE TO FACE GREATER DANGERS THAN THIS. IT'S GOOD PRACTICE.
YOU SHOULD BE THANKING YOUR LUCKY STARS.
WE'RE TALKING ABOUT THE ASSISTANCE OF FUTURE SUPERSTAR FREDRIKA!
TREASURE THIS OPPORTUNITY TO PLAY A SUPPORTING ROLE!!

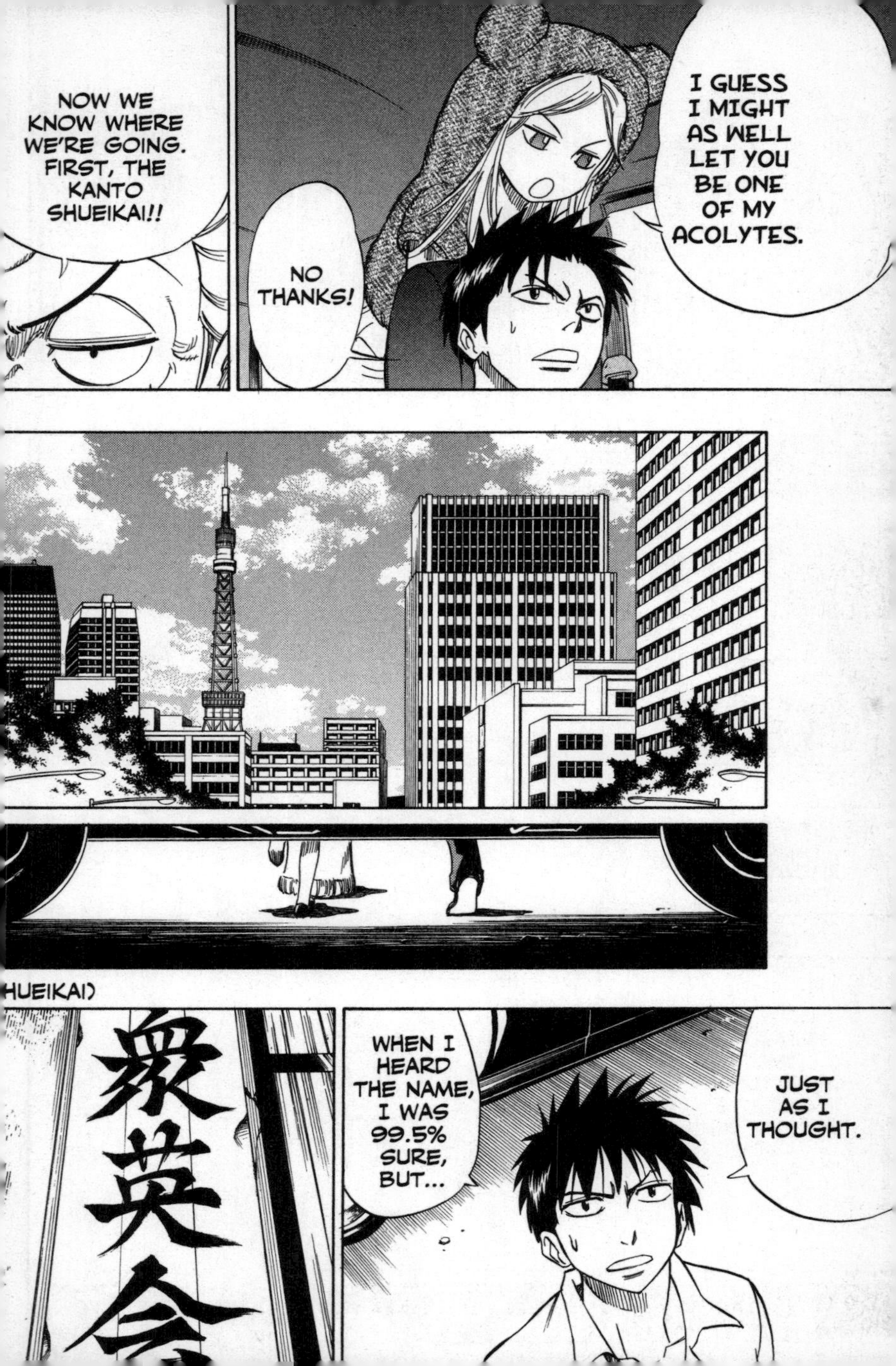
I GUESS I MIGHT AS WELL LET YOU BE ONE OF MY ACOLYTES.
NO THANKS!
NOW WE KNOW WHERE WE'RE GOING. FIRST, THE KANTO SHUEIKAI!!
HUEIKAI)
WHEN I HEARD THE NAME, I WAS 99.5% SURE, BUT...
JUST AS I THOUGHT.
衆英会

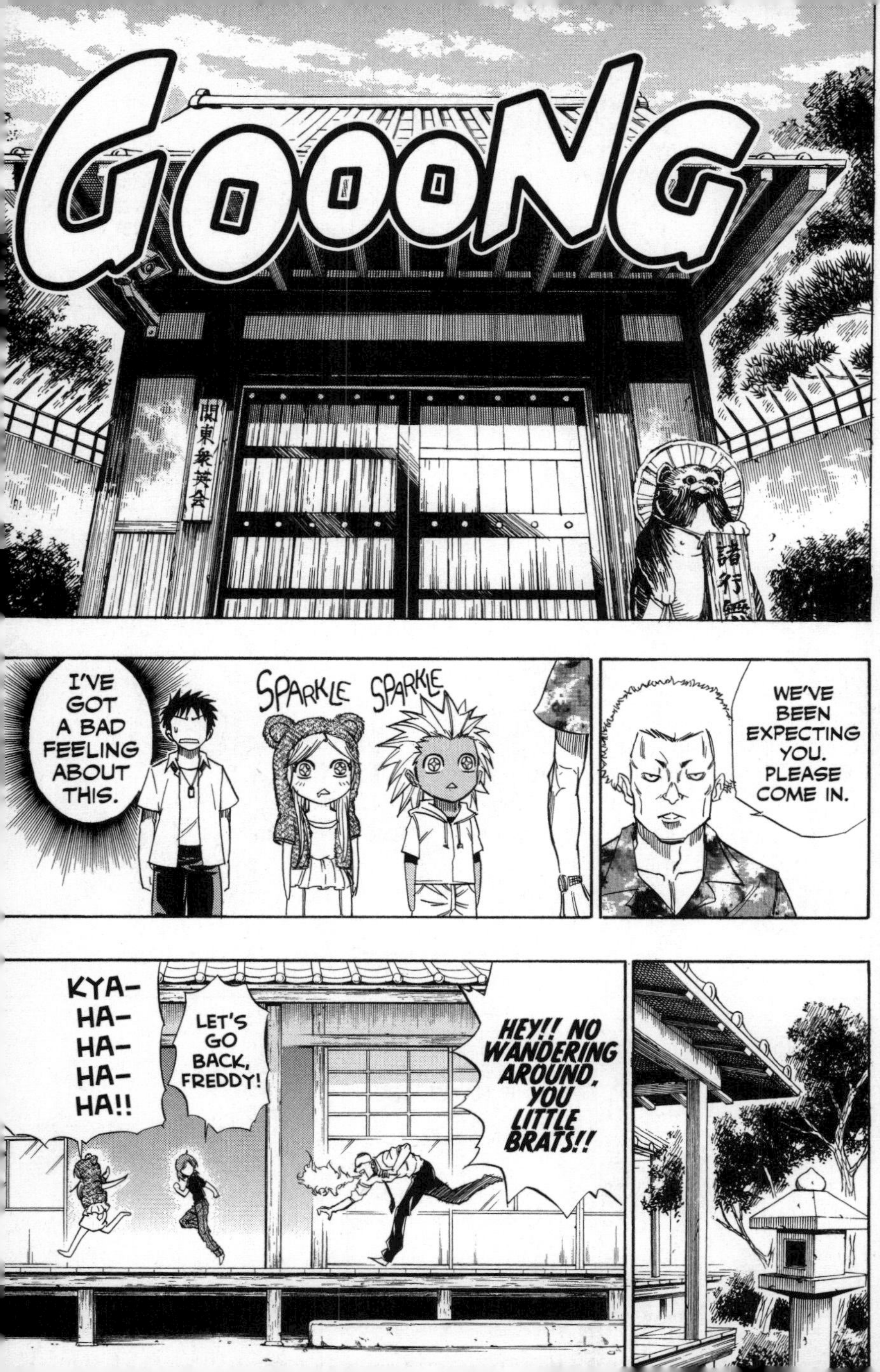
GOOONG
WE'VE BEEN EXPECTING YOU. PLEASE COME IN.
SPARKLE SPARKLE
I'VE GOT A BAD FEELING ABOUT THIS.
HEY!! NO WANDERING AROUND, YOU LITTLE BRATS!!
LET'S GO BACK, FREDDY!
KYA-HA-HA-HA-HA!!

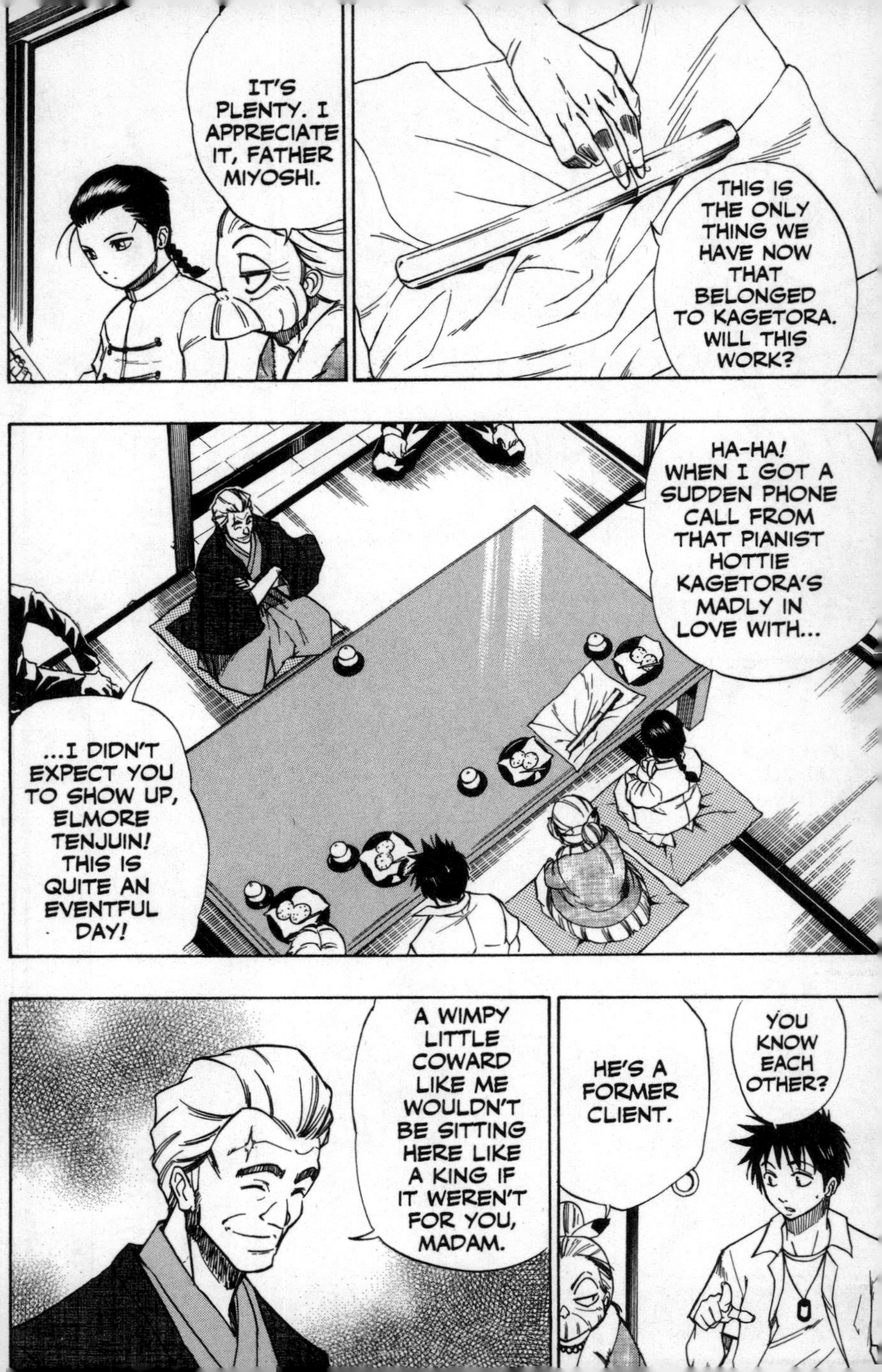
THIS IS THE ONLY THING WE HAVE NOW THAT BELONGED TO KAGETORA. WILL THIS WORK?
IT'S PLENTY. I APPRECIATE IT, FATHER MIYOSHI.
HA-HA! WHEN I GOT A SUDDEN PHONE CALL FROM THAT PIANIST HOTTIE KAGETORA'S MADLY IN LOVE WITH...
...I DIDN'T EXPECT YOU TO SHOW UP, ELMORE TENJUIN! THIS IS QUITE AN EVENTFUL DAY!
YOU KNOW EACH OTHER?
HE'S A FORMER CLIENT.
A WIMPY LITTLE COWARD LIKE ME WOULDN'T BE SITTING HERE LIKE A KING IF IT WEREN'T FOR YOU, MADAM.

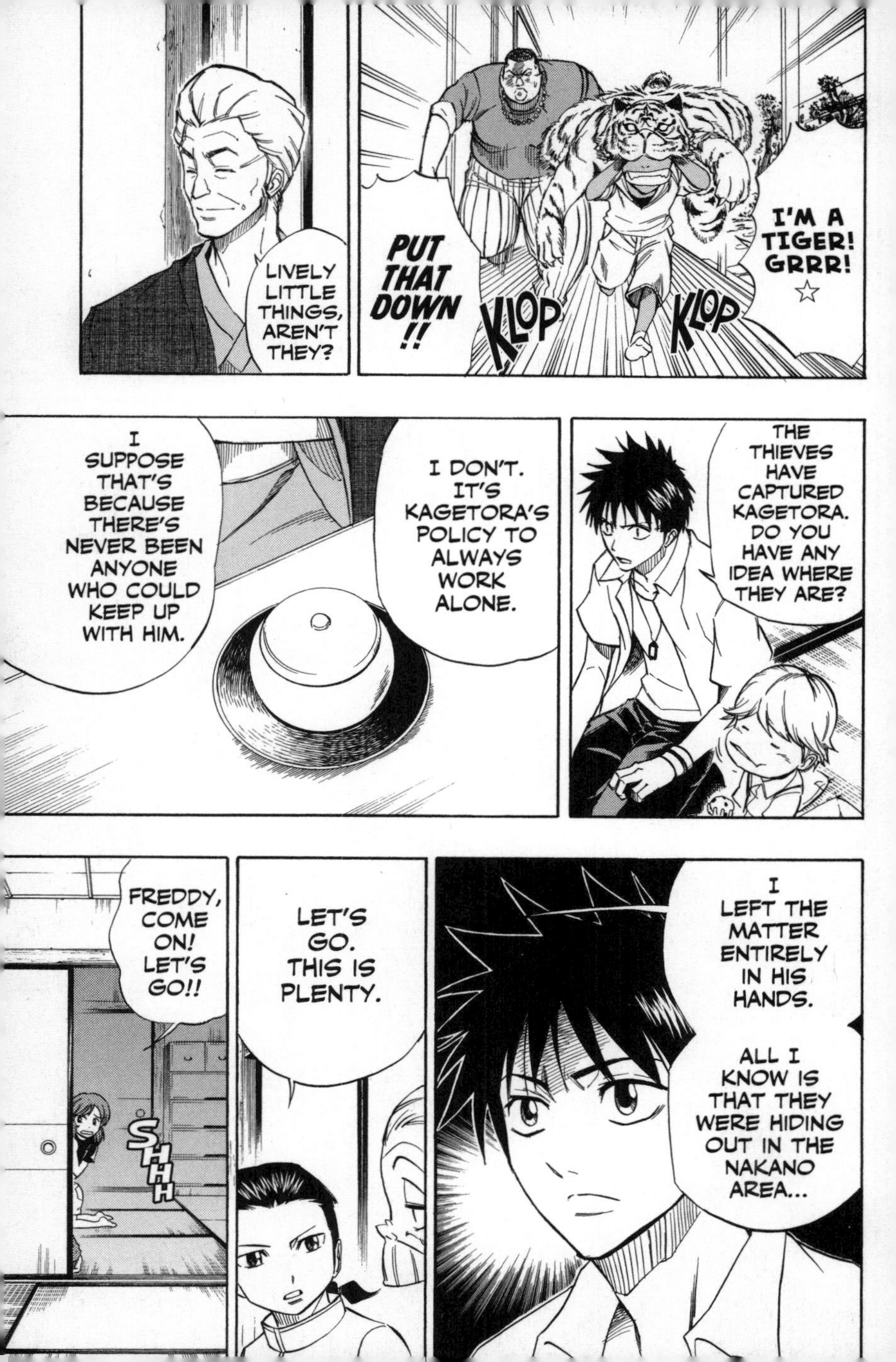
I'M A TIGER! GRRR! ☆
KLOP
KLOP
PUT THAT DOWN!!
LIVELY LITTLE THINGS, AREN'T THEY?
THE THIEVES HAVE CAPTURED KAGETORA. DO YOU HAVE ANY IDEA WHERE THEY ARE?
I DON'T. IT'S KAGETORA'S POLICY TO ALWAYS WORK ALONE.
I SUPPOSE THAT'S BECAUSE THERE'S NEVER BEEN ANYONE WHO COULD KEEP UP WITH HIM.
I LEFT THE MATTER ENTIRELY IN HIS HANDS.
ALL I KNOW IS THAT THEY WERE HIDING OUT IN THE NAKANO AREA...
LET'S GO. THIS IS PLENTY.
FREDDY, COME ON! LET'S GO!!
SHHH

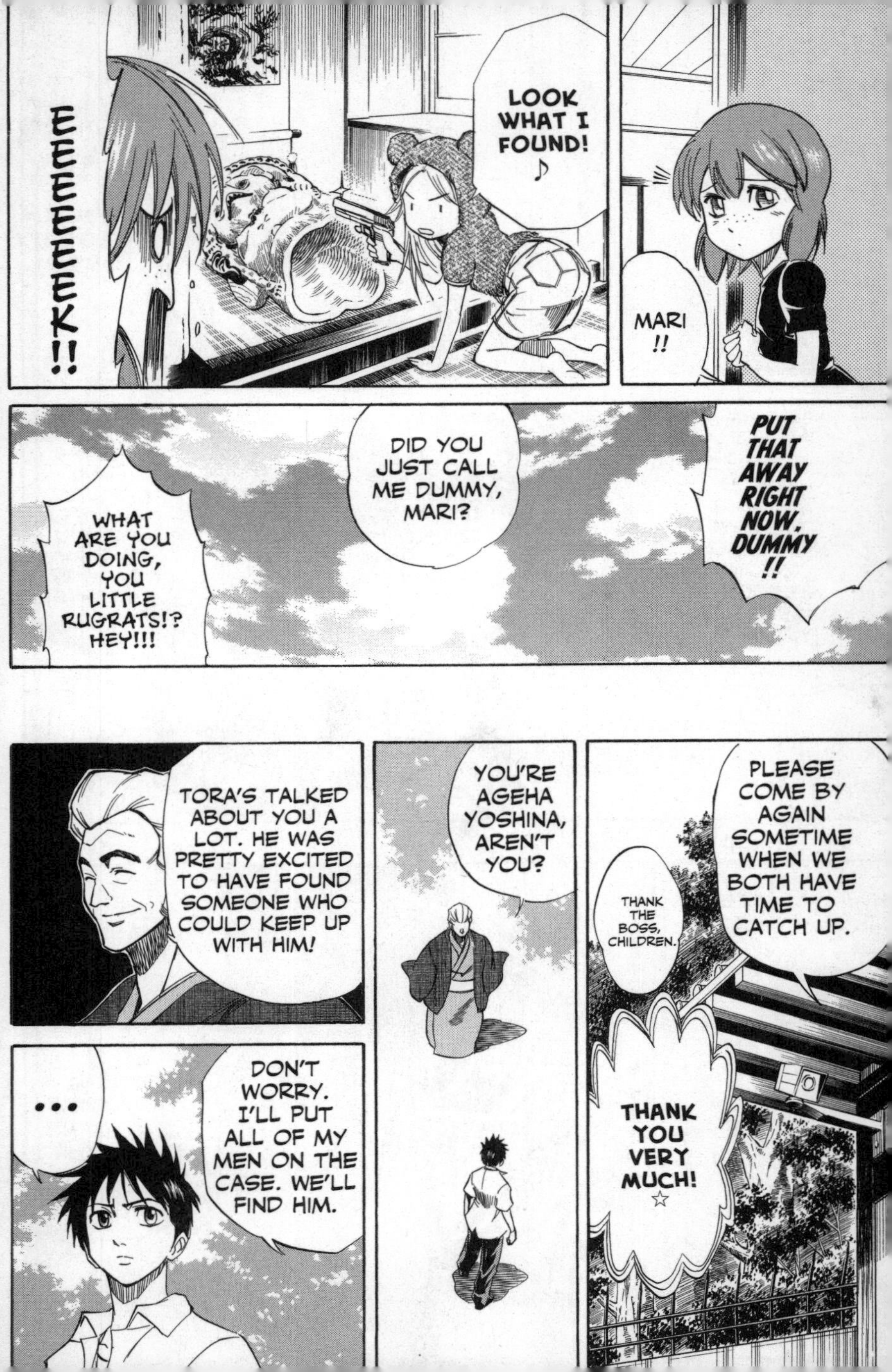
MARI!!
LOOK WHAT I FOUND! ♪
EEEEEEEK!!
PUT THAT AWAY RIGHT NOW, DUMMY!!
DID YOU JUST CALL ME DUMMY, MARI?
WHAT ARE YOU DOING, YOU LITTLE RUGRATS!? HEY!!!
PLEASE COME BY AGAIN SOMETIME WHEN WE BOTH HAVE TIME TO CATCH UP.
THANK THE BOSS, CHILDREN.
THANK YOU VERY MUCH! ☆
YOU'RE AGEHA YOSHINA, AREN'T YOU?
TORA'S TALKED ABOUT YOU A LOT. HE WAS PRETTY EXCITED TO HAVE FOUND SOMEONE WHO COULD KEEP UP WITH HIM!
DON'T WORRY. I'LL PUT ALL OF MY MEN ON THE CASE. WE'LL FIND HIM.
...

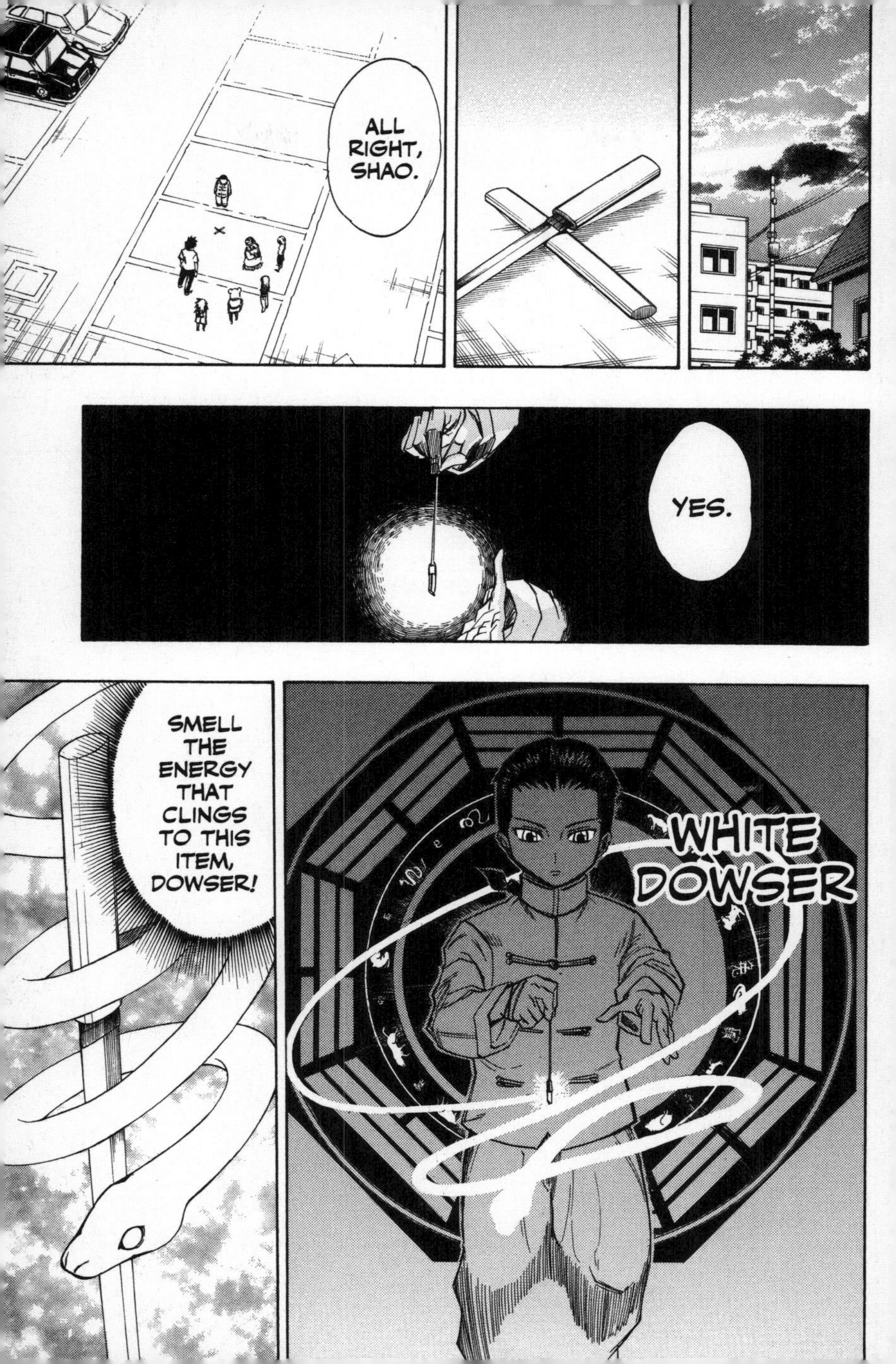
ALL RIGHT, SHAO.
YES.
WHITE DOWSER
SMELL THE ENERGY THAT CLINGS TO THIS ITEM, DOWSER!

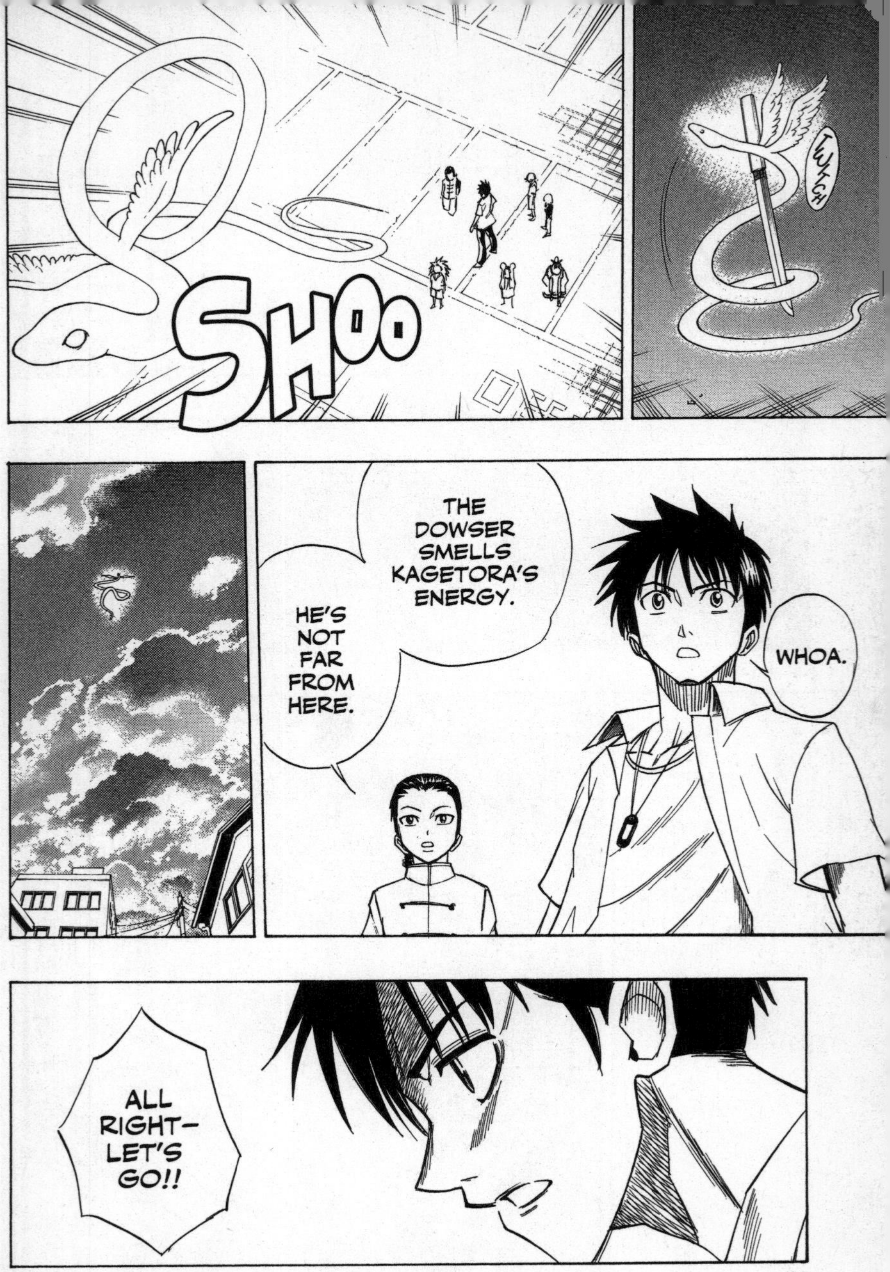
TWITCH
SHOO
WHOA.
THE DOWSER SMELLS KAGETORA'S ENERGY.
HE'S NOT FAR FROM HERE.
ALL RIGHT—LET'S GO!!

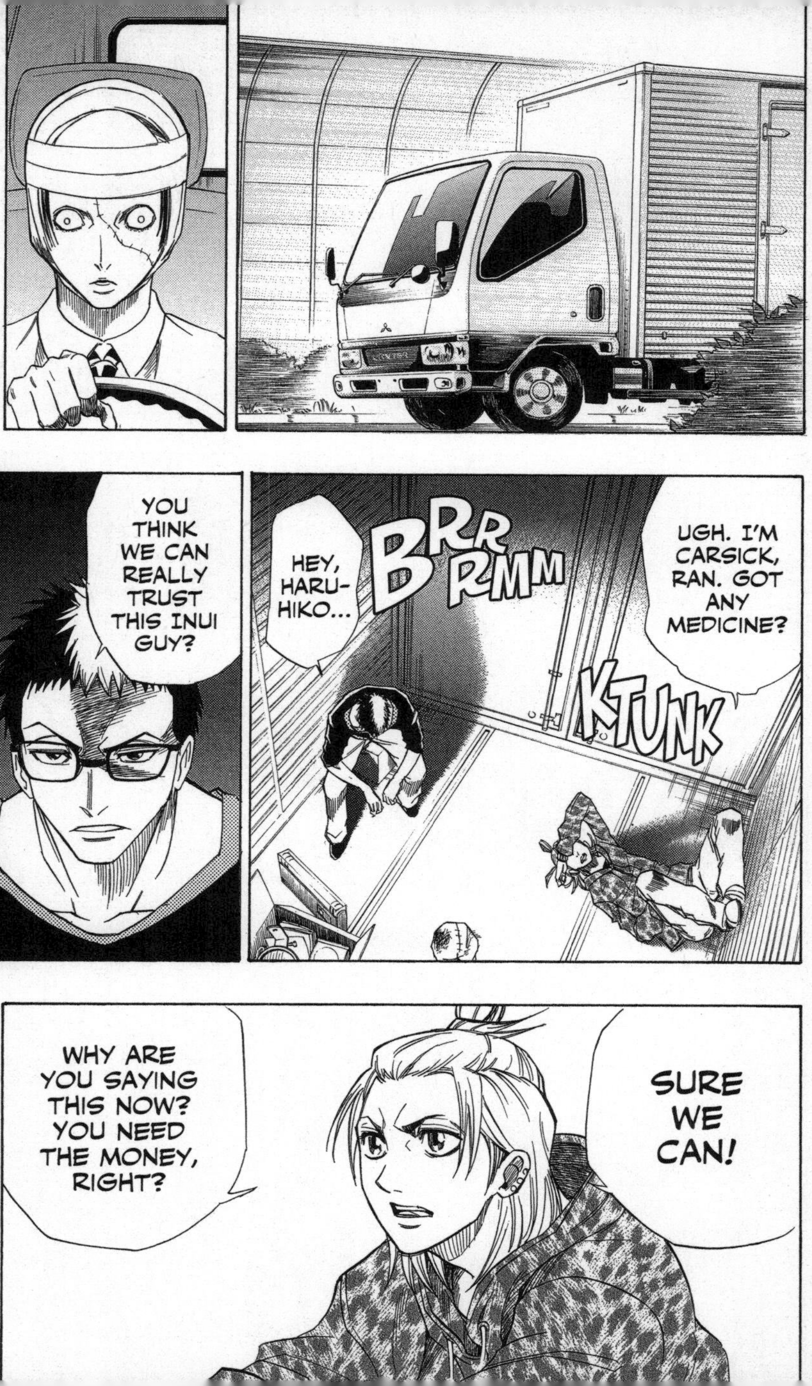
UGH. I'M CARSICK, RAN. GOT ANY MEDICINE?
BRRRMM
HEY, HARU-HIKO...
KTUNK
YOU THINK WE CAN REALLY TRUST THIS INUI GUY?
SURE WE CAN!
WHY ARE YOU SAYING THIS NOW? YOU NEED THE MONEY, RIGHT?

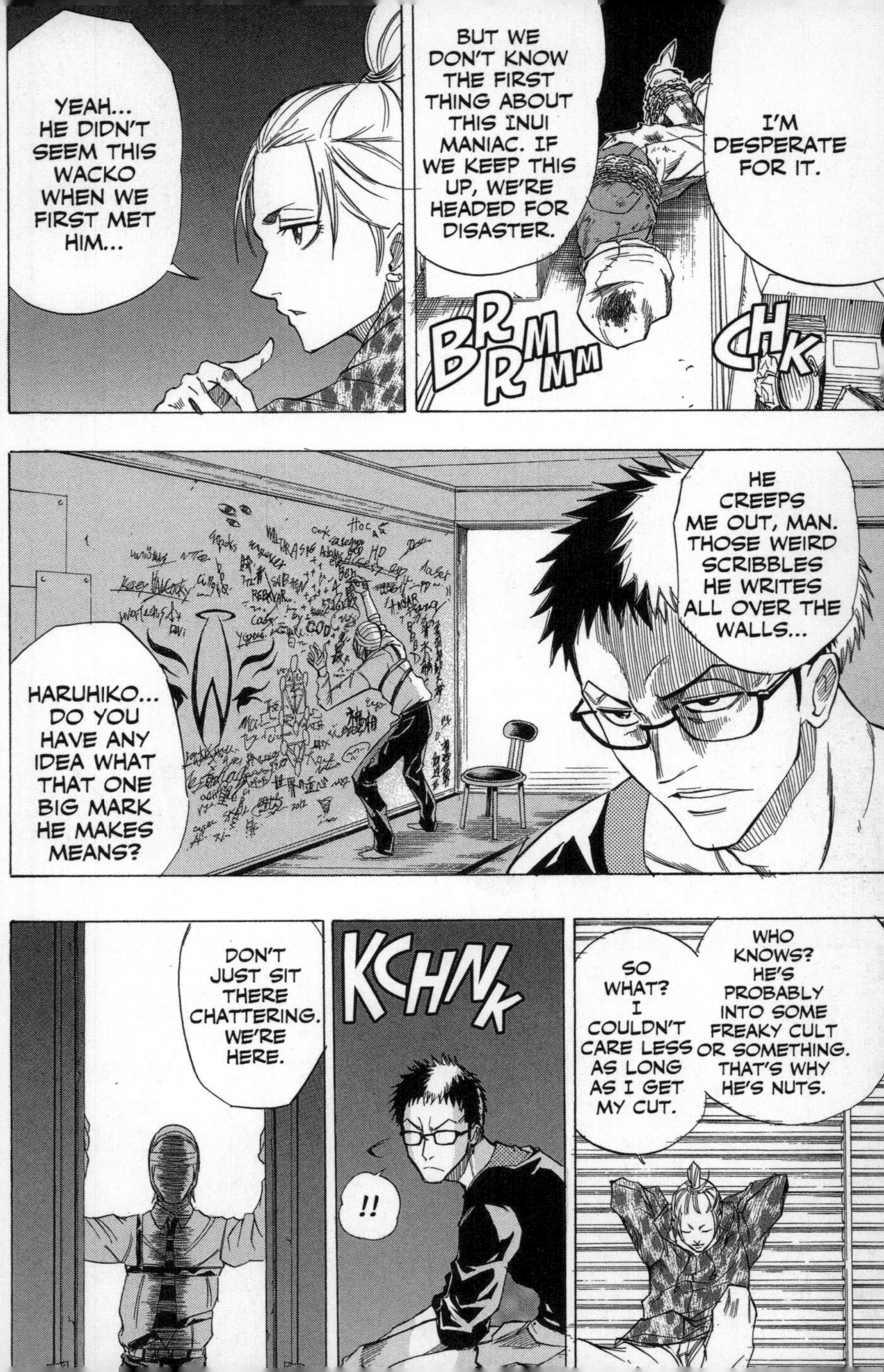
I'M DESPERATE FOR IT.
CHK
BUT WE DON'T KNOW THE FIRST THING ABOUT THIS INUI MANIAC. IF WE KEEP THIS UP, WE'RE HEADED FOR DISASTER.
BRRMMMM
YEAH... HE DIDN'T SEEM THIS WACKO WHEN WE FIRST MET HIM...
HE CREEPS ME OUT, MAN. THOSE WEIRD SCRIBBLES HE WRITES ALL OVER THE WALLS...
HARUHIKO... DO YOU HAVE ANY IDEA WHAT THAT ONE BIG MARK HE MAKES MEANS?
WHO KNOWS? HE'S PROBABLY INTO SOME FREAKY CULT OR SOMETHING. THAT'S WHY HE'S NUTS.
SO WHAT? I COULDN'T CARE LESS AS LONG AS I GET MY CUT.
KCHNK
!!
DON'T JUST SIT THERE CHATTERING. WE'RE HERE.

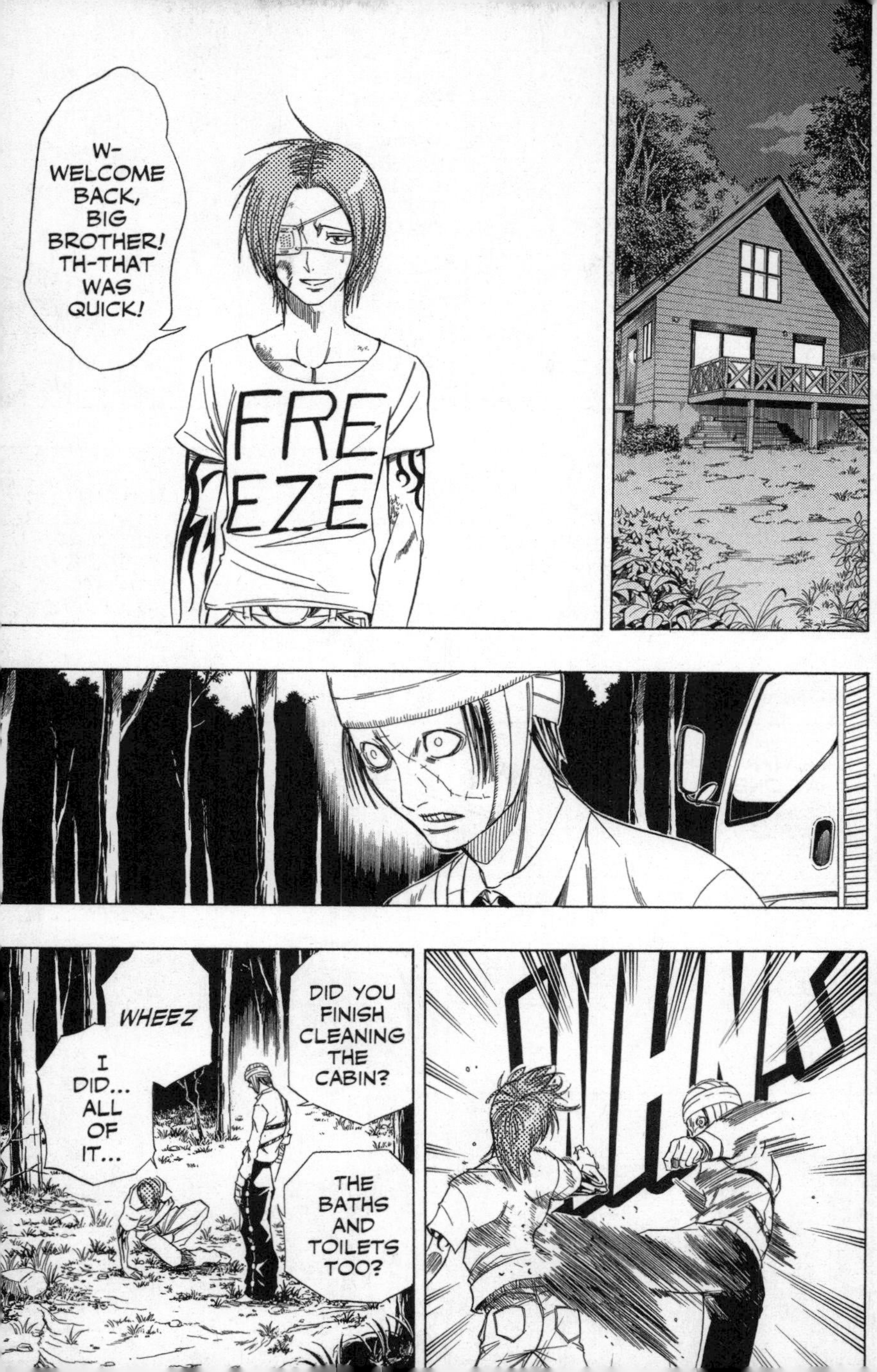
W-WELCOME BACK, BIG BROTHER! TH-THAT WAS QUICK!
FRE EZE
DID YOU FINISH CLEANING THE CABIN?
THE BATHS AND TOILETS TOO?
WHEEZ
I DID... ALL OF IT...

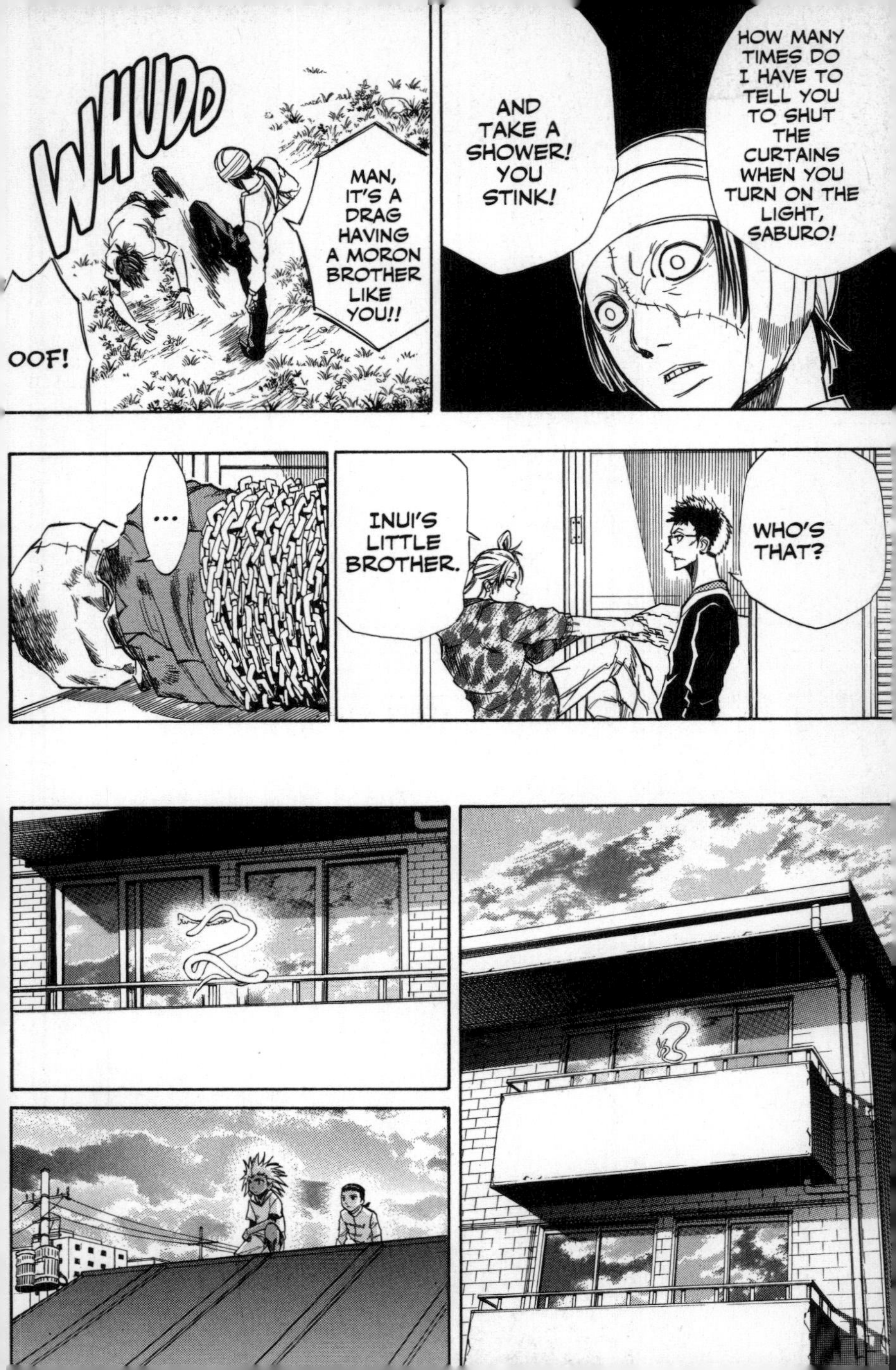
HOW MANY TIMES DO I HAVE TO TELL YOU TO SHUT THE CURTAINS WHEN YOU TURN ON THE LIGHT, SABURO!
AND TAKE A SHOWER! YOU STINK!
MAN, IT'S A DRAG HAVING A MORON BROTHER LIKE YOU!!
WHUDD
OOF!
WHO'S THAT?
INUI'S LITTLE BROTHER.
...

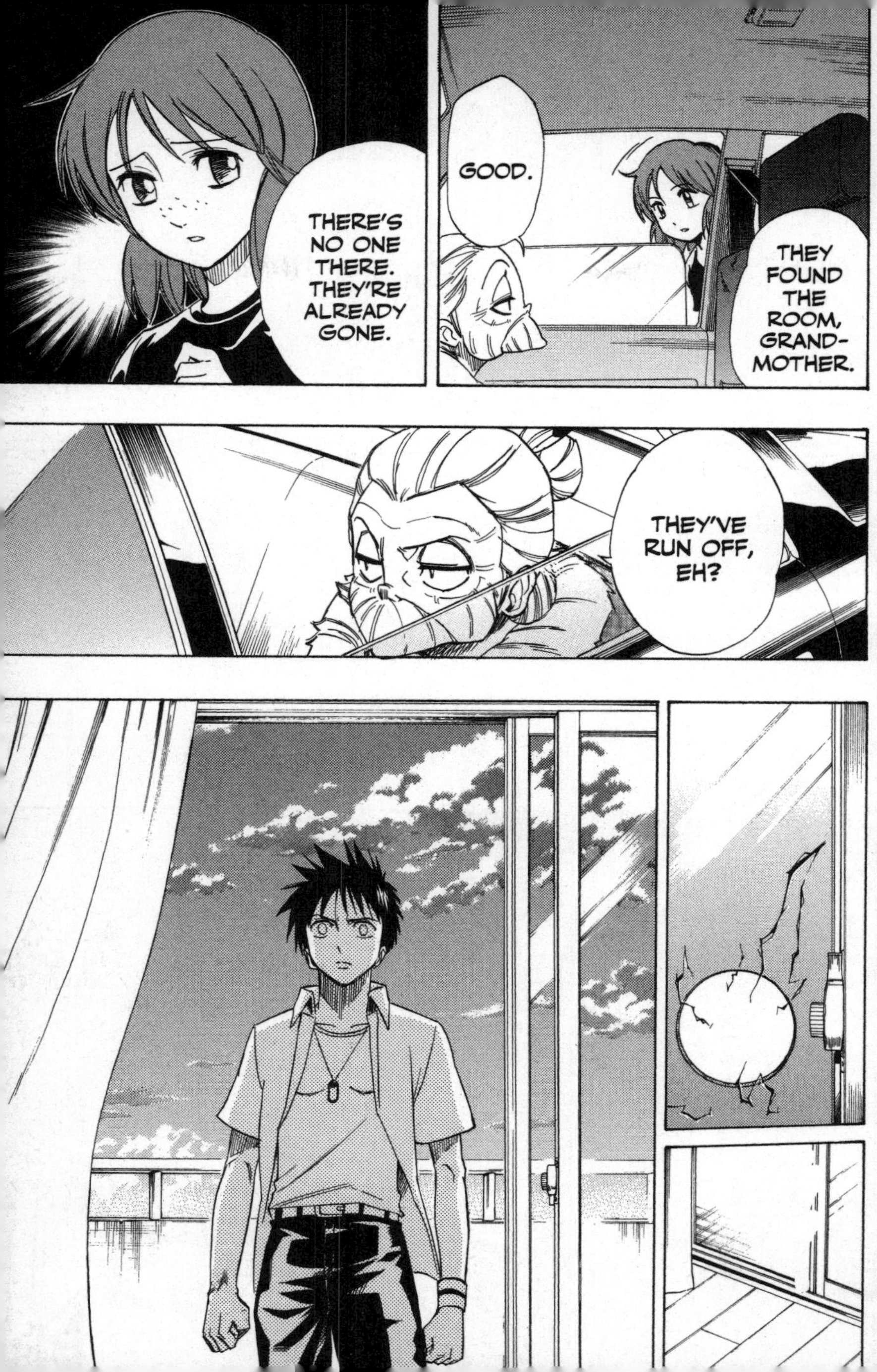
THEY FOUND THE ROOM, GRAND-MOTHER.
GOOD.
THERE'S NO ONE THERE. THEY'RE ALREADY GONE.
THEY'VE RUN OFF, EH?

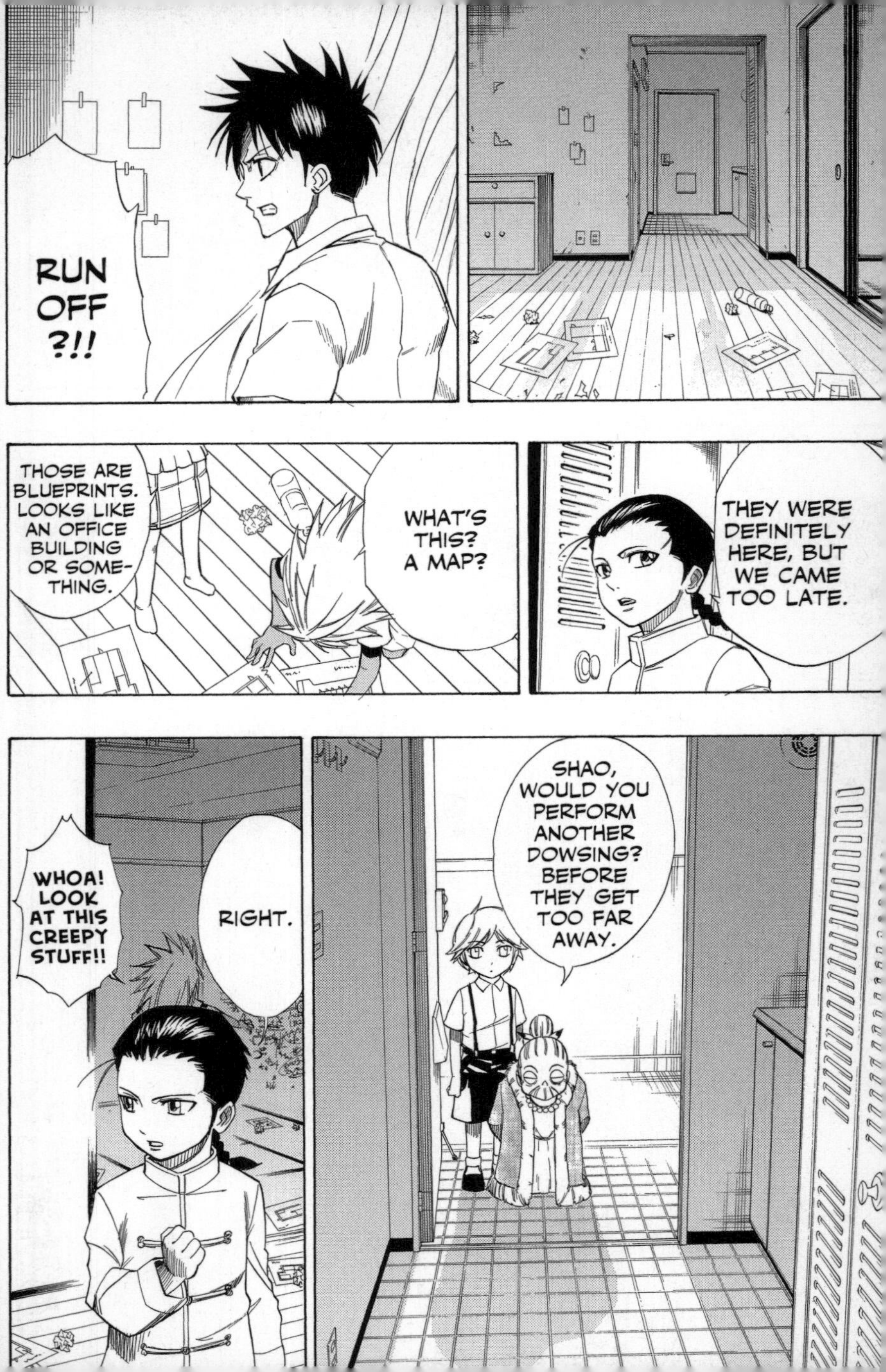
RUN OFF ?!!
THEY WERE DEFINITELY HERE, BUT WE CAME TOO LATE.
WHAT'S THIS? A MAP?
THOSE ARE BLUEPRINTS. LOOKS LIKE AN OFFICE BUILDING OR SOME-THING.
SHAO, WOULD YOU PERFORM ANOTHER DOWSING? BEFORE THEY GET TOO FAR AWAY.
RIGHT.
WHOA! LOOK AT THIS CREEPY STUFF!!

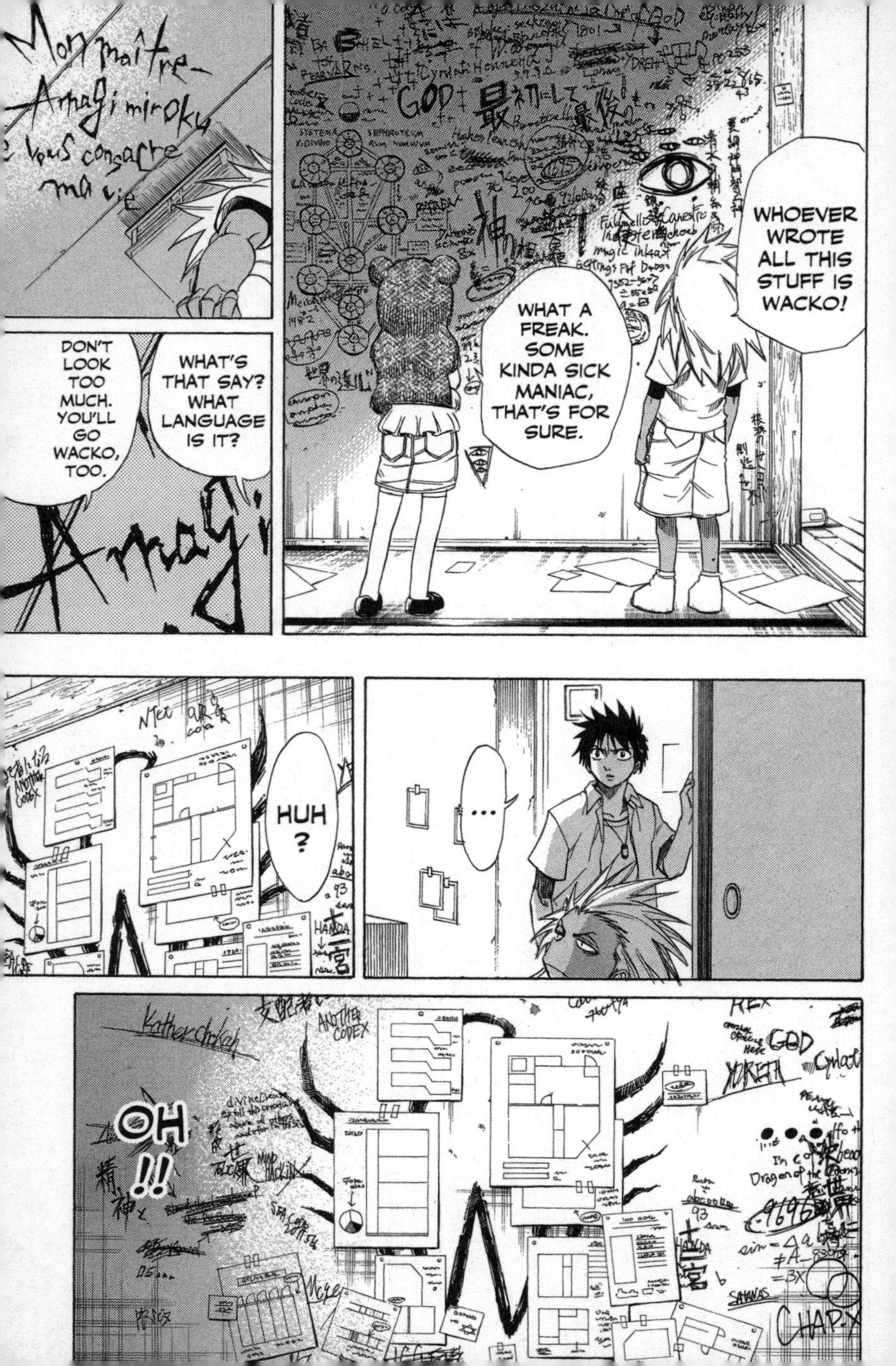
WHOEVER WROTE ALL THIS STUFF IS WACKO!
WHAT A FREAK. SOME KINDA SICK MANIAC, THAT'S FOR SURE.
Mon maître— Amagi miroku je vous consacre ma vie
WHAT'S THAT SAY? WHAT LANGUAGE IS IT?
DON'T LOOK TOO MUCH. YOU'LL GO WACKO, TOO.
Amagi
...
HUH?
OH!!
ANOTHER CODEX
GOD

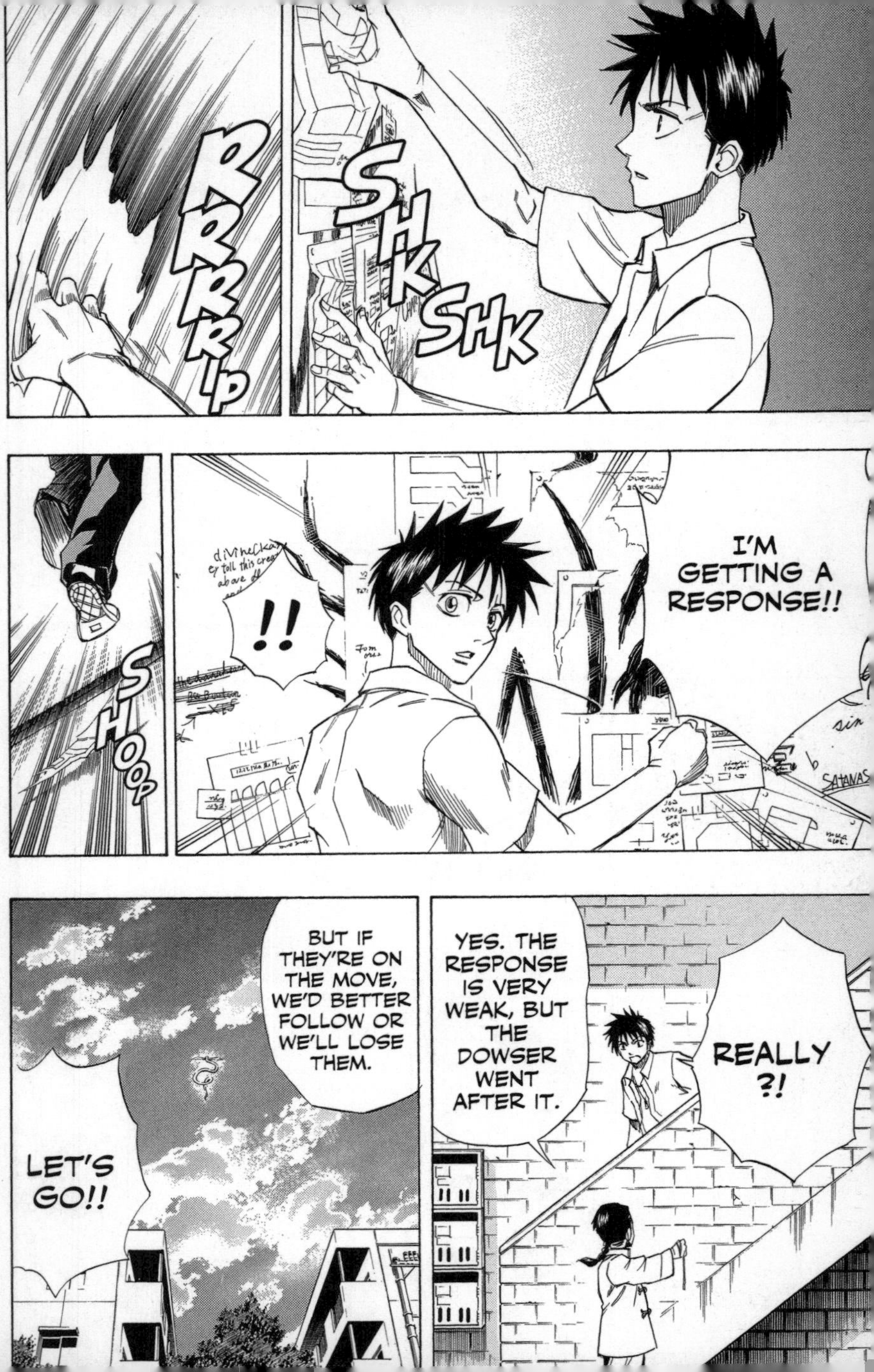
SHK SHK
RRRRRIP
I'M GETTING A RESPONSE!!
!!
SHOOP
REALLY?!
YES. THE RESPONSE IS VERY WEAK, BUT THE DOWSER WENT AFTER IT.
BUT IF THEY'RE ON THE MOVE, WE'D BETTER FOLLOW OR WE'LL LOSE THEM.
LET'S GO!!

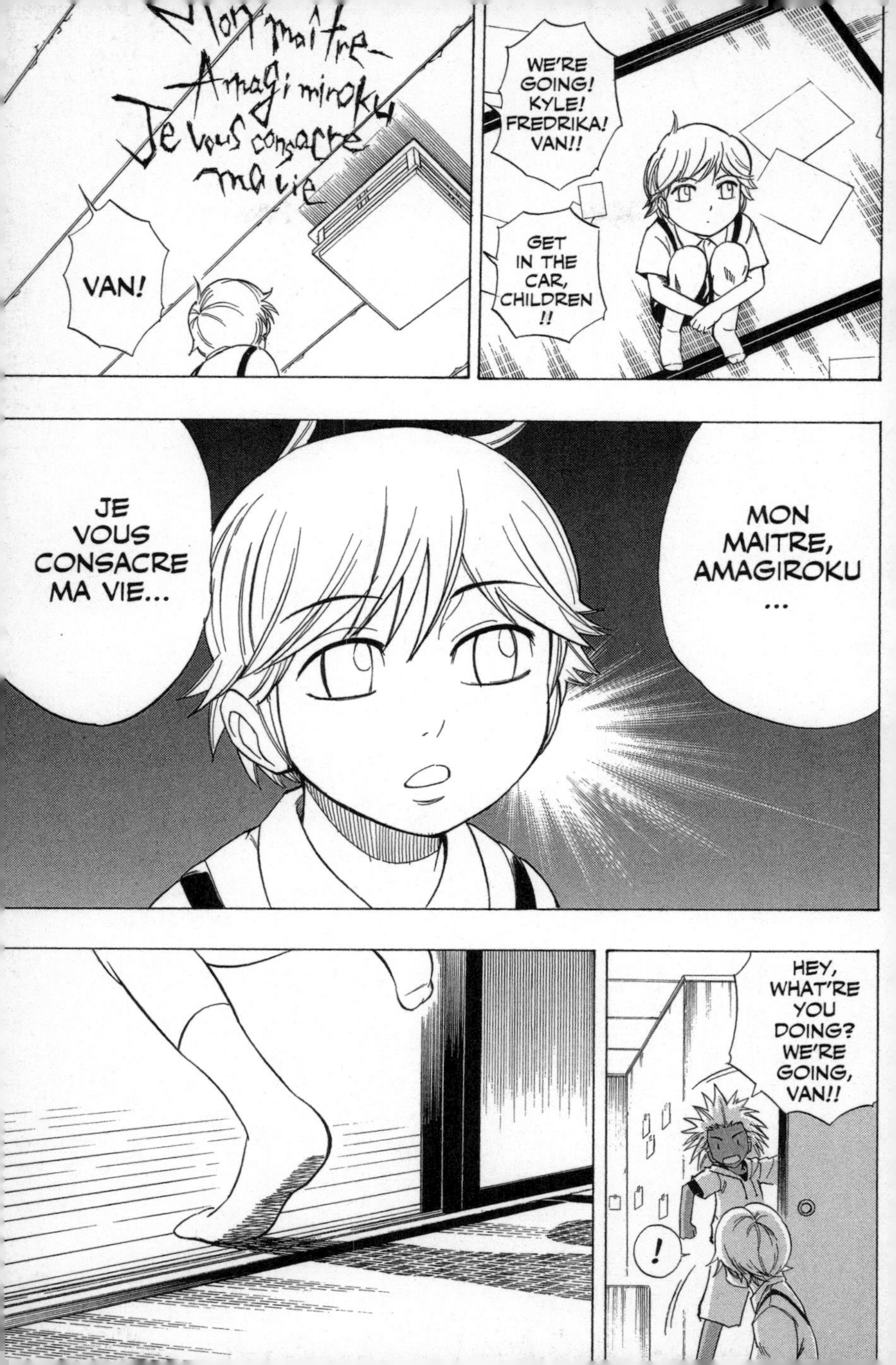
WE'RE GOING! KYLE! FREDRIKA! VAN!!
GET IN THE CAR, CHILDREN!!
Mon maitre- Amagi miroku Je vous consacre ma vie
VAN!
MON MAITRE, AMAGIROKU ...
JE VOUS CONSACRE MA VIE...
HEY, WHAT'RE YOU DOING? WE'RE GOING, VAN!!
!

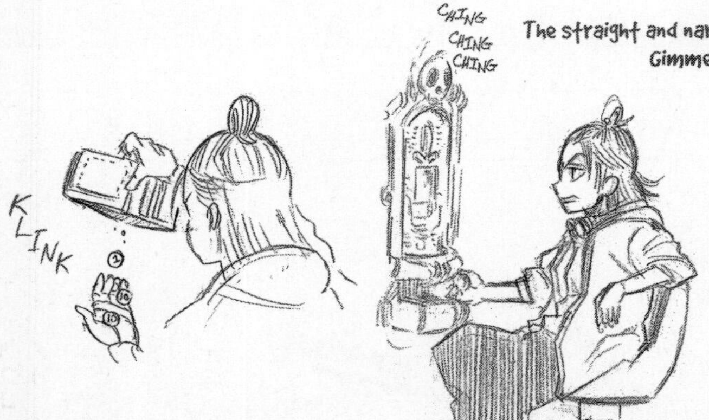
The straight and narrow?
Gimme a break.
CHING
CHING
CHING
KLINK

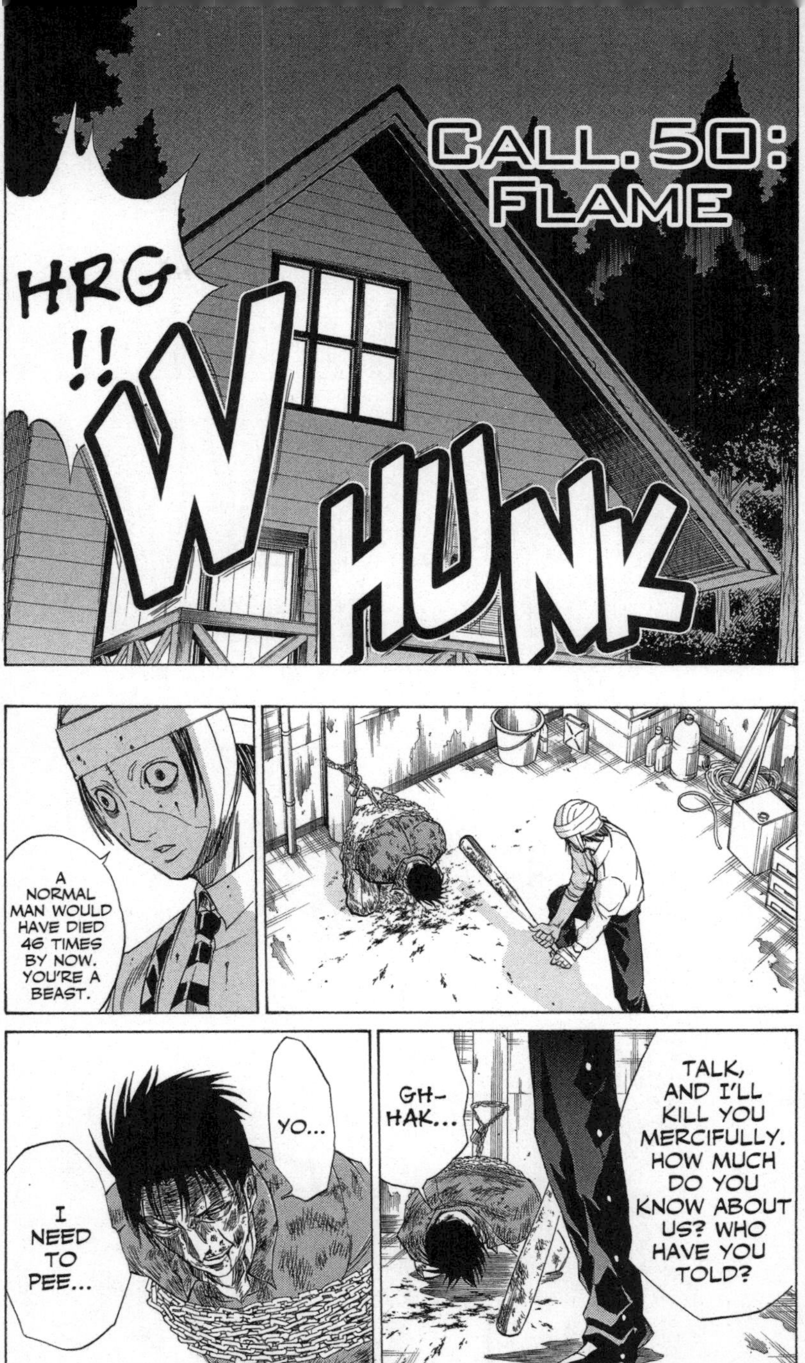
CALL. 50: FLAME
HRG !!
WHUNK
A NORMAL MAN WOULD HAVE DIED 46 TIMES BY NOW. YOU'RE A BEAST.
TALK, AND I'LL KILL YOU MERCIFULLY. HOW MUCH DO YOU KNOW ABOUT US? WHO HAVE YOU TOLD?
GH-HAK...
YO...
I NEED TO PEE...

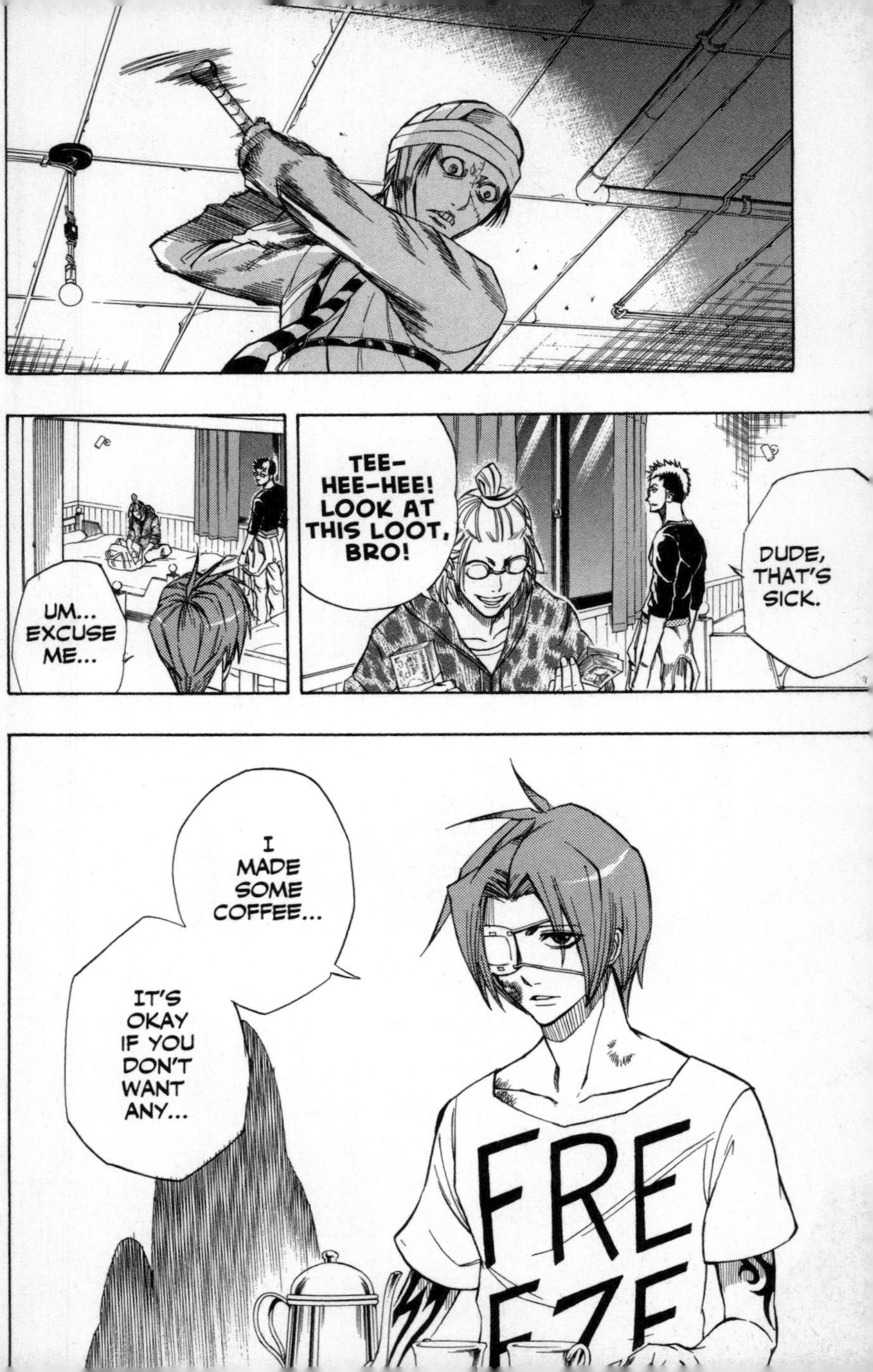

TEE-HEE-HEE! LOOK AT THIS LOOT, BRO!
DUDE, THAT'S SICK.
UM... EXCUSE ME...
I MADE SOME COFFEE...
IT'S OKAY IF YOU DON'T WANT ANY...
FRE

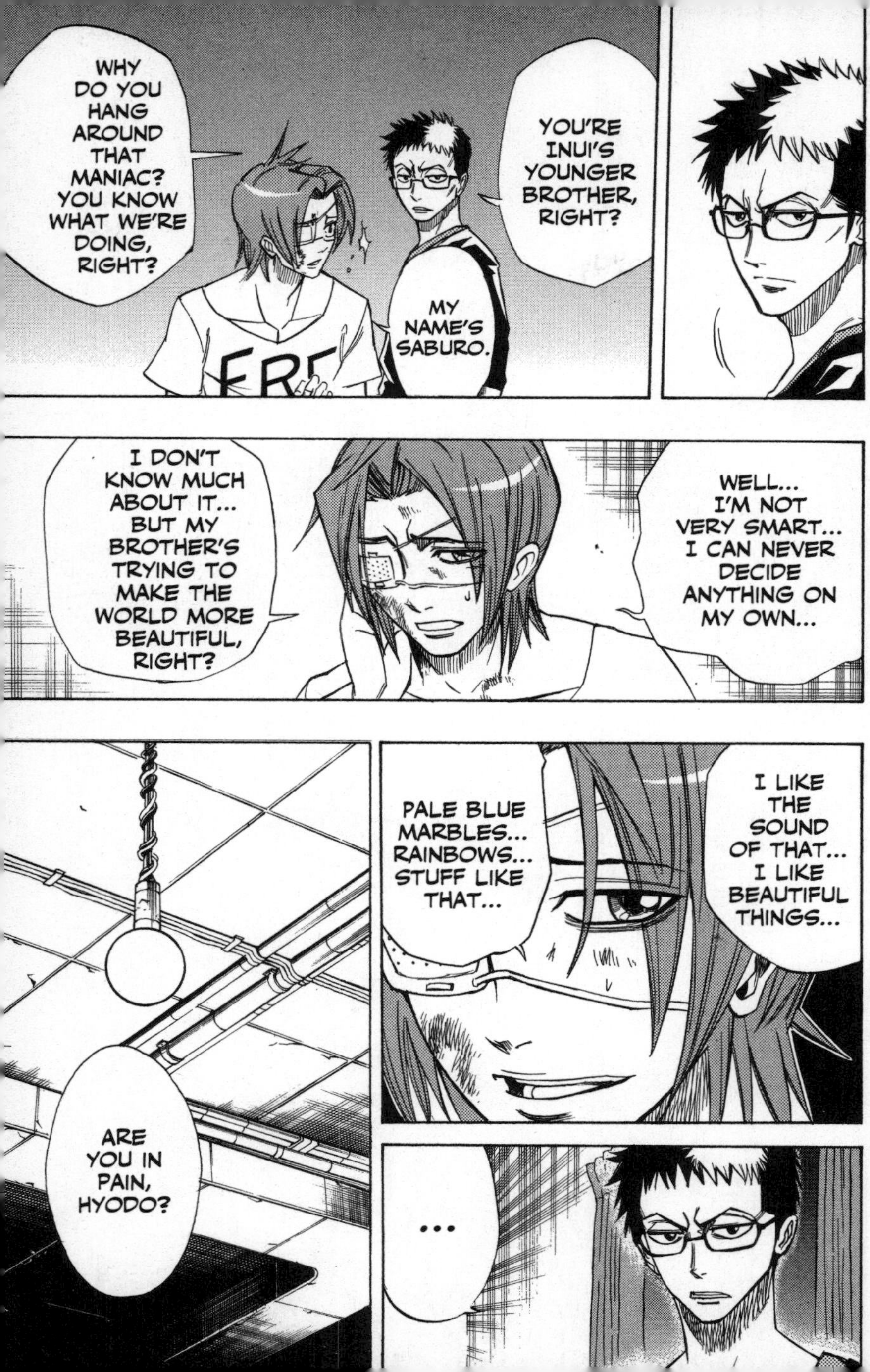
YOU'RE INUI'S YOUNGER BROTHER, RIGHT?
MY NAME'S SABURO.
WHY DO YOU HANG AROUND THAT MANIAC? YOU KNOW WHAT WE'RE DOING, RIGHT?
WELL... I'M NOT VERY SMART... I CAN NEVER DECIDE ANYTHING ON MY OWN...
I DON'T KNOW MUCH ABOUT IT... BUT MY BROTHER'S TRYING TO MAKE THE WORLD MORE BEAUTIFUL, RIGHT?
I LIKE THE SOUND OF THAT... I LIKE BEAUTIFUL THINGS...
PALE BLUE MARBLES... RAINBOWS... STUFF LIKE THAT...
...
ARE YOU IN PAIN, HYODO?

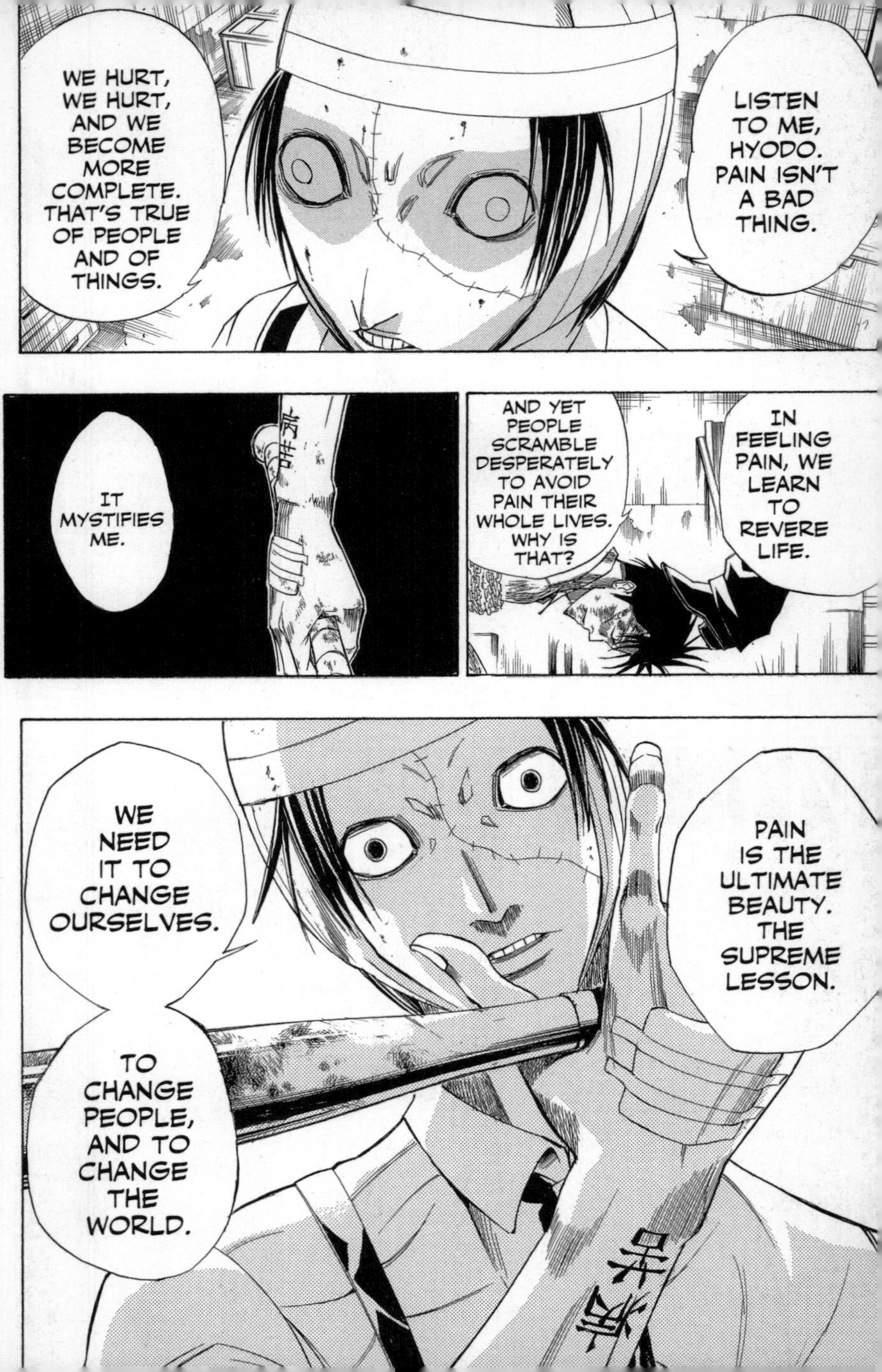
LISTEN TO ME, HYODO. PAIN ISN'T A BAD THING.
WE HURT, WE HURT, AND WE BECOME MORE COMPLETE. THAT'S TRUE OF PEOPLE AND OF THINGS.
IN FEELING PAIN, WE LEARN TO REVERE LIFE.
AND YET PEOPLE SCRAMBLE DESPERATELY TO AVOID PAIN THEIR WHOLE LIVES. WHY IS THAT?
IT MYSTIFIES ME.
PAIN IS THE ULTIMATE BEAUTY. THE SUPREME LESSON.
WE NEED IT TO CHANGE OURSELVES.
TO CHANGE PEOPLE, AND TO CHANGE THE WORLD.

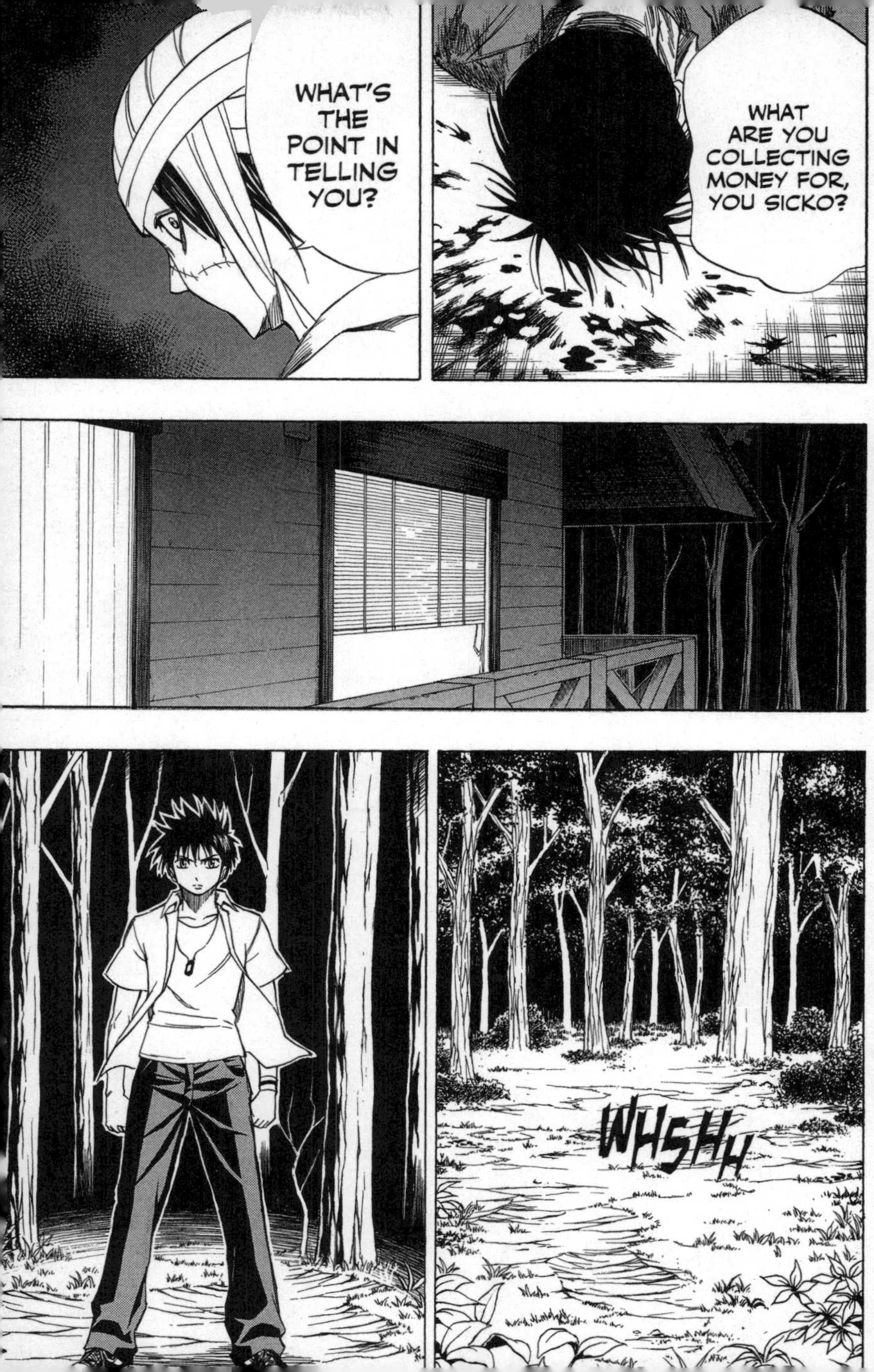
WHAT ARE YOU COLLECTING MONEY FOR, YOU SICKO?
WHAT'S THE POINT IN TELLING YOU?
WHSHH

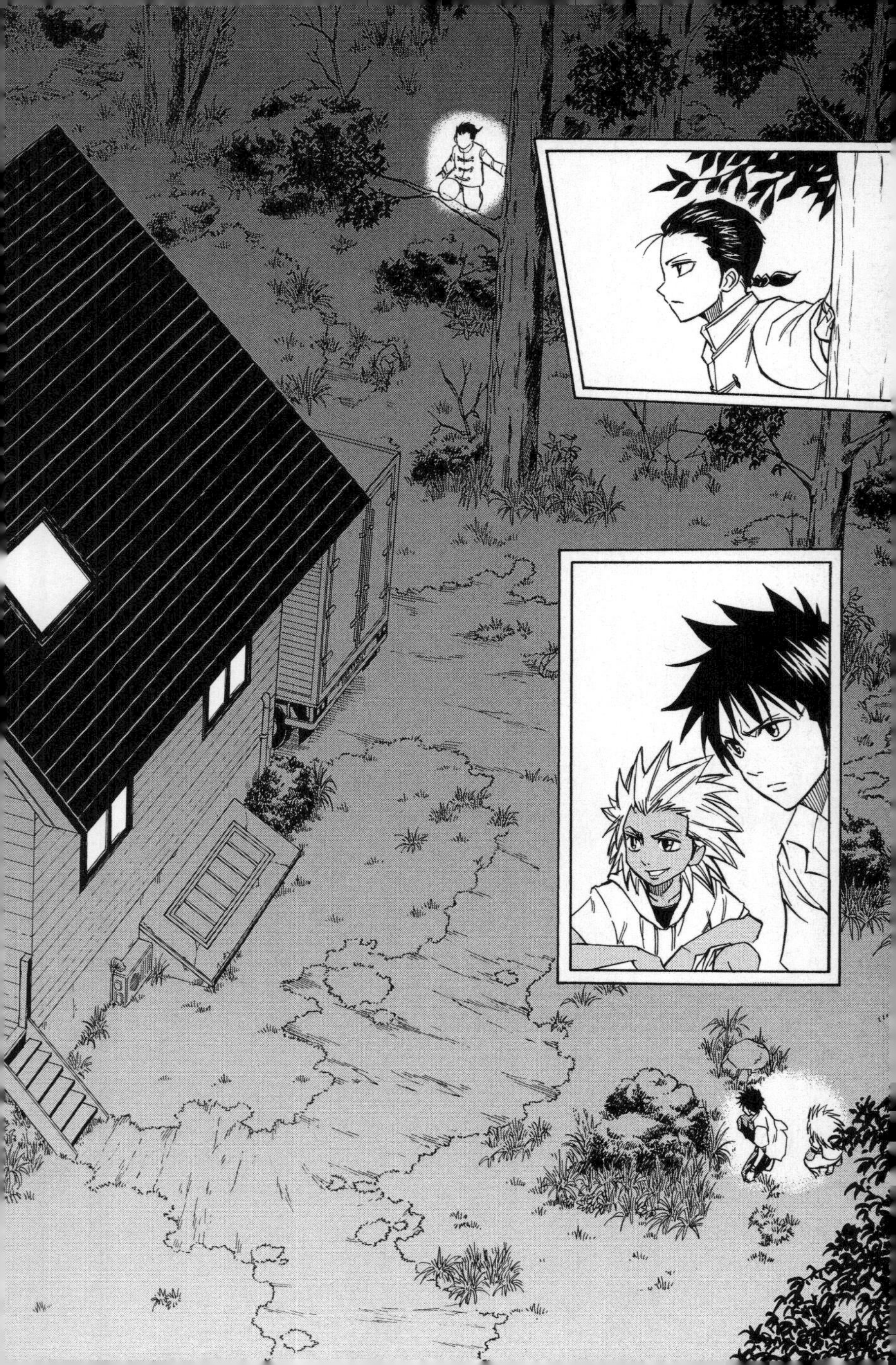

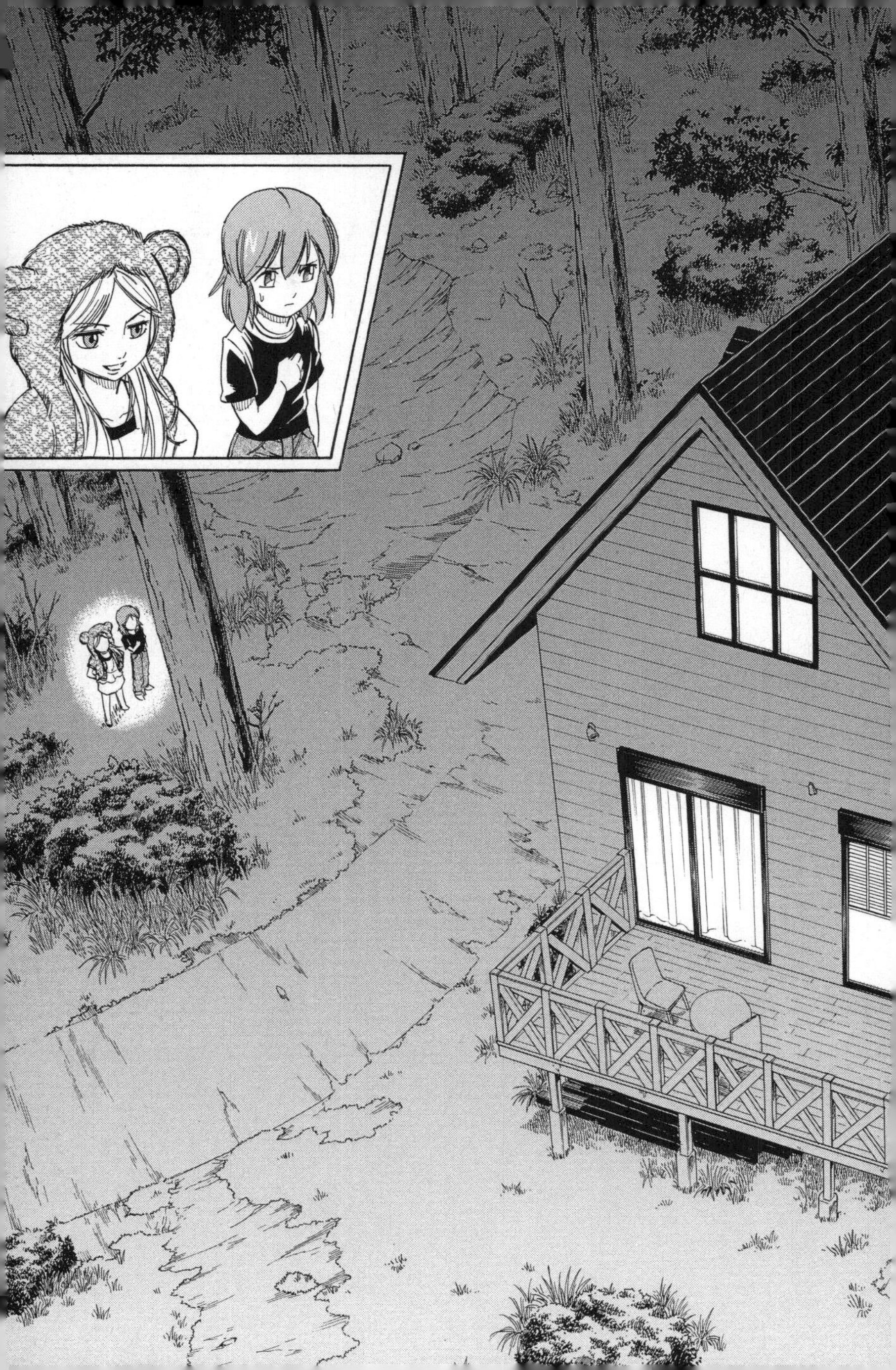

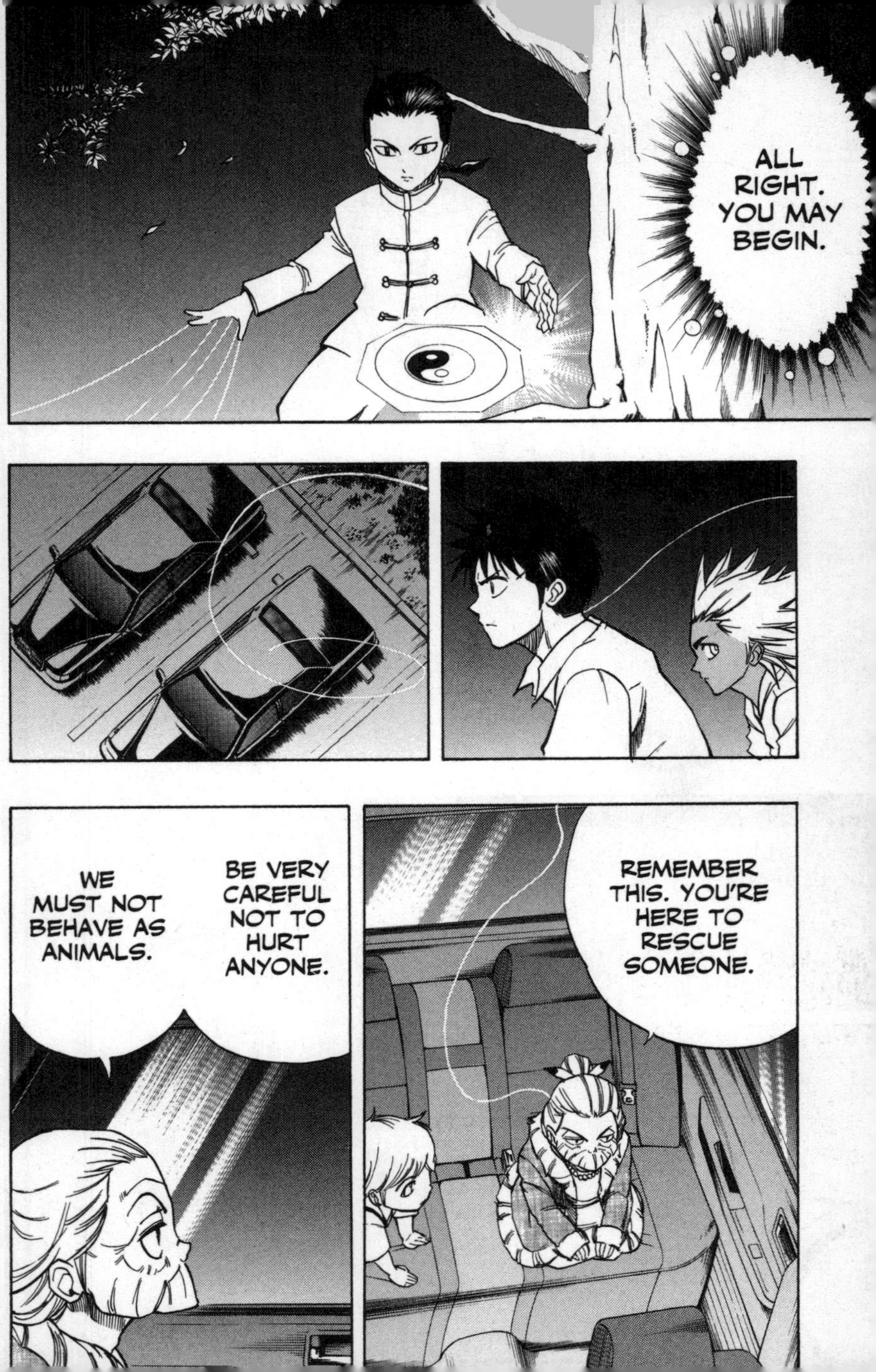
ALL RIGHT. YOU MAY BEGIN.
REMEMBER THIS. YOU'RE HERE TO RESCUE SOMEONE.
BE VERY CAREFUL NOT TO HURT ANYONE.
WE MUST NOT BEHAVE AS ANIMALS.

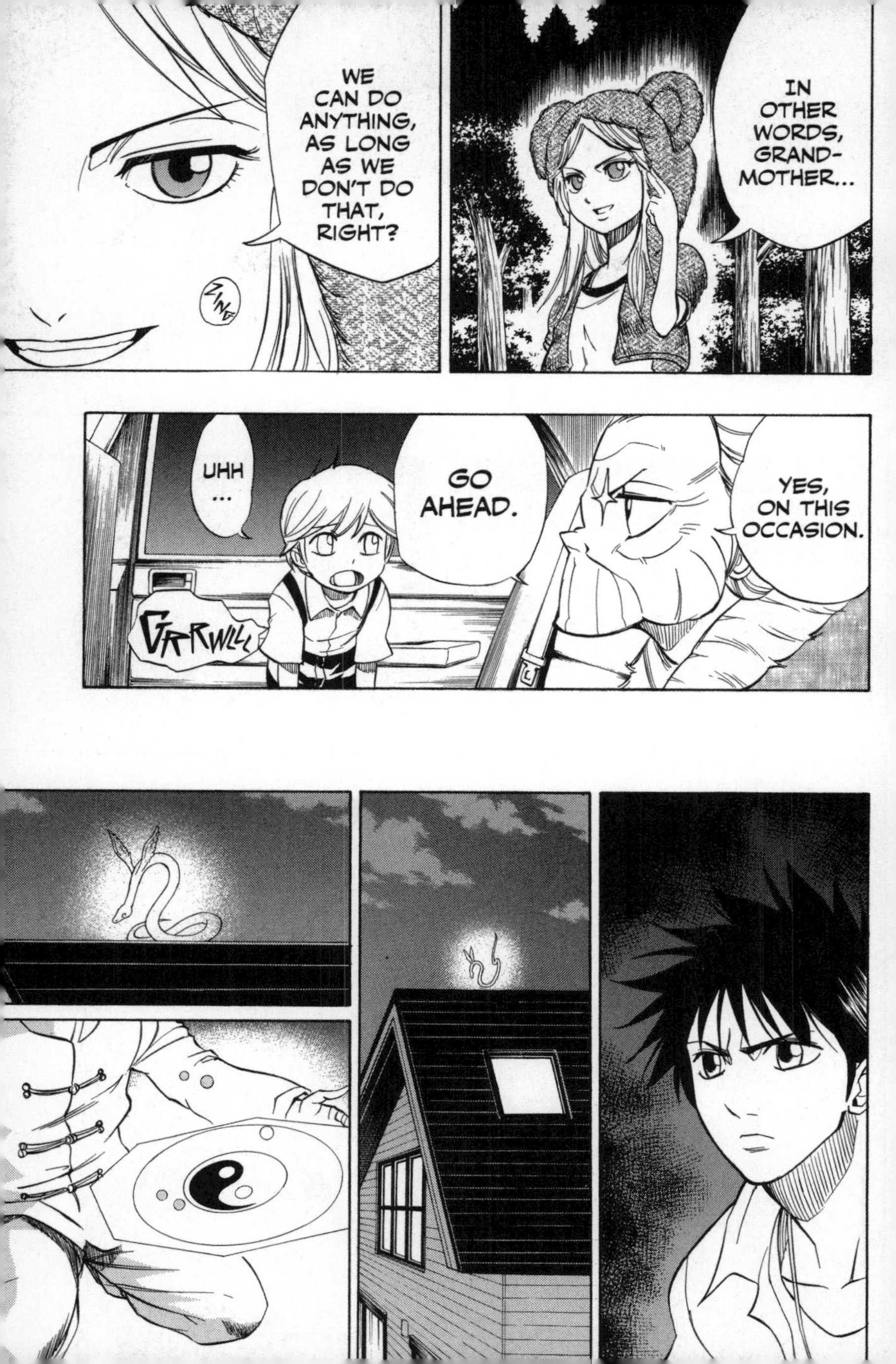
IN OTHER WORDS, GRAND-MOTHER...
WE CAN DO ANYTHING, AS LONG AS WE DON'T DO THAT, RIGHT?
ZING
YES, ON THIS OCCASION.
GO AHEAD.
UHH ...
GRRWLLL

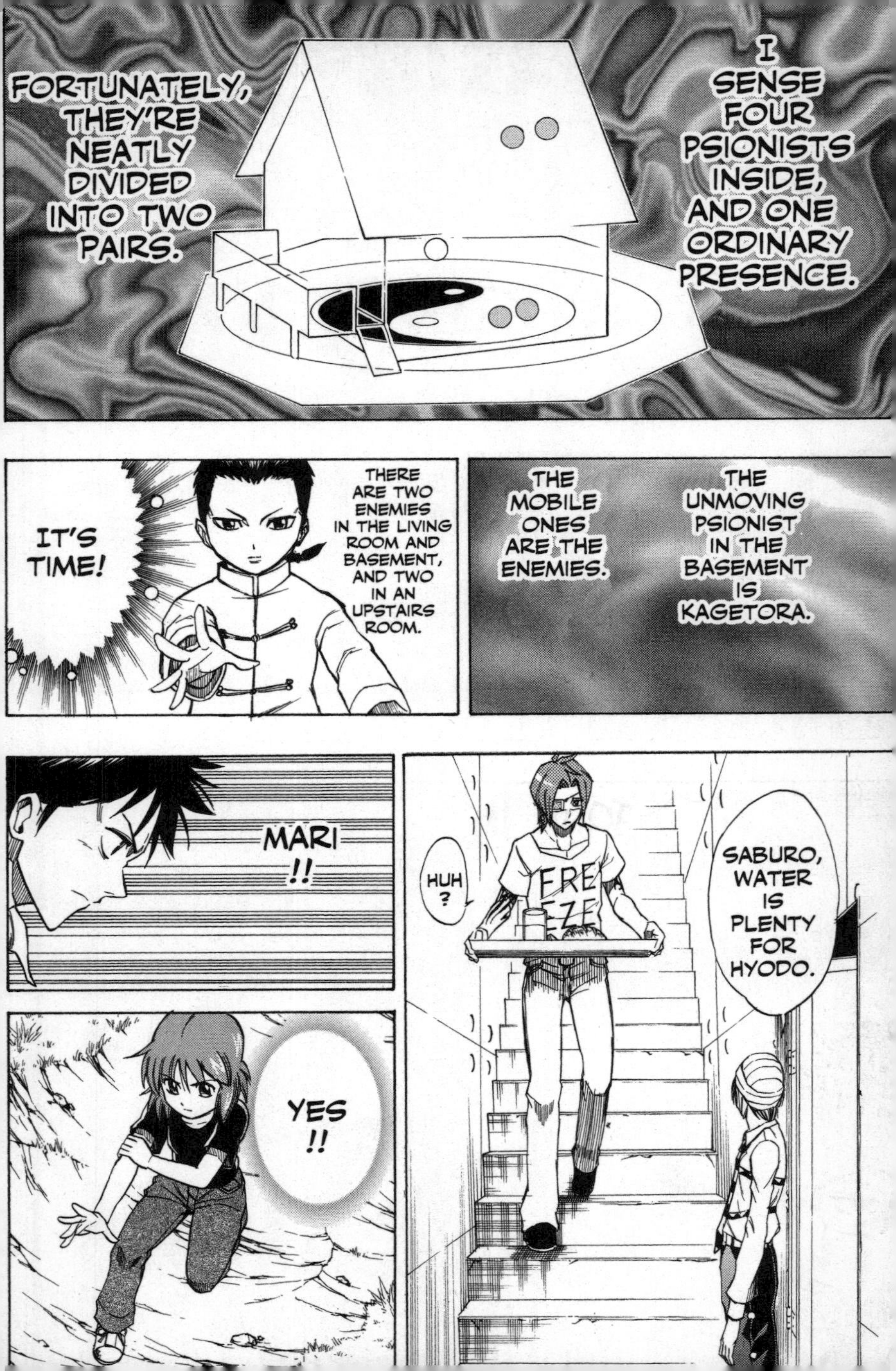
I SENSE FOUR PSIONISTS INSIDE, AND ONE ORDINARY PRESENCE.
FORTUNATELY, THEY'RE NEATLY DIVIDED INTO TWO PAIRS.
THE UNMOVING PSIONIST IN THE BASEMENT IS KAGETORA.
THE MOBILE ONES ARE THE ENEMIES.
THERE ARE TWO ENEMIES IN THE LIVING ROOM AND BASEMENT, AND TWO IN AN UPSTAIRS ROOM.
IT'S TIME!
SABURO, WATER IS PLENTY FOR HYODO.
HUH?
FREEZE
MARI!!
YES!!

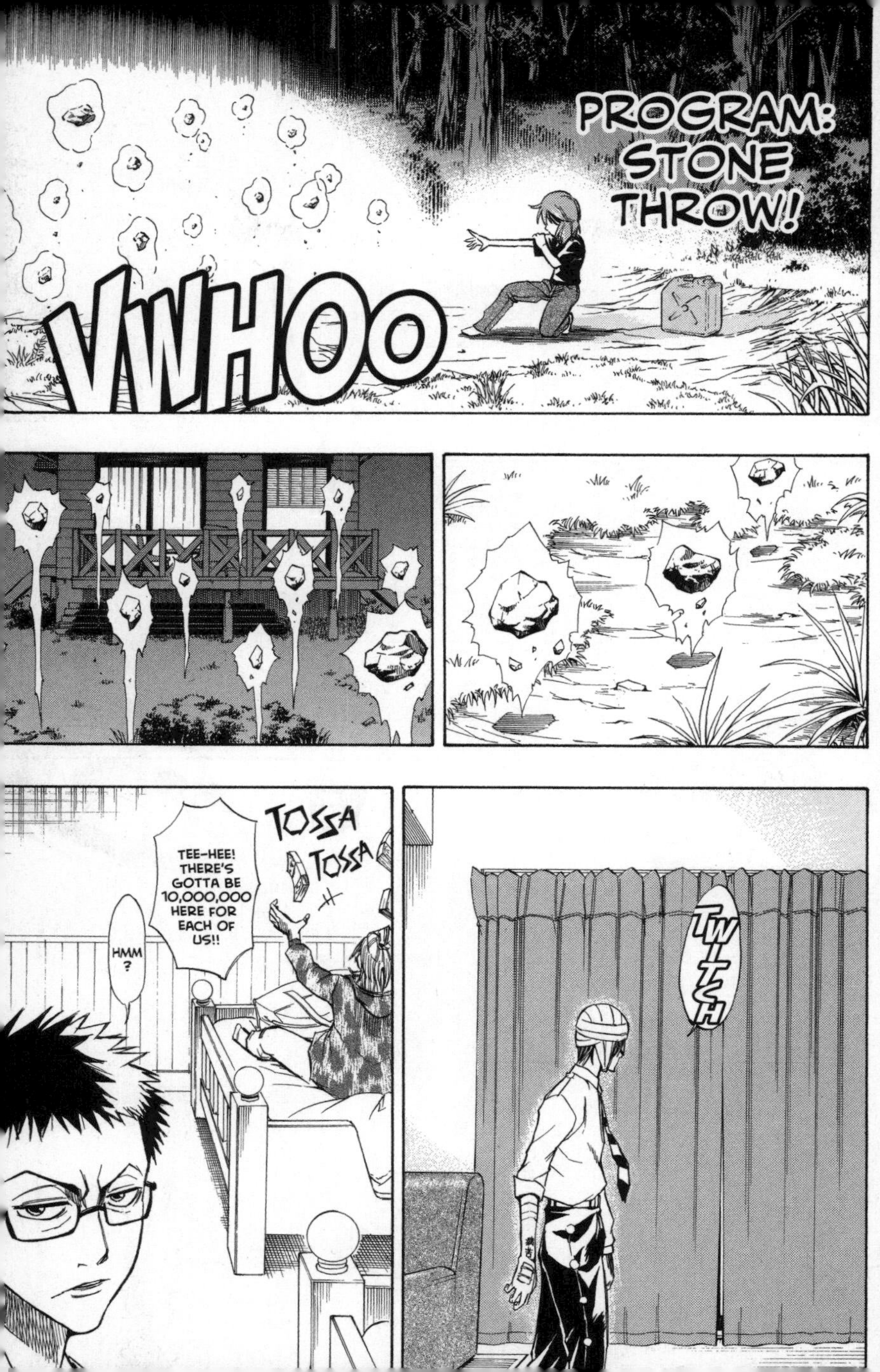
PROGRAM: STONE THROW!
VWHOO
TWITCH
TOSSA TOSSA
TEE-HEE! THERE'S GOTTA BE 10,000,000 HERE FOR EACH OF US!!
HMM?

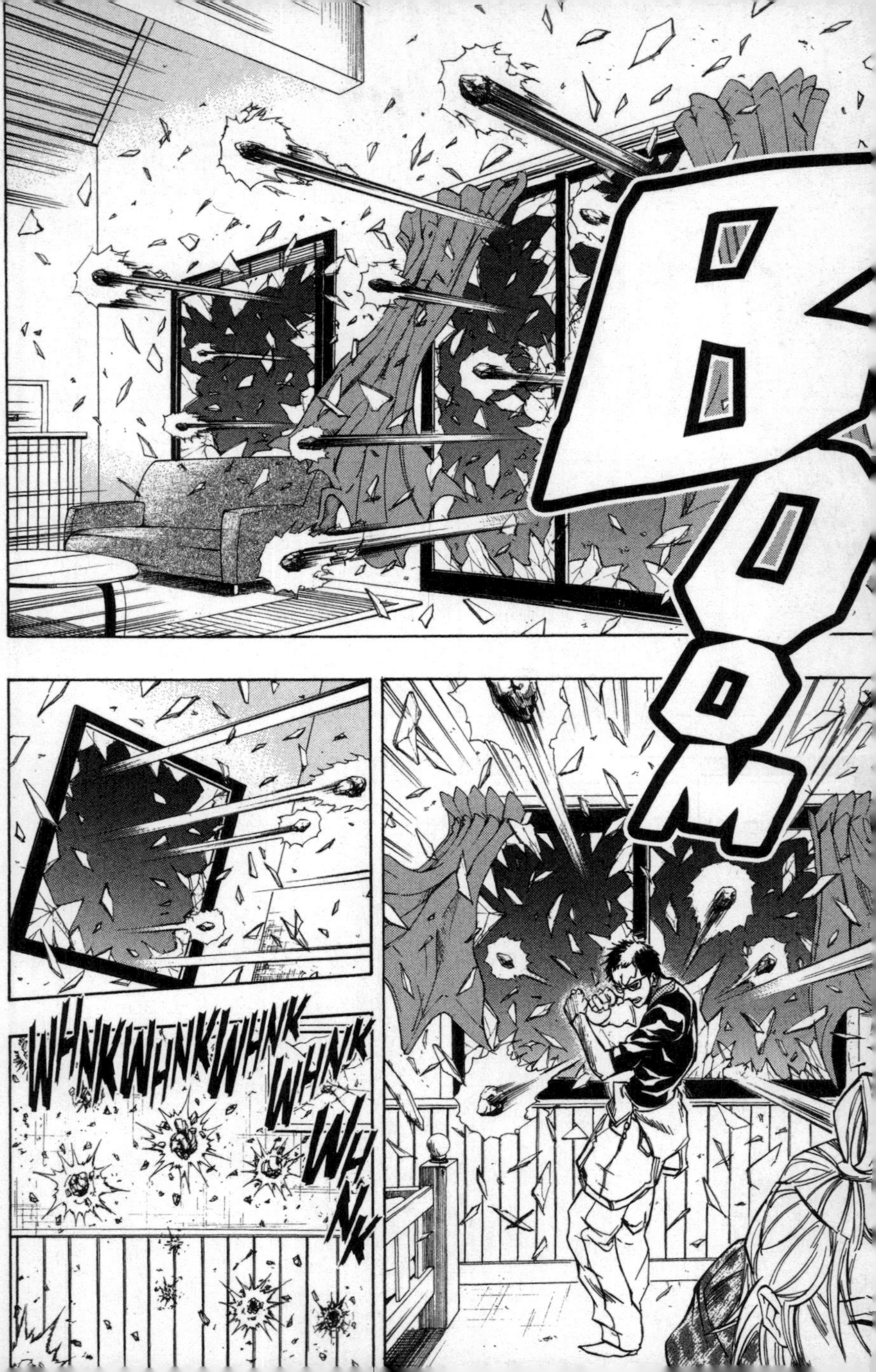
BOOM
WHNKWHNKWHNK
WHNK
WHNK

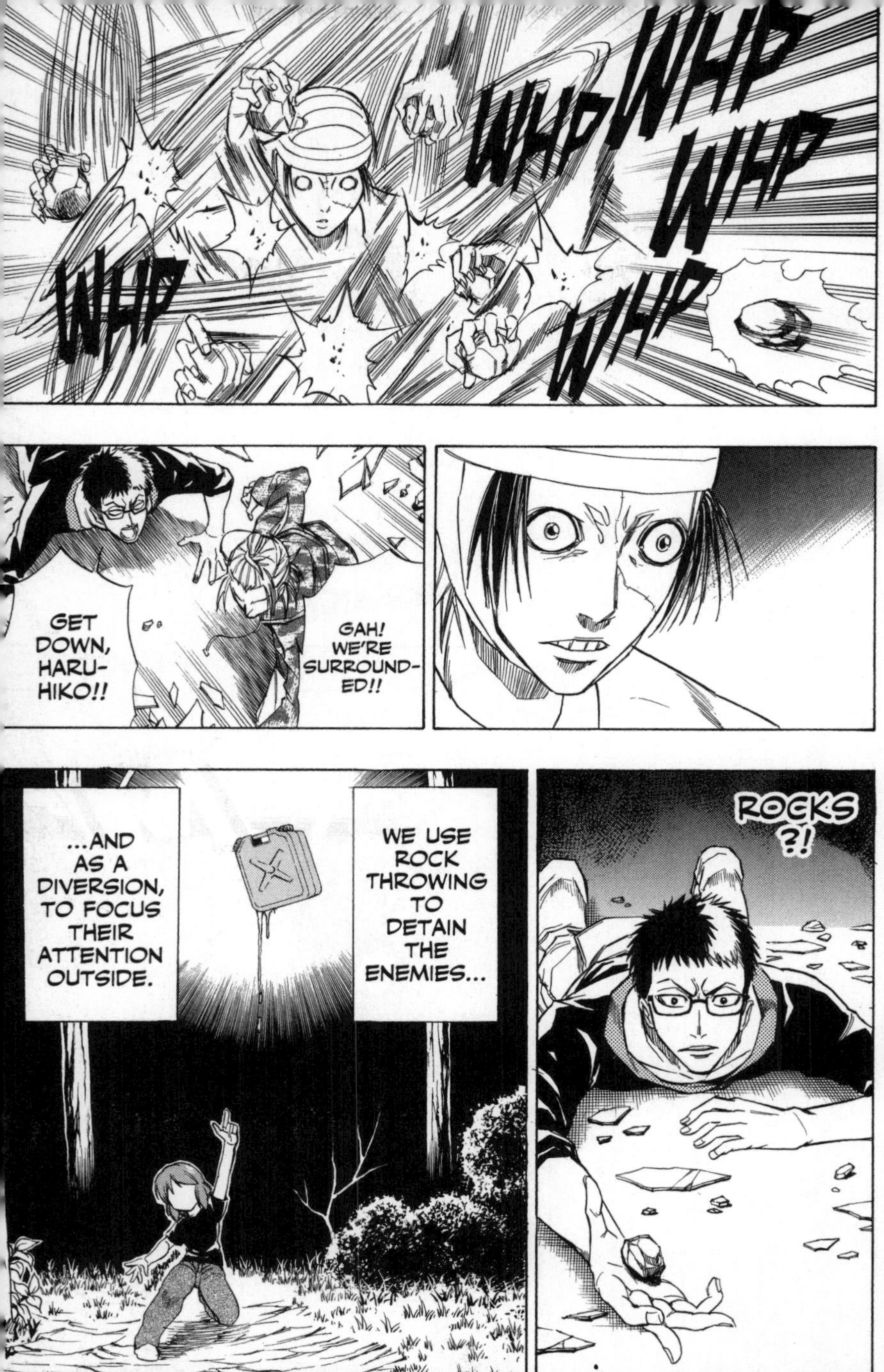
WHP
WHP
WHP
WHP
WHP
GAH! WE'RE SURROUND-ED!!
GET DOWN, HARU-HIKO!!
ROCKS ?!
WE USE ROCK THROWING TO DETAIN THE ENEMIES...
...AND AS A DIVERSION, TO FOCUS THEIR ATTENTION OUTSIDE.

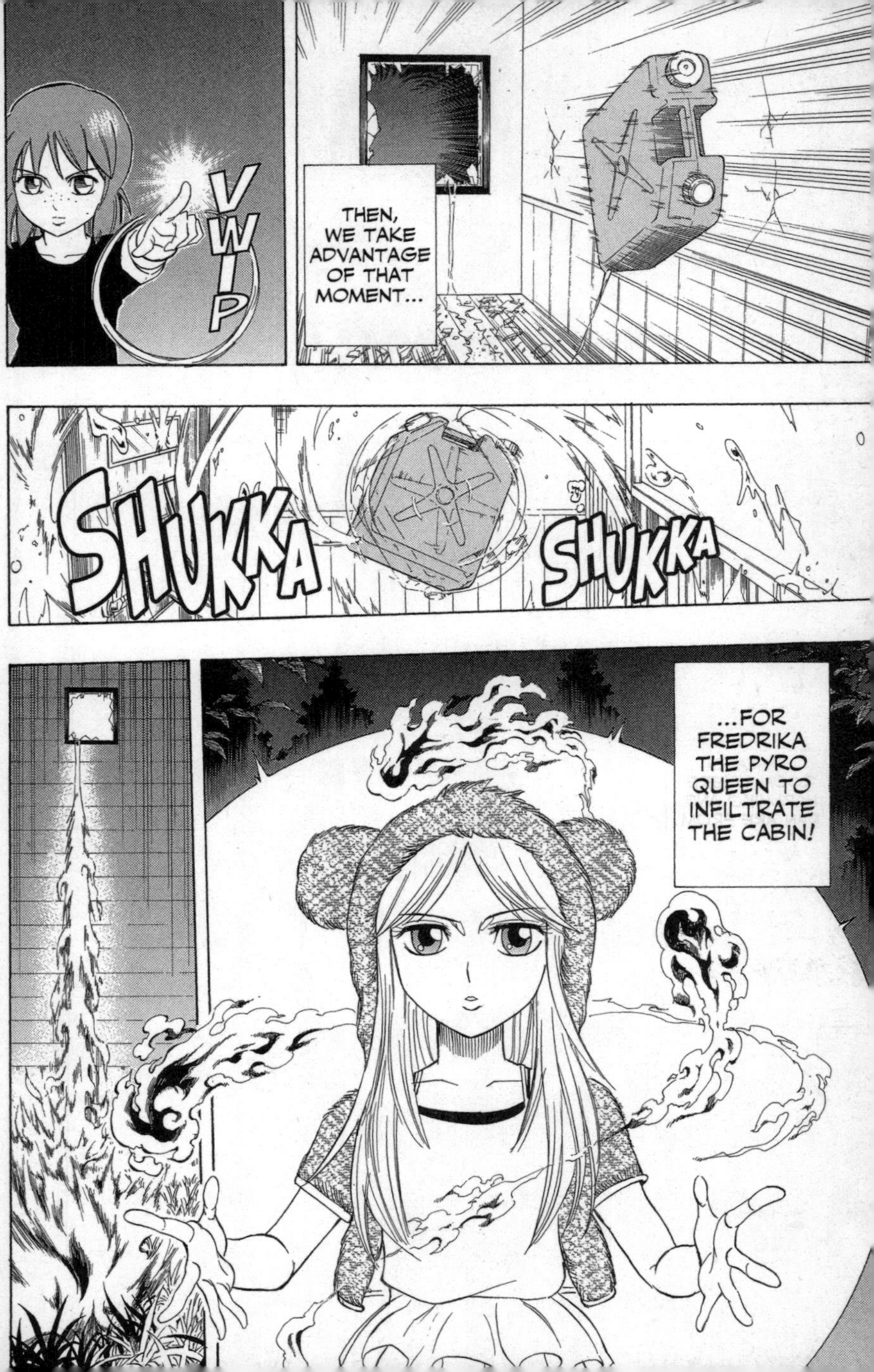
THEN, WE TAKE ADVANTAGE OF THAT MOMENT...
VWIP
SHUKKA
SHUKKA
...FOR FREDRIKA THE PYRO QUEEN TO INFILTRATE THE CABIN!

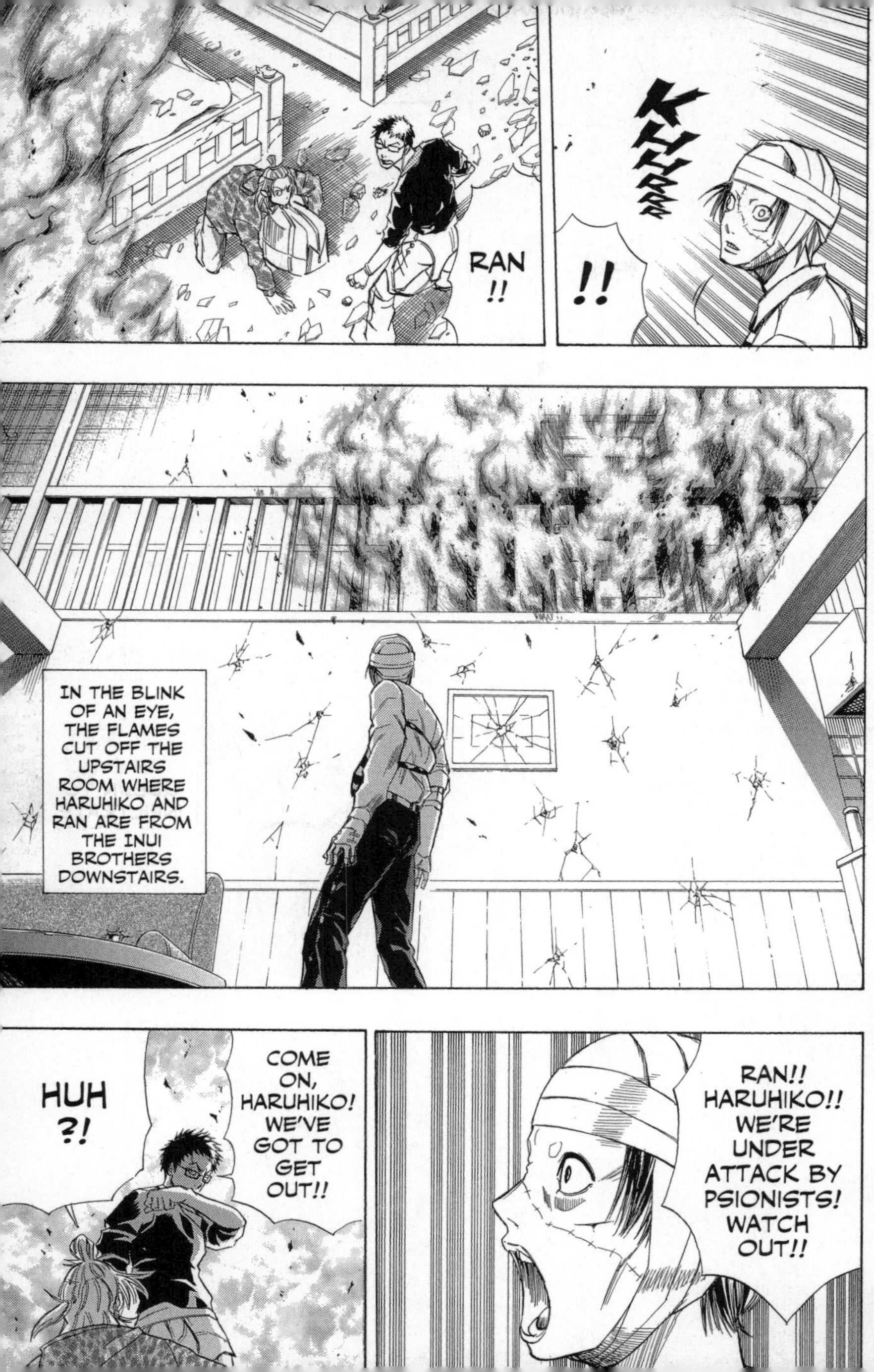

KHHRRR
!!
RAN!!
IN THE BLINK OF AN EYE, THE FLAMES CUT OFF THE UPSTAIRS ROOM WHERE HARUHIKO AND RAN ARE FROM THE INUI BROTHERS DOWNSTAIRS.
RAN!! HARUHIKO!! WE'RE UNDER ATTACK BY PSIONISTS! WATCH OUT!!
COME ON, HARUHIKO! WE'VE GOT TO GET OUT!!
HUH ?!

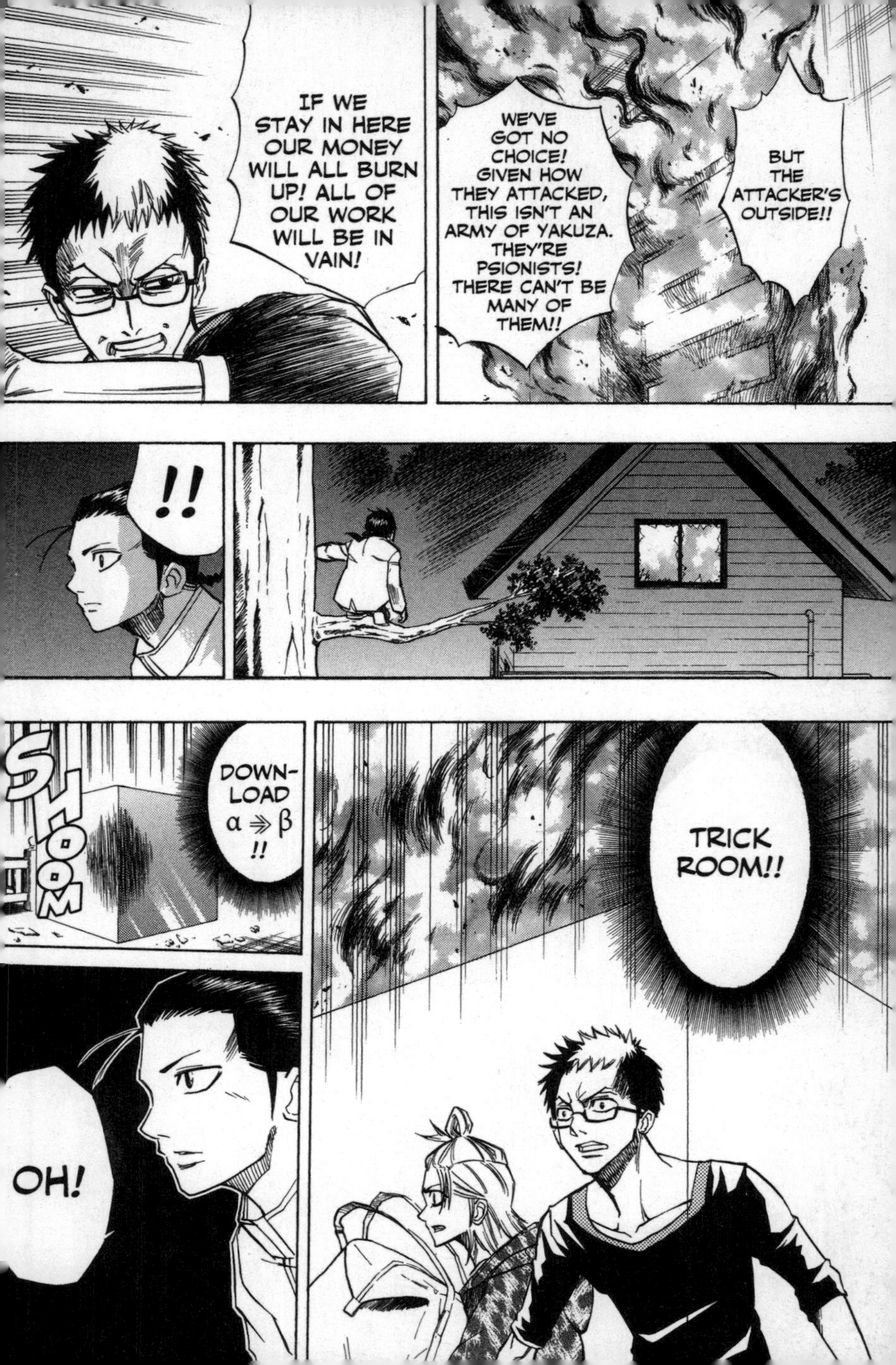
BUT THE ATTACKER'S OUTSIDE!!
WE'VE GOT NO CHOICE! GIVEN HOW THEY ATTACKED, THIS ISN'T AN ARMY OF YAKUZA. THEY'RE PSIONISTS! THERE CAN'T BE MANY OF THEM!!
IF WE STAY IN HERE OUR MONEY WILL ALL BURN UP! ALL OF OUR WORK WILL BE IN VAIN!
!!
TRICK ROOM!!
DOWN-LOAD α ⇛ β !!
SHOOM
OH!

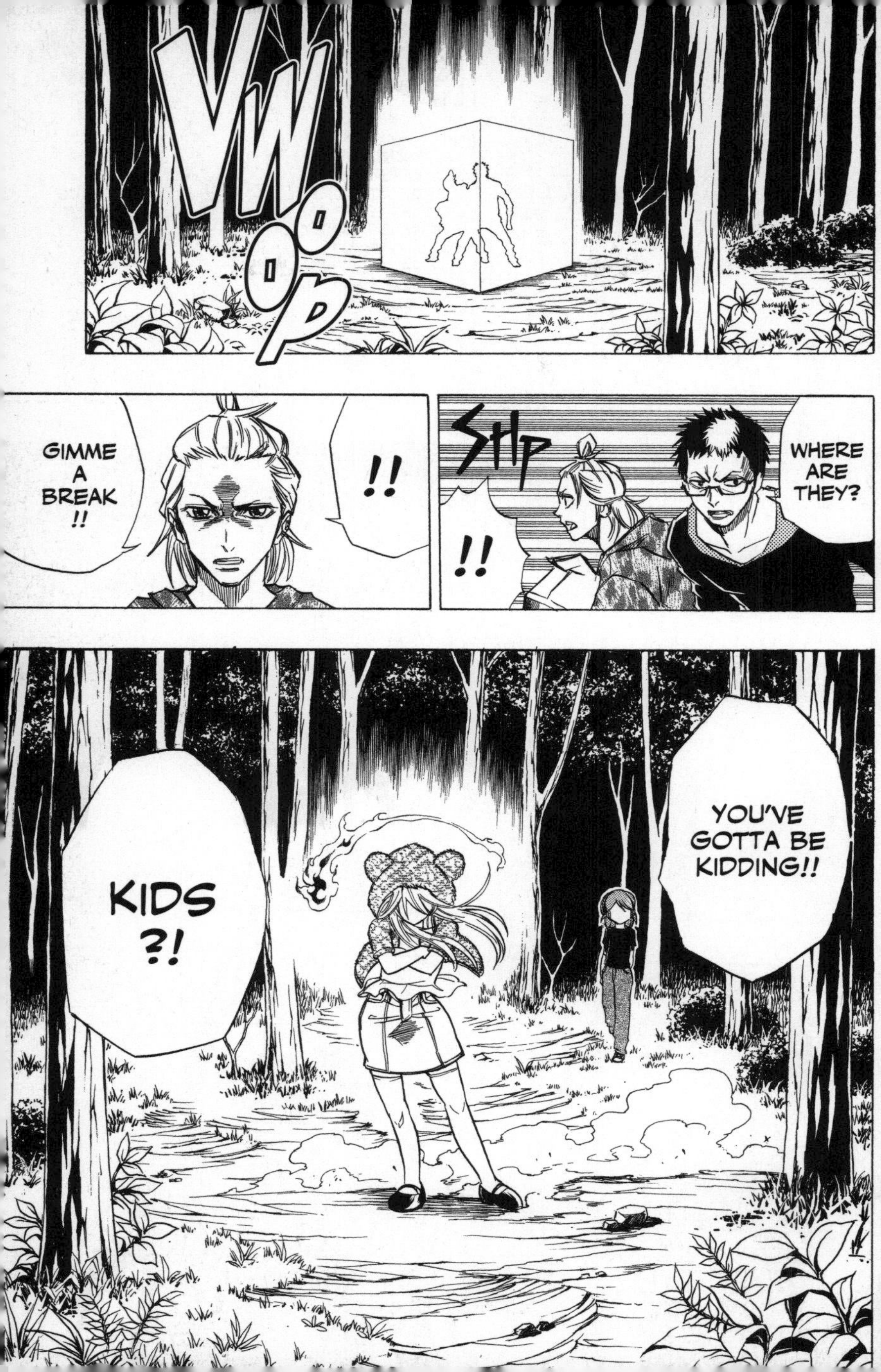
VWOOOP
WHERE ARE THEY?
SHP
!!
!!
GIMME A BREAK !!
YOU'VE GOTTA BE KIDDING!!
KIDS ?!

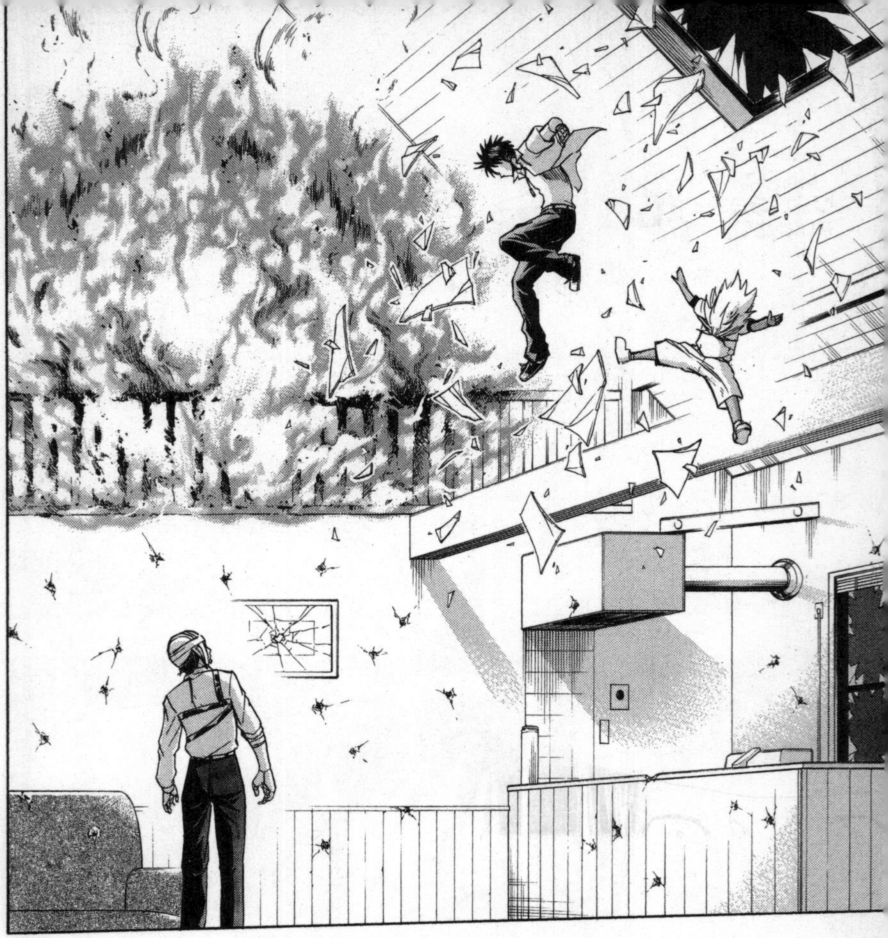
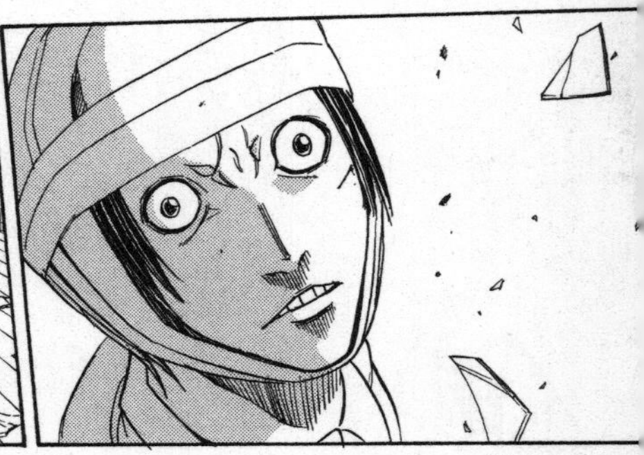
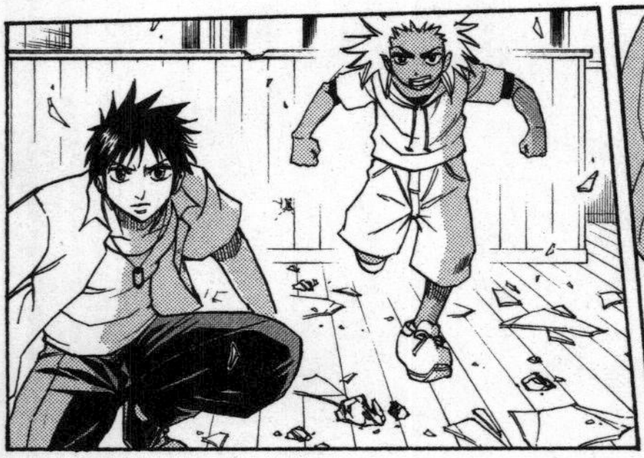

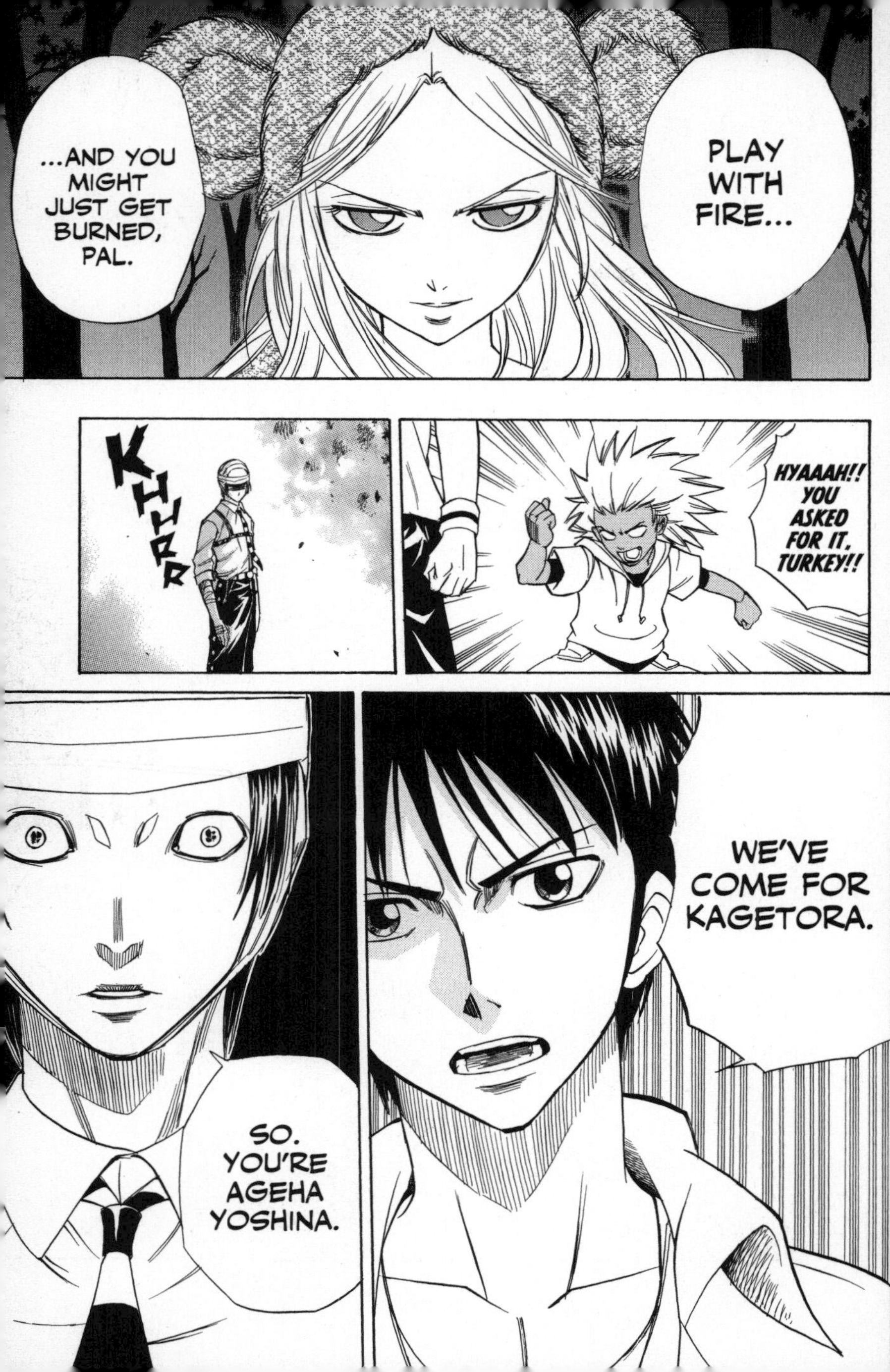
PLAY WITH FIRE...
...AND YOU MIGHT JUST GET BURNED, PAL.
HYAAAH!! YOU ASKED FOR IT, TURKEY!!
KHURR
WE'VE COME FOR KAGETORA.
SO. YOU'RE AGEHA YOSHINA.

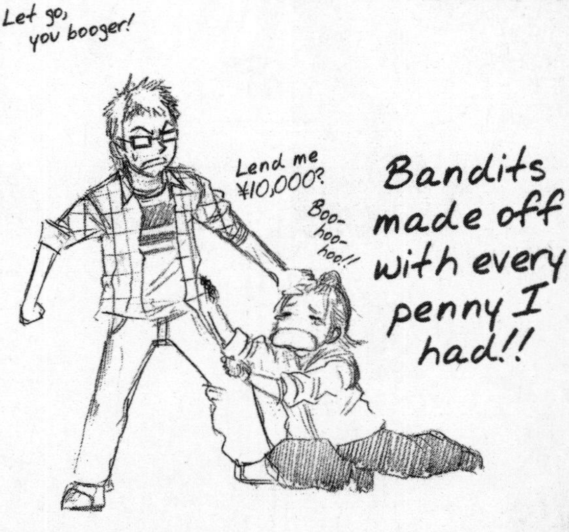
Bandits made off with every penny I had!!
Lend me ¥10,000?
Boo-hoo-hoo!!
Let go, you booger!

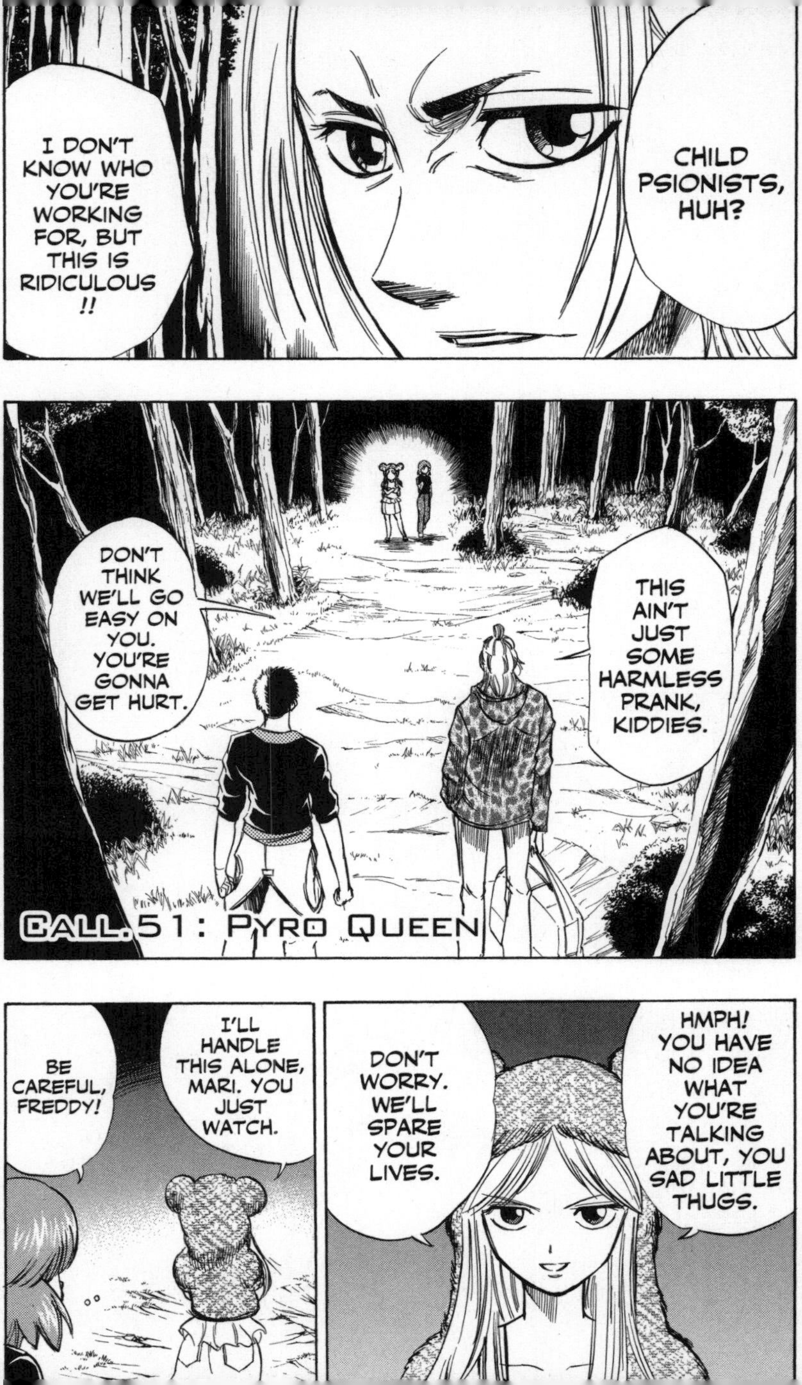
CHILD PSIONISTS, HUH?
I DON'T KNOW WHO YOU'RE WORKING FOR, BUT THIS IS RIDICULOUS!!
THIS AIN'T JUST SOME HARMLESS PRANK, KIDDIES.
DON'T THINK WE'LL GO EASY ON YOU. YOU'RE GONNA GET HURT.
CALL.51: PYRO QUEEN
HMPH! YOU HAVE NO IDEA WHAT YOU'RE TALKING ABOUT, YOU SAD LITTLE THUGS.
DON'T WORRY. WE'LL SPARE YOUR LIVES.
I'LL HANDLE THIS ALONE, MARI. YOU JUST WATCH.
BE CAREFUL, FREDDY!

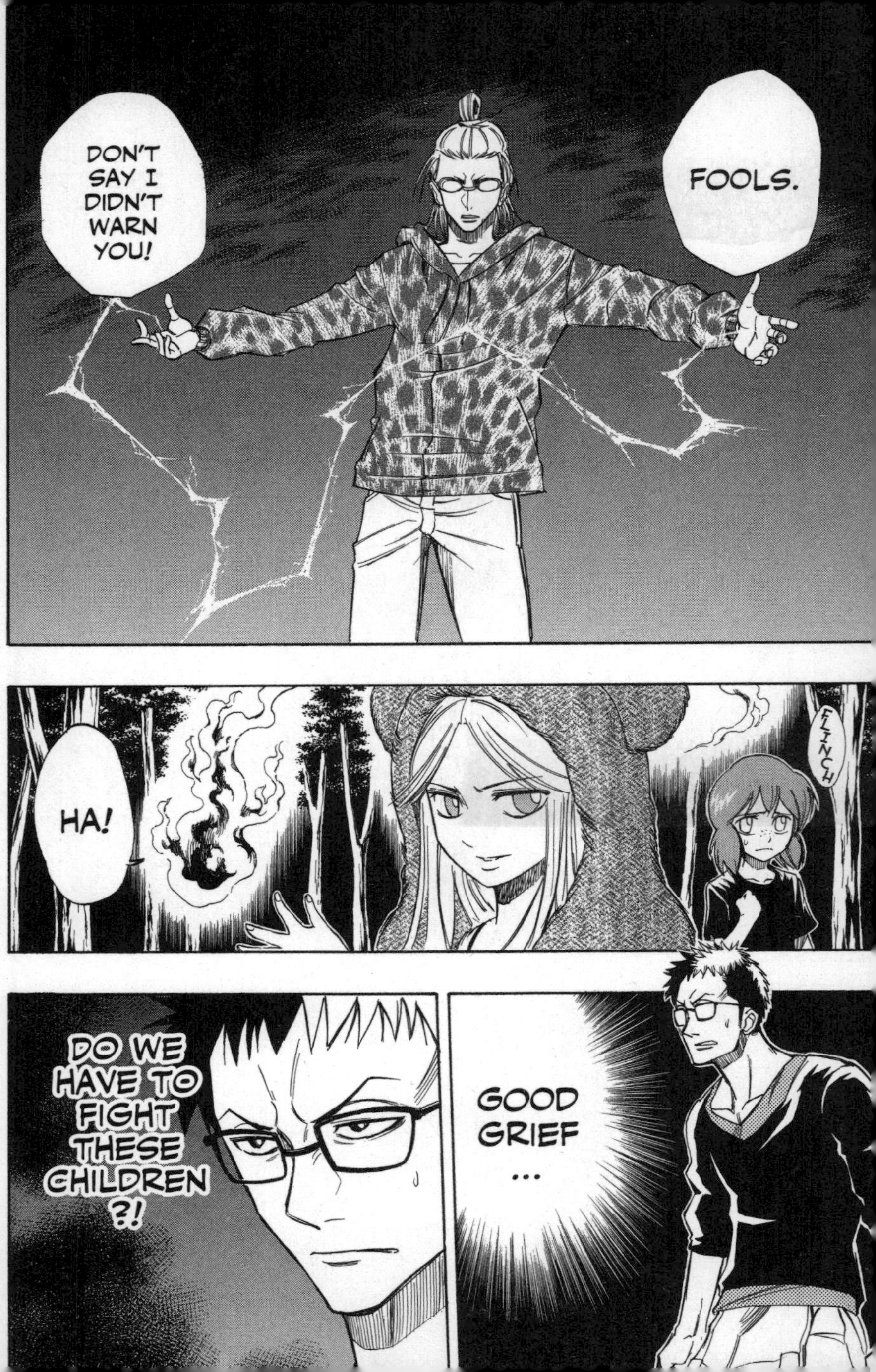
FOOLS.
DON'T SAY I DIDN'T WARN YOU!
FLINCH
HA!
GOOD GRIEF ...
DO WE HAVE TO FIGHT THESE CHILDREN ?!

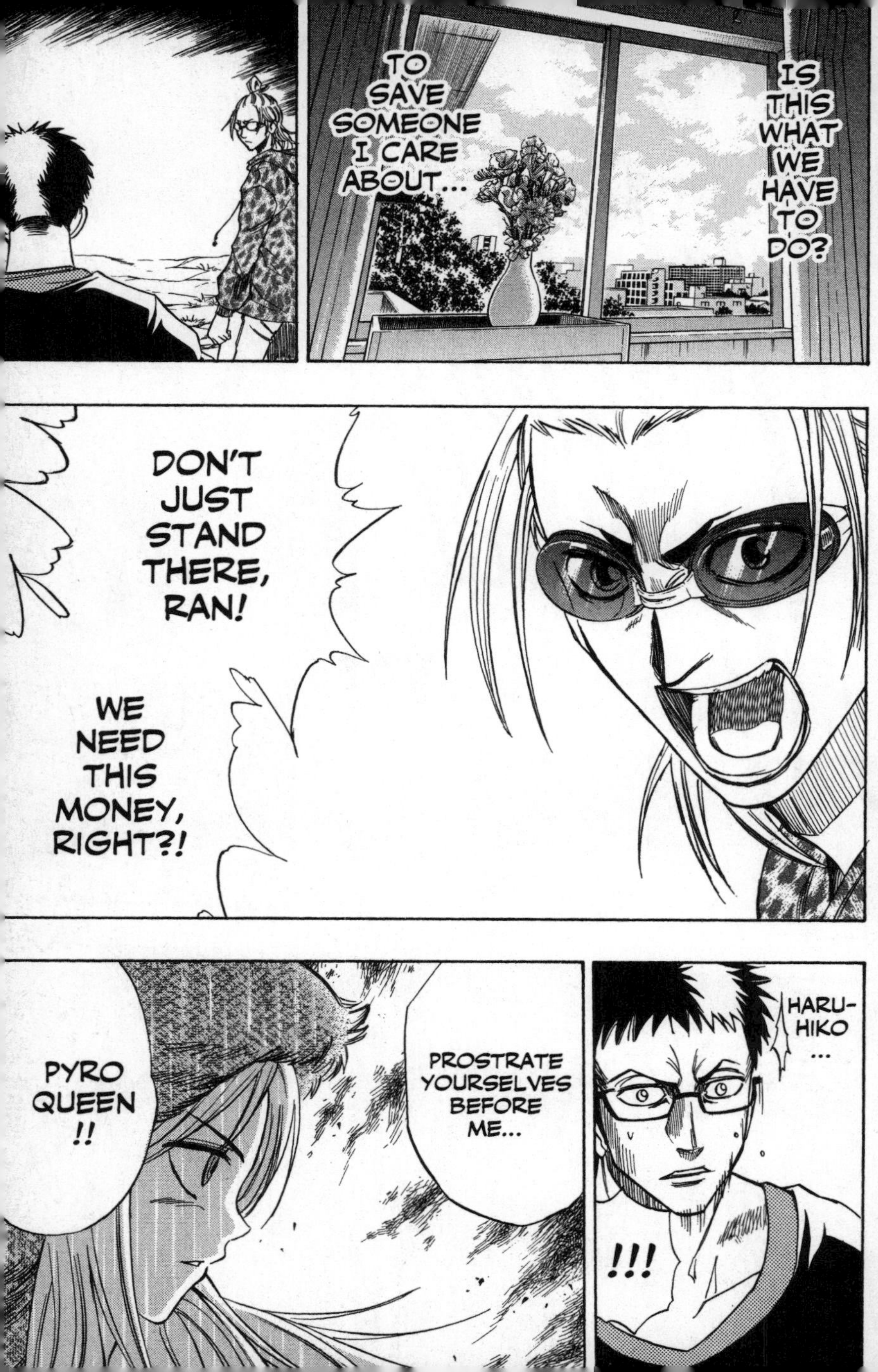
TO SAVE SOMEONE I CARE ABOUT...
IS THIS WHAT WE HAVE TO DO?
DON'T JUST STAND THERE, RAN!
WE NEED THIS MONEY, RIGHT?!
HARU-HIKO...
!!!
PROSTRATE YOURSELVES BEFORE ME...
PYRO QUEEN !!

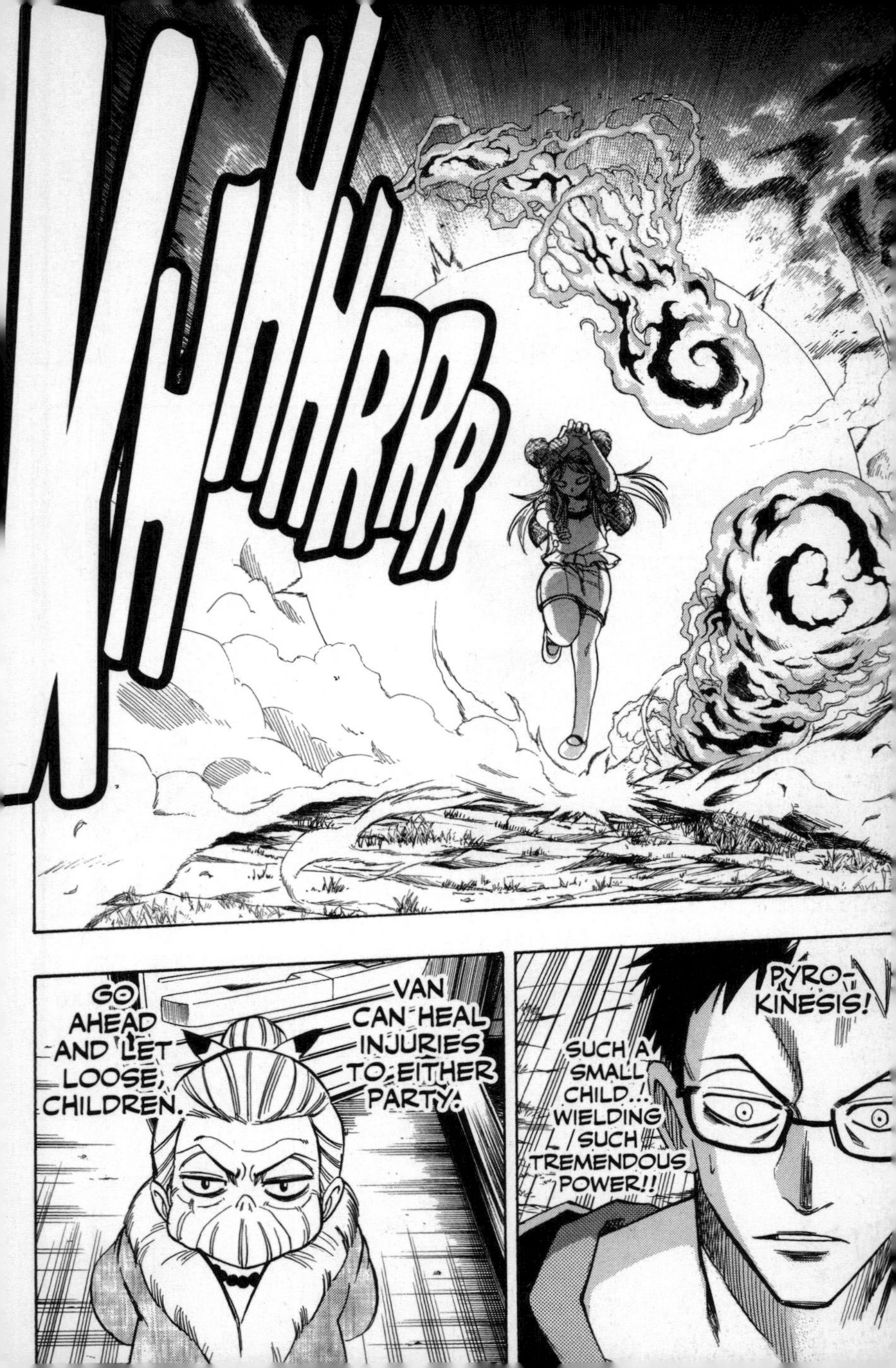

PYRO-KINESIS!
SUCH A SMALL CHILD... WIELDING SUCH TREMENDOUS POWER!!
VAN CAN HEAL INJURIES TO EITHER PARTY.
GO AHEAD AND LET LOOSE, CHILDREN.

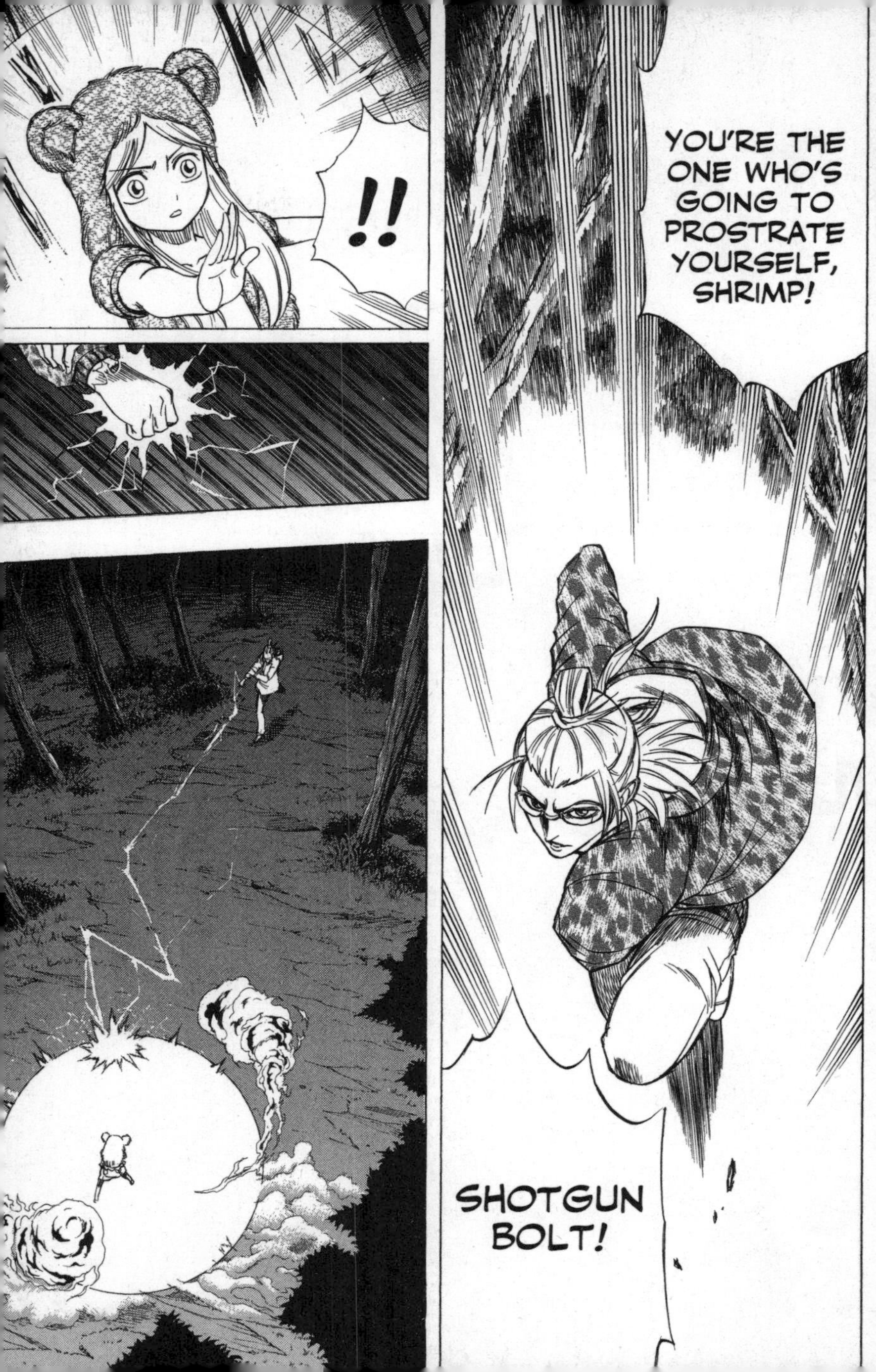
YOU'RE THE ONE WHO'S GOING TO PROSTRATE YOURSELF, SHRIMP!
SHOTGUN BOLT!
!!

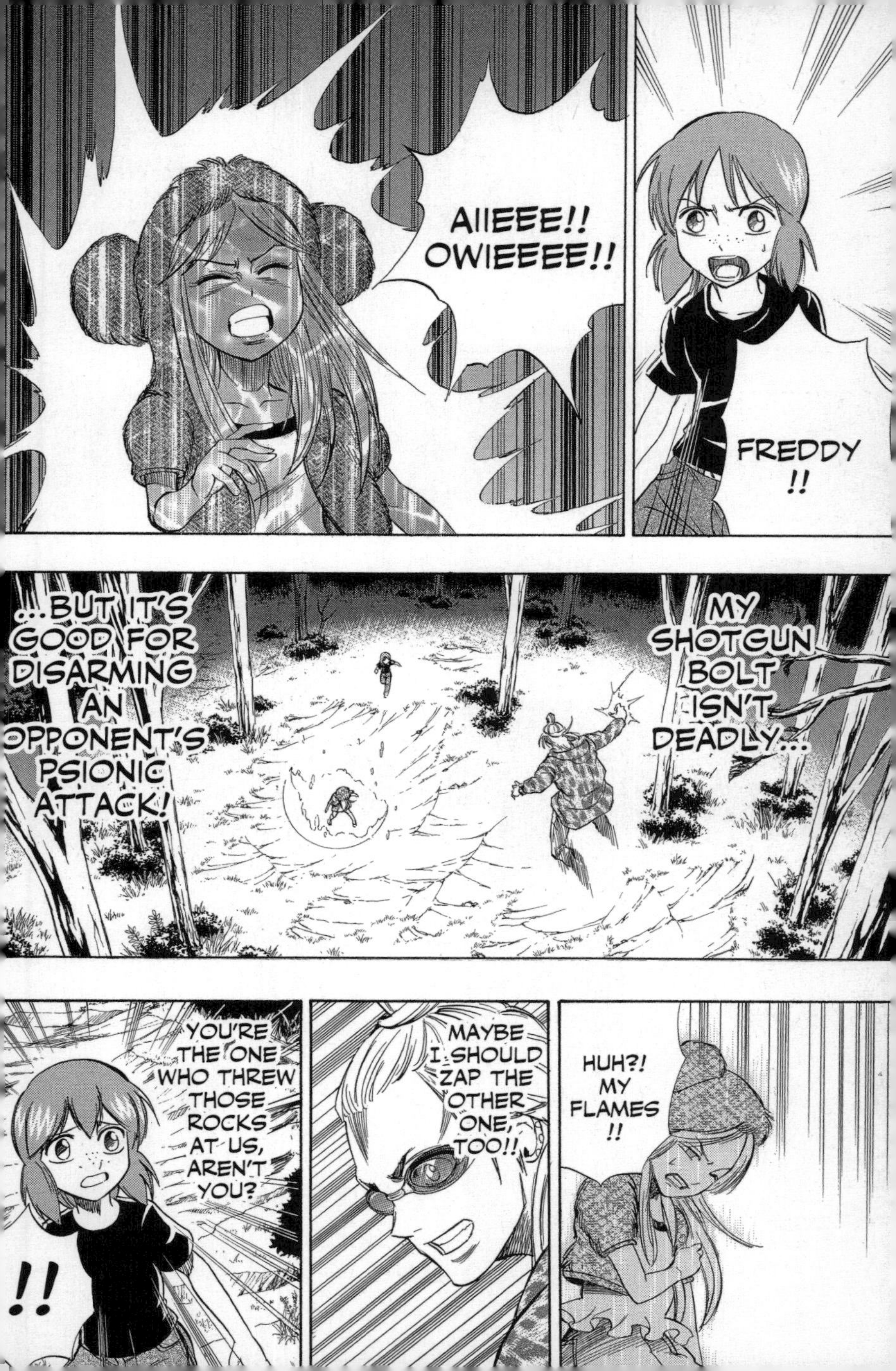
FREDDY !!
AIIEEE!! OWIEEEE!!
MY SHOTGUN BOLT ISN'T DEADLY...
...BUT IT'S GOOD FOR DISARMING AN OPPONENT'S PSIONIC ATTACK!
HUH?! MY FLAMES !!
MAYBE I SHOULD ZAP THE OTHER ONE, TOO!!
YOU'RE THE ONE WHO THREW THOSE ROCKS AT US, AREN'T YOU?
!!

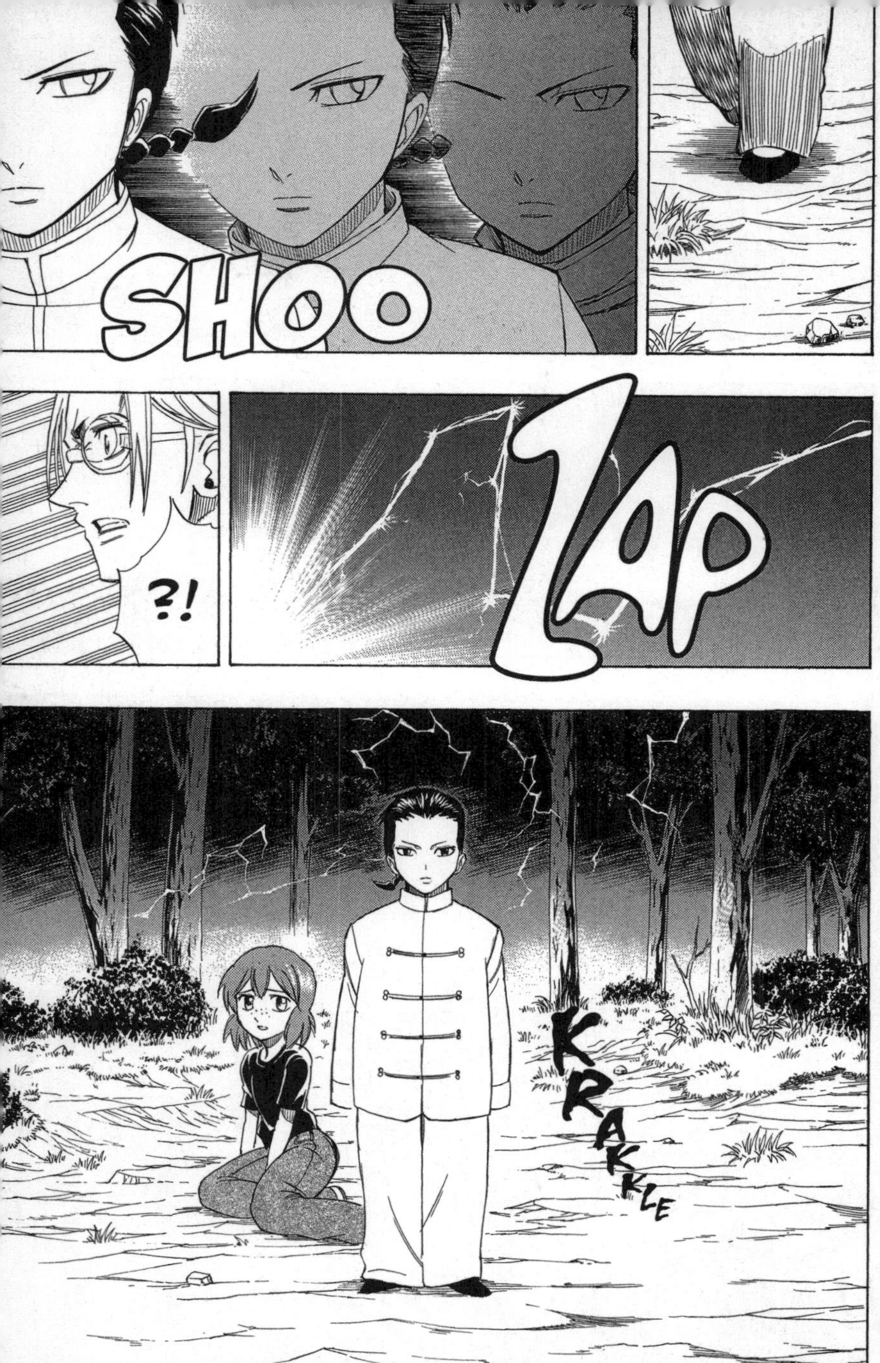
SHOO
ZAP
?!
KRAKKLE

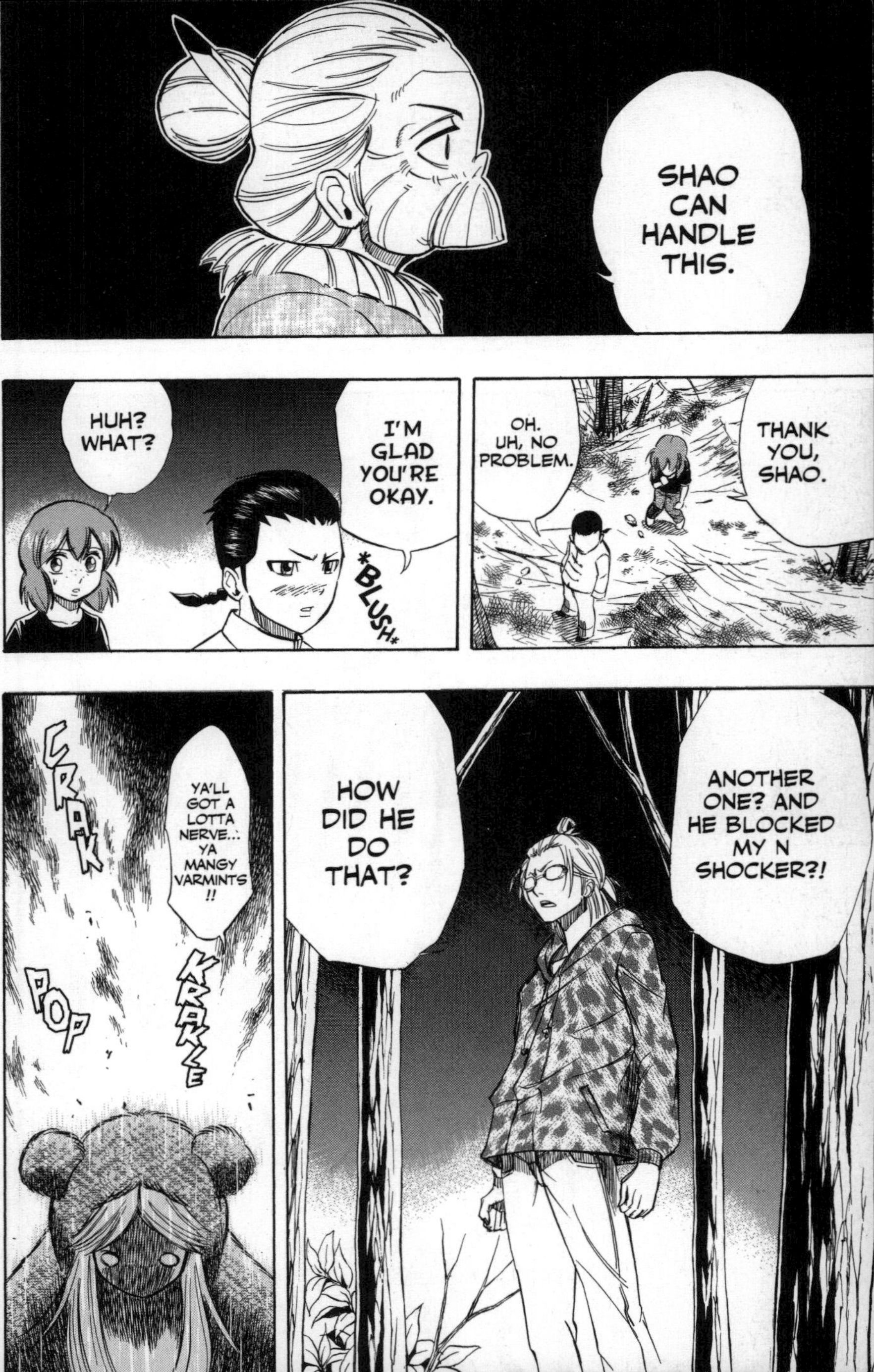
SHAO CAN HANDLE THIS.
THANK YOU, SHAO.
OH. UH, NO PROBLEM.
I'M GLAD YOU'RE OKAY.
BLUSH
HUH? WHAT?
ANOTHER ONE? AND HE BLOCKED MY N SHOCKER?!
HOW DID HE DO THAT?
YA'LL GOT A LOTTA NERVE... YA MANGY VARMINTS!!
CRAK
KRAKLE
POP

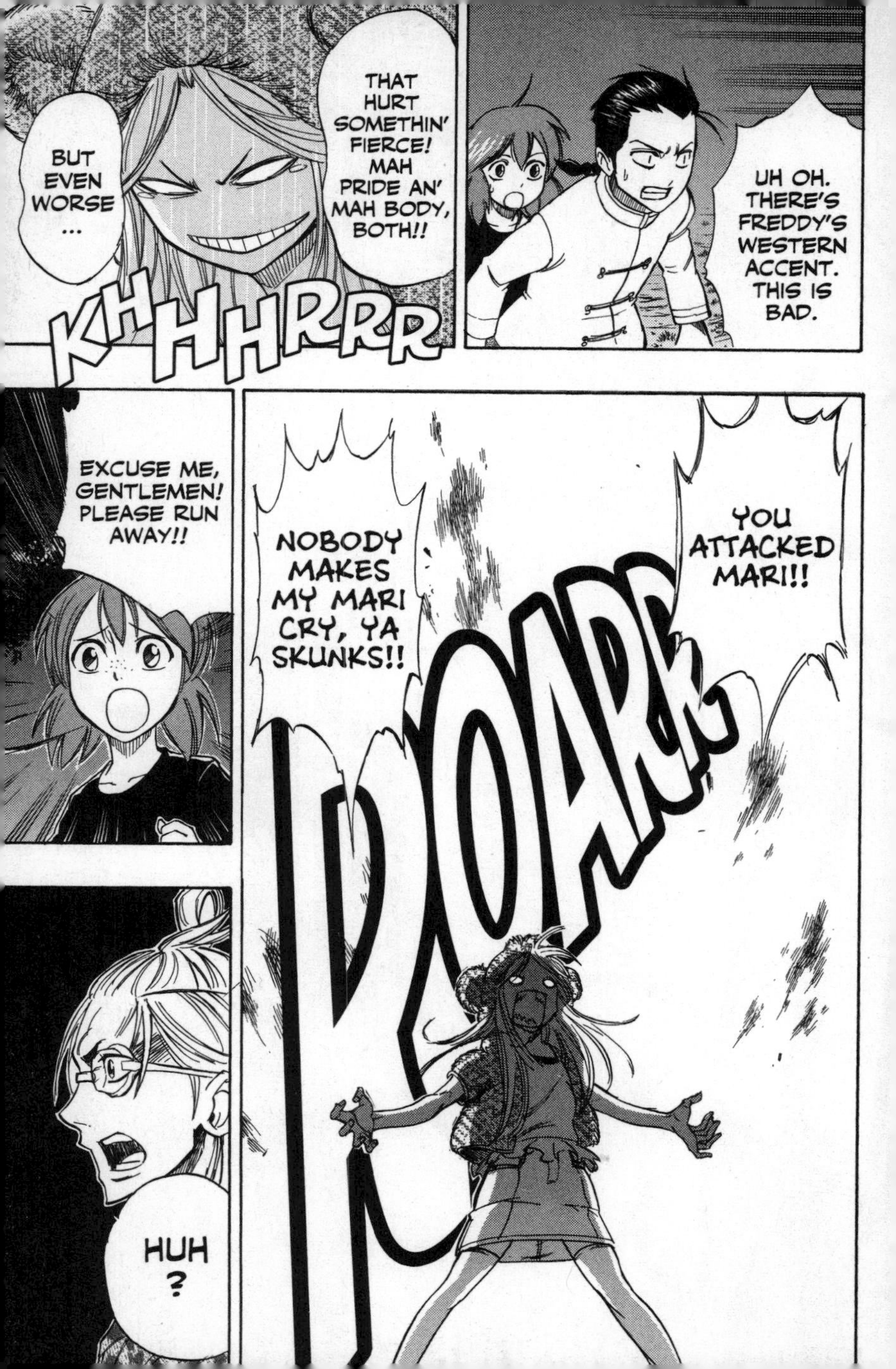
UH OH. THERE'S FREDDY'S WESTERN ACCENT. THIS IS BAD.
THAT HURT SOMETHIN' FIERCE! MAH PRIDE AN' MAH BODY, BOTH!!
BUT EVEN WORSE ...
KHHHRRR
YOU ATTACKED MARI!!
NOBODY MAKES MY MARI CRY, YA SKUNKS!!
ROARR
EXCUSE ME, GENTLEMEN! PLEASE RUN AWAY!!
HUH ?

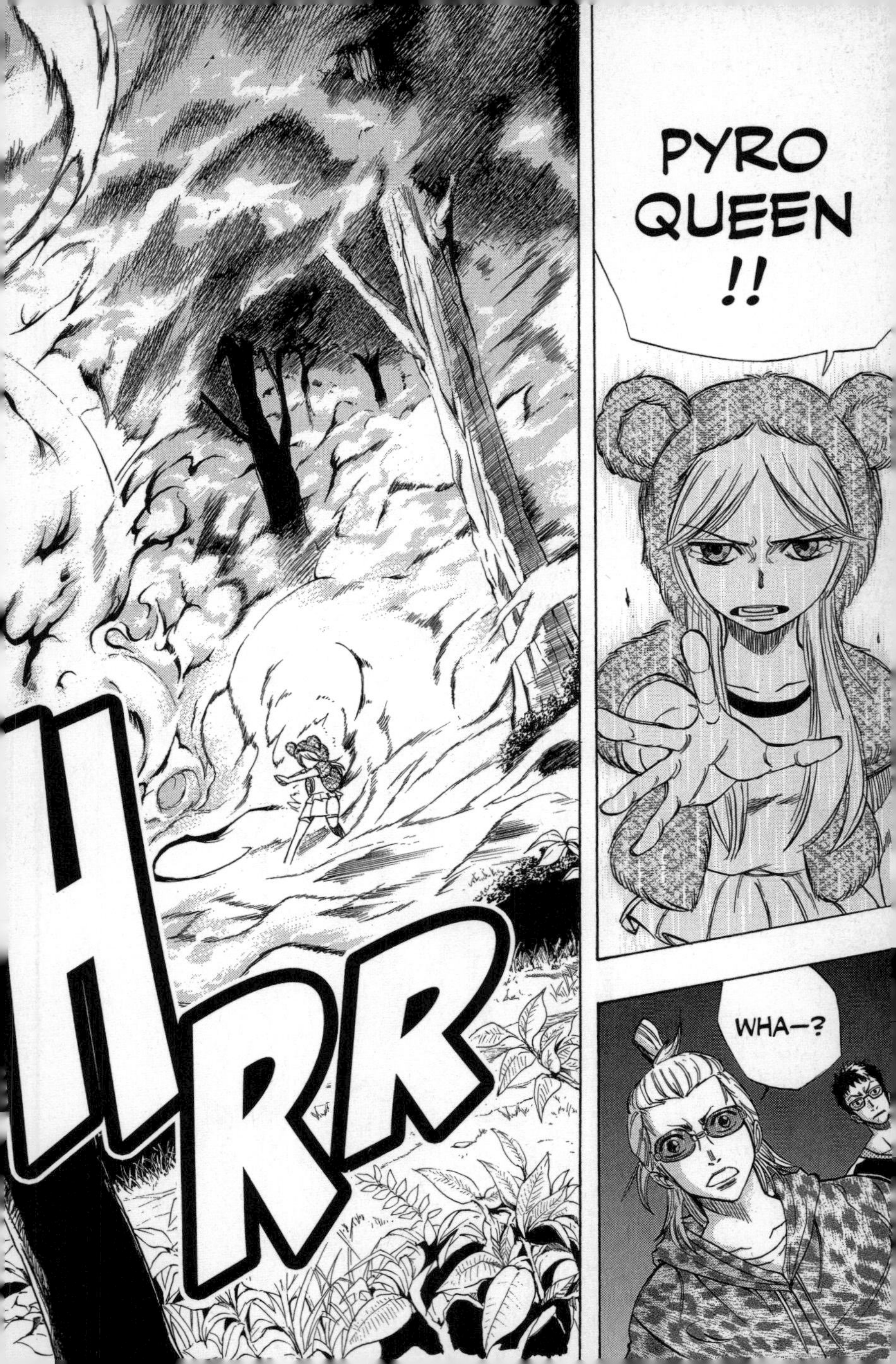
PYRO QUEEN !!
WHA—?
HRR

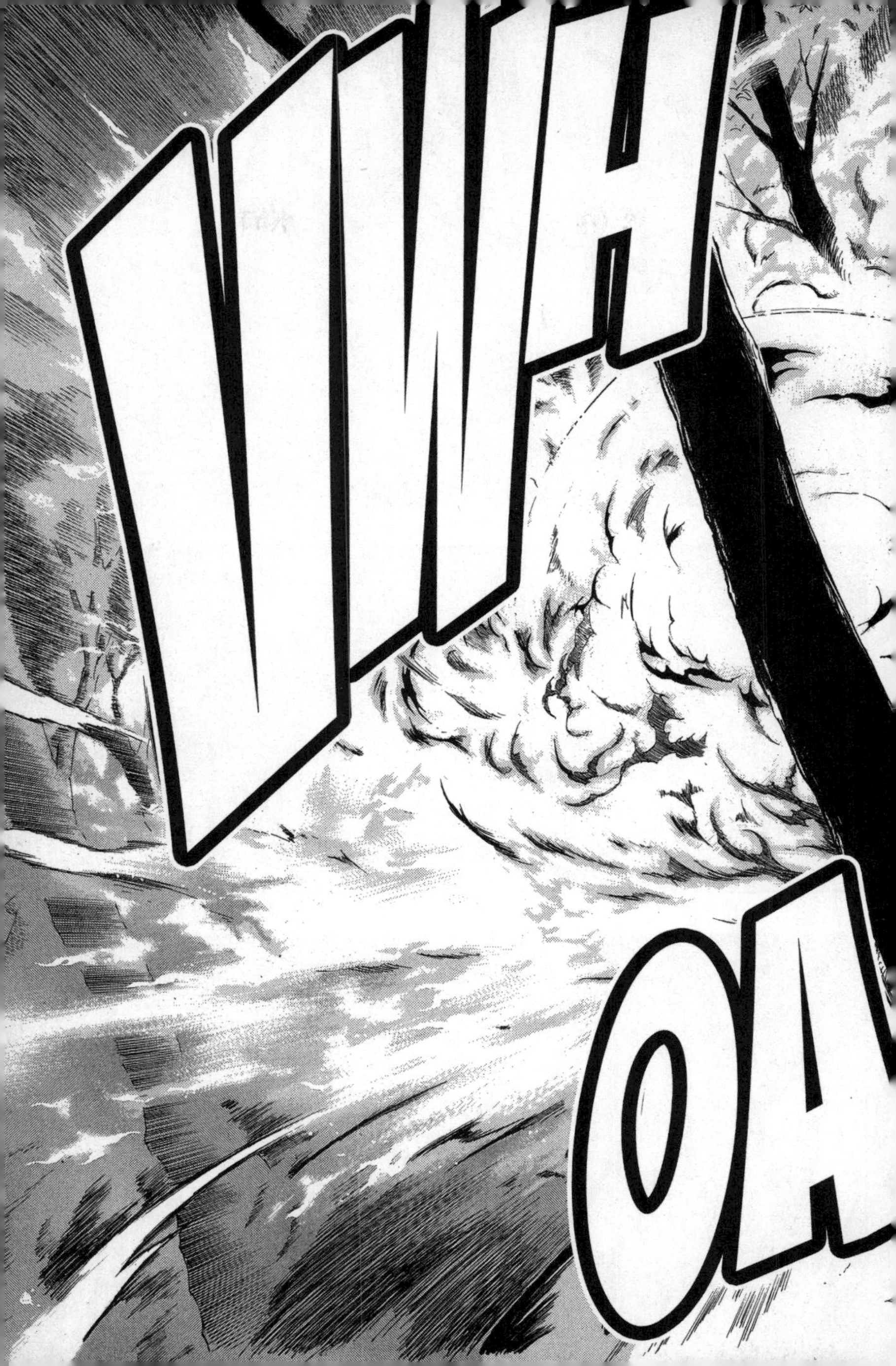
WHOA

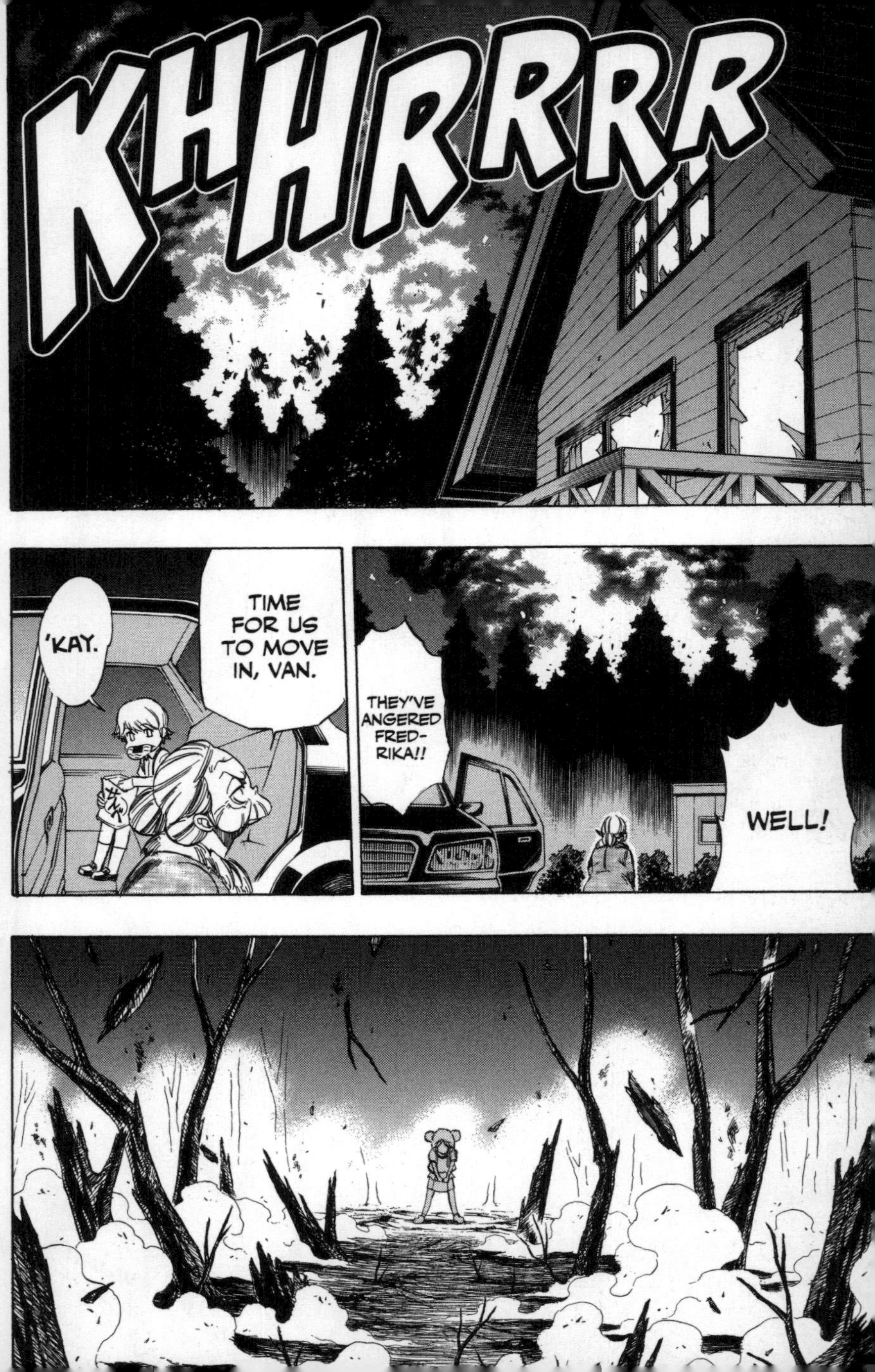
KHRRRRR
WELL!
THEY'VE ANGERED FRED-RIKA!!
TIME FOR US TO MOVE IN, VAN.
'KAY.

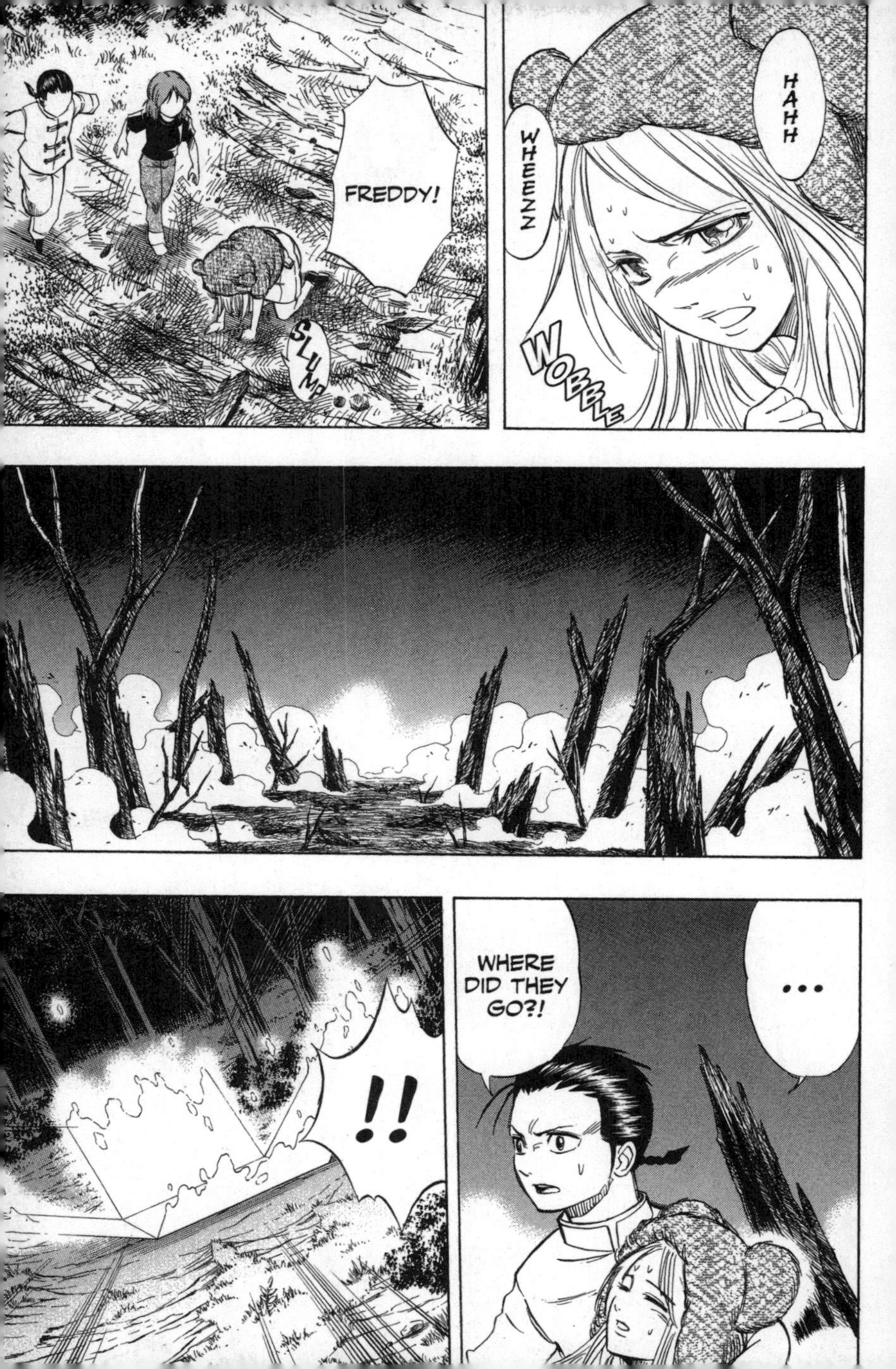
HAHH
WHEEZZ
WOBBLE
FREDDY!
SLUMP
...
WHERE DID THEY GO?!
!!

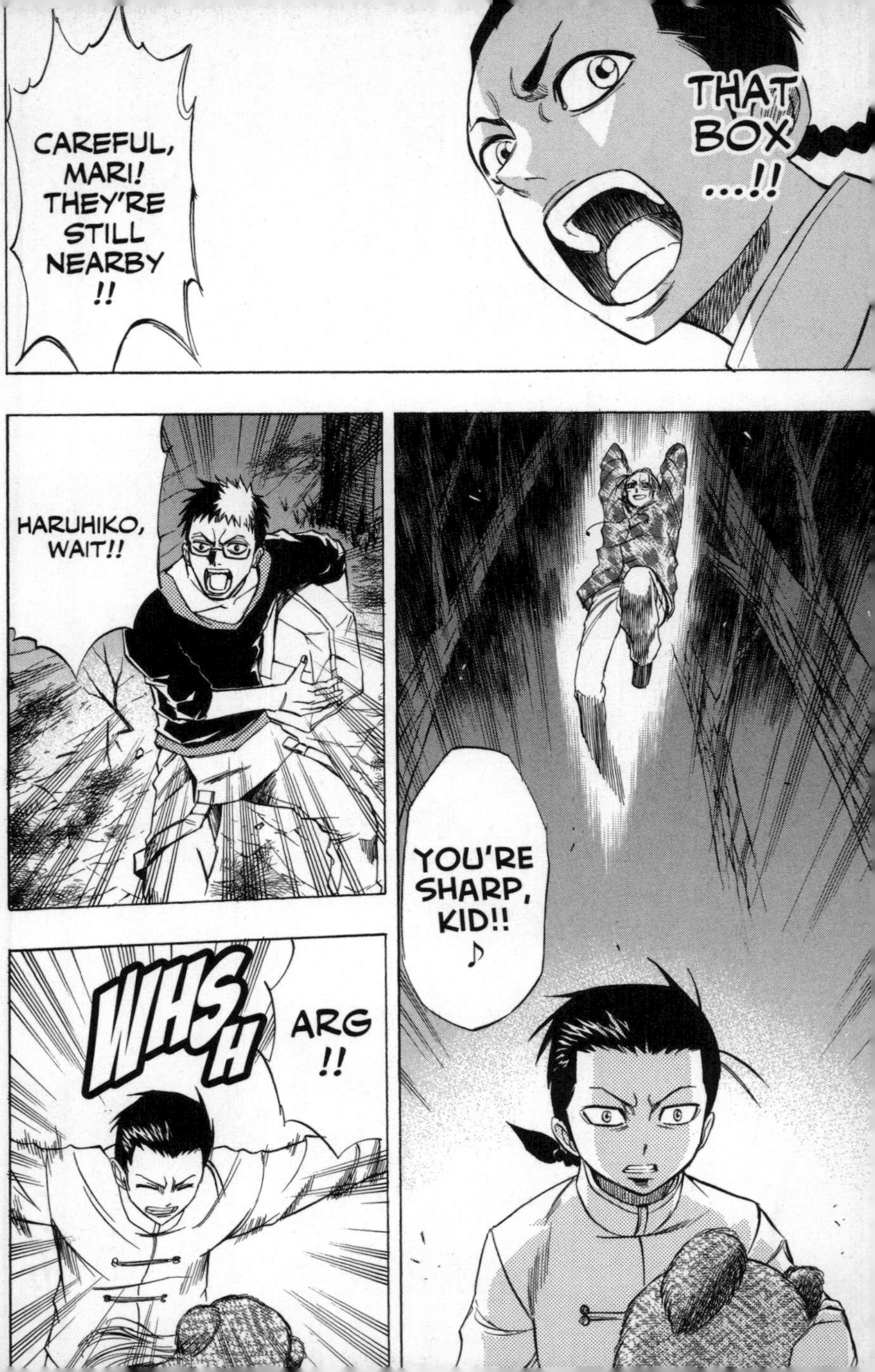
THAT BOX ...!!
CAREFUL, MARI! THEY'RE STILL NEARBY !!
YOU'RE SHARP, KID!! ♪
HARUHIKO, WAIT!!
WHSH
ARG !!

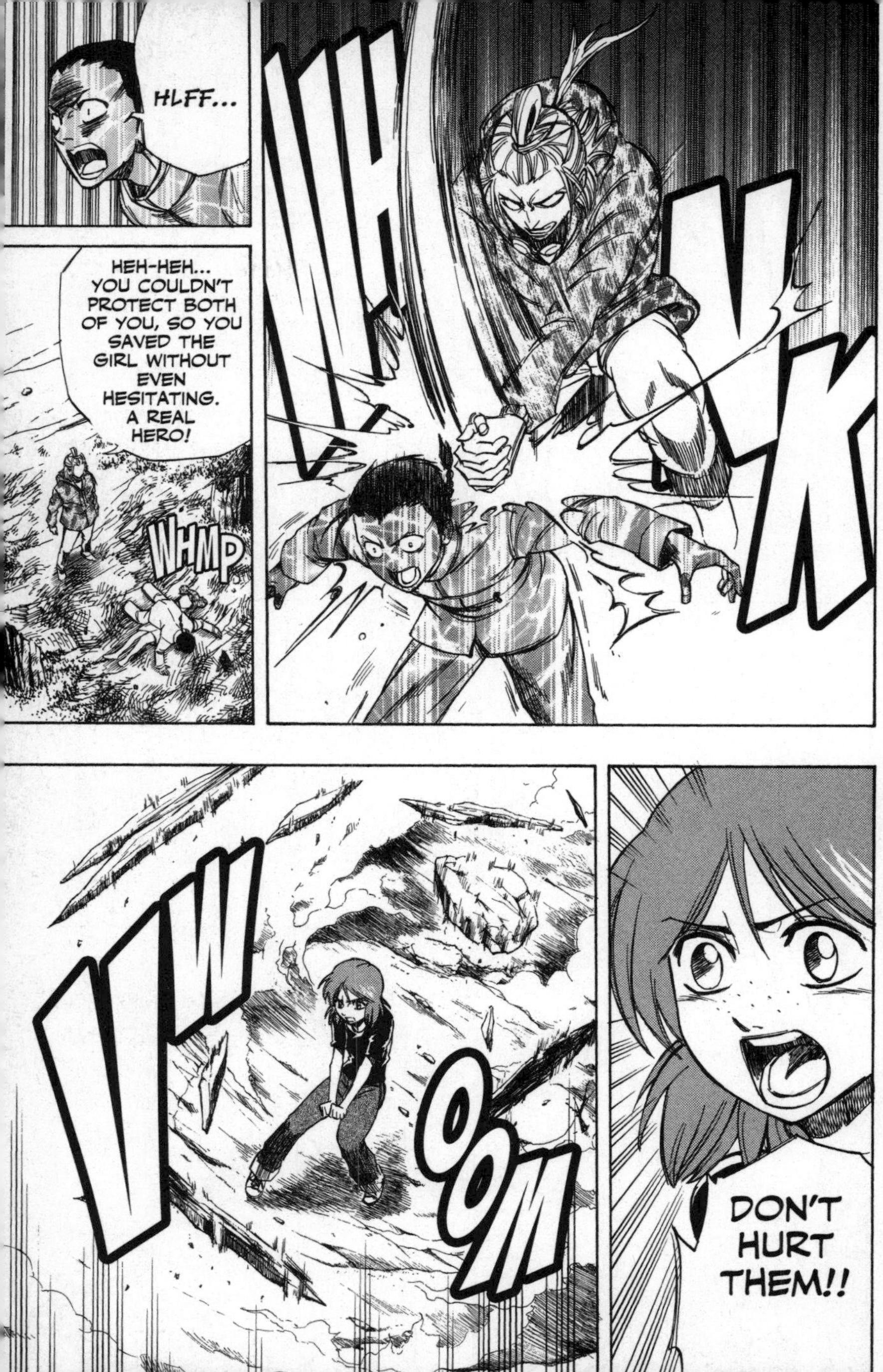
HLFF...
HEH-HEH... YOU COULDN'T PROTECT BOTH OF YOU, SO YOU SAVED THE GIRL WITHOUT EVEN HESITATING. A REAL HERO!
WHMP
DON'T HURT THEM!!

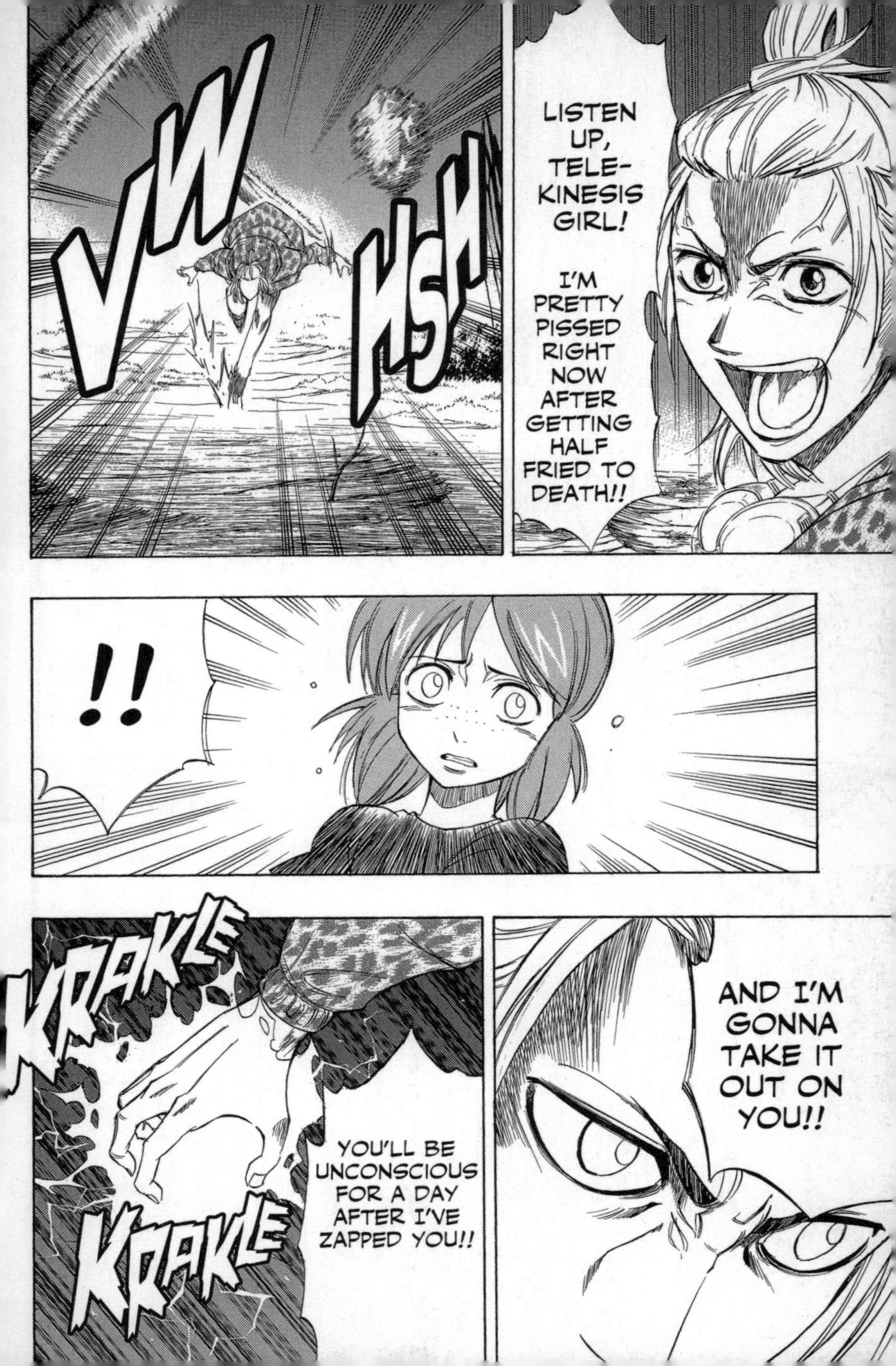
LISTEN UP, TELE-KINESIS GIRL!
I'M PRETTY PISSED RIGHT NOW AFTER GETTING HALF FRIED TO DEATH!!
VW
HSH
!!
AND I'M GONNA TAKE IT OUT ON YOU!!
KRAKLE
YOU'LL BE UNCONSCIOUS FOR A DAY AFTER I'VE ZAPPED YOU!!
KRAKLE

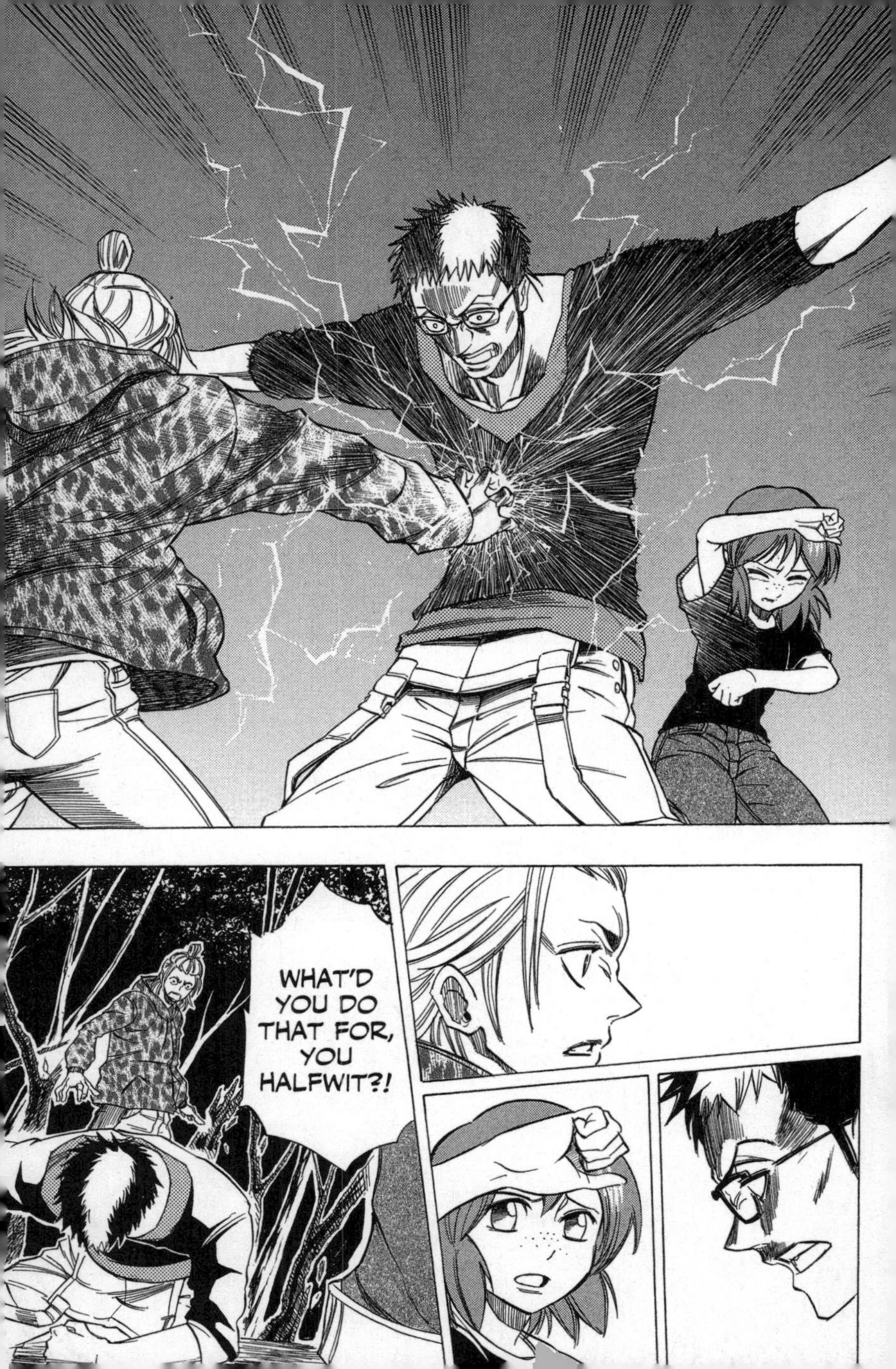
WHAT'D YOU DO THAT FOR, YOU HALFWIT?!

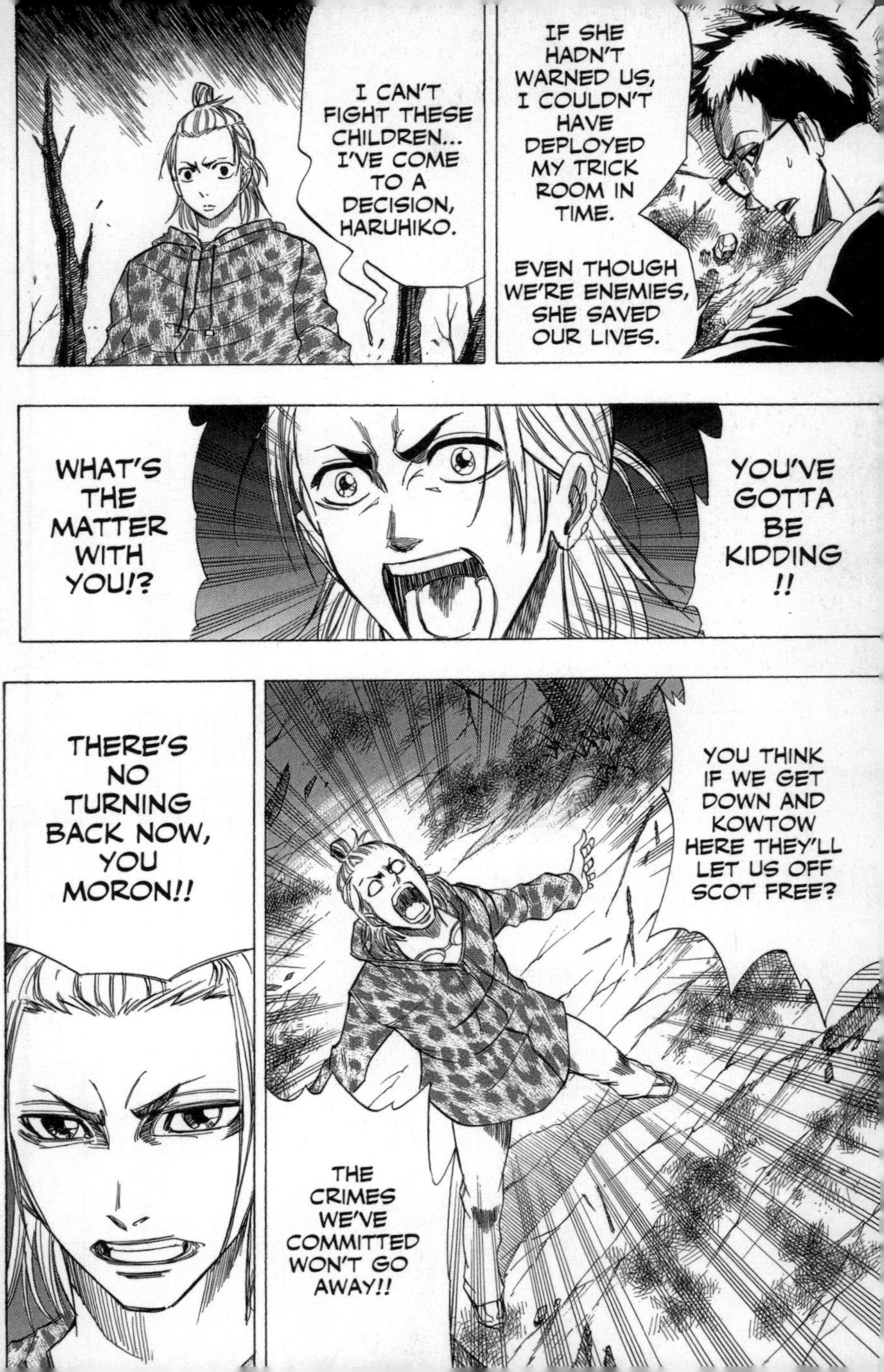
IF SHE HADN'T WARNED US, I COULDN'T HAVE DEPLOYED MY TRICK ROOM IN TIME.
EVEN THOUGH WE'RE ENEMIES, SHE SAVED OUR LIVES.
I CAN'T FIGHT THESE CHILDREN... I'VE COME TO A DECISION, HARUHIKO.
YOU'VE GOTTA BE KIDDING!!
WHAT'S THE MATTER WITH YOU!?
YOU THINK IF WE GET DOWN AND KOWTOW HERE THEY'LL LET US OFF SCOT FREE?
THE CRIMES WE'VE COMMITTED WON'T GO AWAY!!
THERE'S NO TURNING BACK NOW, YOU MORON!!

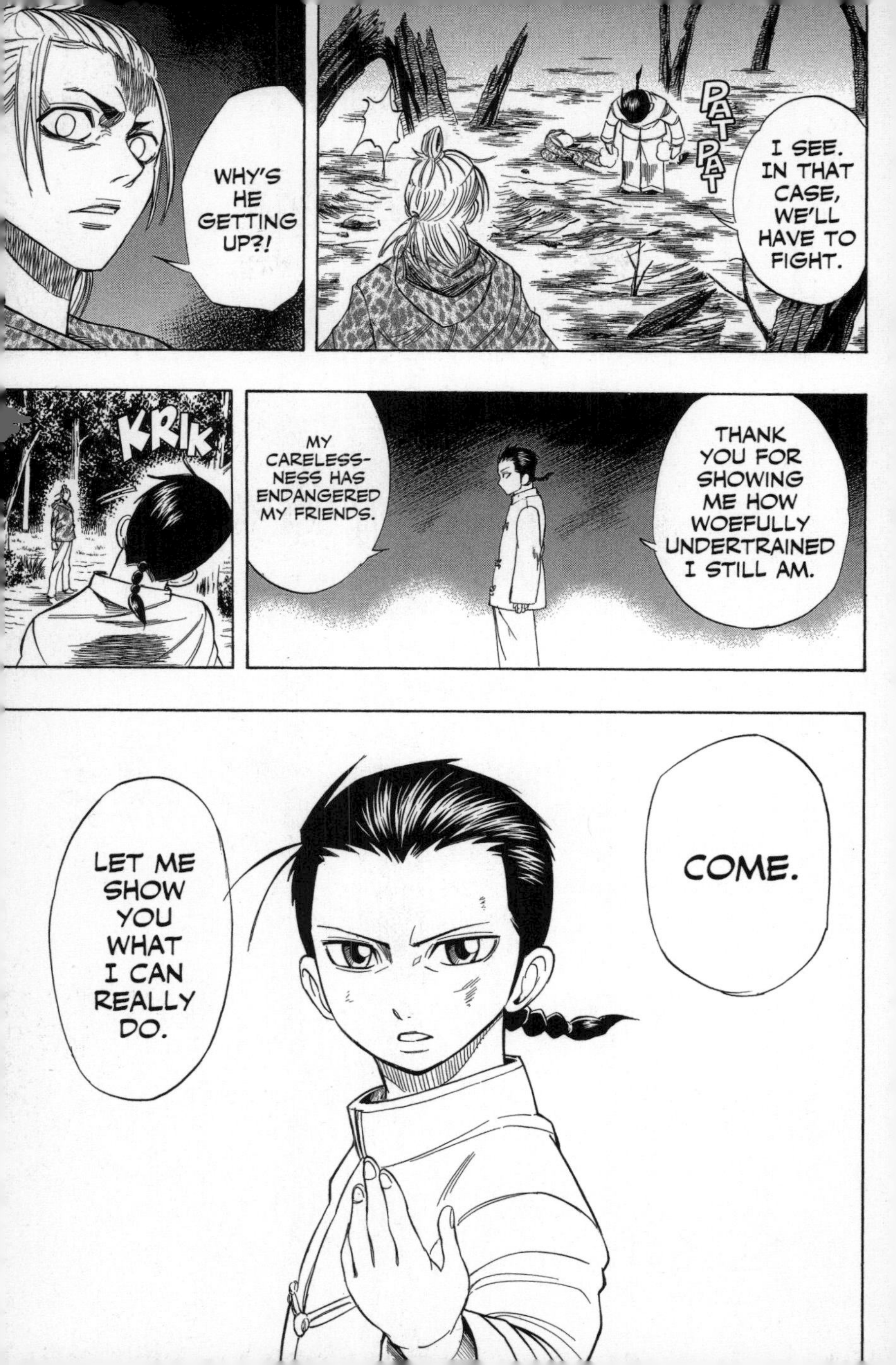
I SEE. IN THAT CASE, WE'LL HAVE TO FIGHT.
PAT PAT
WHY'S HE GETTING UP?!
THANK YOU FOR SHOWING ME HOW WOEFULLY UNDERTRAINED I STILL AM.
MY CARELESS-NESS HAS ENDANGERED MY FRIENDS.
KRIK
COME.
LET ME SHOW YOU WHAT I CAN REALLY DO.

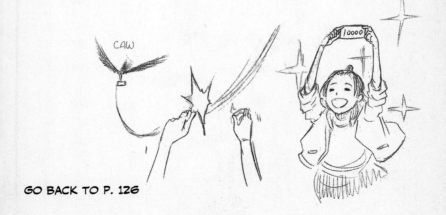

CAW

GO BACK TO P. 126

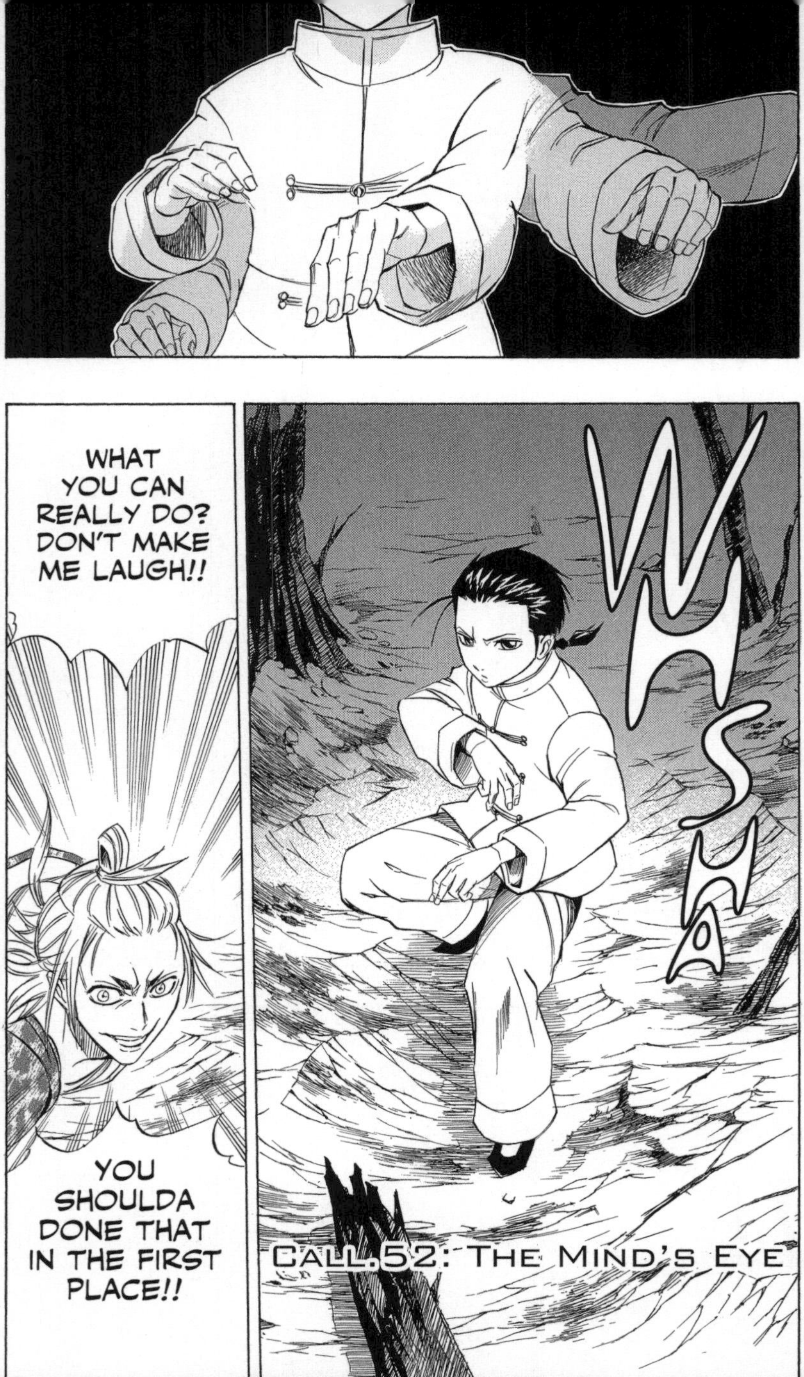
WHSHA
CALL.52: THE MIND'S EYE
WHAT YOU CAN REALLY DO? DON'T MAKE ME LAUGH!!
YOU SHOULDA DONE THAT IN THE FIRST PLACE!!

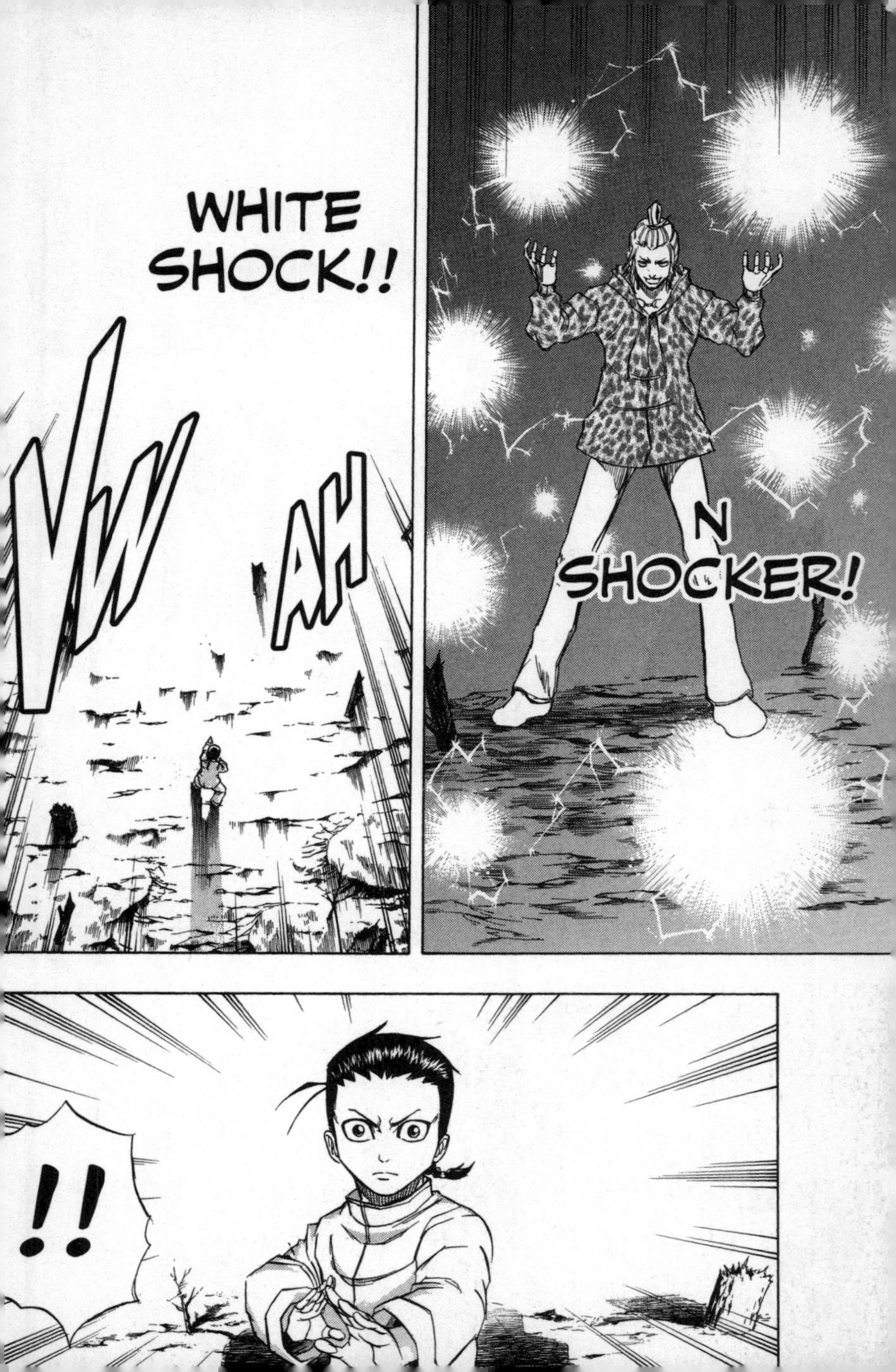
N
SHOCKER!
WHITE SHOCK!!
VWAH
!!

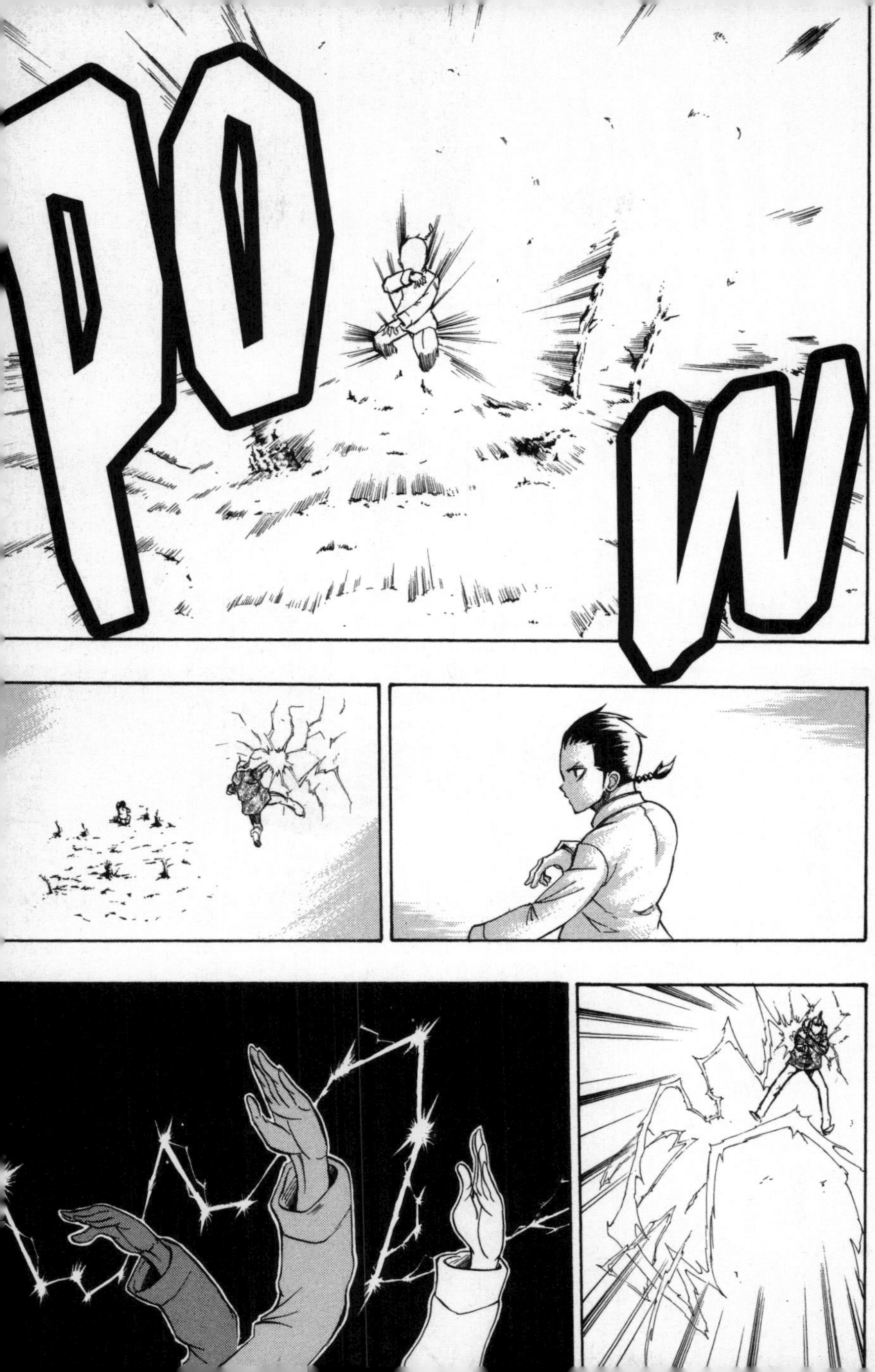
POW

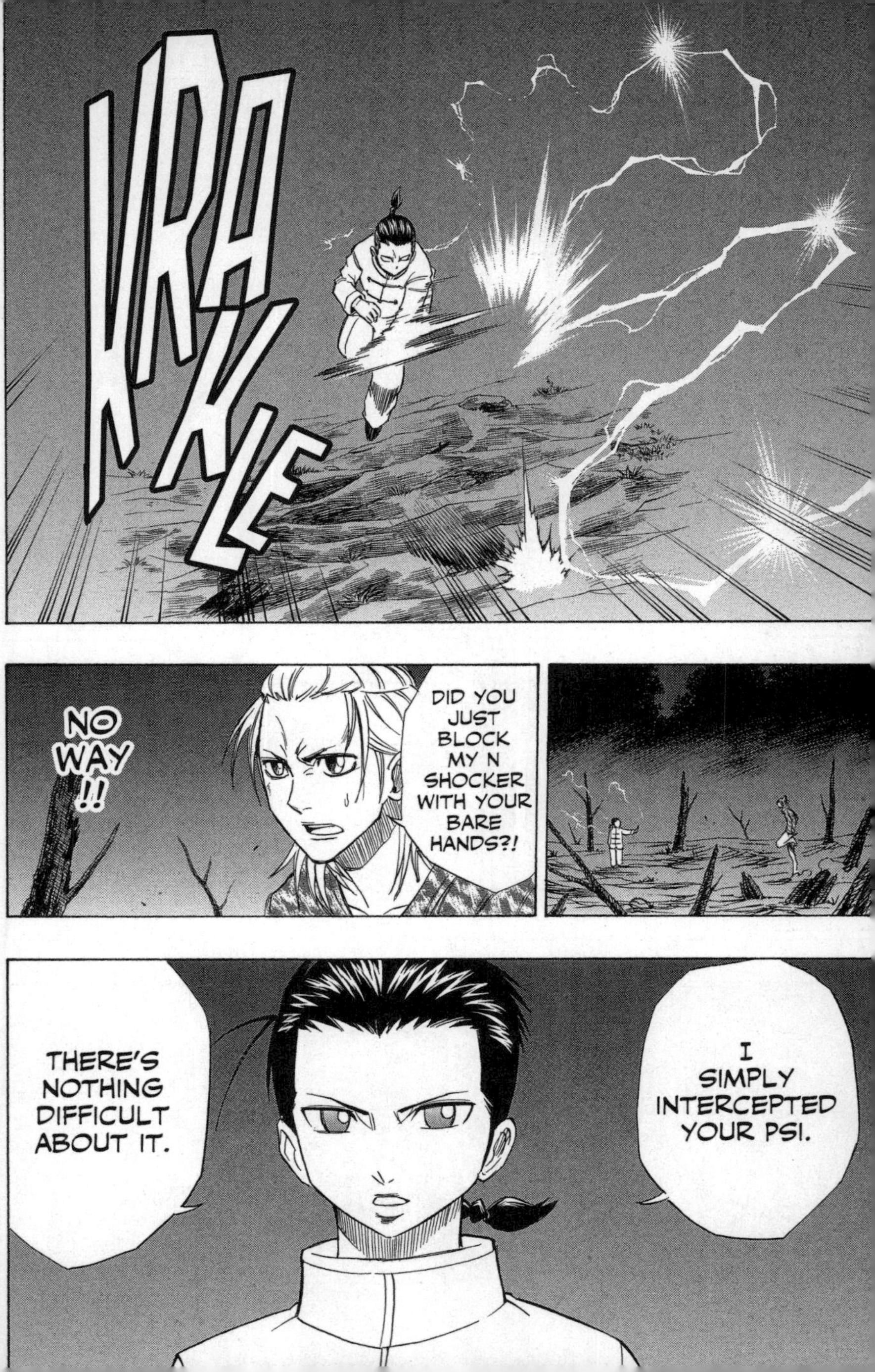
KRAKLE
DID YOU JUST BLOCK MY N SHOCKER WITH YOUR BARE HANDS?!
NO WAY!!
I SIMPLY INTERCEPTED YOUR PSI.
THERE'S NOTHING DIFFICULT ABOUT IT.

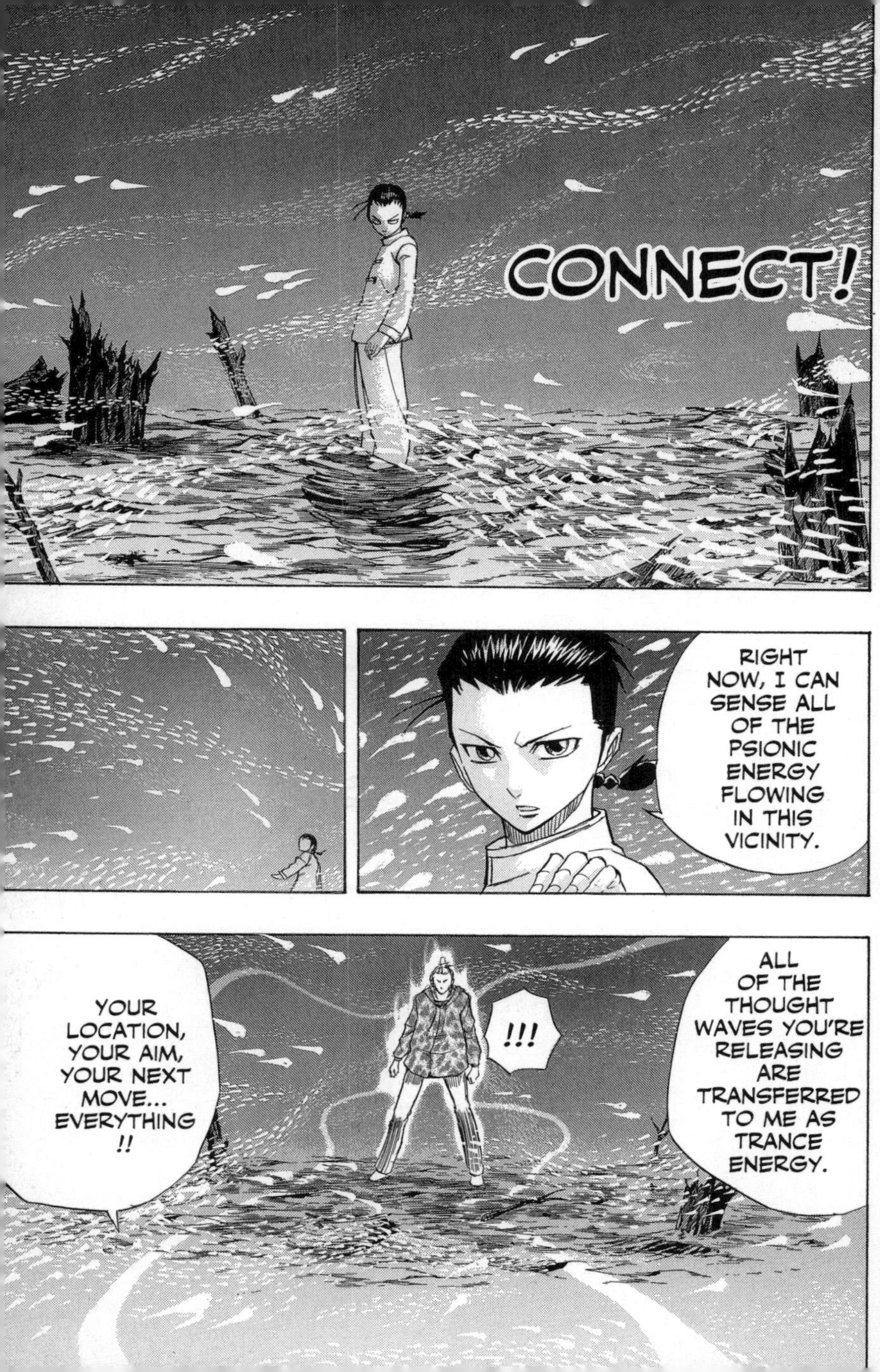
CONNECT!
RIGHT NOW, I CAN SENSE ALL OF THE PSIONIC ENERGY FLOWING IN THIS VICINITY.
ALL OF THE THOUGHT WAVES YOU'RE RELEASING ARE TRANSFERRED TO ME AS TRANCE ENERGY.
!!!
YOUR LOCATION, YOUR AIM, YOUR NEXT MOVE... EVERYTHING !!

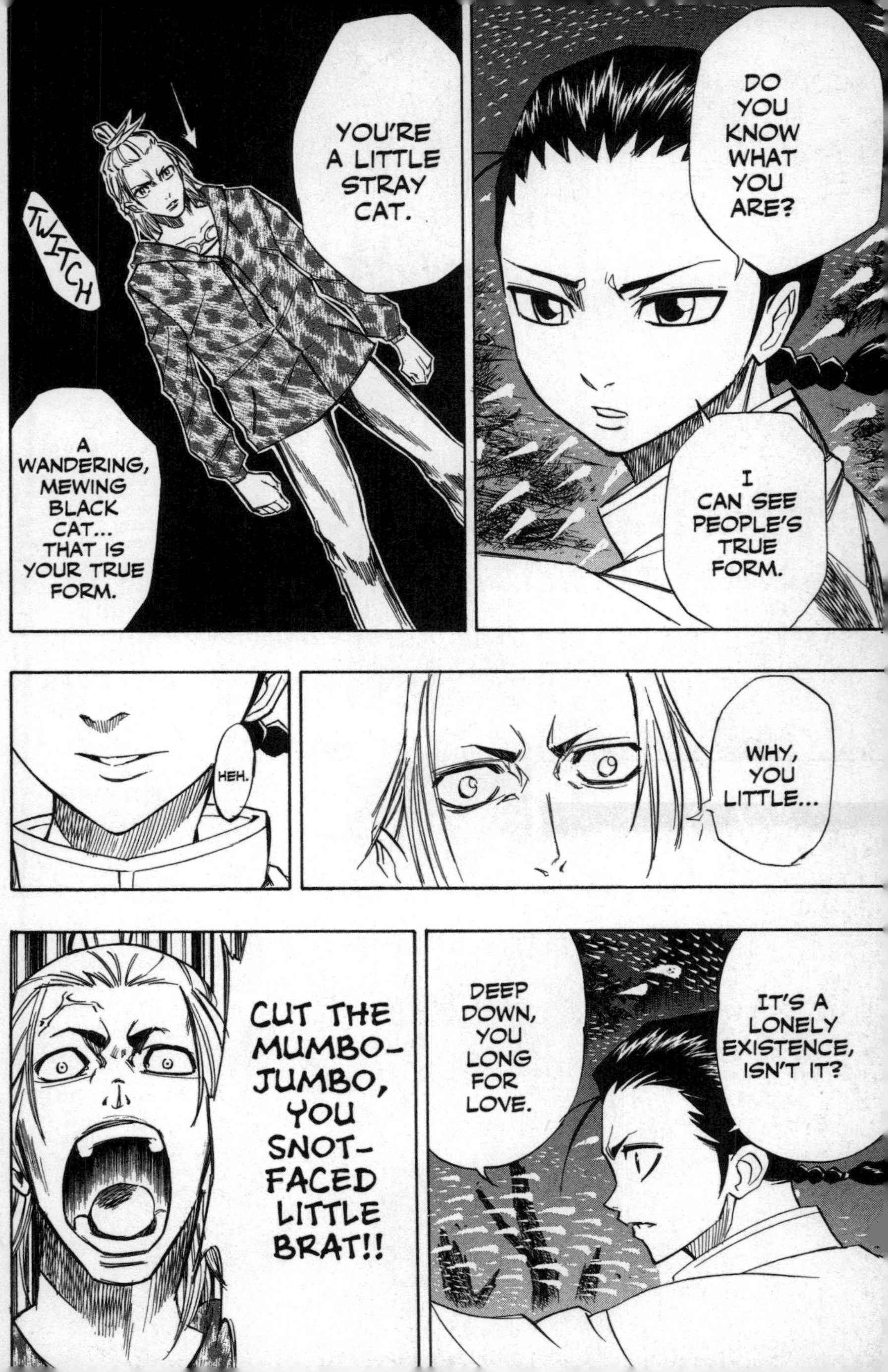
DO YOU KNOW WHAT YOU ARE?
I CAN SEE PEOPLE'S TRUE FORM.
YOU'RE A LITTLE STRAY CAT.
TWITCH
A WANDERING, MEWING BLACK CAT... THAT IS YOUR TRUE FORM.
WHY, YOU LITTLE...
HEH.
IT'S A LONELY EXISTENCE, ISN'T IT?
DEEP DOWN, YOU LONG FOR LOVE.
CUT THE MUMBO-JUMBO, YOU SNOT-FACED LITTLE BRAT!!

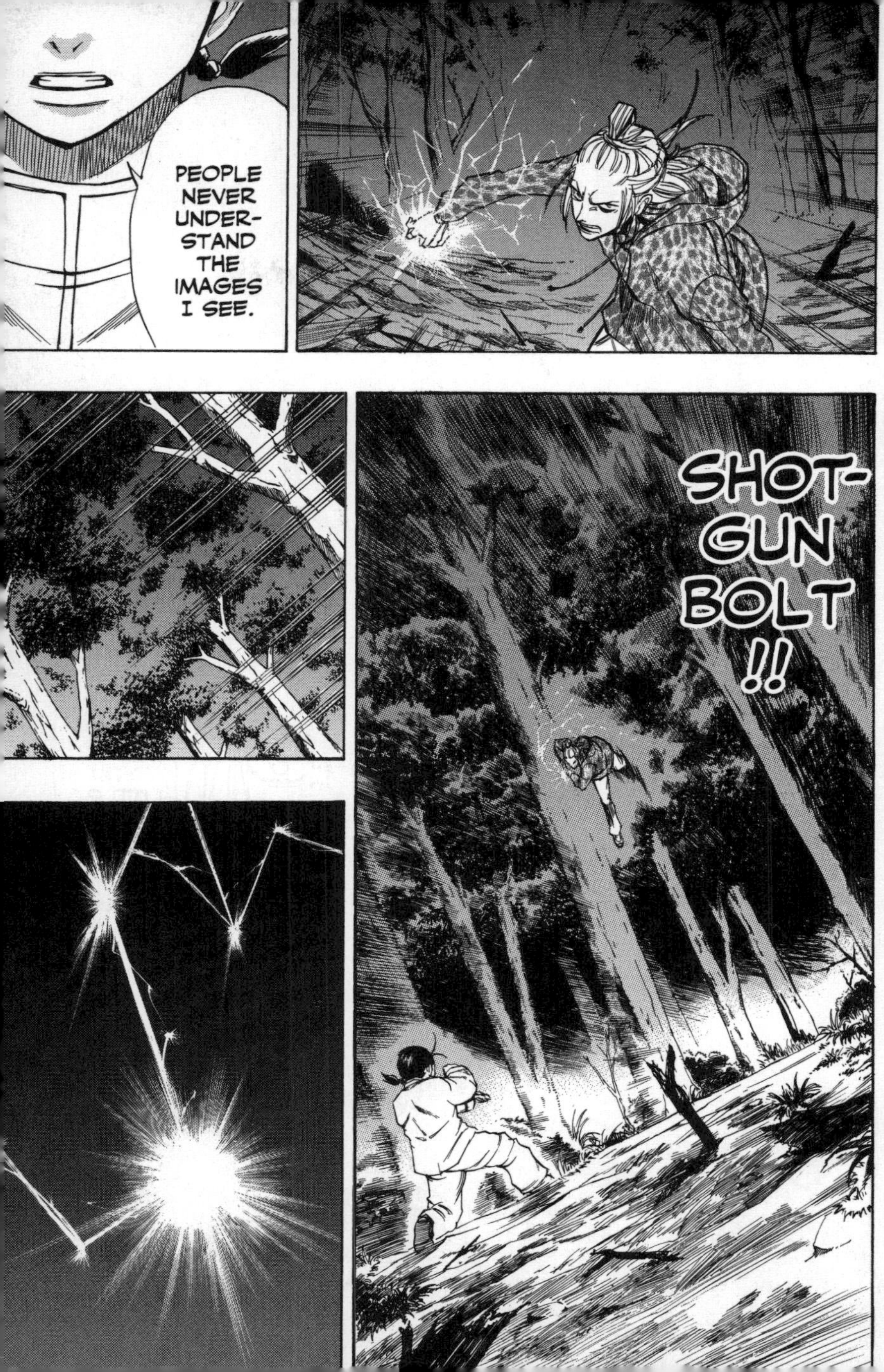
PEOPLE NEVER UNDER-STAND THE IMAGES I SEE.
SHOT-GUN BOLT !!

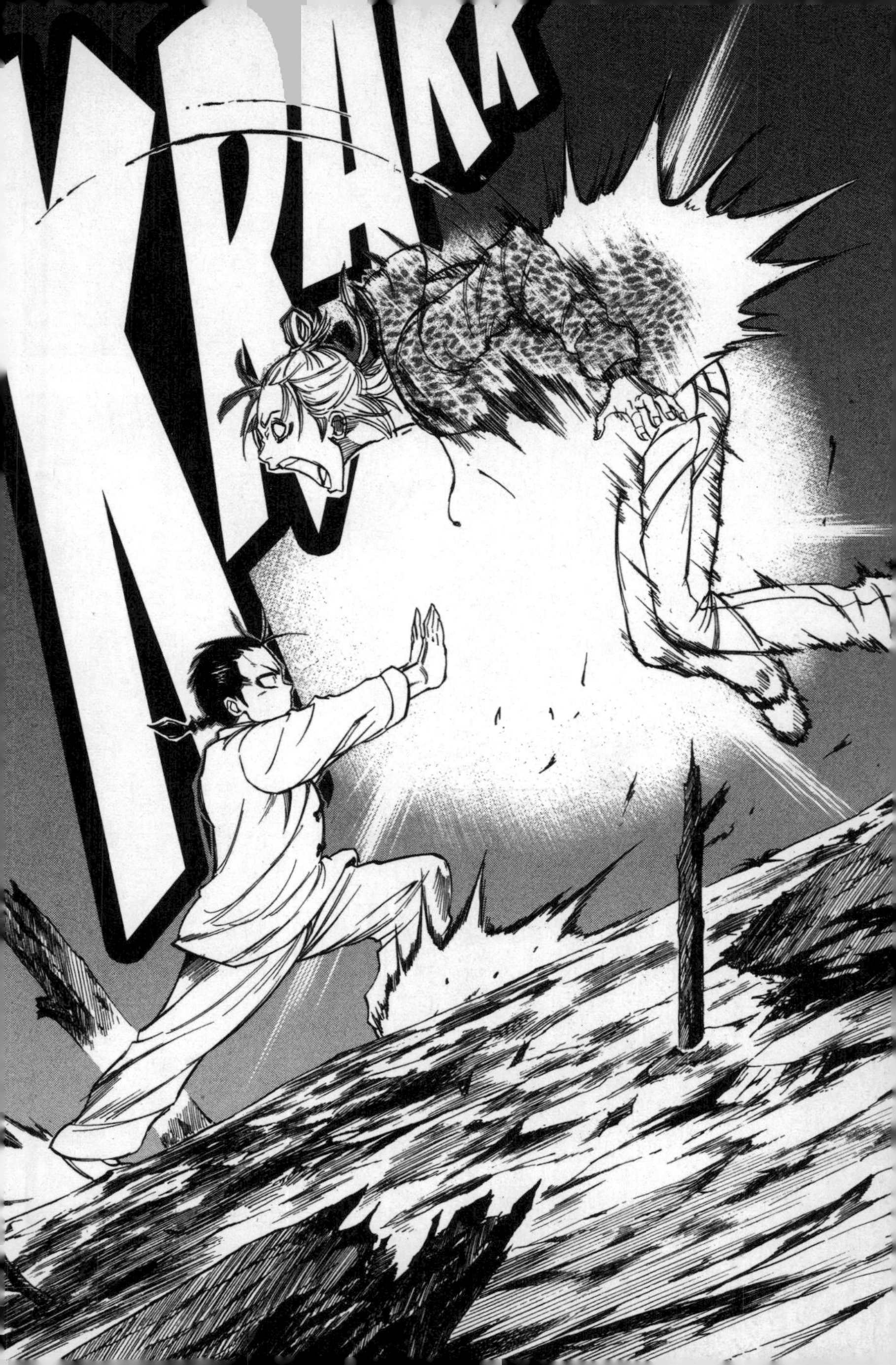

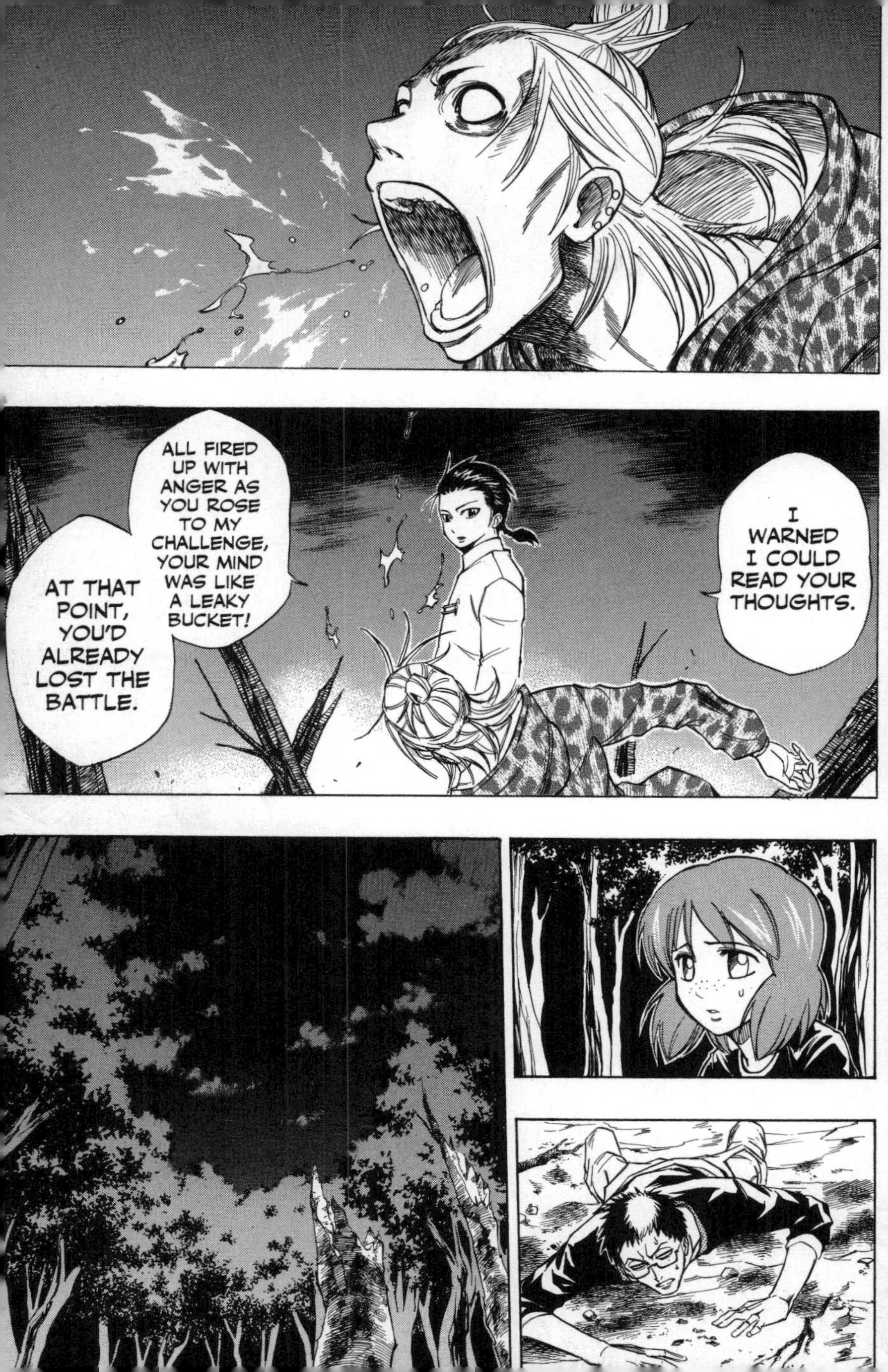
I WARNED I COULD READ YOUR THOUGHTS.
ALL FIRED UP WITH ANGER AS YOU ROSE TO MY CHALLENGE, YOUR MIND WAS LIKE A LEAKY BUCKET!
AT THAT POINT, YOU'D ALREADY LOST THE BATTLE.

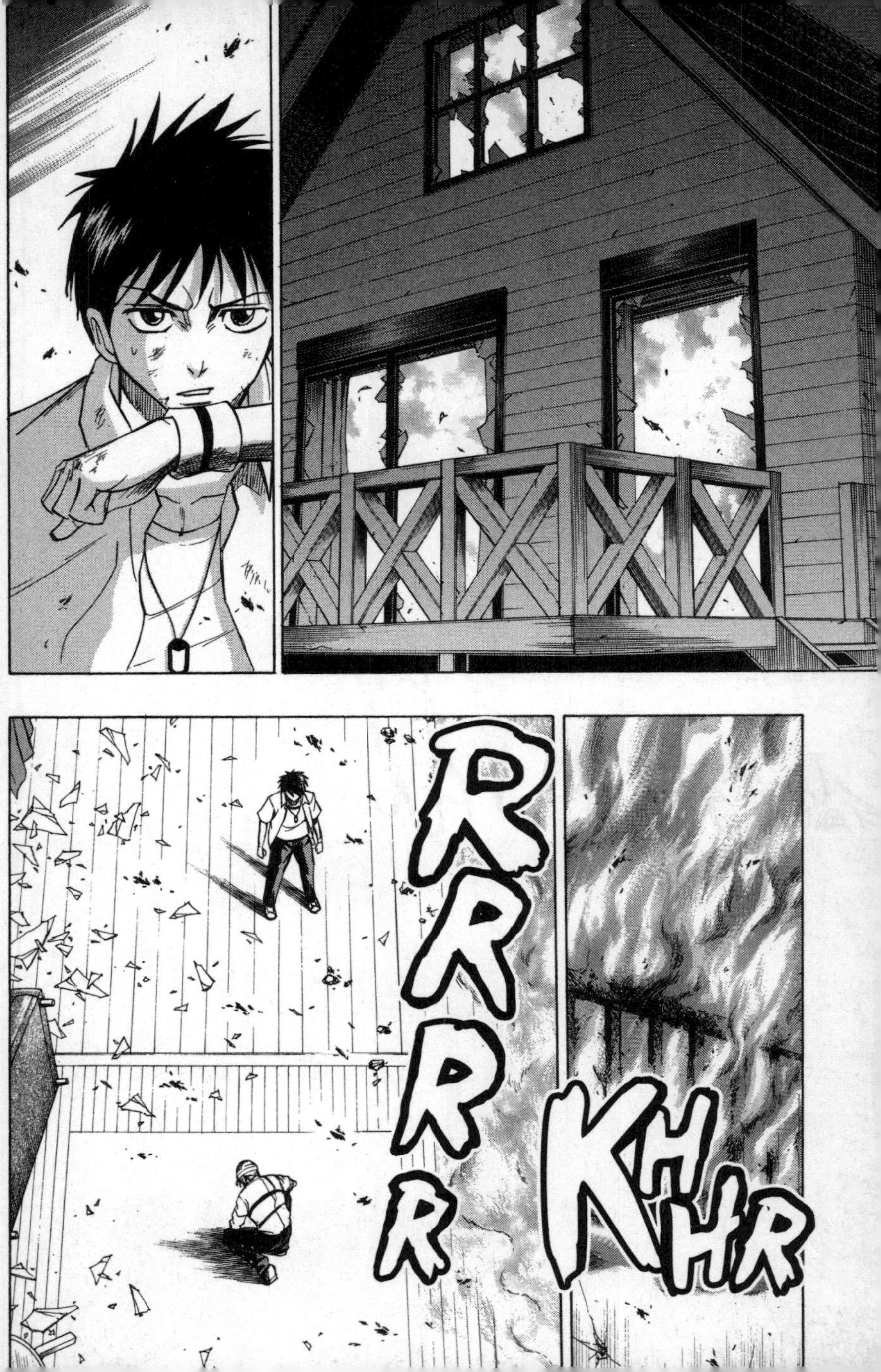
KHHR
RRRR

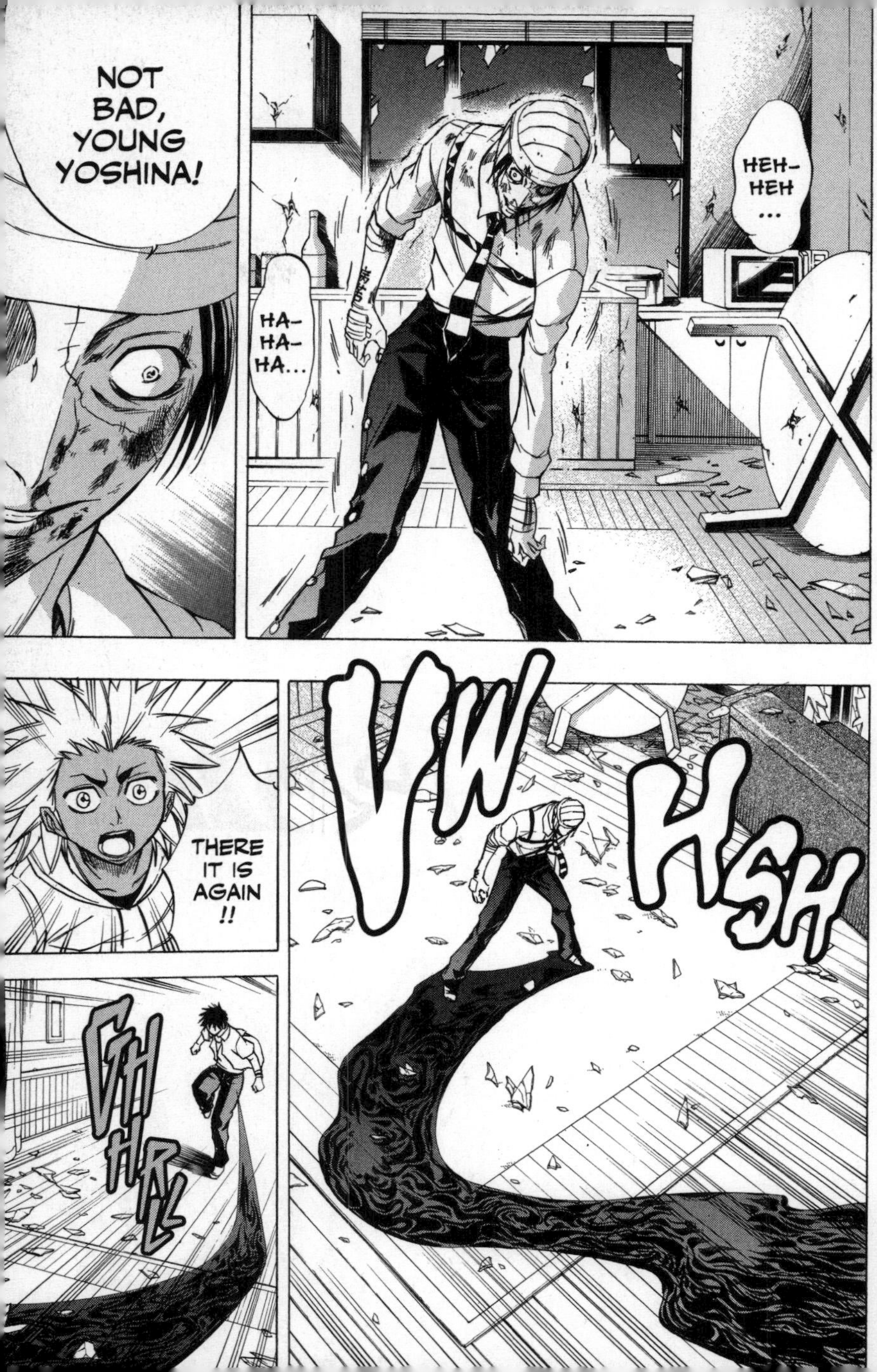
HEH-HEH...
HA-HA-HA...
NOT BAD, YOUNG YOSHINA!
VWHSH
THERE IT IS AGAIN!!

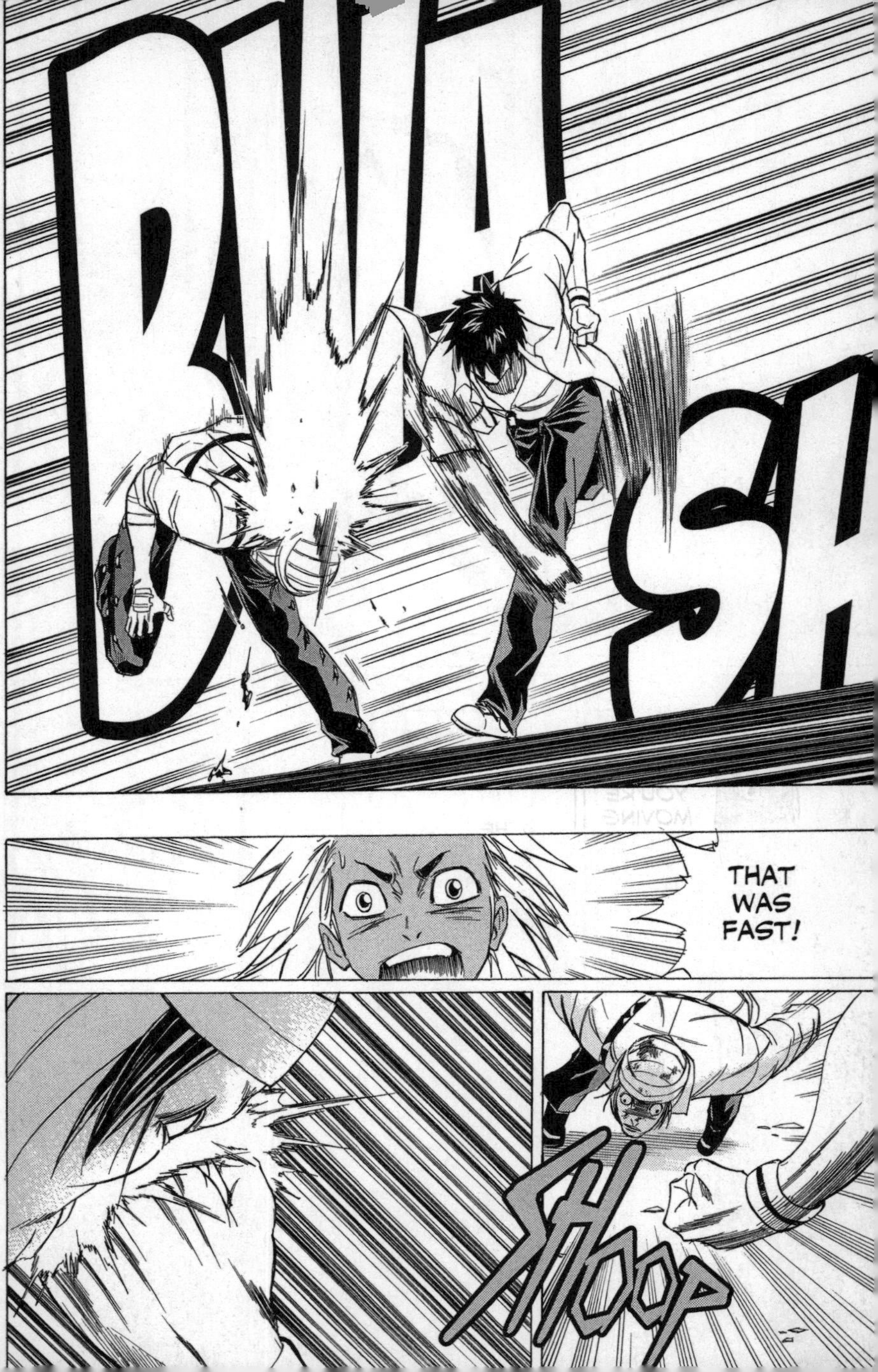
DWASH
THAT WAS FAST!
SHOOP

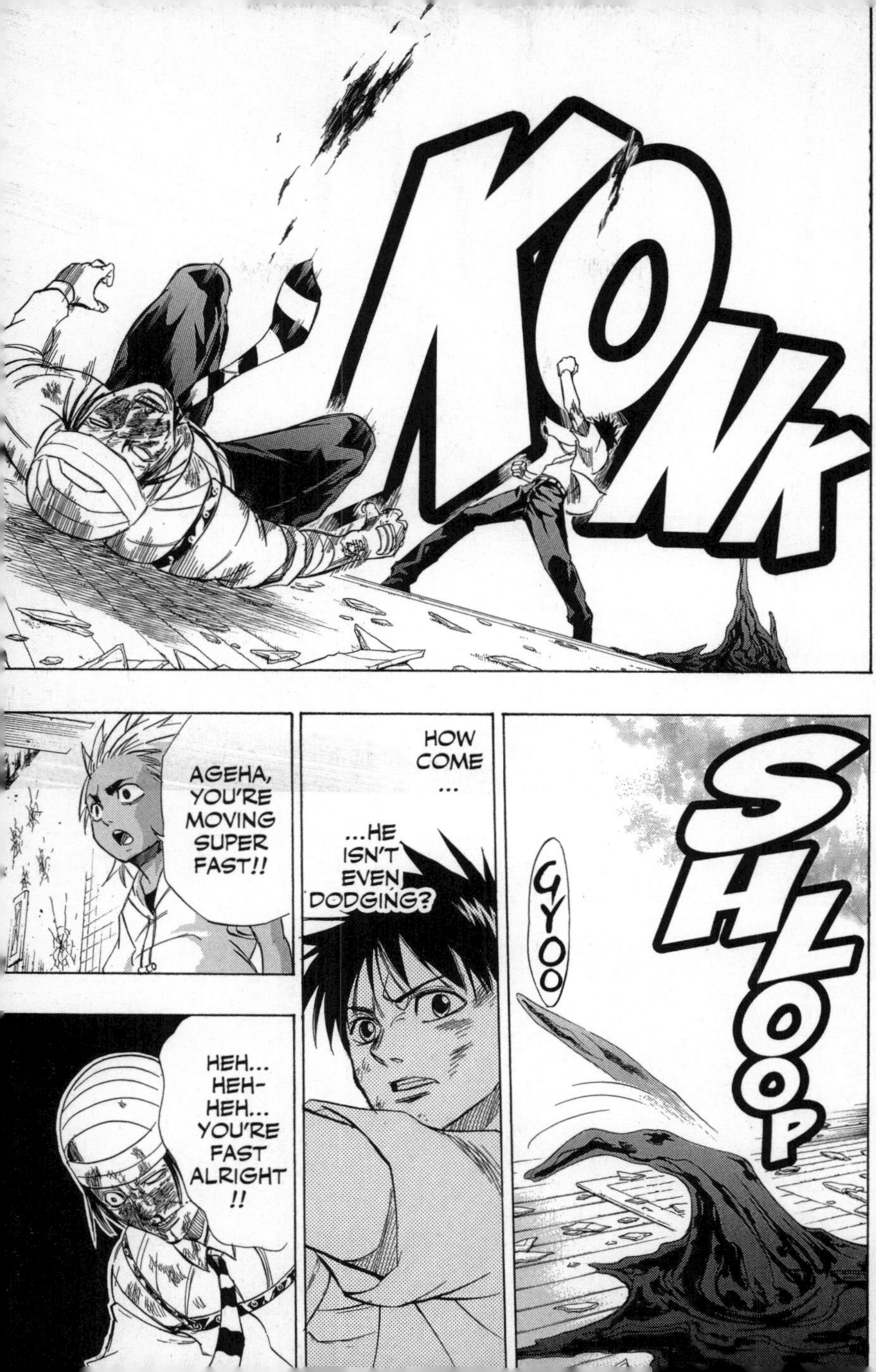
KONK
SHLOOP
GYOO
HOW COME ...
...HE ISN'T EVEN DODGING?
AGEHA, YOU'RE MOVING SUPER FAST!!
HEH... HEH-HEH... YOU'RE FAST ALRIGHT!!

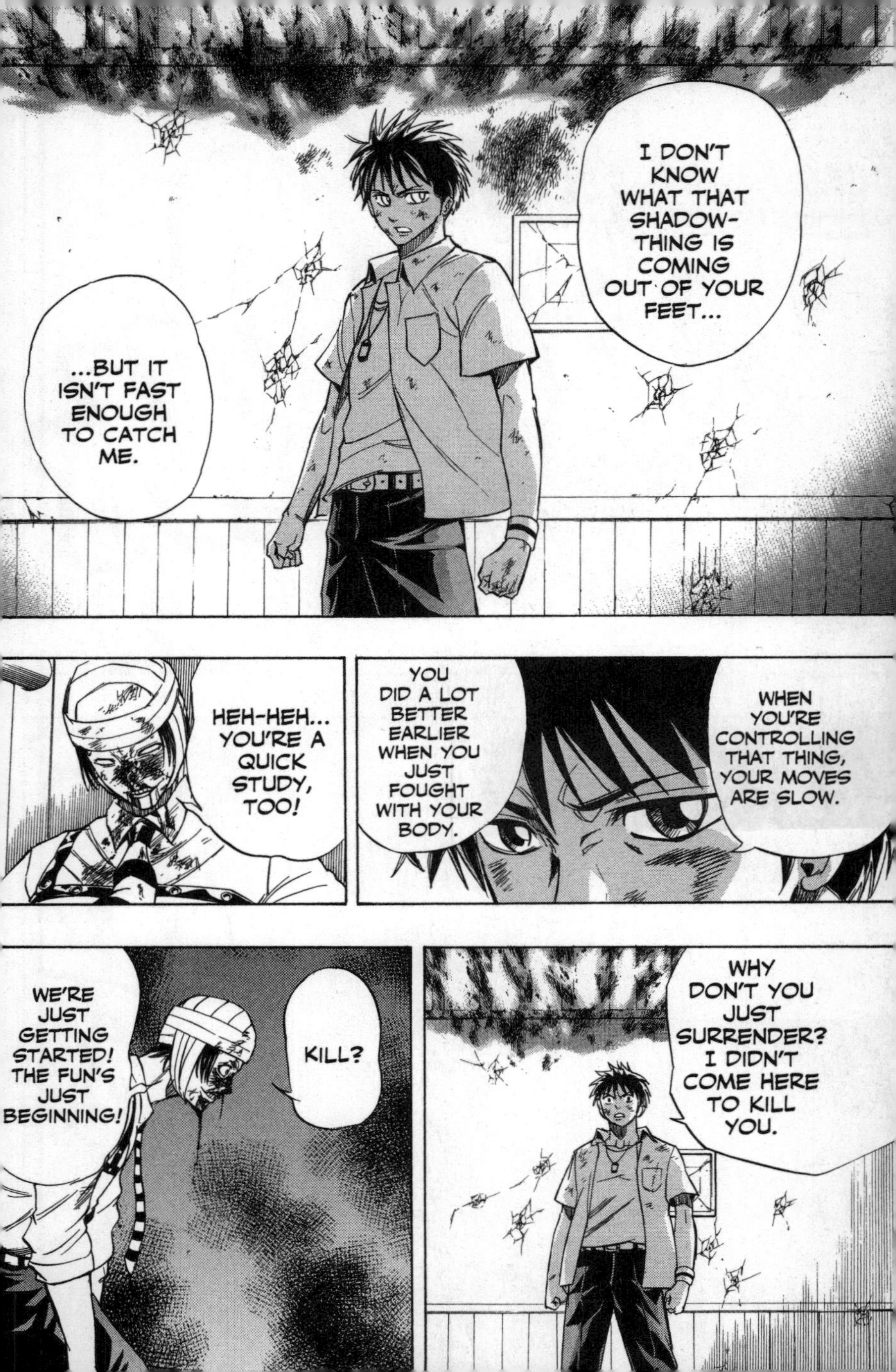
I DON'T KNOW WHAT THAT SHADOW-THING IS COMING OUT OF YOUR FEET...
...BUT IT ISN'T FAST ENOUGH TO CATCH ME.
WHEN YOU'RE CONTROLLING THAT THING, YOUR MOVES ARE SLOW.
YOU DID A LOT BETTER EARLIER WHEN YOU JUST FOUGHT WITH YOUR BODY.
HEH-HEH... YOU'RE A QUICK STUDY, TOO!
WHY DON'T YOU JUST SURRENDER? I DIDN'T COME HERE TO KILL YOU.
KILL?
WE'RE JUST GETTING STARTED! THE FUN'S JUST BEGINNING!

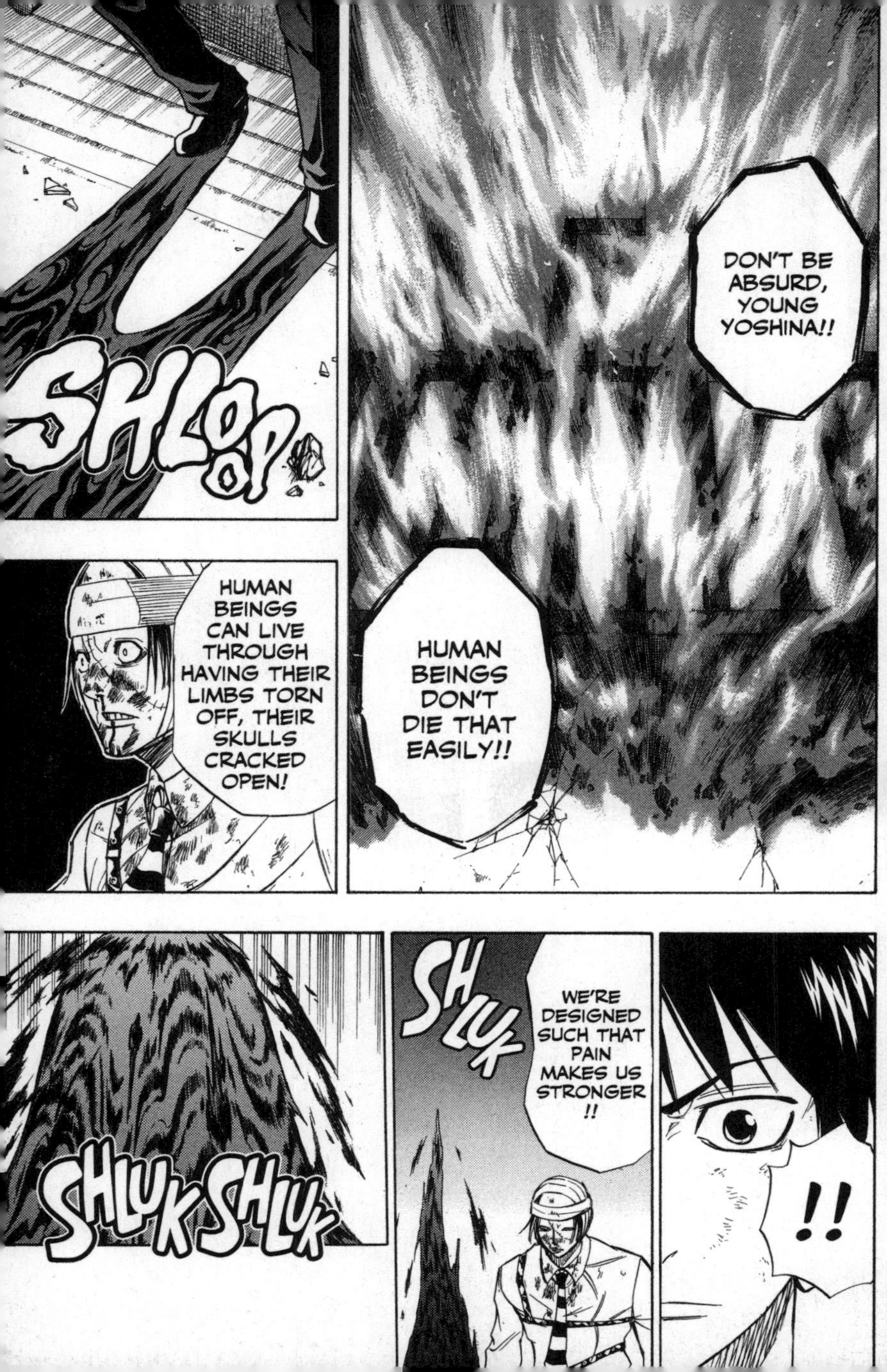
DON'T BE ABSURD, YOUNG YOSHINA!!
HUMAN BEINGS DON'T DIE THAT EASILY!!
SHLOOP
HUMAN BEINGS CAN LIVE THROUGH HAVING THEIR LIMBS TORN OFF, THEIR SKULLS CRACKED OPEN!
!!
WE'RE DESIGNED SUCH THAT PAIN MAKES US STRONGER!!
SHLUK
SHLUK SHLUK

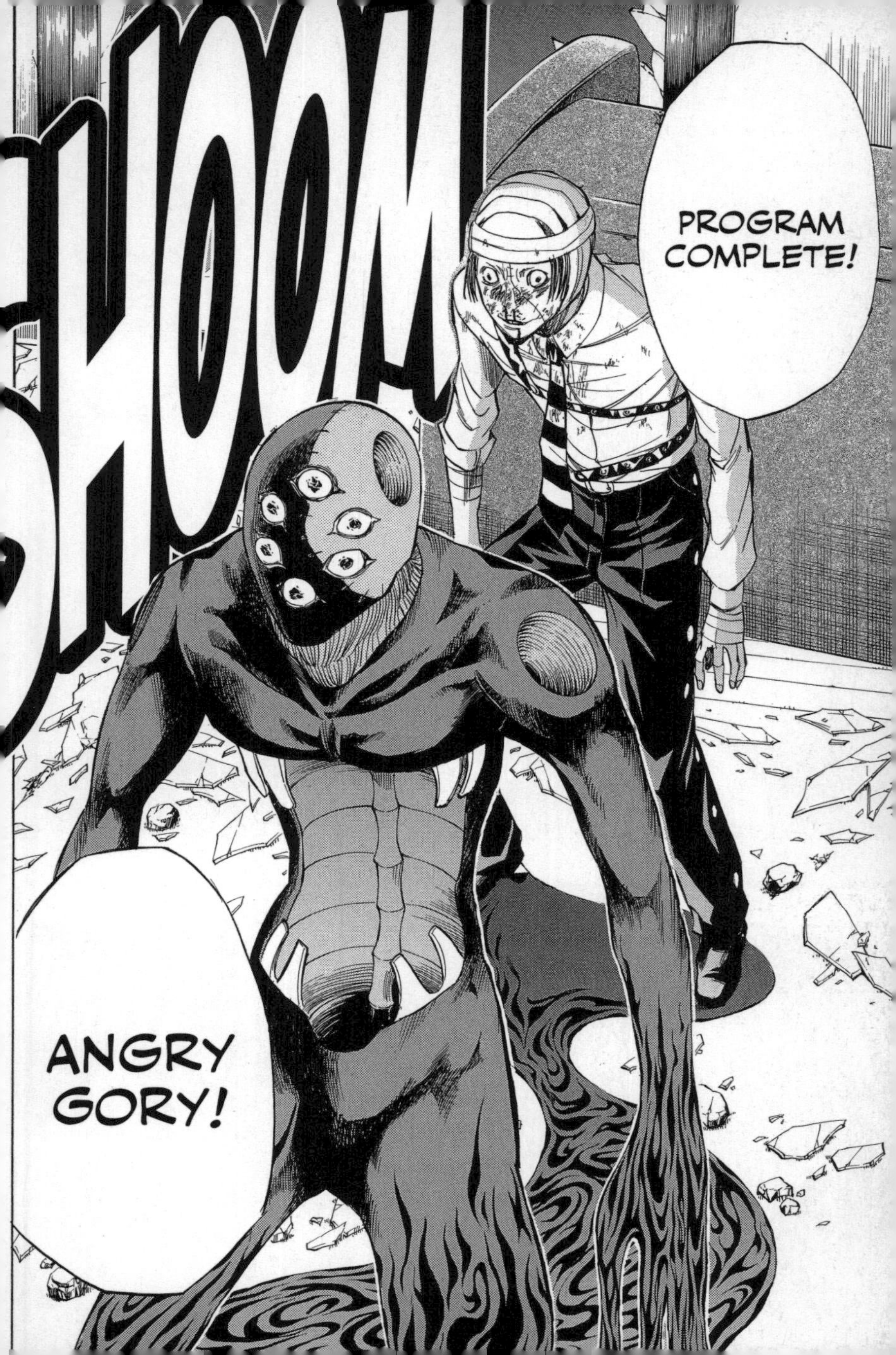
PROGRAM COMPLETE!
SHOOM
ANGRY GORY!

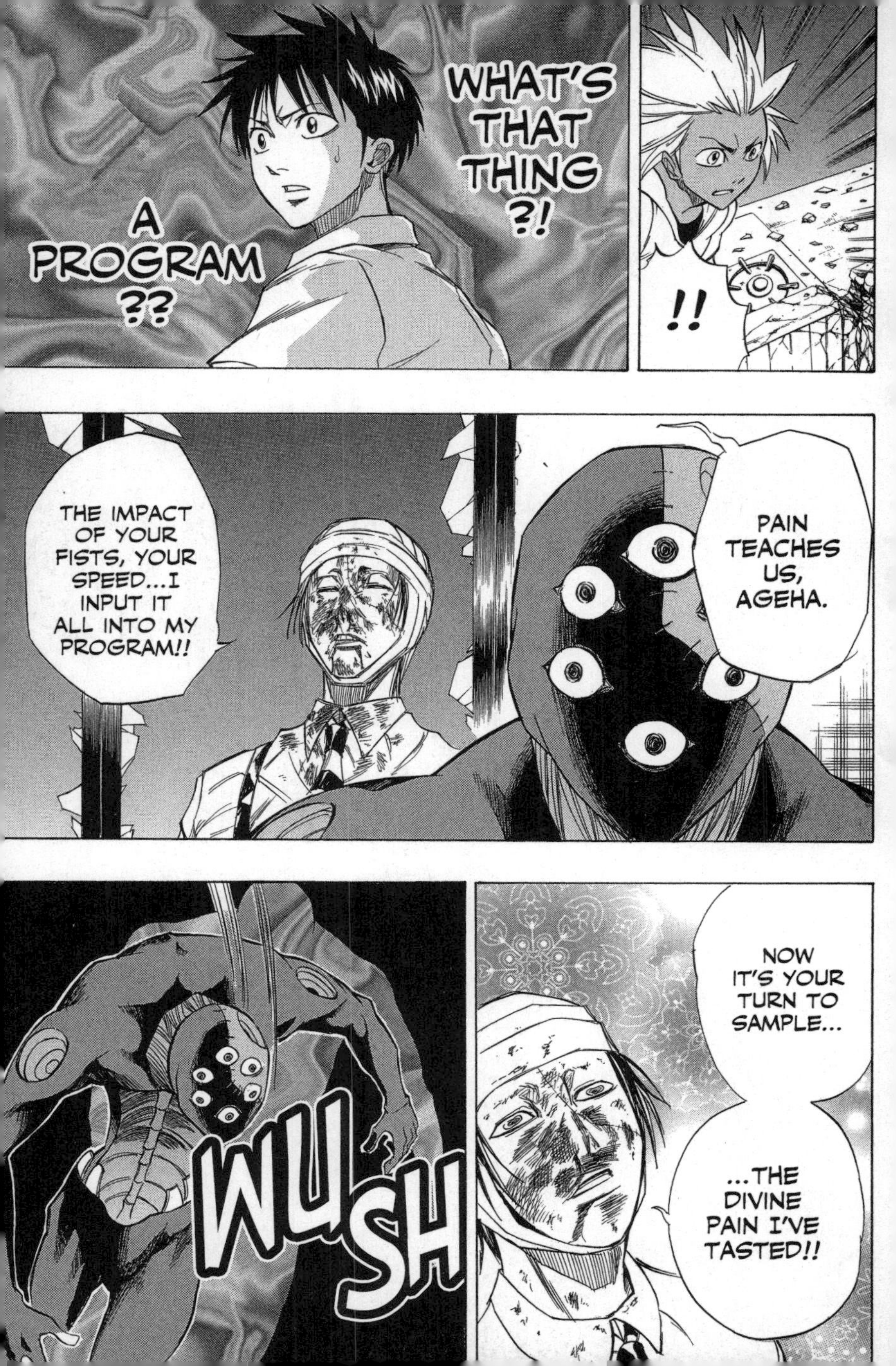
!!
WHAT'S THAT THING ?!
A PROGRAM ??
PAIN TEACHES US, AGEHA.
THE IMPACT OF YOUR FISTS, YOUR SPEED...I INPUT IT ALL INTO MY PROGRAM!!
NOW IT'S YOUR TURN TO SAMPLE...
...THE DIVINE PAIN I'VE TASTED!!
WUSH

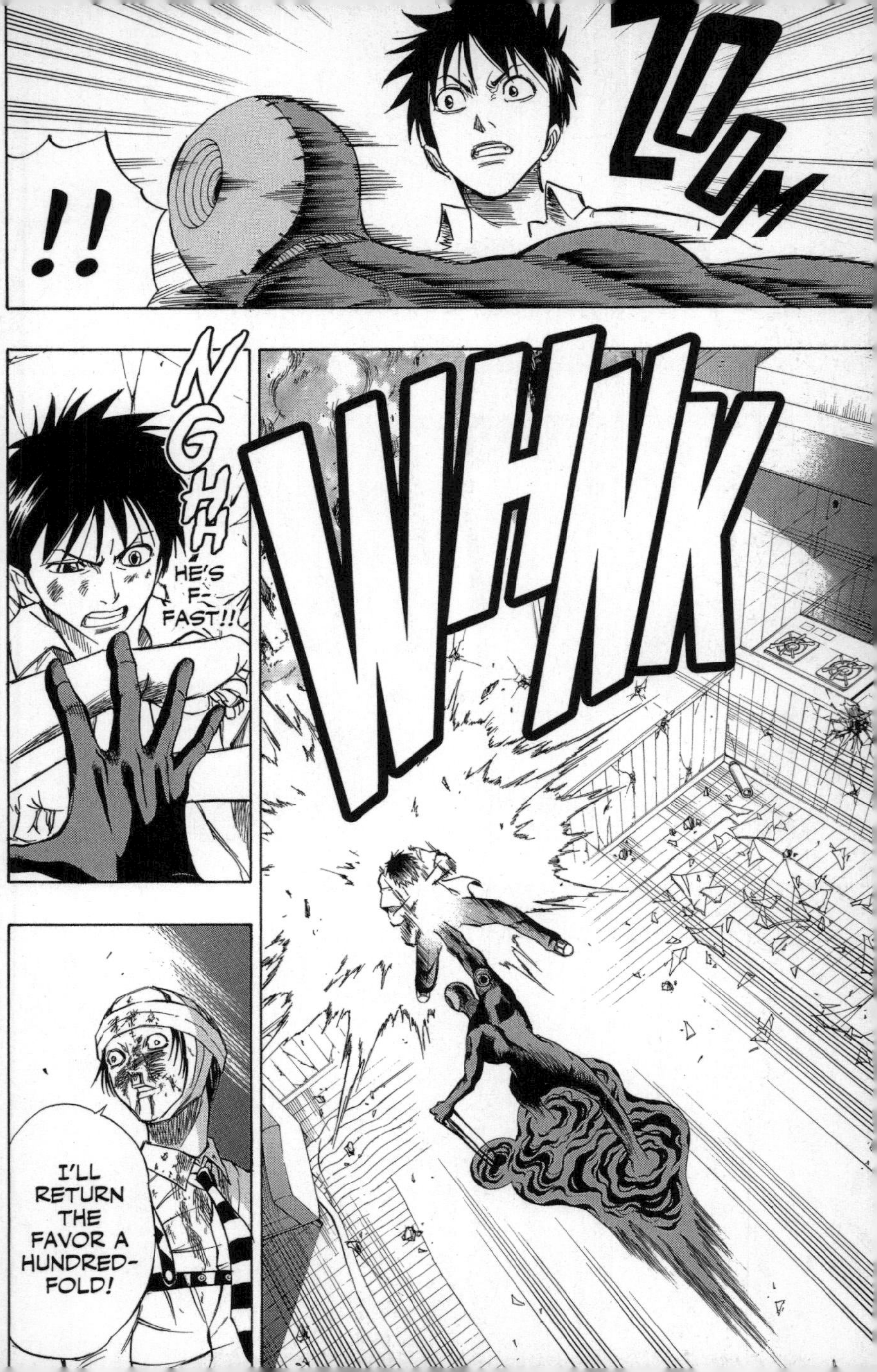
ZOOM
!!
WHNK
NGHH
HE'S F-FAST!!
I'LL RETURN THE FAVOR A HUNDRED-FOLD!

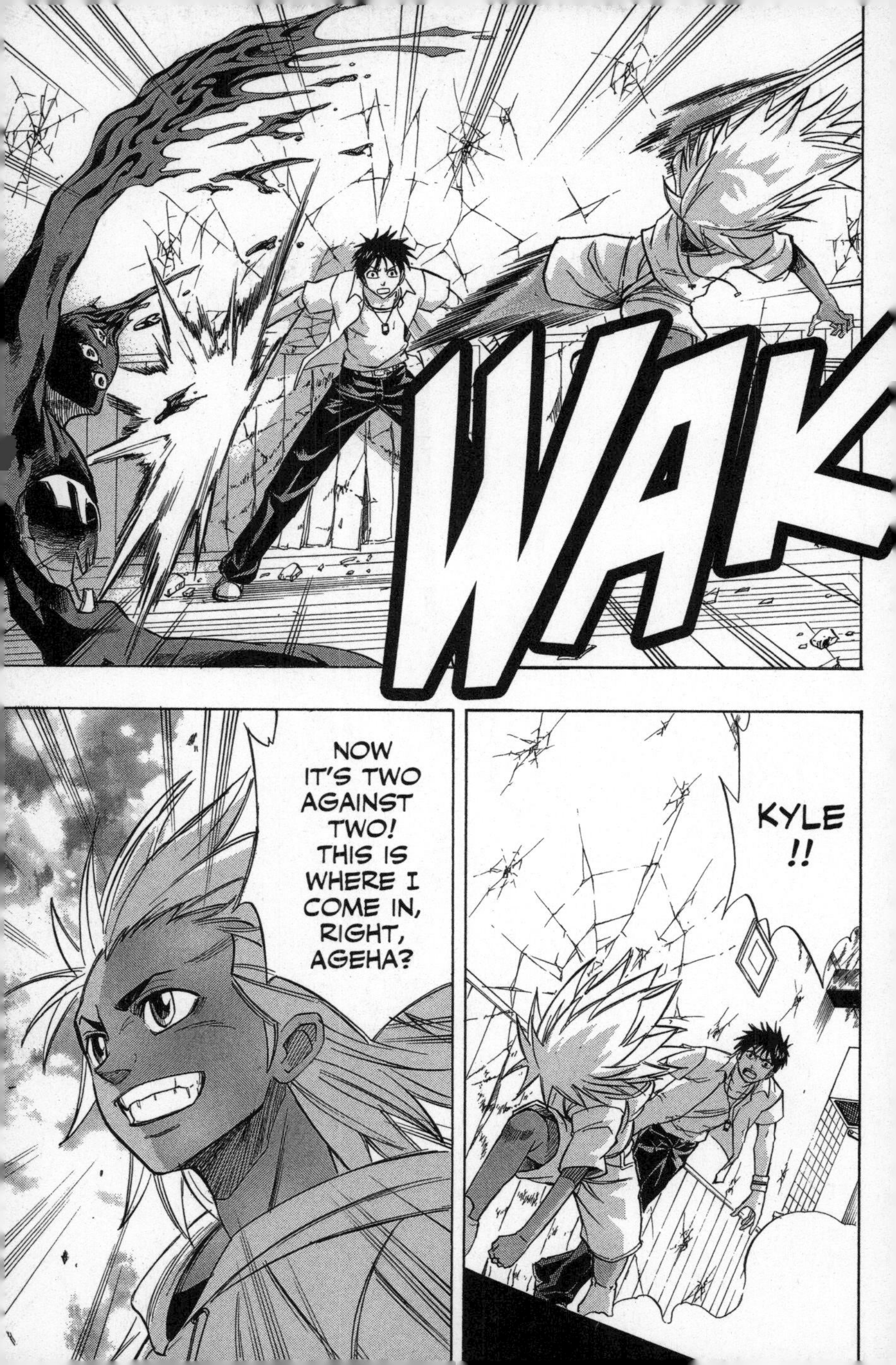
WAK
KYLE !!
NOW IT'S TWO AGAINST TWO! THIS IS WHERE I COME IN, RIGHT, AGEHA?

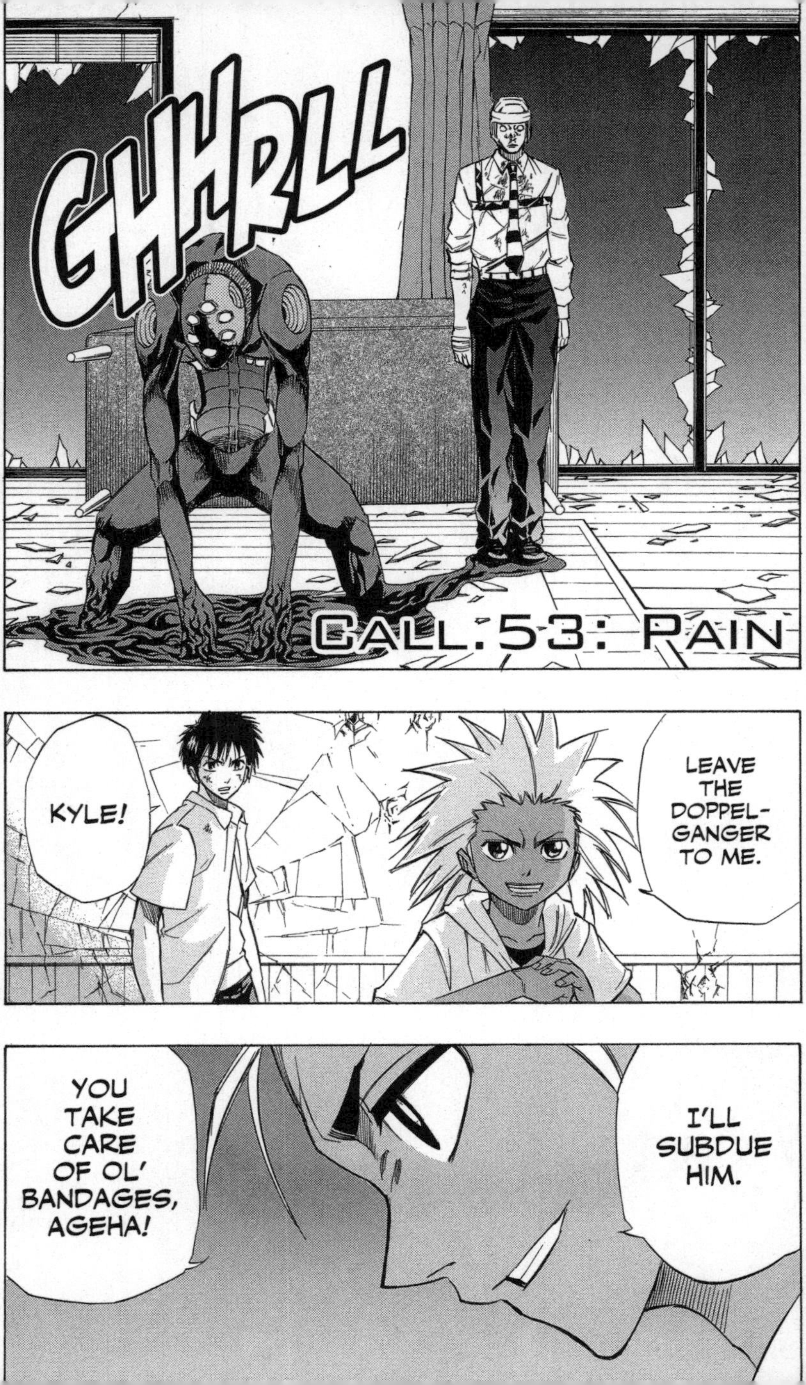
GHHRLL
CALL.53: PAIN
LEAVE THE DOPPEL-GANGER TO ME.
KYLE!
I'LL SUBDUE HIM.
YOU TAKE CARE OF OL' BANDAGES, AGEHA!

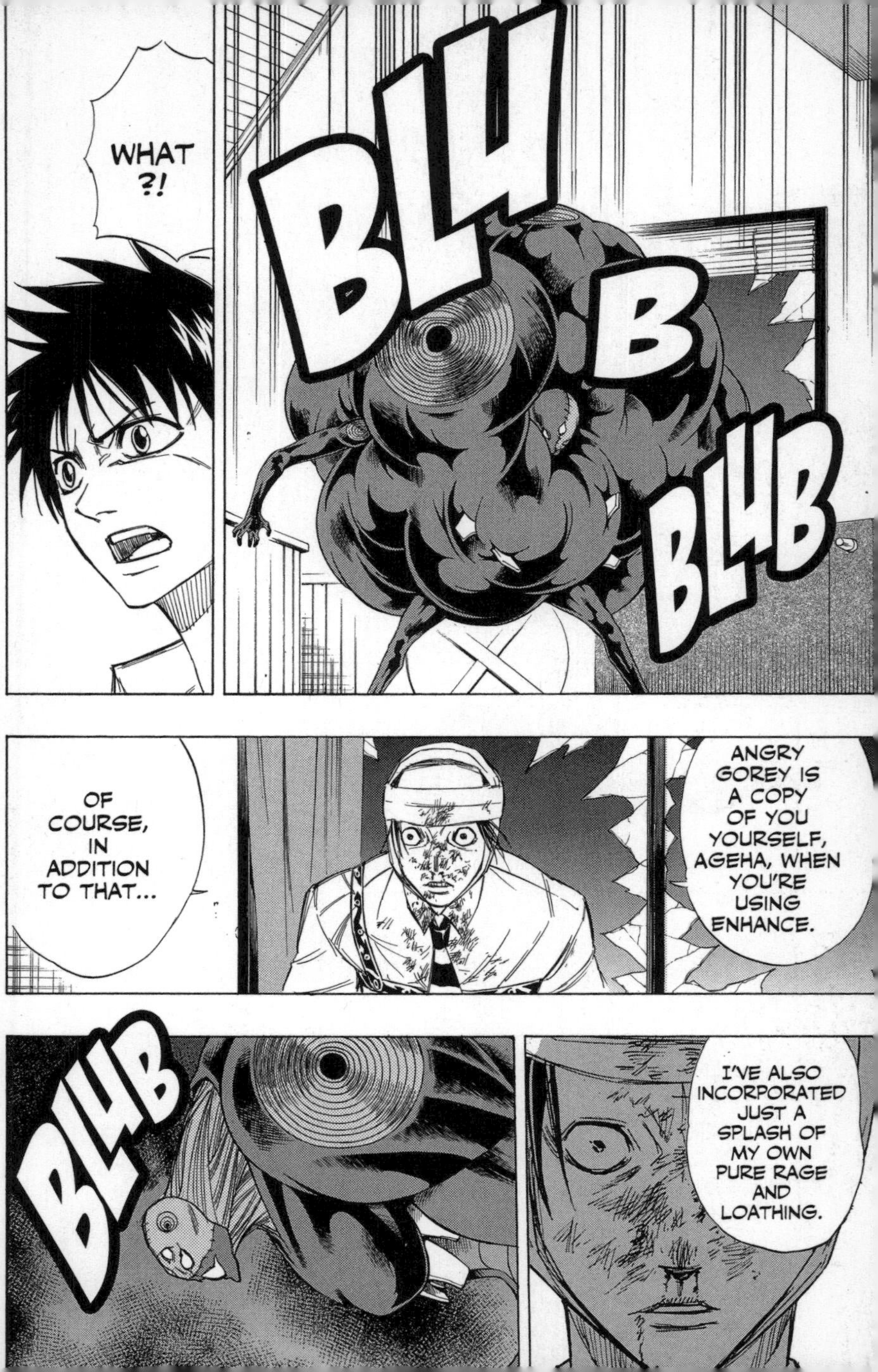
BLUB
BLUB
WHAT ?!
ANGRY GOREY IS A COPY OF YOU YOURSELF, AGEHA, WHEN YOU'RE USING ENHANCE.
OF COURSE, IN ADDITION TO THAT...
I'VE ALSO INCORPORATED JUST A SPLASH OF MY OWN PURE RAGE AND LOATHING.
BLUB

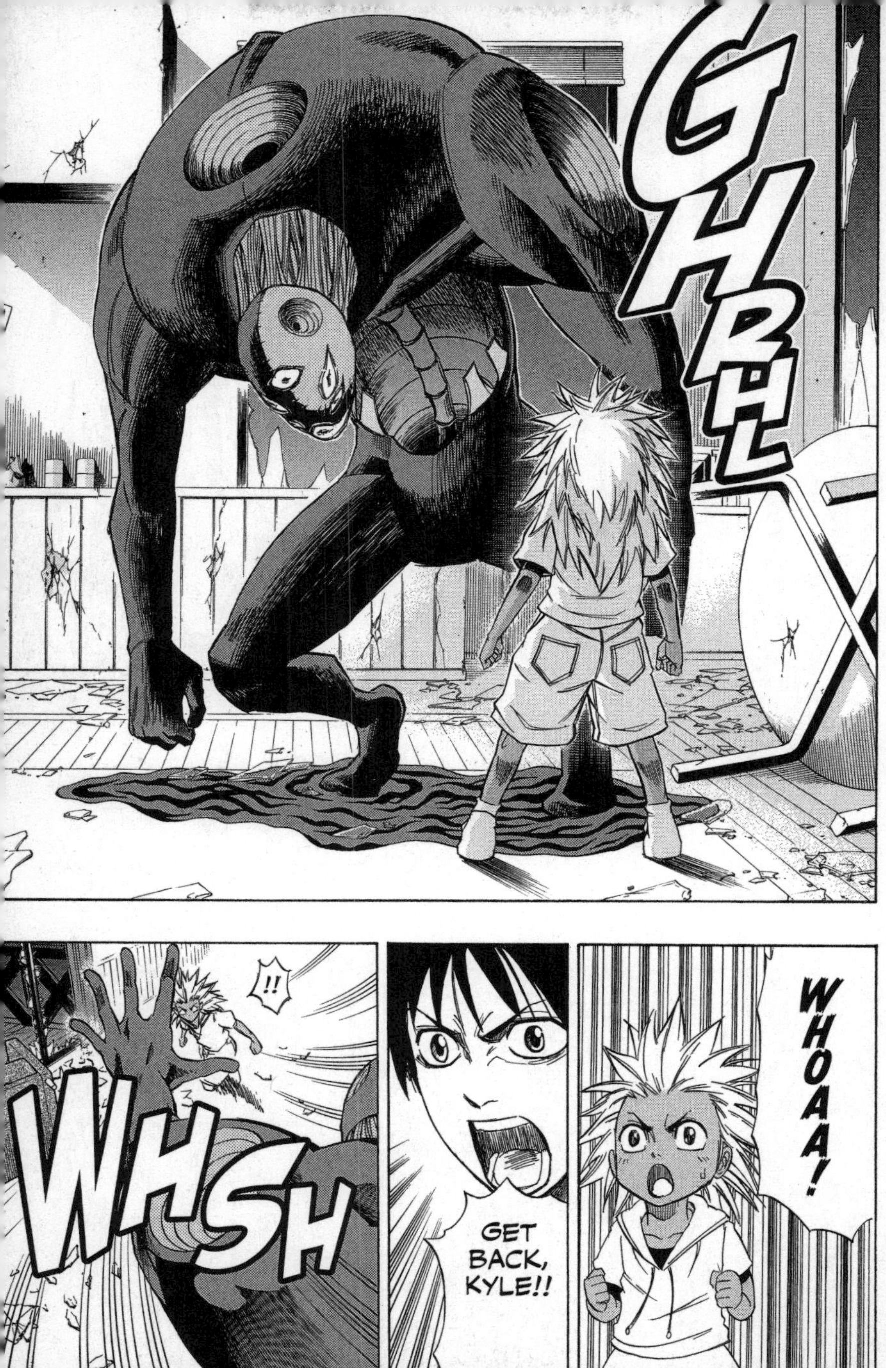
GHRHL
WHOAA!
GET BACK, KYLE!!
!!
WHSH

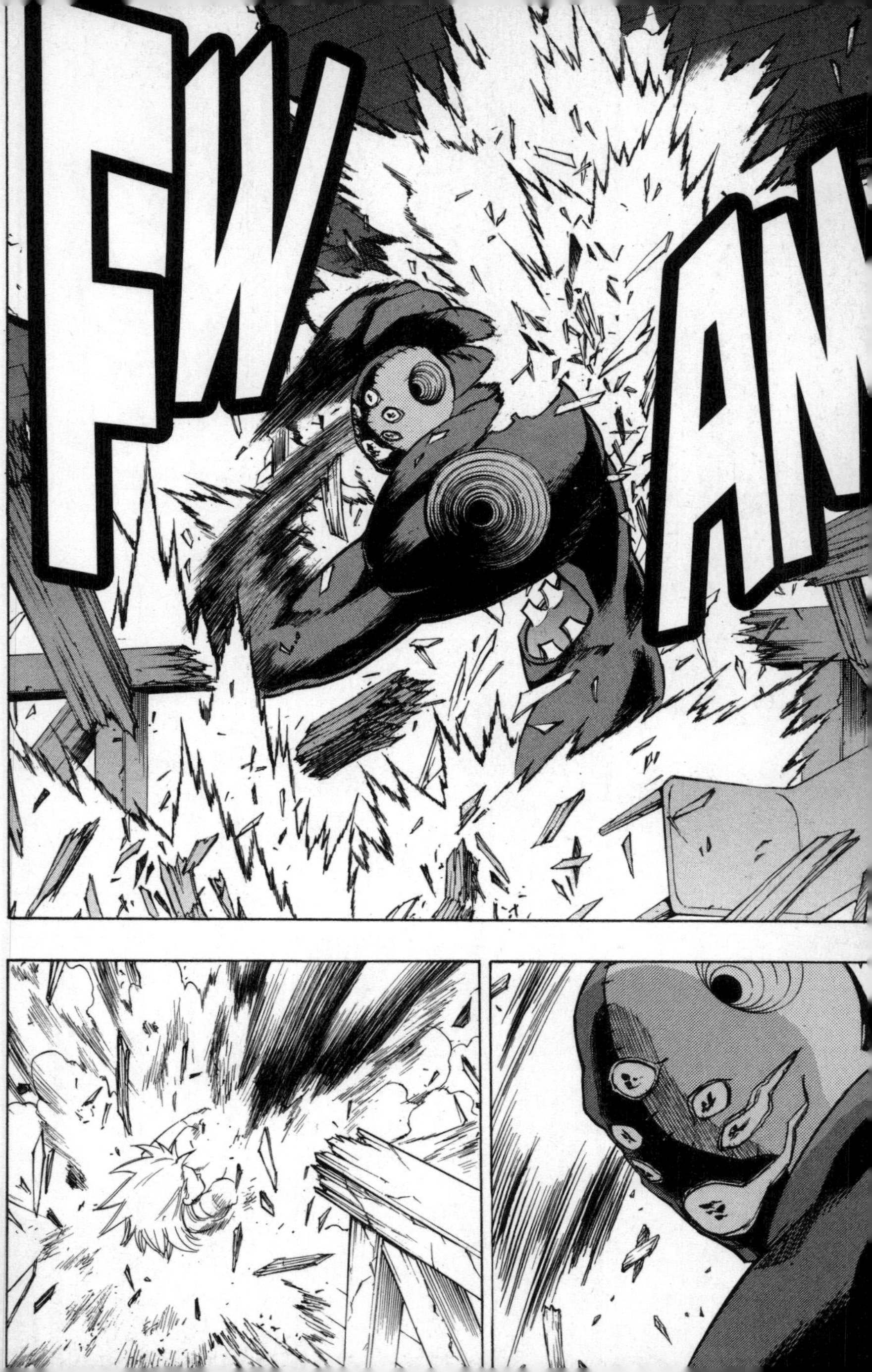
FWAM

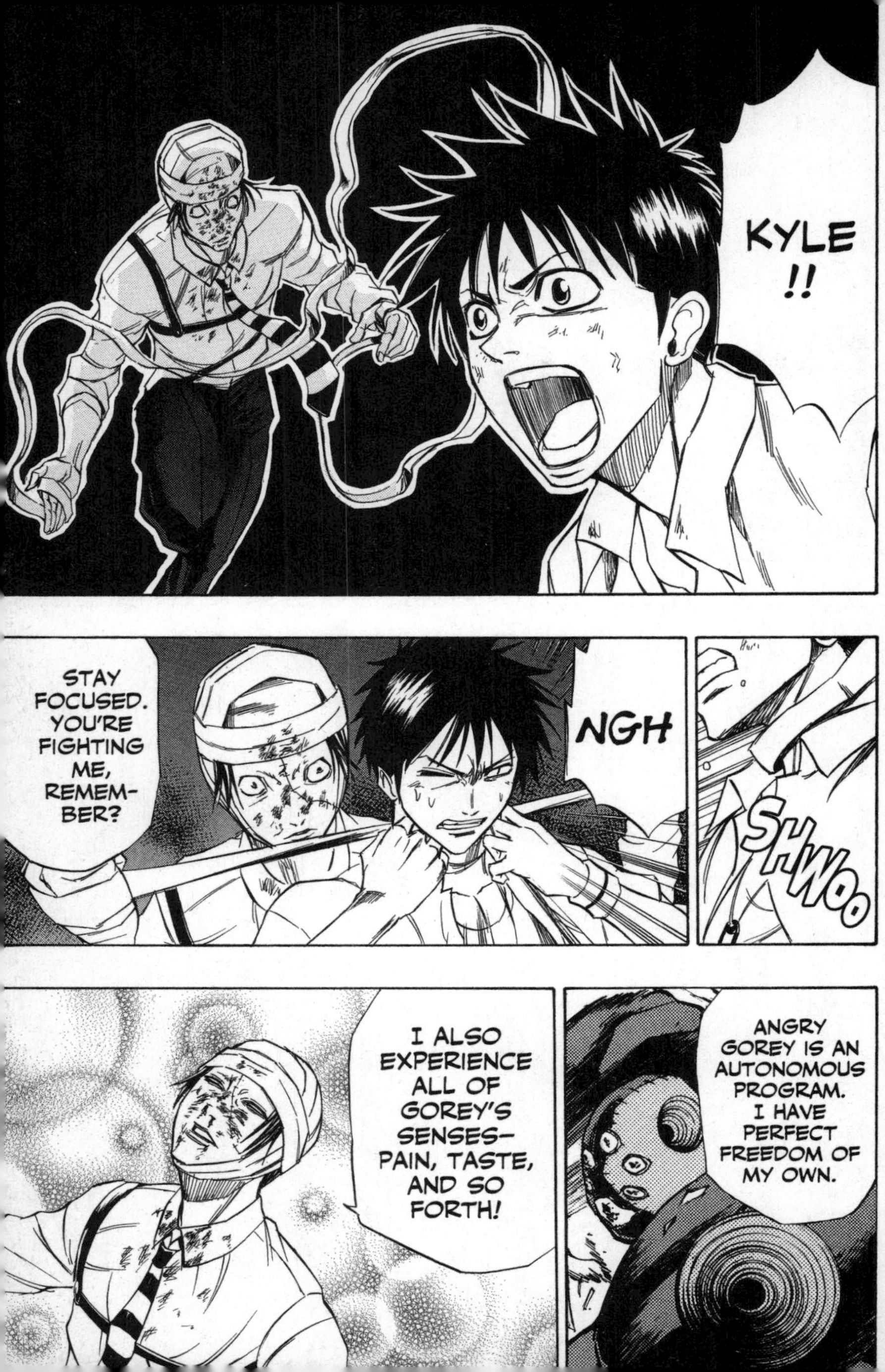
KYLE !!
SHWOO
NGH
STAY FOCUSED. YOU'RE FIGHTING ME, REMEMBER?
ANGRY GOREY IS AN AUTONOMOUS PROGRAM. I HAVE PERFECT FREEDOM OF MY OWN.
I ALSO EXPERIENCE ALL OF GOREY'S SENSES— PAIN, TASTE, AND SO FORTH!

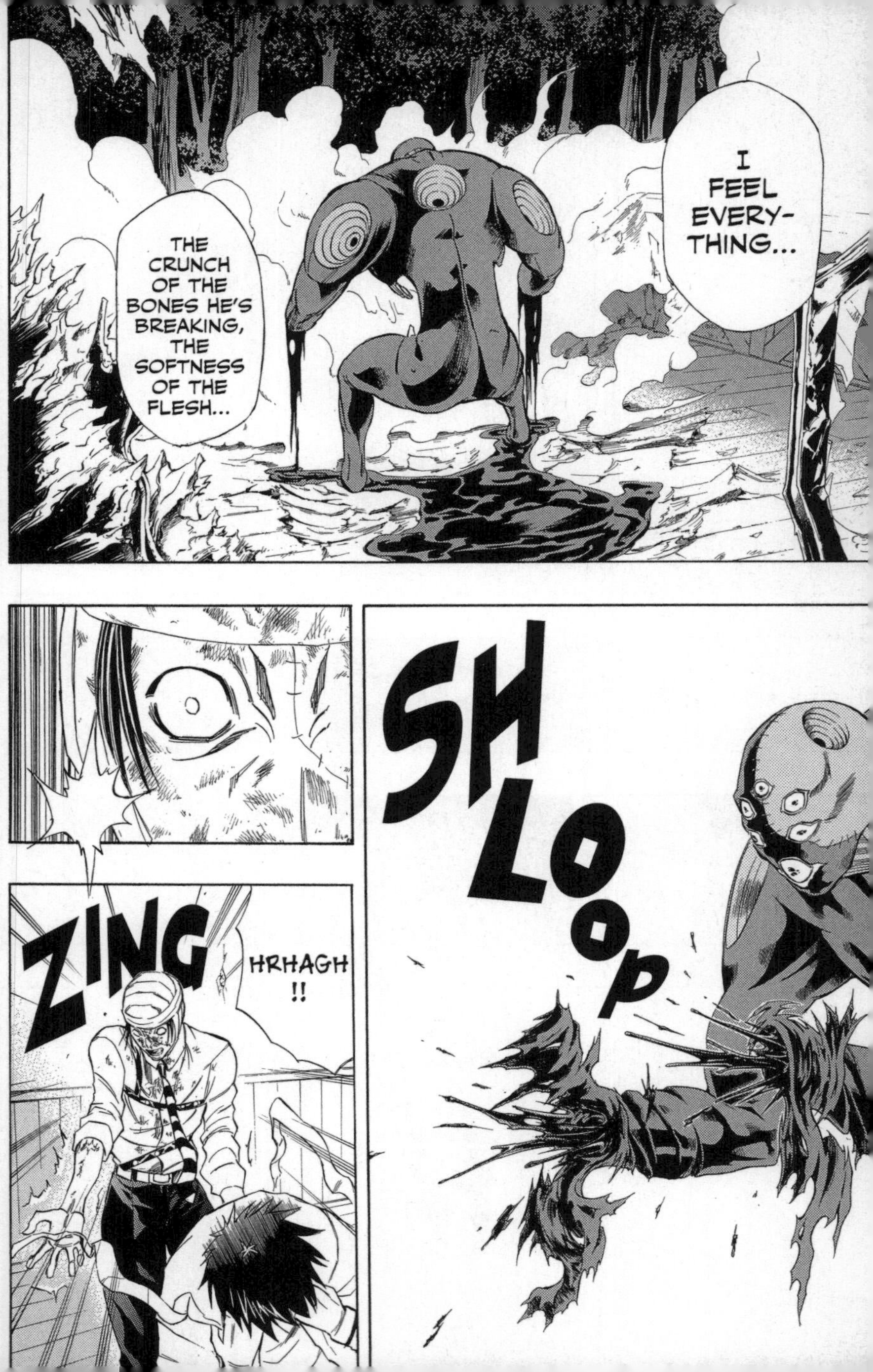
I FEEL EVERY-THING...
THE CRUNCH OF THE BONES HE'S BREAKING, THE SOFTNESS OF THE FLESH...
SHLOOP
ZING
HRHAGH !!

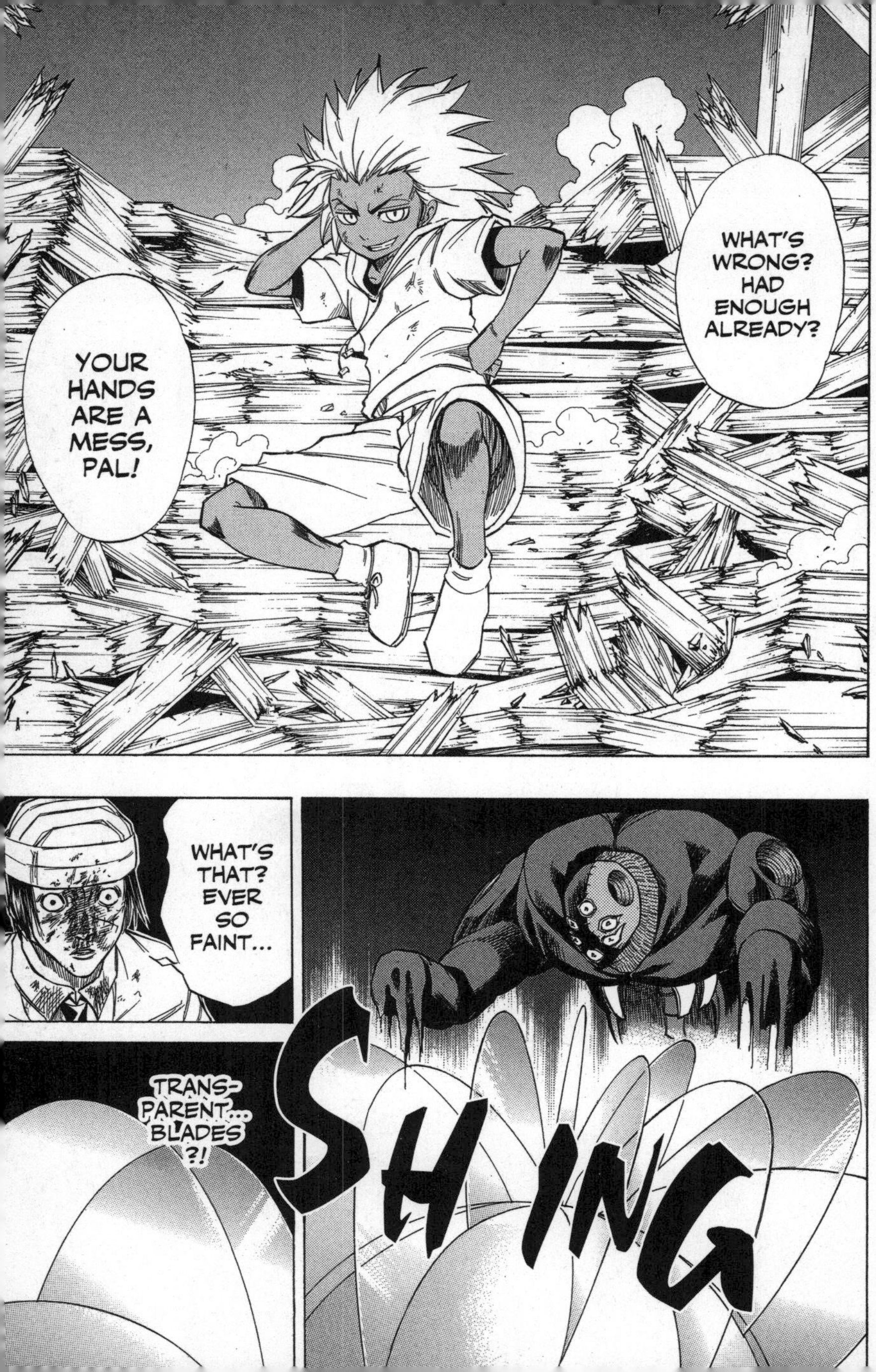
WHAT'S WRONG? HAD ENOUGH ALREADY?
YOUR HANDS ARE A MESS, PAL!
SHING
WHAT'S THAT? EVER SO FAINT...
TRANS-PARENT... BLADES?!

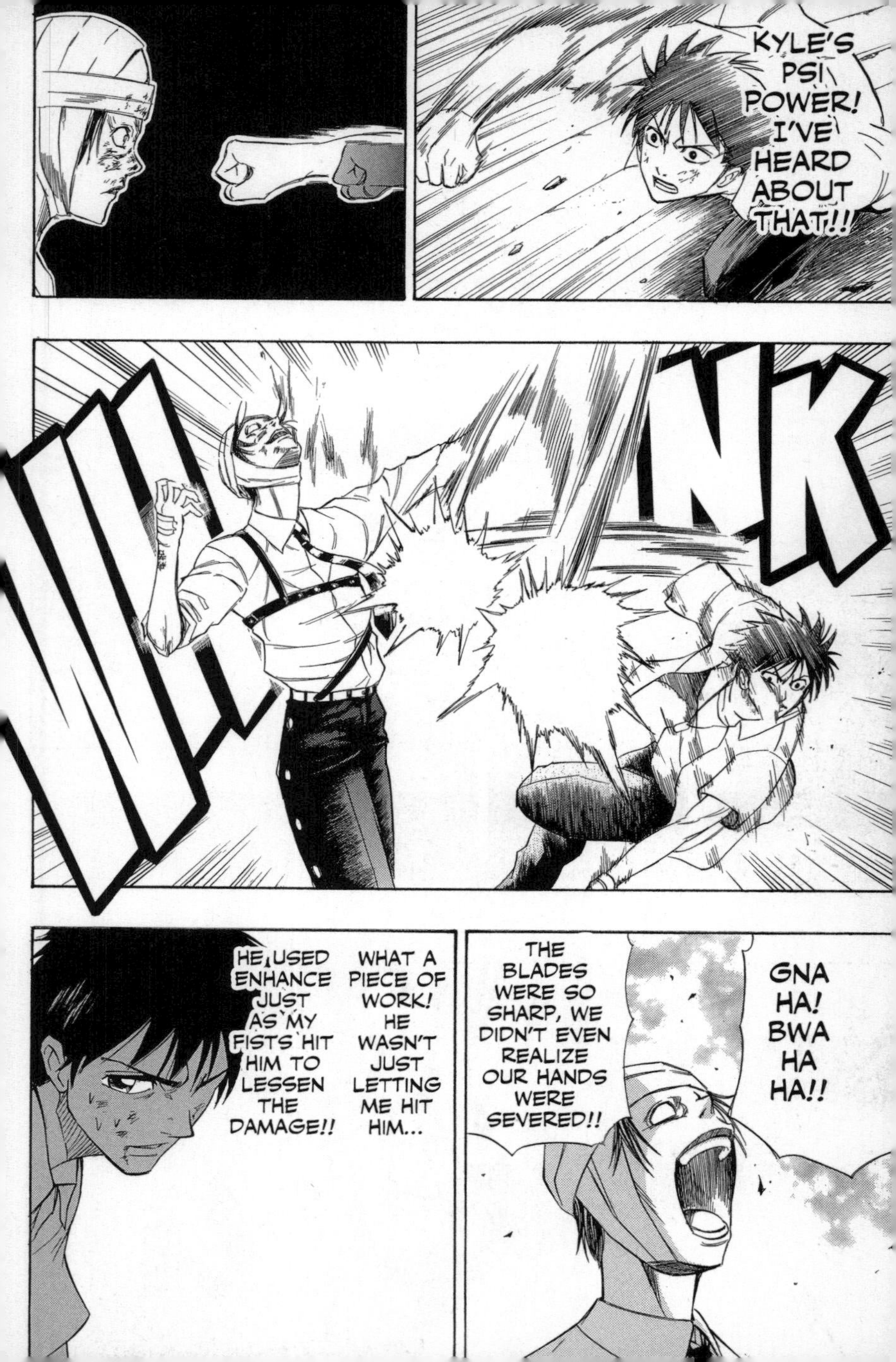
KYLE'S PSI POWER! I'VE HEARD ABOUT THAT!!
NK
GNA HA! BWA HA HA!!
THE BLADES WERE SO SHARP, WE DIDN'T EVEN REALIZE OUR HANDS WERE SEVERED!!
WHAT A PIECE OF WORK! HE WASN'T JUST LETTING ME HIT HIM...
HE USED ENHANCE JUST AS MY FISTS HIT HIM TO LESSEN THE DAMAGE!!

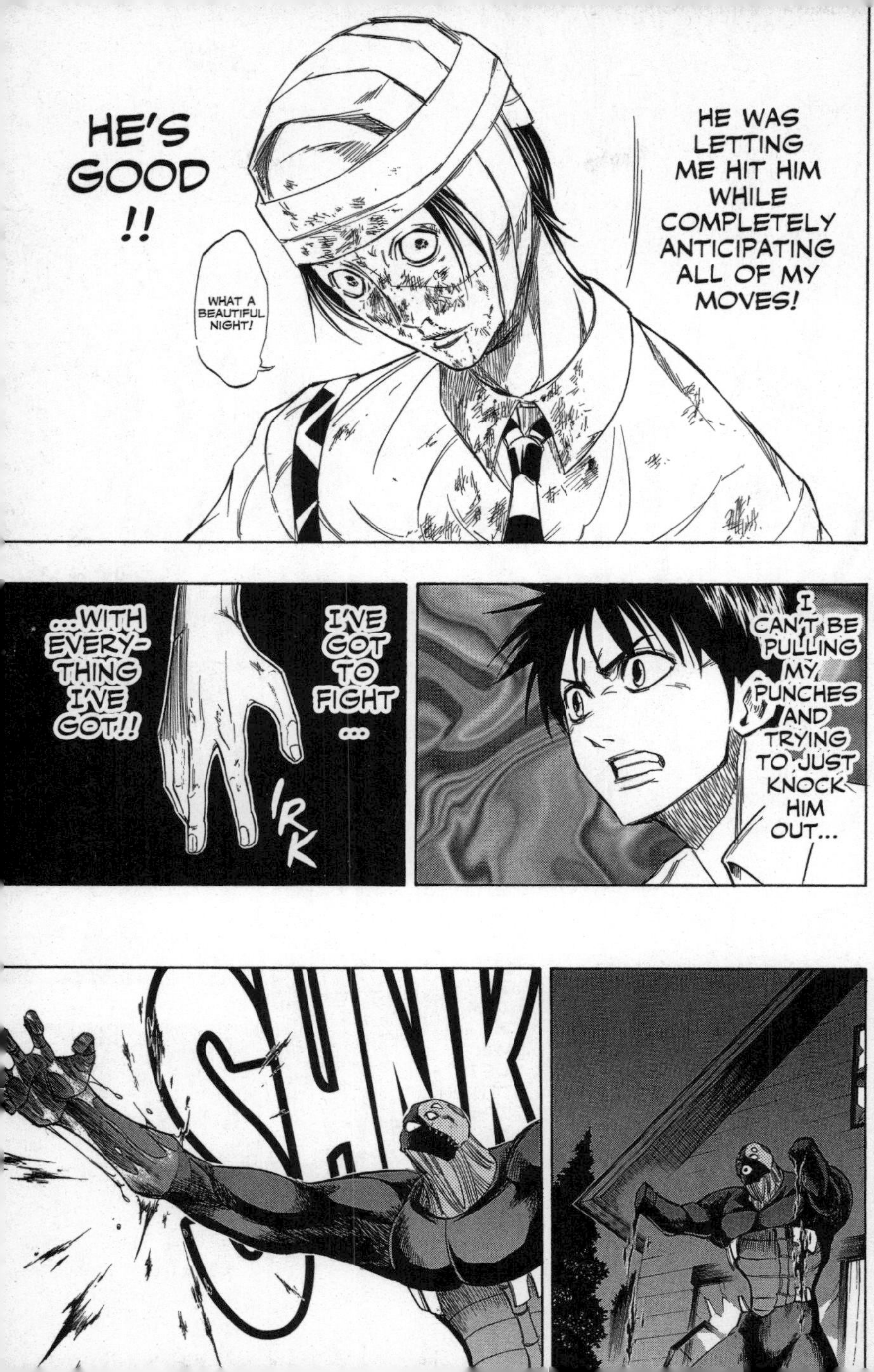
HE WAS LETTING ME HIT HIM WHILE COMPLETELY ANTICIPATING ALL OF MY MOVES!
HE'S GOOD!!
WHAT A BEAUTIFUL NIGHT!
I CAN'T BE PULLING MY PUNCHES AND TRYING TO JUST KNOCK HIM OUT...
I'VE GOT TO FIGHT...
...WITH EVERYTHING I'VE GOT!!
IRK

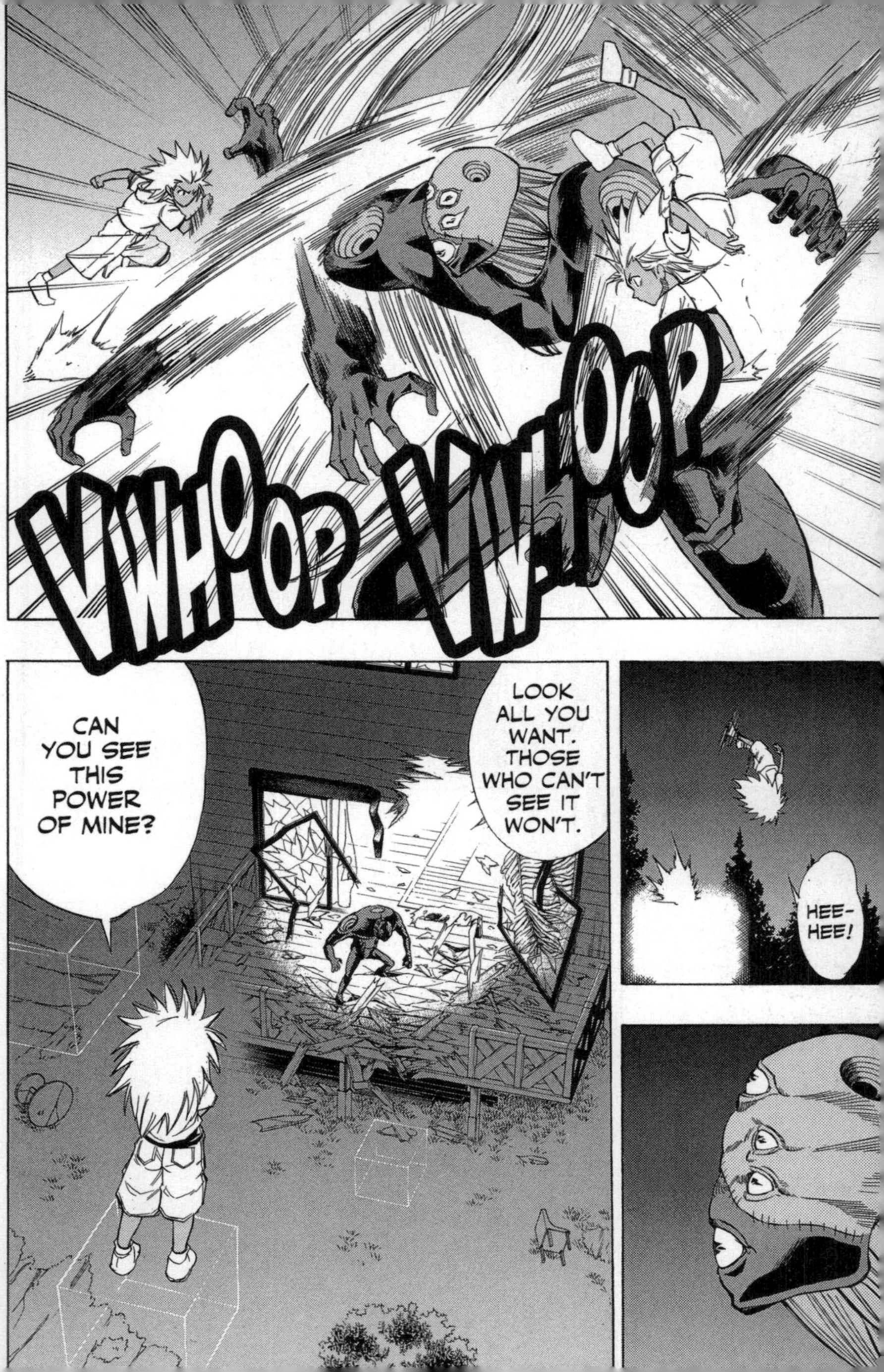
VWHOOP VWHOOP
HEE-HEE!
LOOK ALL YOU WANT. THOSE WHO CAN'T SEE IT WON'T.
CAN YOU SEE THIS POWER OF MINE?

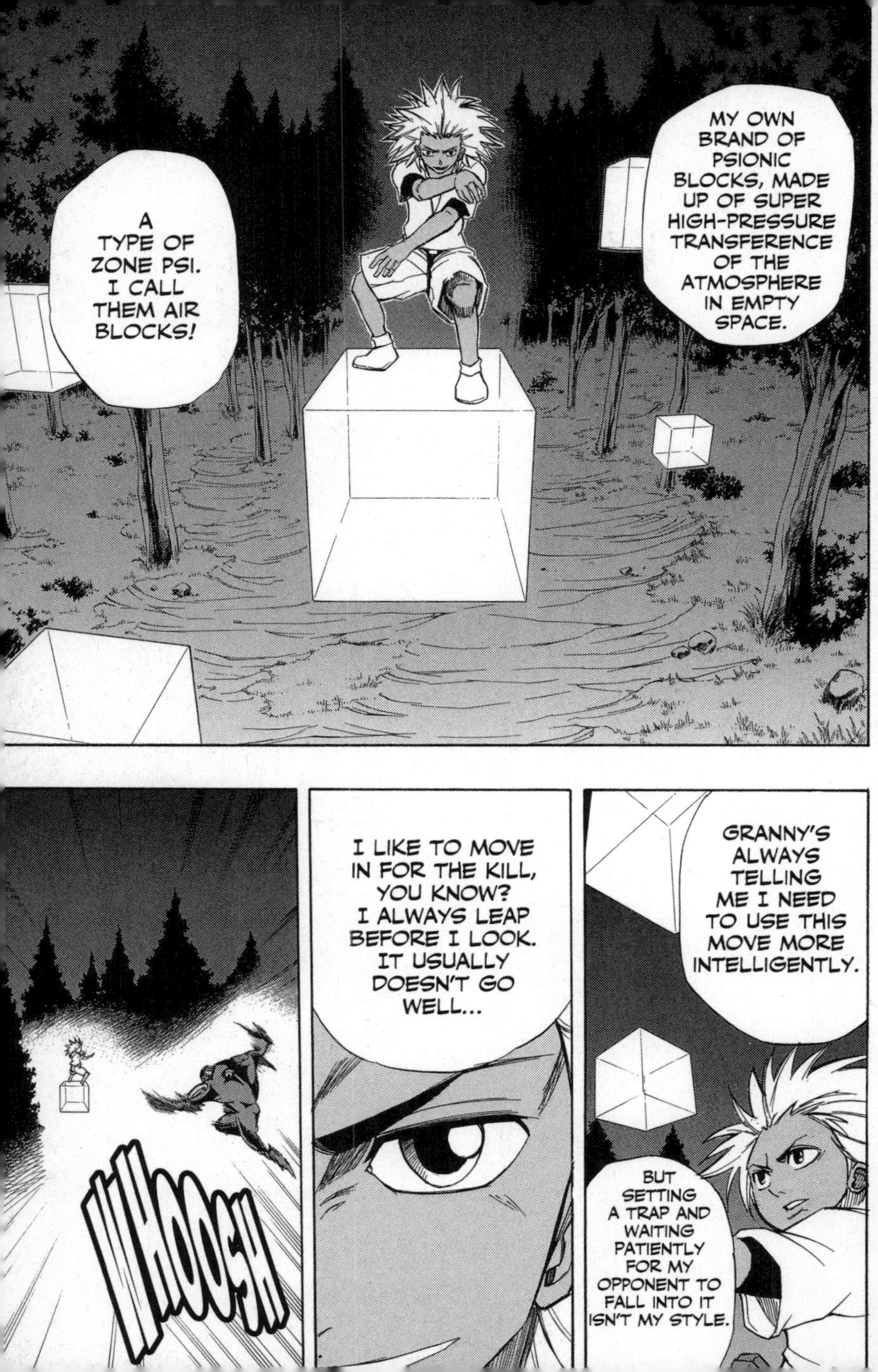
MY OWN BRAND OF PSIONIC BLOCKS, MADE UP OF SUPER HIGH-PRESSURE TRANSFERENCE OF THE ATMOSPHERE IN EMPTY SPACE.
A TYPE OF ZONE PSI. I CALL THEM AIR BLOCKS!
GRANNY'S ALWAYS TELLING ME I NEED TO USE THIS MOVE MORE INTELLIGENTLY.
BUT SETTING A TRAP AND WAITING PATIENTLY FOR MY OPPONENT TO FALL INTO IT ISN'T MY STYLE.
I LIKE TO MOVE IN FOR THE KILL, YOU KNOW? I ALWAYS LEAP BEFORE I LOOK. IT USUALLY DOESN'T GO WELL...
WHOOSH

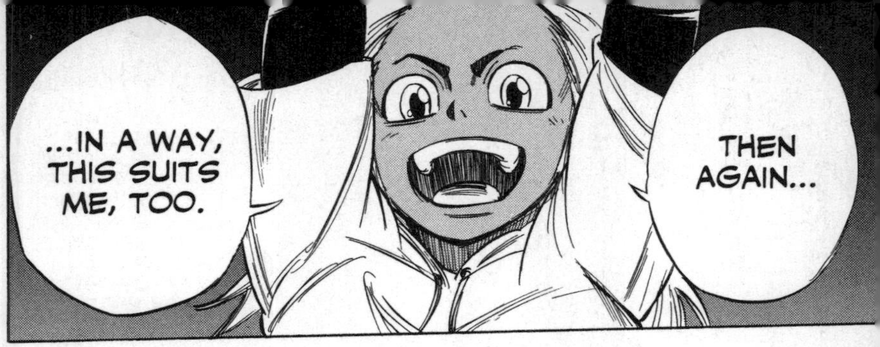
THEN AGAIN...
...IN A WAY, THIS SUITS ME, TOO.

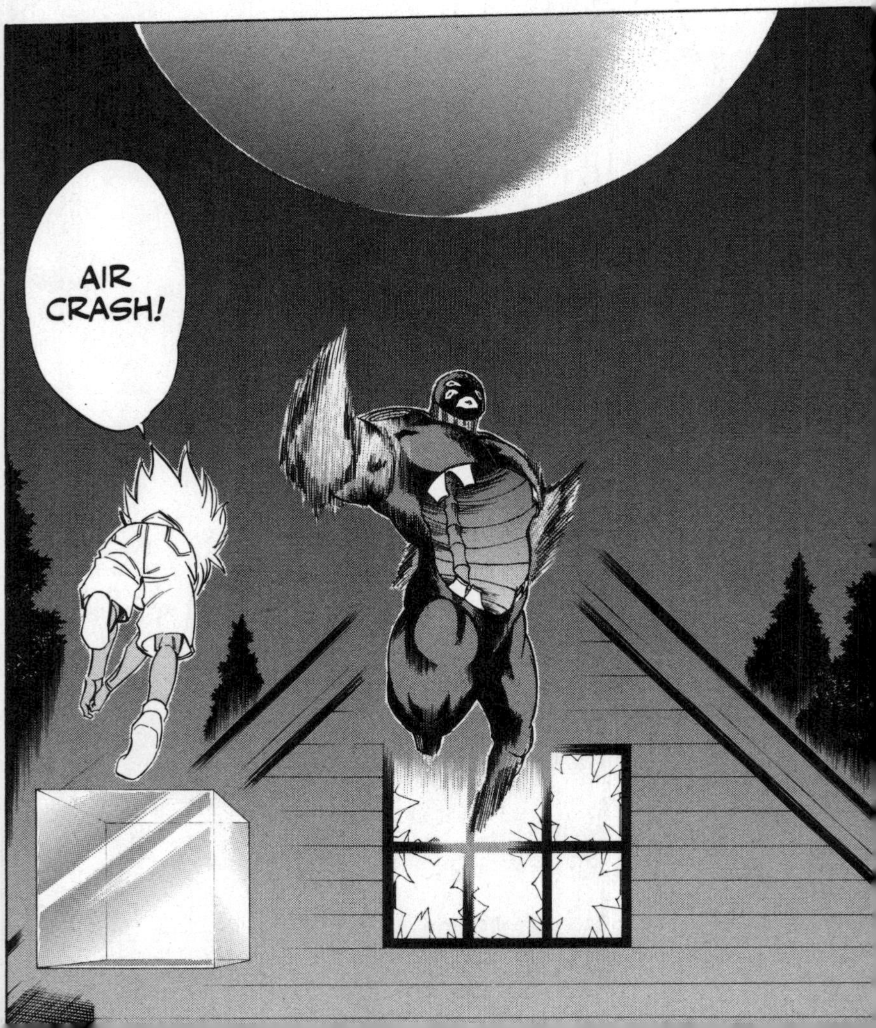
AIR CRASH!

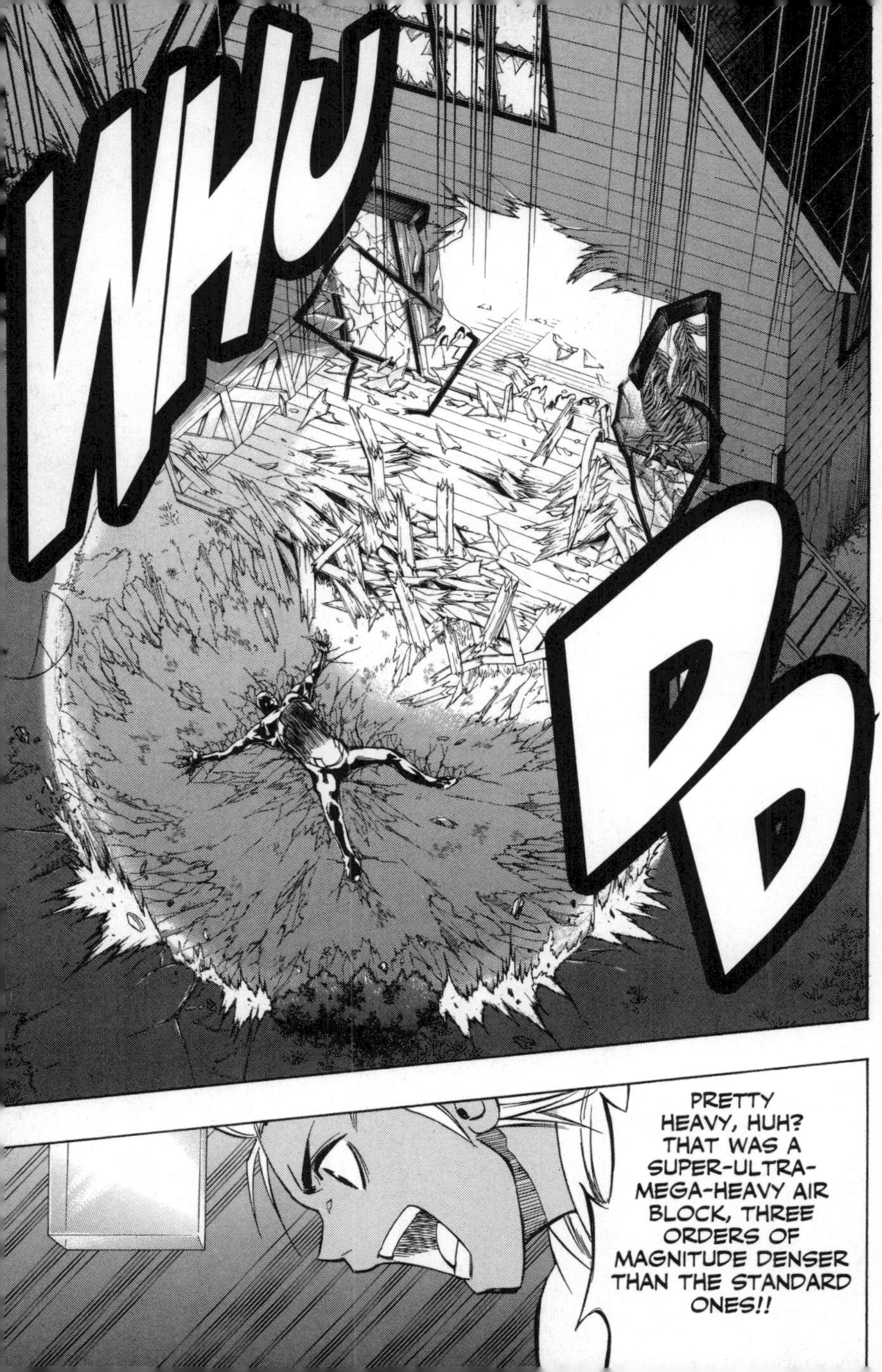
WHUDD
PRETTY HEAVY, HUH? THAT WAS A SUPER-ULTRA-MEGA-HEAVY AIR BLOCK, THREE ORDERS OF MAGNITUDE DENSER THAN THE STANDARD ONES!!

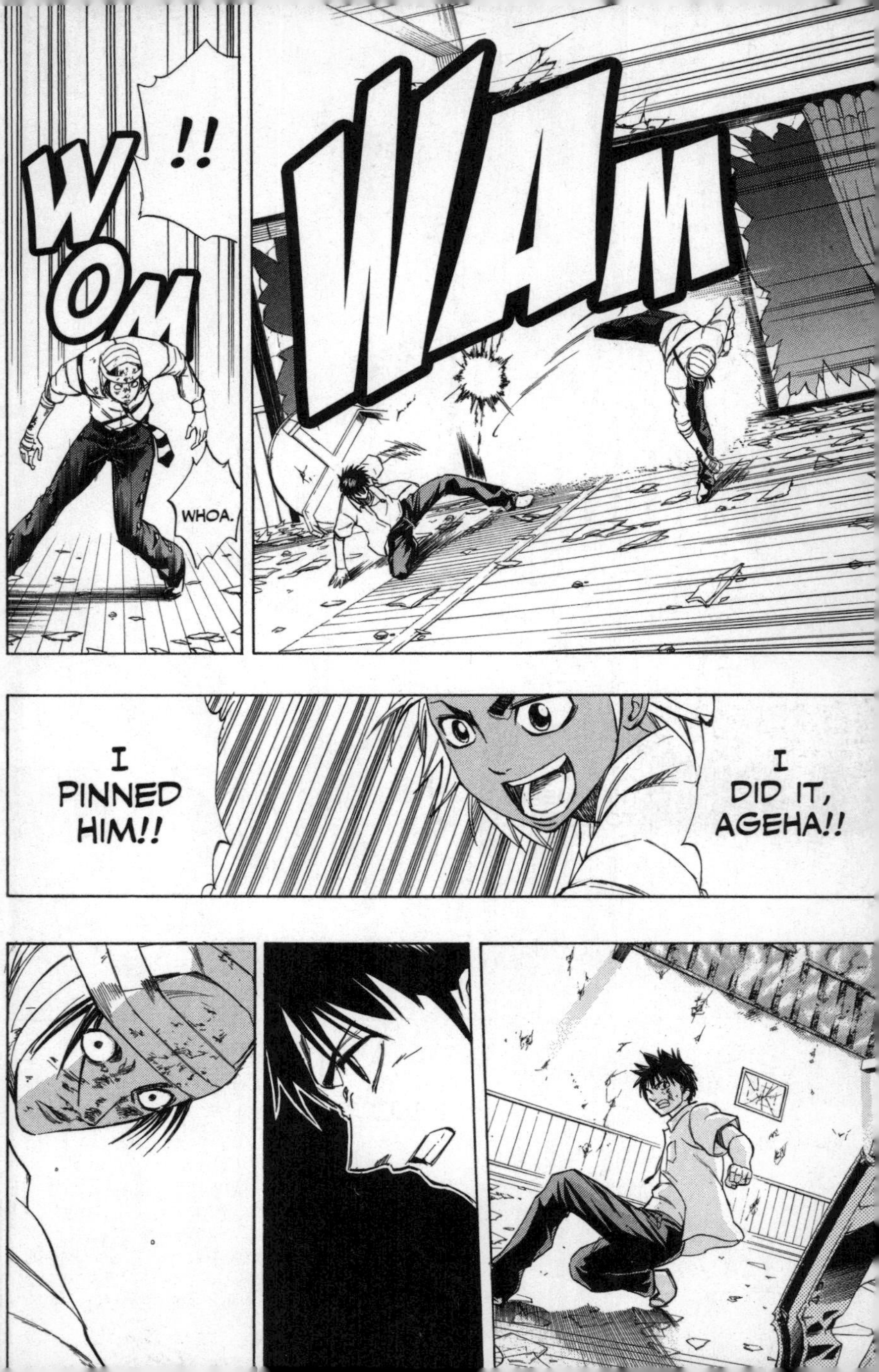
WAM
WOM !!
WHOA.
I DID IT, AGEHA!!
I PINNED HIM!!

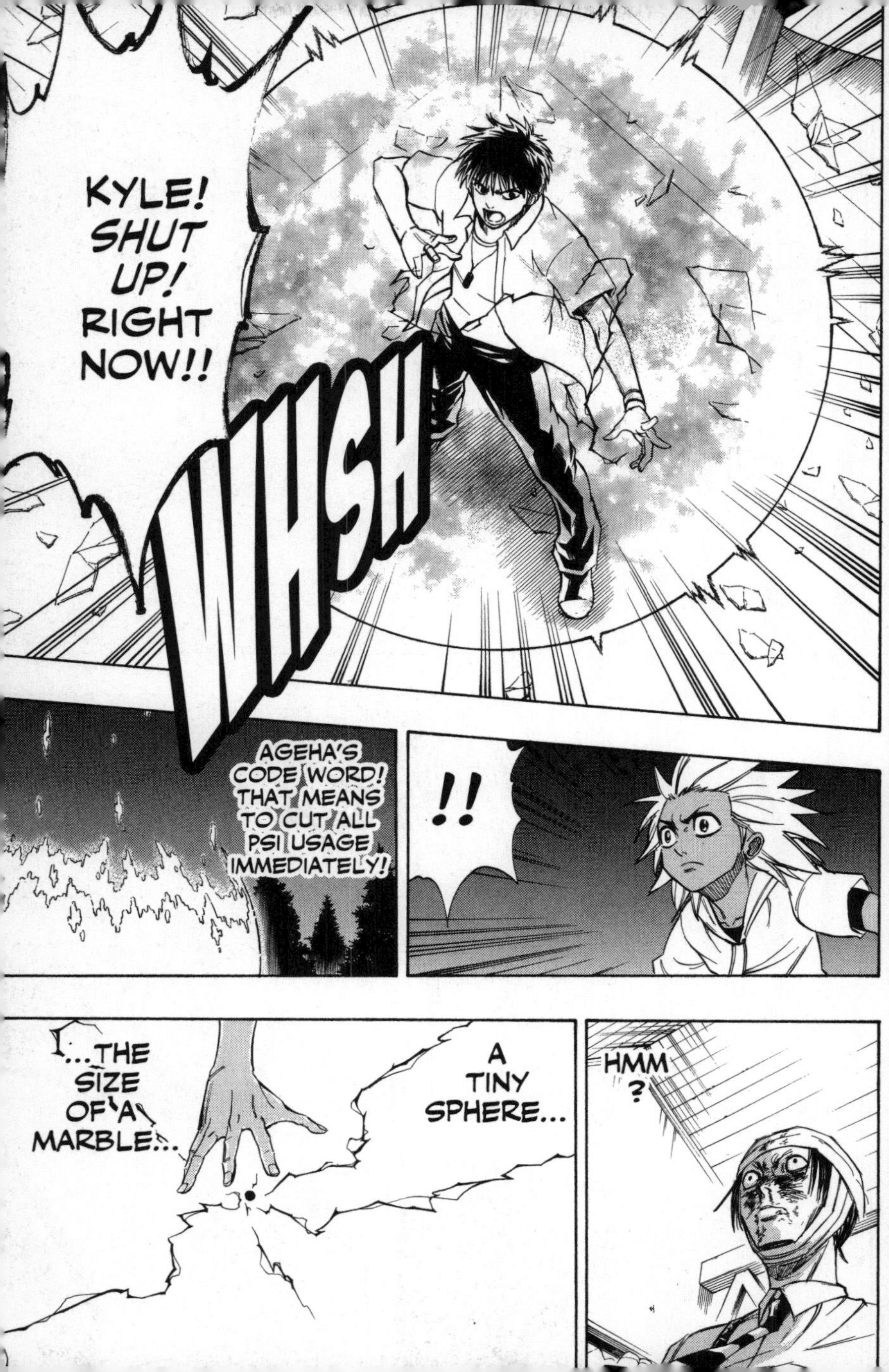
KYLE! SHUT UP! RIGHT NOW!!
WHSH
!!
AGEHA'S CODE WORD! THAT MEANS TO CUT ALL PSI USAGE IMMEDIATELY!
HMM ?
A TINY SPHERE...
...THE SIZE OF A MARBLE...

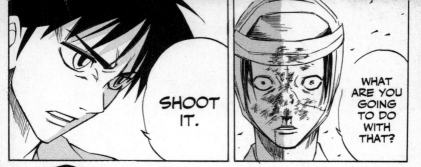

SHOOT IT.

WHAT ARE YOU GOING TO DO WITH THAT?

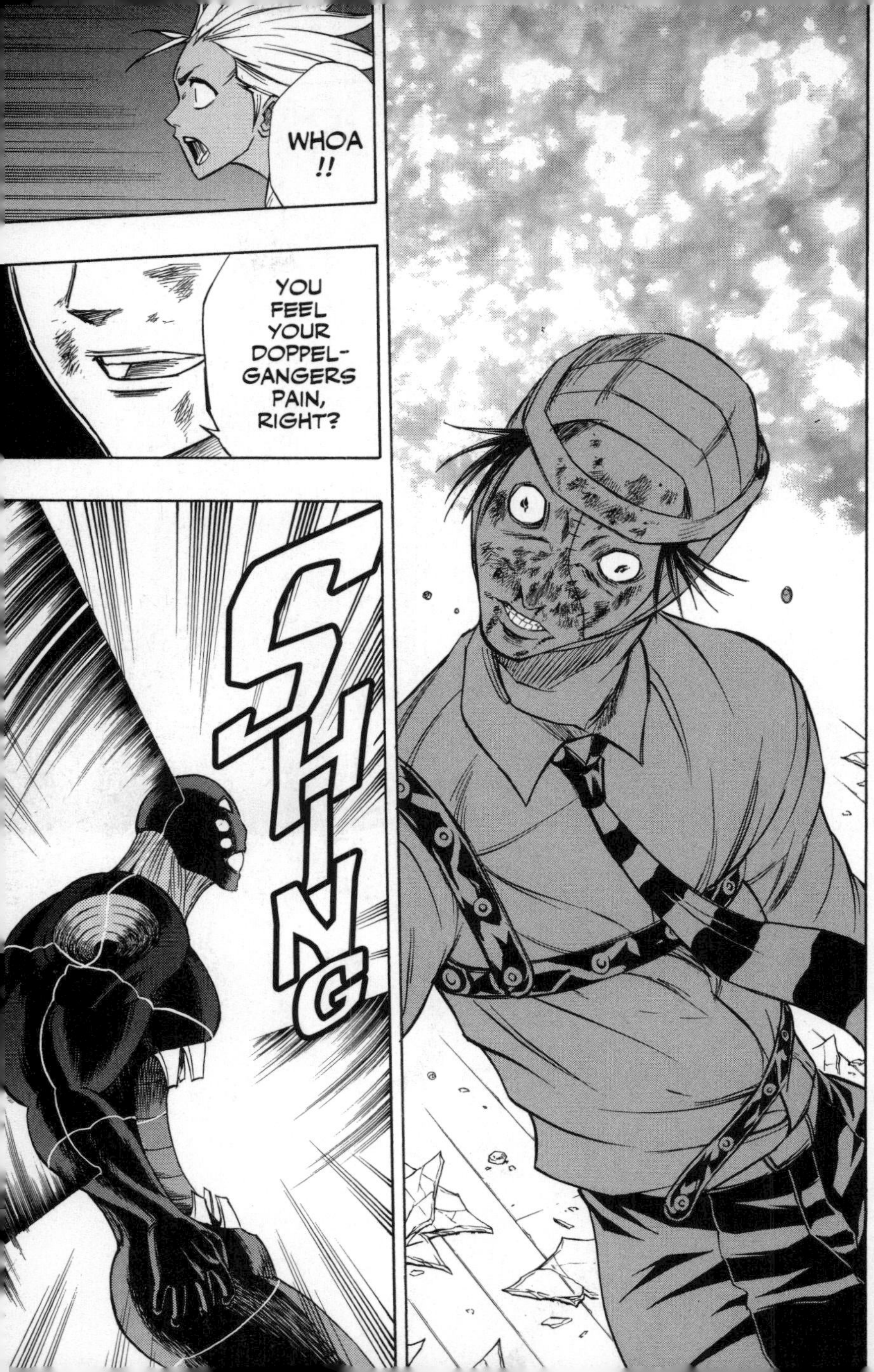
WHOA !!
YOU FEEL YOUR DOPPEL-GANGERS PAIN, RIGHT?
SHING

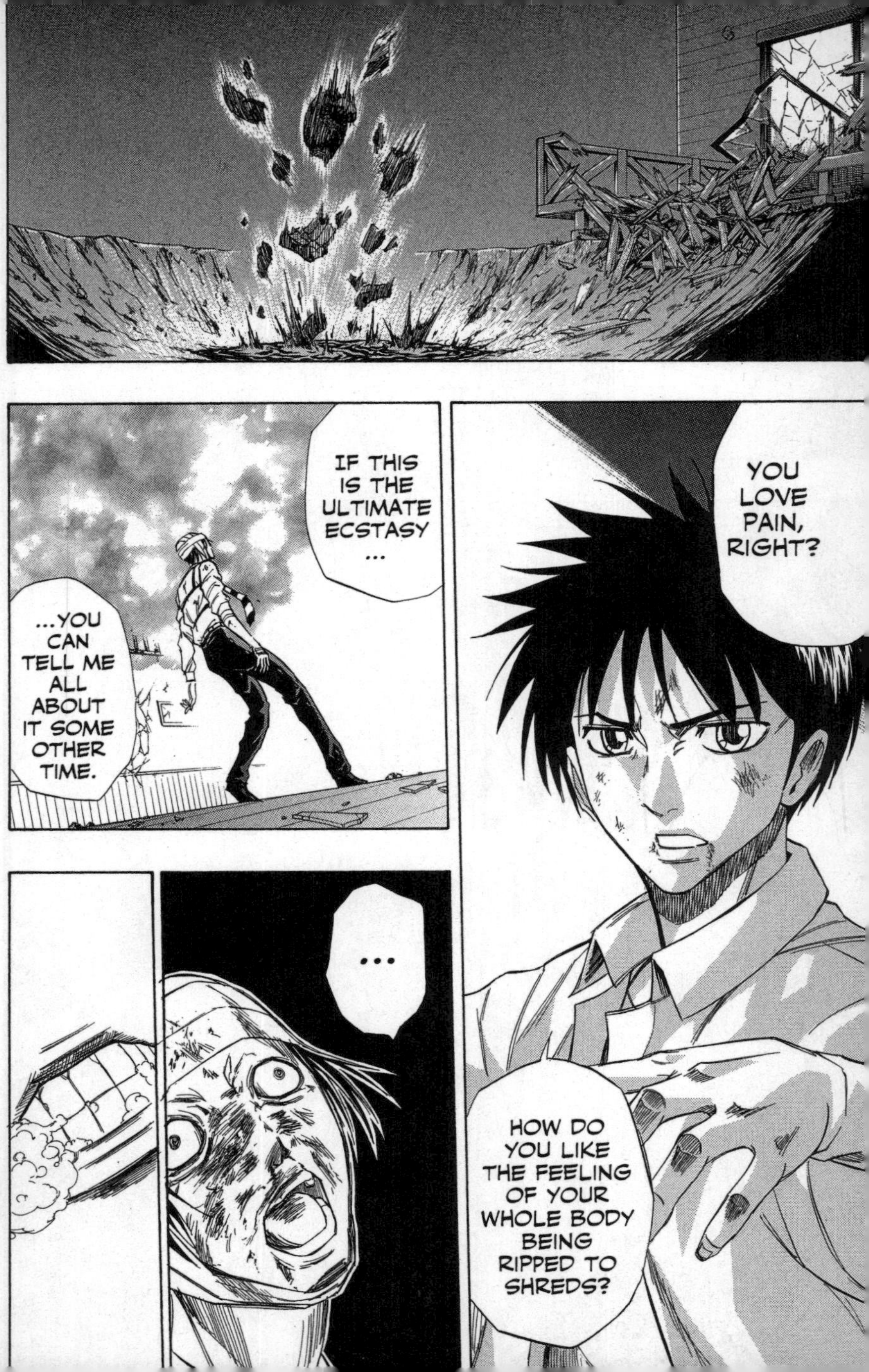
YOU LOVE PAIN, RIGHT?
HOW DO YOU LIKE THE FEELING OF YOUR WHOLE BODY BEING RIPPED TO SHREDS?
IF THIS IS THE ULTIMATE ECSTASY ...
...YOU CAN TELL ME ALL ABOUT IT SOME OTHER TIME.
...

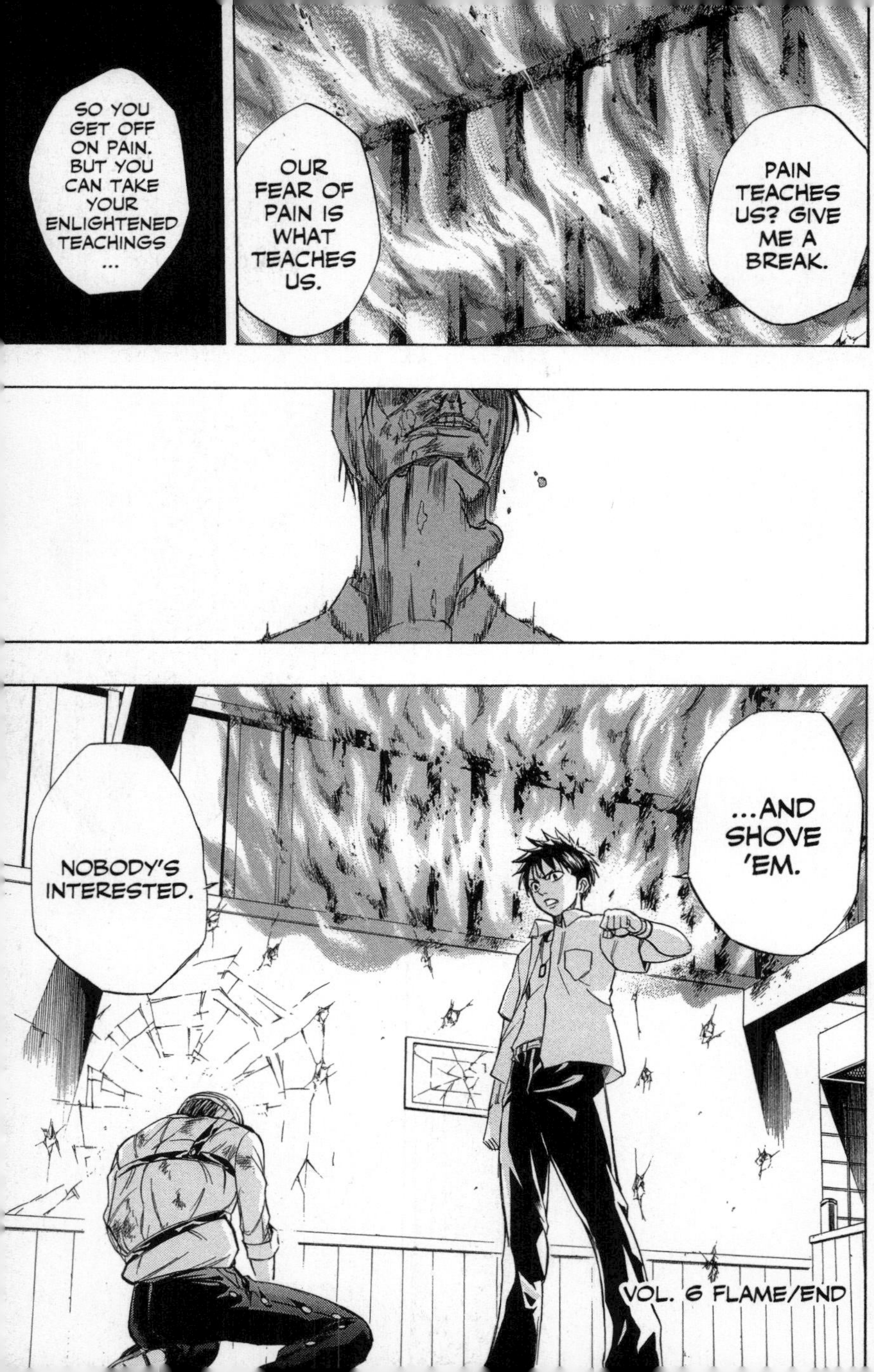
PAIN TEACHES US? GIVE ME A BREAK.
OUR FEAR OF PAIN IS WHAT TEACHES US.
SO YOU GET OFF ON PAIN. BUT YOU CAN TAKE YOUR ENLIGHTENED TEACHINGS ...
...AND SHOVE 'EM.
NOBODY'S INTERESTED.
VOL. 6 FLAME/END

PSYREN BONUS SECTION

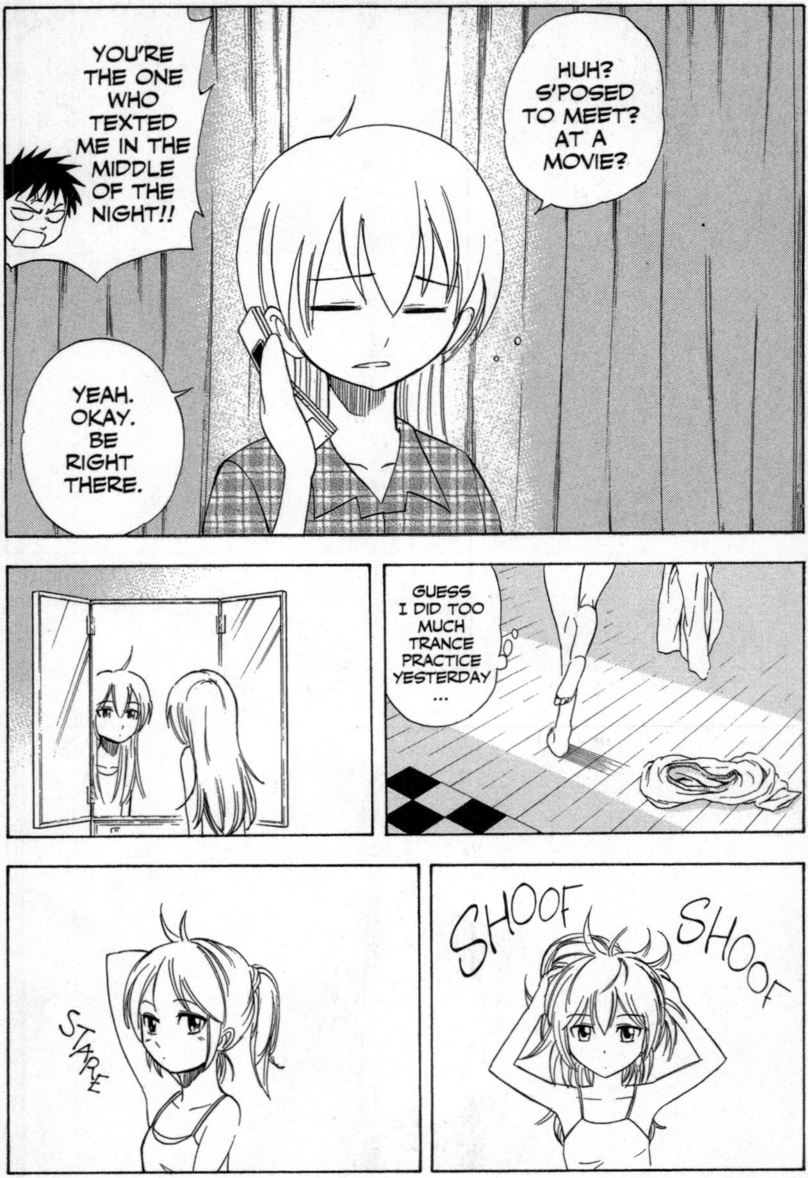
HUH? S'POSED TO MEET? AT A MOVIE?
YOU'RE THE ONE WHO TEXTED ME IN THE MIDDLE OF THE NIGHT!!
YEAH. OKAY. BE RIGHT THERE.
GUESS I DID TOO MUCH TRANCE PRACTICE YESTERDAY ...
SHOOF
SHOOF
STARE

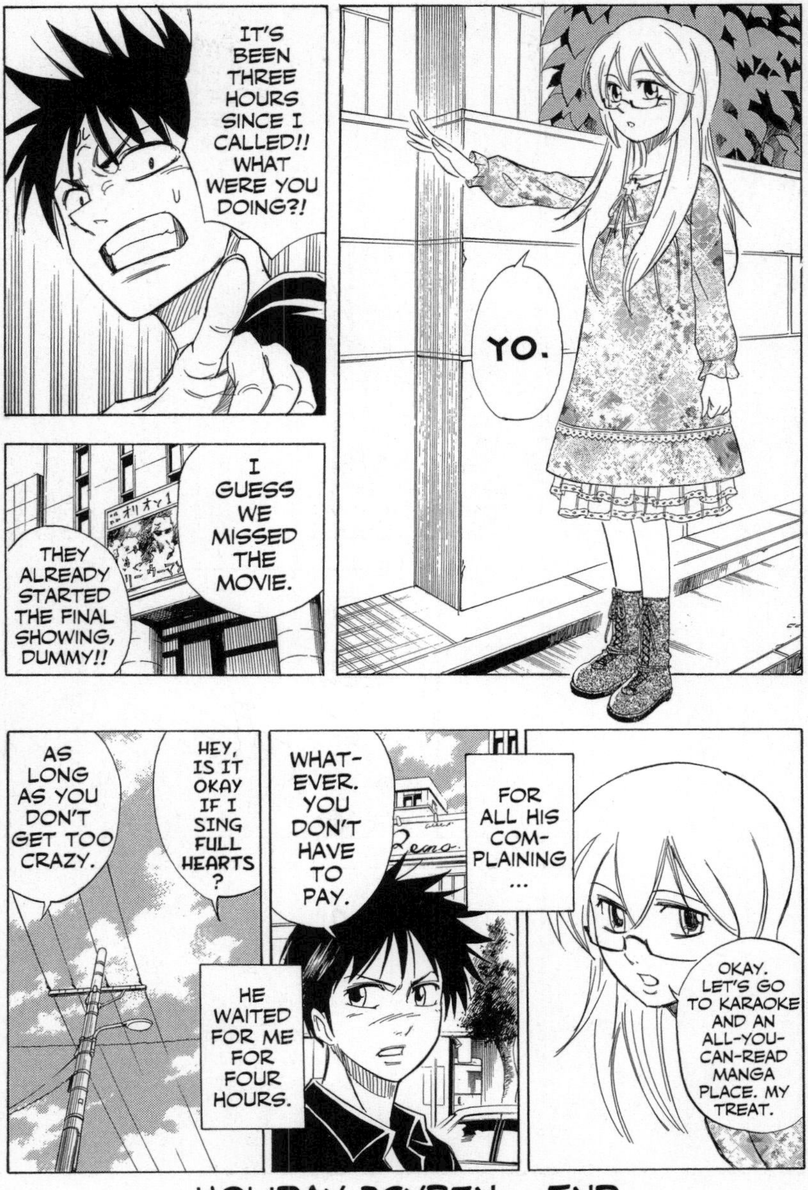
YO.
IT'S BEEN THREE HOURS SINCE I CALLED!! WHAT WERE YOU DOING?!
I GUESS WE MISSED THE MOVIE.
THEY ALREADY STARTED THE FINAL SHOWING, DUMMY!!
FOR ALL HIS COMPLAINING...
OKAY. LET'S GO TO KARAOKE AND AN ALL-YOU-CAN-READ MANGA PLACE. MY TREAT.
WHAT-EVER. YOU DON'T HAVE TO PAY.
HE WAITED FOR ME FOR FOUR HOURS.
HEY, IS IT OKAY IF I SING FULL HEARTS?
AS LONG AS YOU DON'T GET TOO CRAZY.

HOLIDAY PSYREN - END

PSYREN

6

Afterword

THANK YOU SO MUCH FOR READING
PSYREN VOLUME 6!

WORK HAS BEEN GOING SMOOTHLY
THESE DAYS, AND I'VE MANAGED
NOT TO GET SICK. WHEN I LOOK
OVER THE STORYBOARDS AND
DRAWINGS, I GET THE SENSE THAT
THE STYLE HAS CHANGED
SOMEWHAT SINCE VOLUME 1.

IN THE BEGINNING, I TRIED TO
EXPLAIN EVERYTHING 100%, BUT
THAT'S LOOSENED UP OVER TIME.

I INTEND TO HAVE FUN DRAWING
THIS MANGA.

SEE YOU NEXT TIME!

MAY 2009
TOSHIAKI IWASHIRO

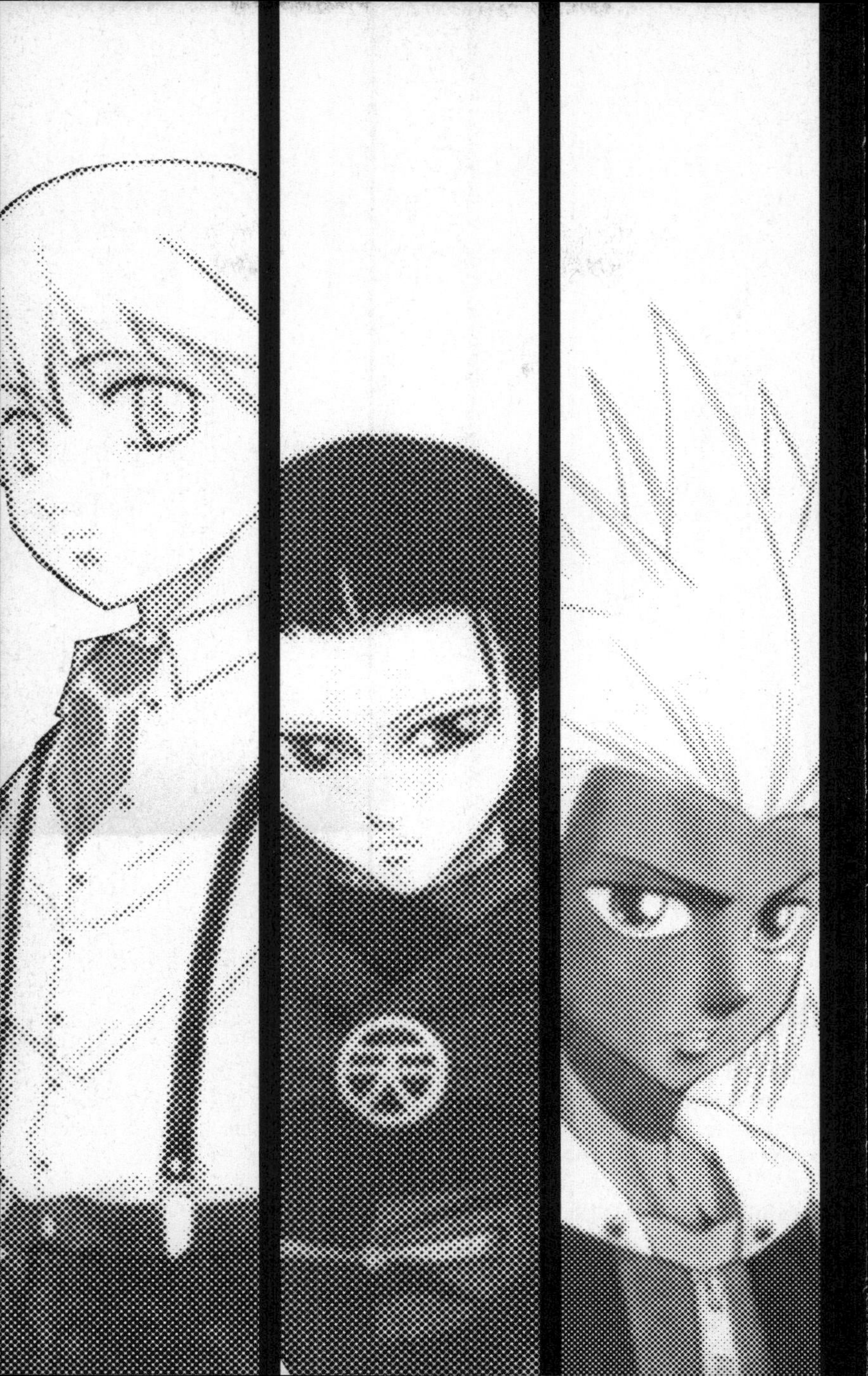

IN THE NEXT VOLUME...

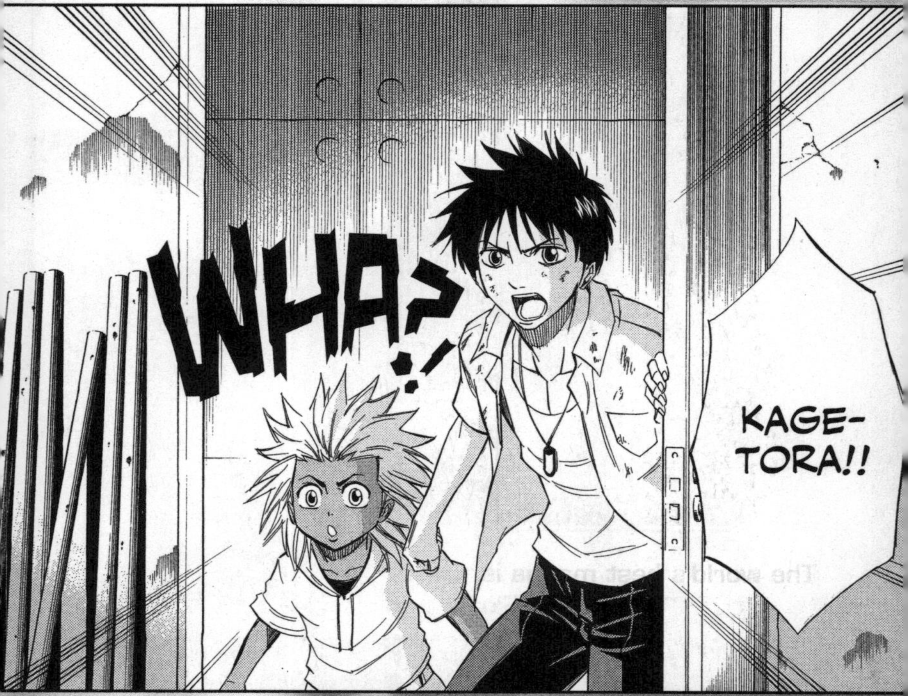
KAGE-
TORA!!
WHA?!

THE DECEMBER 2ND REVOLUTION

Ageha and his fellow Psionists discover that their actions in the present may be altering the outcome of the future. Now everything they know—and everyone they love—is in danger, including their mentor Elmore Tenjuin. But their attempt to save their beloved Elmore is interrupted...by a jolting sudden return to Psyren!

Available NOVEMBER 2012!

The VIZ Manga App has some new friends...

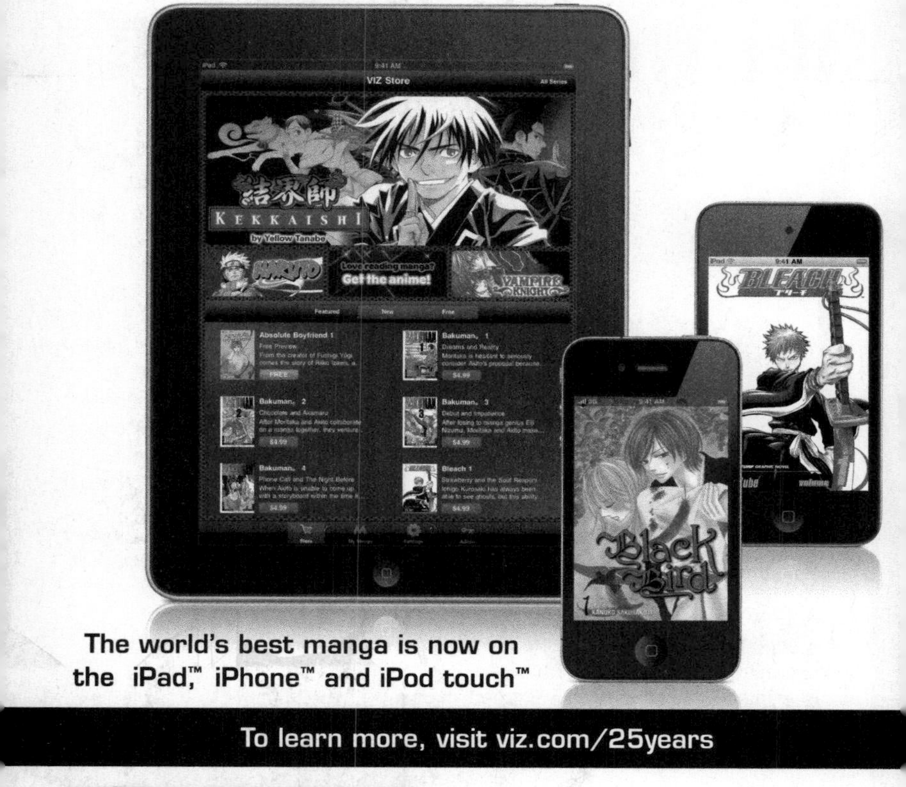

VIZ Store
KEKKAISHI
by Yellow Tanabe
Love reading manga?
Get the anime!
Absolute Boyfriend 1
Bakuman。 1
Bakuman。 2
Bakuman。 3
Bakuman。 4
Bleach 1
BLEACH
Black Bird

The world's best manga is now on the iPad,™ iPhone™ and iPod touch™

To learn more, visit viz.com/25years

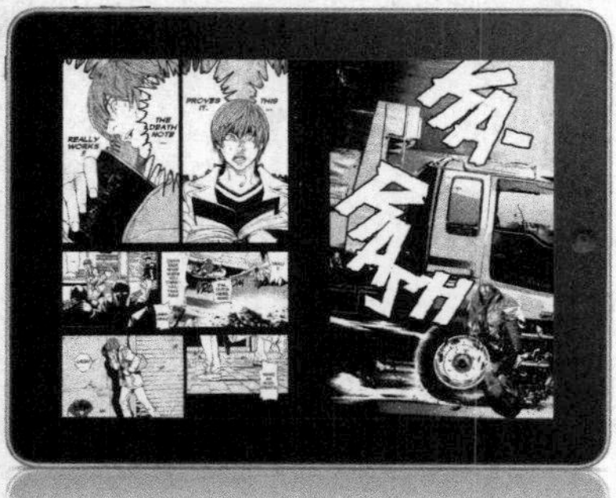

From legendary manga like *Death Note* to *Absolute Boyfriend*, the best manga in the world is now available on multiple devices through the official VIZ Manga app.

- Hundreds of volumes available
- Free App
- New content weekly
- Free chapter 1 previews

HEROES OF MANGA
VIZ media 25 YEARS
viz.com/25years

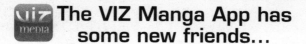

You're Reading in the Wrong Direction!!

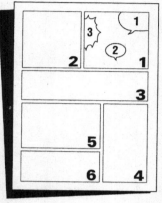

Whoops! Guess what? You're starting at the wrong end of the comic!

...It's true! In keeping with the original Japanese format, **Psyren** is meant to be read from right to left, starting in the upper-right corner.

Unlike English, which is read from left to right, Japanese is read from right to left, meaning that action, sound effects and word-balloon order are completely reversed—something which can make readers unfamiliar with Japanese feel pretty backwards themselves. For this reason, manga or Japanese comics published in the U.S. in English have sometimes been published "flopped"—that is, printed in exact reverse order, as though seen from the other side of a mirror.

By flopping pages, U.S. publishers can avoid confusing readers, but the compromise is not without its downside. For one thing, a character in a flopped manga series who once wore in the original Japanese version a T-shirt emblazoned with "M A Y" (as in "the merry month of") now wears one which reads "Y A M"! Additionally, many manga creators in Japan are themselves unhappy with the process, as some feel the mirror-imaging of their art changes their original intentions.

We are proud to bring you Toshiaki Iwashiro's **Psyren** in the original unflopped format. For now, though, turn to the other side of the book and let the fun begin...!

—Editor

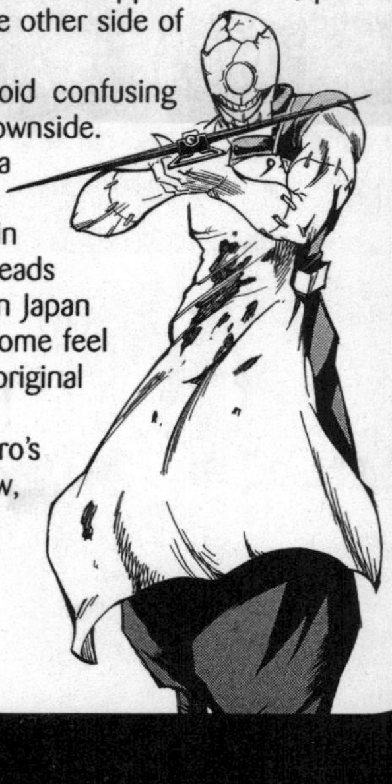